Microsoft Official Academic Course: Microsoft Office Outlook 2003

Microsoft Corporation

PUBLISHED BY
Microsoft Press
A Division of Microsoft Corporation
One Microsoft Way
Redmond, Washington 98052-6399

Copyright © 2004 by Microsoft Corporation

All rights reserved. No part of the contents of this book may be reproduced or transmitted in any form or by any means without the written permission of the publisher.

Library of Congress Cataloging-in-Publication Data pending.
 ISBN 0-7356-2090-3
 (Microsoft Press)
 ISBN 0-07-225577-3
 (McGraw-Hill)

Printed and bound in the United States of America.

1 2 3 4 5 6 7 8 9   QWE   8 7 6 5 4

Distributed in Canada by H.B. Fenn and Company Ltd.

A CIP catalogue record for this book is available from the British Library.

Microsoft Press books are available through booksellers and distributors worldwide. For further information about international editions, contact your local Microsoft Corporation office or contact Microsoft Press International directly at fax (425) 936-7329. Visit our Web site at www.microsoft.com/learning/. Send comments to *mspinput@microsoft.com*.

Hotmail, Microsoft, MSN, Outlook, PowerPoint, Windows, and the Windows logo are either registered trademarks or trademarks of Microsoft Corporation in the United States and/or other countries. Other product and company names mentioned herein may be the trademarks of their respective owners.

The example companies, organizations, products, domain names, e-mail addresses, logos, people, places, and events depicted herein are fictitious. No association with any real company, organization, product, domain name, e-mail address, logo, person, place, or event is intended or should be inferred.

This book expresses the author's views and opinions. The information contained in this book is provided without any express, statutory, or implied warranties. Neither the authors, Microsoft Corporation, nor its resellers or distributors will be held liable for any damages caused or alleged to be caused either directly or indirectly by this book.

Acquisitions Editor: Linda Engelman
Project Editor: Dick Brown

Body Part No. X10-42275

Contents

Contents iii

Course Overview vii

Conventions and Features Used in This Book xii

Using the CD-ROMs xiv

MOS Objectives xx

Taking a Microsoft Office Specialist Certification Test xxi

Microsoft e-Learning Library xxv

LESSON 1   Introduction to Outlook 1

Starting Outlook 2 ▪ Navigating Within Outlook 4 ▪ Using Personalized Menus 5 ▪ Using the Navigation Pane 7 ▪ Using the Folder List 12 ▪ Using the Office Assistant 14 ▪ Key Points 16 ▪ Quick Quiz 16 ▪ On Your Own 18 ▪ One Step Further 18

LESSON 2   Using E-Mail in Outlook 19

Composing, Addressing, and Sending Messages 20 ▪ Formatting a Message 24 ▪ Flagging Messages 25 ▪ Setting Message Priority 26 ▪ Saving Drafts 27 ▪ Attaching a File to a Message 27 ▪ Checking for E-Mail Messages 30 ▪ View Messages 32 ▪ Reading Messages 35 ▪ Replying to and Forwarding Messages 37 ▪ Printing Messages 40 ▪ Finding Messages 42 ▪ Recalling Messages 44 ▪ Deleting Messages 45 ▪ Key Points 46 ▪ Quick Quiz 47 ▪ On Your Own 48 ▪ One Step Further 48

LESSON 3   Customizing E-Mail 49

Specifying E-Mail Options 50 ▪ Customizing the Appearance of E-Mail Messages 56 ▪ Using Stationery 62 ▪ Adding a Signature to an E-Mail Message 65 ▪ Sorting Messages 69 ▪ Filtering an Arrangement 72 ▪ Creating Folders 76 ▪ Moving Messages Between Folders 78 ▪ Color-Coding Message Headers 83 ▪ Filtering Junk E-Mail Messages 85 ▪ Archiving Messages 88 ▪ Key Points 90 ▪ Quick Quiz 90 ▪ On Your Own 91 ▪ One Step Further 92

LESSON 4   Using Contacts 93

Viewing Contacts 94 ▪ Creating and Editing a New Contact 98 ▪ Creating Multiple Contacts for the Same Company 102 ▪ Deleting and Restoring Contacts 105 ▪ Using Folders to Organize Contacts 107 ▪ Using Views to Organize Contacts 109 ▪ Using Categories to Organize Contacts 114 ▪ Assigning Items to a New Category 114 ▪ Assigning Items to Multiple Categories 117 ■ Modifying the Outlook Master Category List 119 ■ Sorting Contacts 121 ■ Using the Address Book to Send E-Mail 124 ■ Using Contacts to Send E-Mail 127 ■ Sending and Receiving Contact Information via E-Mail 129 ■ Creating a Letter for a Contact 134 ■ Key Points 136 ■ Quick Quiz 136 ■ On Your Own 137 ■ One Step Further 138

LESSON 5   Using the Calendar 139

Using the Outlook Calendar 140 ■ Changing the Calendar View 144 ■ Scheduling Appointments and Events 146 ■ Creating Recurring Appointments 151 ■ Setting Reminders 154 ■ Editing Appointments 156 ■ Deleting Appointments 158 ■ Organizing Appointments by Using Categories 159 ■ Organizing Appointments by Using Arrangements 161 ■ Planning Meetings 164 ■ Printing Calendars 172 ■ Saving a Calendar as a Web Page 174 ■ Integrating the Calendar with Other Outlook Components 176 ■ Key Points 178 ■ Quick Quiz 178 ■ On Your Own 180 ■ One Step Further 180

LESSON 6   Using Tasks 181

Creating Tasks 182 ■ Changing Task Views 185 ■ Adding Task Details 187 ■ Sorting Tasks 190 ■ Printing a Task List 192 ■ Organizing Tasks by Using Folders 193 ■ Organizing Tasks by Using Categories 195 ■ Assigning Tasks to Others 198 ■ Accepting or Declining Tasks 201 ■ Marking Tasks as Complete 204 ■ Manually Recording a Task in the Journal 206 ■ Deleting Tasks 209 ■ Key Points 210 ■ Quick Quiz 210 ■ On Your Own 212 ■ One Step Further 212

LESSON 7   Using Notes 213

Creating Notes 214 ■ Editing Notes 217 ■ Copying Notes 218 ■ Forwarding Notes 221 ■ Organizing Notes by View 223 ■ Organizing Notes by Folder 225 ■ Deleting Notes 228 ■ Key Points 229 ■ Quick Quiz 229 ■ On Your Own 230 ■ One Step Further 230

LESSON 8   Customizing Outlook 231

Setting Outlook Startup Options 232 ■ Customizing the Navigation Pane 235 ■ Creating a Shortcut on the Navigation Pane 239 ■ Using and Customizing Outlook Today 243 ■ Create Personal Folders 247 ■ Importing a Microsoft Access Database into Outlook 249 ■ Exporting Outlook Data to a Microsoft Excel Database 256 ■ Key Points 259 ■ Quick Quiz 259 ■ On Your Own 260 ■ One Step Further 260

LESSON 9   Using Advanced E-Mail Features 261

Creating and Using Message Templates 262 ■ Creating a Distribution List 267 ■ Protecting Your Privacy 271 ■ Using the Rules Wizard 273 ■ Tracking When Messages are Delivered and Read 281 ■ Preparing to Access a Newsgroup 284 ■ Viewing Newsgroups and Newsgroup Messages 288 ■ Subscribing to a Newsgroup 290 ■ Key Points 291 ■ Quick Quiz 292 ■ On Your Own 293 ■ One Step Further 293

LESSON 10 Using Advanced Calendar Features 295

Customizing Calendar Options 296 ■ Changing Time Zone Settings 301 ■ Setting Private Appointments 304 ■ Updating Meetings 305 ■ Scheduling Online Meetings Using NetMeeting 311 ■ Sharing Calendar Information Over the Internet 314 ■ Side-by-Side Calendars 317 ■ Key Points 320 ■ Quick Quiz 321 ■ On Your Own 322 ■ One Step Further 322

LESSON 11 Managing Information 323

Working Offline 324 ■ Modifying Mail Service 327 ■ Creating and Using Outlook Forms 328 ■ Searching for Information 332 ■ Granting Permissions to Your Folders 336 ■ Using Outlook with Windows SharePoint Services 339 ■ Key Points 344 ■ Quick Quiz 344 ■ On Your Own 346 ■ One Step Further 346

LESSON 12 Managing Contacts and Tasks 347

Viewing and Sending Task Information for Other Users 347 ■ Sending and Receiving Instant Messages 352 ■ Key Points 354 ■ Quick Quiz 354 ■ On Your Own 356 ■ One Step Further 356

APPENDIX A Setting Up Outlook 357

GLOSSARY 361

INDEX 365

Course Overview

Welcome to the *Microsoft Official Academic Course* series for Microsoft Office System 2003 Edition. This series facilitates classroom learning, enabling you to develop competence and confidence in using Office applications. In completing courses taught with the *Microsoft Official Academic Course* series, you learn to use the software productively and discover how to make the software work for you. This series addresses core-level and expert-level skills in Microsoft Office Word 2003, Microsoft Office Excel 2003, Microsoft Office Access 2003, Microsoft Office PowerPoint 2003, Microsoft Office Outlook 2003, Microsoft FrontPage 2002/2003, and Microsoft Project 2002/2003.

The *Microsoft Official Academic Course* series provides:

- A time-tested, integrated approach to learning.
- Task-based, results-oriented learning strategies.
- Exercises based on realistic business scenarios.
- Complete preparation for Microsoft Office Specialist (MOS) certification.
- Attractive student guides with full-featured lessons.
- Lessons with accurate, logical, and sequential instructions.
- Comprehensive coverage of skills from the basic to the expert level.
- Review of core-level skills provided in expert-level guides.
- A CD-ROM with Microsoft's e-learning tool as well as practice files.

A Task-Based Approach Using Business Scenarios

The *Microsoft Official Academic Course* uses the time-tested approach of learning by doing. By studying with a task-based approach, you learn more than just the features of the software. You learn how to accomplish real-world tasks so that you can immediately increase your productivity using the software application.

The lessons are based on tasks that you might encounter in the everyday work world. This approach allows you to quickly see the relevance of the training beyond just the classroom. The business focus is woven throughout the series, from business examples within procedures, to scenarios chosen for practice files, to examples shown in the e-learning tool.

An Integrated Approach to Training

The *Microsoft Official Academic Course* series distinguishes itself from other series on the market with its consistent delivery and completely integrated approach to learning across print and online training media.

The textbook component of the *Microsoft Official Academic Course* series uses easily digested units of learning so that you can stop and restart lessons easily.

For those who prefer online training, this series includes an e-learning tool, the Microsoft e-Learning Library Version 2 (MELL 2). MELL 2 offers highly interactive online training in a simulated work environment, complete with graphics, sound, video, and animation. Icons in the margin of the textbook direct you to related topics within the e-learning tool so that you can choose to reinforce your learning more visually. MELL 2 also includes an assessment feature that students and teachers can use to gauge preliminary knowledge about the application.

Preparation for Microsoft Office Specialist (MOS) Certification

This series has been certified as approved courseware for the Microsoft Office Specialist certification program. Students who have completed this training are prepared to take the related MOS exam. By passing the exam for a particular Office application, students demonstrate proficiency in that application to their employers or prospective employers. Exams are offered at participating test centers. For more information, see *www.microsoft.com/traincert/mcp/officespecialist/requirements.asp*.

Designed for Optimal Learning

Lessons in the *Microsoft Official Academic Course* series are presented in a logical, easy-to-follow format, helping you find information quickly and learn as efficiently as possible. The colorful and highly visual series design makes it easy for you to see what to read and what to do when practicing new skills.

Lessons break training into easily assimilated sessions. Each lesson is self-contained, and lessons can be completed in sequences other than the one presented in the table of contents. Sample files for the lessons don't depend on completion of other lessons. Sample files within a lesson assume only that you are working sequentially through a complete lesson.

Each book within the *Microsoft Official Academic Course* series features:

- **Lesson objectives.** Objectives clearly state the instructional goals for the lesson so that you understand what skills you will master. Each lesson objective is covered in its own section, and each section or topic in the lesson is covered in a consistent way. Lesson objectives preview the lesson structure, helping you grasp key information and prepare for learning skills.

- **Key terms.** Terms with which you might not be familiar are listed at the beginning of the lesson. When these terms are used later in the lesson, they appear in boldface type and are defined. The Glossary contains all of the key terms and their definitions.

- **Informational text for each topic.** For each objective, the lesson provides easy-to-read, technique-focused information.

- **The Bottom Line.** Each main topic within the lesson has a summary of what makes the topic relevant to you.

- **Hands-on practice.** Numbered steps give detailed, step-by-step instructions to help you learn skills. The steps also show results and screen images to match what you should see on your computer screen. The accompanying CD contains the sample files needed for each lesson.

- **Full-color illustrations.** Illustrated screen images give visual feedback as you work through exercises. The images reinforce key concepts, provide visual clues about the steps, and give you something to check your progress against.
- **MOS icon.** Each section or sidebar that covers a MOS certification objective has a MOS icon in the margin at the beginning of the section. The complete list of MOS objectives and the location in the text where they are covered can be found in the MOS Objectives section of this book.
- **Reader aids.** Helpful hints and alternate ways to accomplish tasks are located throughout the lesson text. Reader aids provide additional related or background information that adds value to the lesson. These also include things to watch out for or things to avoid.
- **Check This Out.** These sidebars contain parenthetical topics or additional information that you might find interesting.
- **Button images in the margin.** When the text instructs you to click a particular button, an image of the button is shown in the margin.
- **Quick Reference.** Each main section contains a condensed version of the steps used in its procedures. This section is helpful if you want only a fast reminder of how to complete a certain task.
- **Quick Check.** These questions and answers provide a chance to review material covered in that section of the lesson.
- **Quick Quiz.** You can use the true/false, multiple choice, or short-answer Quick Quiz questions to test or reinforce your understanding of key topics within each lesson.
- **On Your Own exercises.** These exercises give you another opportunity to practice skills that you learned in the lesson. Completing these exercises helps you to verify whether you understand the lesson and to reinforce your learning.
- **One Step Further exercises.** These exercises give you an opportunity to build upon what you have learned by applying that knowledge in a different way. These might also require researching on the Internet.
- **Glossary.** Terms with which you might not be familiar are defined in the glossary. Terms in the glossary appear in boldface type within the lessons and are also defined within the lessons.
- **Index.** Student guides are completely indexed. All glossary terms and application features appear in the index.
- **MELL icons in the margin.** These icons direct you to related topics within the Microsoft e-Learning Library. For more information on MELL, please see the Microsoft e-Learning Library section later in this book.

x   Course Overview

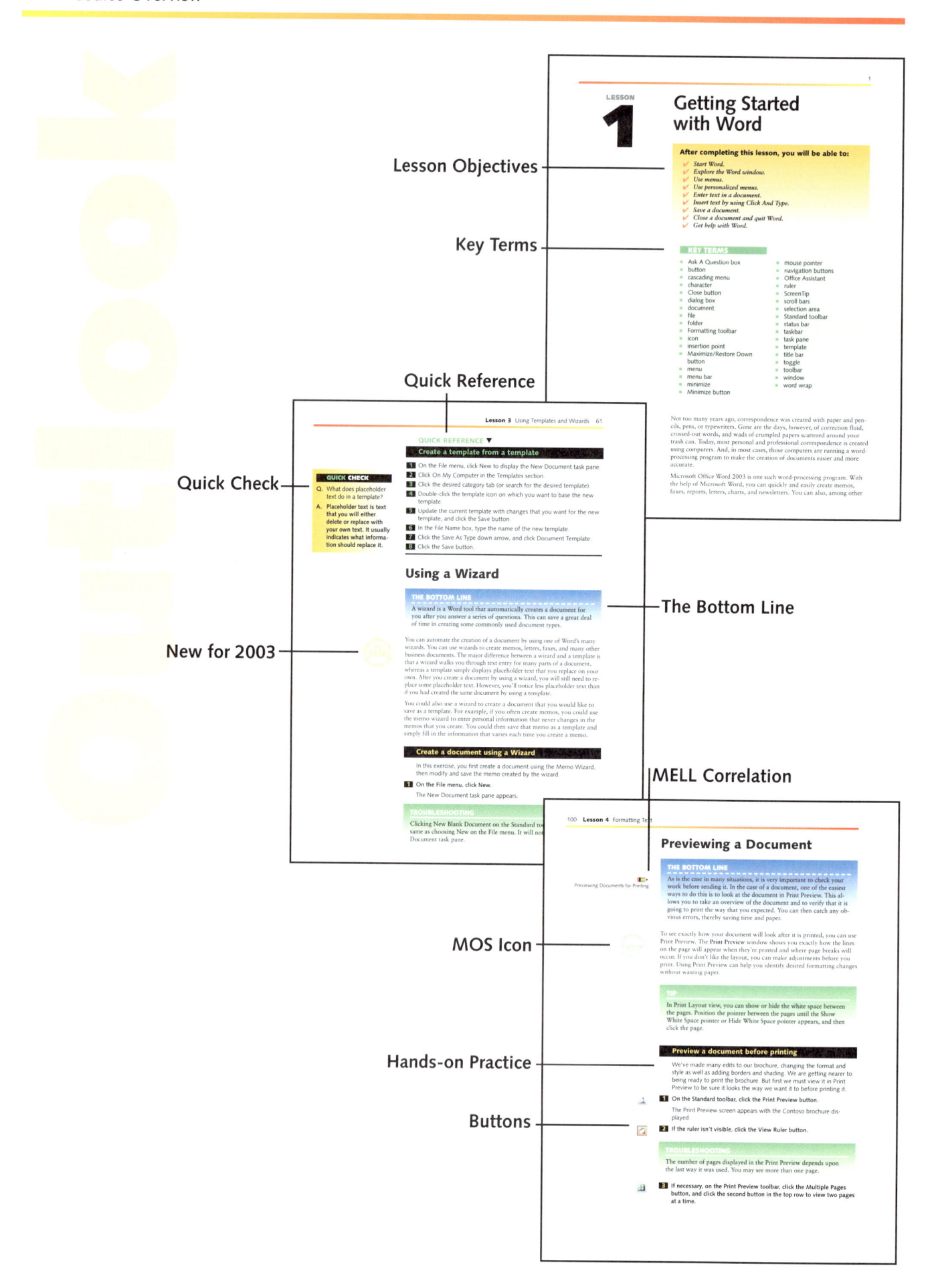

Annotations pointing to sample pages:

- Lesson Objectives
- Key Terms
- Quick Reference
- Quick Check
- New for 2003
- The Bottom Line
- MELL Correlation
- MOS Icon
- Hands-on Practice
- Buttons

Course Overview   xi

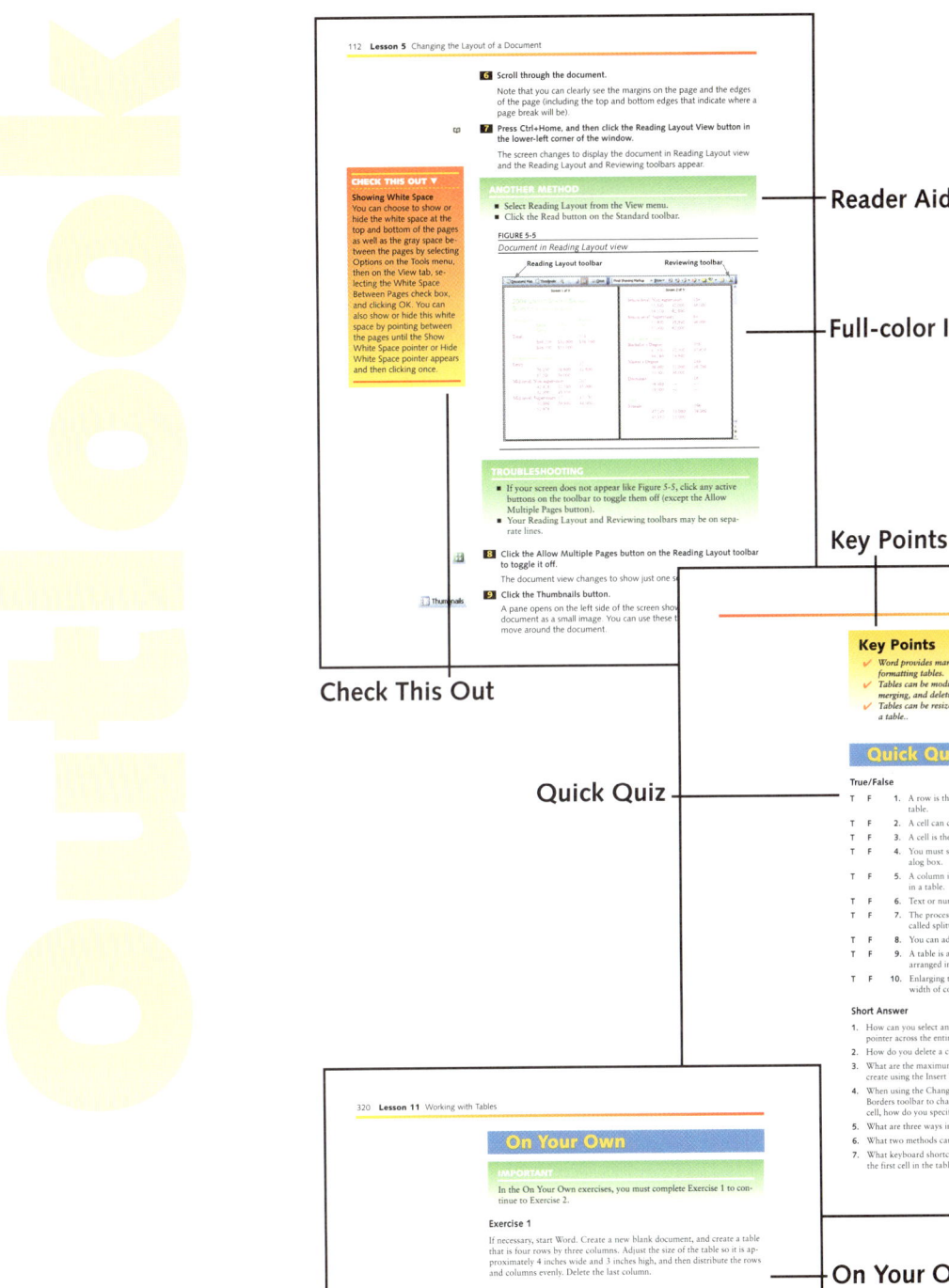

- Reader Aids
- Full-color Illustrations
- Check This Out
- Key Points
- Quick Quiz
- On Your Own
- One Step Further

Conventions and Features Used in This Book

This book uses special fonts, symbols, and heading conventions to highlight important information or to call your attention to special steps. For more information about the features available in each lesson, refer to the "Course Overview" section.

Convention	Meaning
NEW FOR 2003	This icon in the margin indicates a new or greatly improved feature in this version of the software.
MICROSOFT OFFICE SPECIALIST	This icon indicates that the section where it appears covers a Microsoft Office Specialist (MOS) exam objective. For a complete list of the MOS objectives, see the "MOS Objectives" section.
THE BOTTOM LINE	These paragraphs provide a brief summary of the material to be covered in the section that follows.
◆ Close the file.	Words preceded by a yellow diamond in a black box give instructions for opening, saving, or closing files or programs. They also point out items you should check or actions you should carry out.
QUICK REFERENCE ▼	These provide an "at-a-glance" summary of the steps involved to complete a given task. These differ from procedures because they're generic, not scenario-driven, and they're brief.
QUICK CHECK	This is a quick question and answer that serves to reinforce critical points and provides a chance to review the material covered.
TIP	Reader aids appear in green boxes. *Another Method* provides alternative procedures related to particular tasks, *Tip* provides helpful hints related to particular tasks or topics, and *Troubleshooting* covers common mistakes or areas in which you may have trouble. *Important* highlights warnings or cautions that are critical to performing exercises.

Convention	Meaning
CHECK THIS OUT ▼	These notes in the margin area provide pointers to information elsewhere in the book (or another book) or describe interesting features of the program that are not directly discussed in the current topic or used in the exercise.
💾	When a toolbar button is referenced in the lesson, the button's picture is shown in the margin.
Alt+Tab	A plus sign (+) between two key names means that you must press those keys at the same time. For example, "Press Alt+Tab" means that you hold down the Alt key while you press Tab.
Boldface type	Indicates a key term entry that is defined in the Glossary at the end of the book.
Type **Yes**.	Anything you are supposed to type appears in red bold characters.
✏️	This icon alongside a paragraph indicates reated coverage within the Microsoft e-Learning Library, (MELL)the e-learning tool. Find more information on MELL later in this book.

Using the CD-ROMs

There are two CD-ROMs included with this student guide. One contains the practice files that you'll use as you perform the exercises in the book. You can use the other CD-ROM, described below, to install a 180-day trial edition of Microsoft Office Professional Edition 2003. By using the practice files, you won't waste time creating the samples used in the lessons, and you can concentrate on learning how to use Microsoft Office Outlook 2003. With the files and the step-by-step instructions in the lessons, you'll learn by doing, which is an easy and effective way to acquire and remember new skills.

System Requirements

Your computer system must meet the following minimum requirements for you to install the practice files from the CD-ROM and to run Microsoft Outlook 2003.

> **IMPORTANT**
>
> This course assumes that Outlook 2003 has already been installed on the PC you are using. Microsoft Office Professional Edition 2003—180-Day Trial, which includes Outlook, is on the second CD-ROM included with this book. Microsoft Product Support does not support these trial editions.
>
> For information on how to install the trial edition, see "Installing or Uninstalling Microsoft Office Professional Edition 2003—180-Day Trial" later in this part of the book.

- A personal computer running Outlook 2003 on a Pentium 233-megahertz (MHz) or higher processor.
- Microsoft Windows® 2000 with Service Pack 3 (SP3), Windows XP, or later.
- 128 MB of RAM or greater.
- At least 2 MB of available disk space (after installing Outlook 2003 or Microsoft Office).
- A CD-ROM or DVD drive.
- A monitor with Super VGA (800 X 600) or higher resolution with 256 colors.
- A Microsoft mouse, a Microsoft IntelliMouse, or other compatible pointing device.

If You Need to Install or Uninstall the Practice Files

Your instructor might already have installed the practice files before you arrive in class. However, your instructor might ask you to install the practice files on your own at the start of class. Also, if you want to work through any of the exercises in this book on your own at home or at your place of business after class, you will need to first install the practice files.

Install the practice files

1 Insert the CD-ROM in the CD-ROM drive of your computer.

A menu screen appears.

> **IMPORTANT**
>
> If the menu screen does not appear, start Windows Explorer. In the left pane, locate the icon for your CD-ROM, and click this icon. In the right pane, double-click the file StartCD.

2 Click Install Practice Files, and follow the instructions on the screen.

The recommended options are preselected for you.

3 After the files have been installed, click Exit.

A folder called Outlook Practice has been created on your hard disk; the practice files have been placed in that folder.

4 Remove the CD-ROM from the CD-ROM drive.

Use the following steps when you want to delete the lesson practice files from your hard disk. Your instructor might ask you to perform these steps at the end of class. Also, you should perform these steps if you have worked through the exercises at home or at your place of business and want to work through the exercises again. Deleting the practice files and then reinstalling them ensures that all files and folders are in their original condition if you decide to work through the exercises again.

Unistall the practice files from the Windows XP or later operating system

1 On the Windows taskbar, click the Start button and then click Control Panel.

2 If you are in Classic View, double-click the Add Or Remove Programs icon. If you are in Category View, single-click the Add Or Remove Programs link.

3 In the Add Or Remove Programs dialog box, scroll down and select Word Core Practice in the list. Click the Change/Remove button.

4 Click Yes when the confirmation dialog box appears.

Uninstall the practice files from the Windows 2000 operating system

1 On the Windows taskbar, click the Start button, point to Settings, and then click Control Panel.

2 Double-click the Add/Remove icon.

3 Click Word Core Practice in the list, and click the Remove or the Change/Remove button.

4 Click Yes when the confirmation dialog box appears.

Using the Practice Files

Each lesson in this book explains when and how to use any practice files for that lesson. The lessons are built around scenarios that simulate a real work environment, so you can easily apply the skills you learn to your own work. The scenarios in the lessons use the context of the fictitious Contoso, Ltd, a public relations firm, and its client, Adventure Works, a resort located in the mountains of California.

By default, Outlook 2003 places the Standard and Formatting toolbars on the same row below the menu bar to save space. To match the lessons and exercises in this book, the Standard and Formatting toolbars should be separated onto two rows before the start of this course. To separate the Standard and Formatting toolbars:

- Position the mouse pointer over the move handle at the beginning of the Formatting toolbar until it turns into the move pointer (a four-headed arrow), and drag the toolbar down until it appears on its own row.

The following is a list of all files and folders used in the lessons.

File Name	Description
Contact Records	Folder to install before starting
E-mail Messages	Folder to install before starting
Map	Image file used in Lesson 2
Syllabus	Document used in Lesson 2
Eric Lang	Image file used in Lesson 4
AW Address List	Access database used in Lesson 8
Guests	Access database used in Lesson 8

Replying to Install Messages

When you work through some lessons, you might see a message indicating that the feature that you are trying to use is not installed. If you see this message, insert the Microsoft Office Outlook 2003 CD or Microsoft Office CD 1 in your CD-ROM drive, and click Yes to install the feature.

Locating and Opening Files

After you (or your instructor) have installed the practice files, all the files you need for this course will be stored in a folder named Outlook Practice located on your hard disk.

Navigate to the Outlook Practice folder from within Word and open a file

1. On the Standard toolbar, click the Open button.
2. In the Open dialog box, click the Look In down arrow, and click the icon for your hard disk.
3. Double-click the Outlook Practice folder.
4. Double-click the file that you want to open.

All the files for the lessons appear within the Outlook Practice folder.

If You Need Help with the Practice Files

If you have any problems regarding the use of this book's CD-ROM, you should first consult your instructor. If you are using the CD-ROM at home or at your place of business and need additional help with the practice files, contact McGraw-Hill for support:

E-mail: techsup@mcgraw-hill.com

Phone: (800) 331-5094

Post: McGraw-Hill Companies

1333 Burr Ridge Parkway

Burr Ridge, IL 60521

IMPORTANT

For help using Outlook 2003, rather than this book, you can visit support.microsoft.com or call Microsoft Product Support at (425) 635-7070 on weekdays between 5 A.M. and 9 P.M. Pacific Standard Time or on Saturdays and Sundays between 6 A.M. and 3 P.M. Pacific Standard Time. Microsoft Product Support does not provide support for this course. Also please note that Microsoft Product Support does not support trial editions of Office.

Installing or Uninstalling Microsoft Office Professional Edition 2003—180-Day Trial

An installation CD-ROM for Microsoft Office Professional Edition 2003—180-Day Trial is included with this book. Before you install your trial version, please read this entire section for important information on setting up and uninstalling your trial software.

> **CAUTION**
>
> For the best performance, the default selection during Setup is to uninstall previous versions of Office. There is also an option not to remove previous versions of Office. With all trial software, Microsoft recommends that you have your original CDs available to reinstall if necessary. If you want to return to your previous version of Office, you need to uninstall the trial software. This should be done through the Add or Remove Programs icon in Microsoft Windows Control Panel.
>
> Installation of Microsoft Office Professional Edition 2003—180-Day Trial software will remove your existing version of Microsoft Outlook. However, your contacts, calendar, and other personal information will not be deleted. At the end of the trial, if you choose to upgrade or to reinstall your previous version of Outlook, your personal settings and information will be retained.

Setup Instructions

1. Insert the trial software CD into the CD drive on your computer. The CD will be detected, and the Setup.exe file should automatically begin to run on your computer.

2. When prompted for the Office Product Key, enter the Product Key provided with the software, and then click Next.

3. Enter your name and organization user name, and then click Next.

4. Read the End-User License Agreement, select the I Accept The Terms In The License Agreement check box, and then click Next.

> **NOTE**
>
> Copies of the product License Agreements are also available for review at http://www.microsoft.com/office/eula.

5. Select the install option, verify the installation location or click Browse to change the installation location, and then click Next.

   The default setting is Upgrade. You will have the opportunity to specify not to remove previous versions of Office from your computer later in the installation wizard.

6 Verify the program installation preferences, and then click Next.

> **CAUTION**
>
> For best performance, the default selection during setup is to uninstall (remove) previous versions of Office. There is also the option not to remove previous versions of Office. With all trial software, Microsoft recommends that you have your original CDs available to reinstall if necessary.

7 To finish Setup, select the check boxes you want so that you can receive the online updates and downloads or to delete the installation files, then click Finish.

Upgrading Microsoft Office Professional Edition 2003—180-Day Trial Software to the Full Product

You can convert the software into full use without removing or reinstalling software on your computer. When you complete your trial, you can purchase a product license from any Microsoft reseller and enter a valid Product Key when prompted during Setup.

Uninstalling the Trial Software and Returning to Your Previous Office Version

If you want to return to your previous version of Office, you need to uninstall the trial software. This should be done through the Add or Remove Programs icon in Control Panel.

1 Quit any programs that are running, such as Microsoft Word or Outlook.

2 In control Panel, click Add or Remove Programs.

3 Click Microsoft Office Professional Edition 2003, and then click Remove.

> **NOTE**
>
> If you selected the option to remove a previous version of Office during installation of the trial software, you need to reinstall your previous version of Office. If you did not remove your previous version of Office, you can start each of your Office programs either through the Start menu or by opening files for each program, such as Word, Microsoft Excel, and Microsoft PowerPoint files. In some cases, you may have to recreate some of your shortcuts and default settings.

MOS Objectives

Standard	Skill	Page
OLO3S-1	**Messaging**	
OLO3S-1-1	Originate and respond to e-mail and instant messages	20, 24, 37, 50, 56, 62, 124, 127, 129, 262, 352
OLO3S-1-2	Attach files to items	27, 129, 221, 342
OLO3S-1-3	Create and modify a personal signature for messages	65
OLO3S-1-4	Modify e-mail message settings and delivery options	25, 26, 62, 271, 281, 327
OLO3S-1-5	Create and edit contacts	94, 98, 102, 249
OLO3S-1-6	Accept, decline, and delegate tasks	204, 347
OLO3S-2	**Scheduling**	
OLO3S-2-1	Create and modify appointments, meetings, and events	146, 151, 154, 156, 158, 164, 165, 171, 304, 314
OLO3S-2-2	Update, cancel, and respond to meeting requests	168, 305, 311
OLO3S-2-3	Customize Calendar settings	144, 243, 296, 301, 317
OLO3S-2-4	Create, modify, and assign tasks	176, 182, 187, 198, 201, 206, 209
OLO3S-3	**Organizing**	
OLO3S-3-1	Create and modify distribution lists	267
OLO3S-3-2	Link contacts to other items	98
OLO3S-3-3	Create and modify notes	213, 214, 217, 218
OLO3S-3-4	Organize items	50, 69, 72, 83, 85, 88, 105, 109, 114, 119, 159, 161, 185, 190, 223, 239, 247
OLO3S-3-5	Organize items using folders	76, 78, 107, 193, 225, 273
OLO3S-3-6	Search for items	42, 94, 121, 332
OLO3S-3-7	Save items in different file formats	174, 256
OLO3S-3-8	Assign items to categories	114, 117, 119, 195
OLO3S-3-9	Preview and print items	32, 40, 172, 192

Taking a Microsoft Office Specialist Certification Test

The Microsoft Office Specialist (MOS) program is the only Microsoft-approved certification program designed to measure and validate your skills with the Microsoft Office suite of desktop productivity applications: Microsoft Word, Microsoft Excel, Microsoft PowerPoint, Microsoft Access, and Microsoft Outlook.

By becoming certified, you demonstrate to employers that you have achieved a predictable level of skill in the use of a particular Office application. Employers often require certification either as a condition of employment or as a condition of advancement within the company or other organization. The certification examinations are sponsored by Microsoft but administered through Nivo International.

The MOS program typically offers certification exams at the "core" and "expert" levels. For a core-level test, you demonstrate your ability to use an application knowledgeably and without assistance in a day-to-day work environment. For an expert-level test, you demonstrate that you have a thorough knowledge of the application and can effectively apply all or most of the features of the application to solve problems and complete tasks found in business.

Preparing to Take an Exam

Unless you're a very experienced user, you'll need to use a test preparation course to prepare to complete the test correctly and within the time allowed. The *Microsoft Official Academic Course* series is designed to prepare you for either core-level or expert-level knowledge of a particular Microsoft Office application. By the end of this course, you should have a strong knowledge of all exam topics, and with some additional review and practice on your own, you should feel confident in your ability to pass the appropriate exam.

After you decide which exam to take, review the list of objectives for the exam. This list can be found in the "MOS Objectives" section at the front of the appropriate *Microsoft Official Academic Course* student guide. You can also easily identify tasks that are included in the objective list by locating the MOS symbol in the margin of the lessons in this book.

For an expert-level test, you'll need to be able to demonstrate any of the skills from the core-level objective list, too. Expect some of these core-level tasks to appear on the expert-level test.

You can also familiarize yourself with a live MOS certification test by downloading and installing a practice MOS certification test from www.microsoft.com/traincert/mcp/officespecialist/requirements.asp.

To take the MOS test, first see www.microsoft.com/traincert/mcp/office-specialist/requirements.asp to locate your nearest testing center. Then call the testing center directly to schedule your test. The amount of advance notice you should provide will vary for different testing centers, and it typically depends on the number of computers available at the testing center, the number of other testers who have already been scheduled for the day on which you want to take the test, and the number of times per week that the testing center offers MOS testing. In general, you should call to schedule your test at least two weeks prior to the date on which you want to take the test.

When you arrive at the testing center, you might be asked for proof of identity. A driver's license or passport is an acceptable form of identification. If you do not have either of these items of documentation, call your testing center and ask what alternative forms of identification will be accepted. If you are retaking a test, bring your MOS identification number, which will have been given to you when you previously took the test. If you have not prepaid or if your organization has not already arranged to make payment for you, you will need to pay the test-taking fee when you arrive. The current test-taking fee is $75 (U.S.). Prices are subject to change and may vary depending on the testing center.

Test Format

All MOS certification tests are live, performance-based tests. There are no multiple-choice, true/false, or short-answer questions. Instructions are general: you are told the basic tasks to perform on the computer, but you aren't given any help in figuring out how to perform them. You are not permitted to use reference material other than the application's Help system.

As you complete the tasks stated in a particular test question, the testing software monitors your actions. An example question might be:

> Open the file named AW Guests and select the word Welcome in the first paragraph. Change the font to 12 point, and apply bold formatting. Select the words at your convenience in the second paragraph, move them to the end of the first paragraph using drag and drop, and then center the first paragraph.

The sample tests available from www.microsoft.com/traincert/mcp/office-specialist/requirements.asp give you a clear idea of the type of questions that you will be asked on the actual test.

When the test administrator seats you at a computer, you'll see an online form that you use to enter information about yourself (name, address, and other information required to process your exam results). While you complete the form, the software will generate the test from a master test bank and then prompt you to continue. The first test question will appear in a window. Read the question carefully, and then perform all the tasks stated in the test question. When you have finished completing all tasks for a question, click the Next Question button.

You have 45 to 60 minutes to complete all questions, depending on the test that you are taking. The testing software assesses your results as soon as you complete the test, and the test administrator can print the results of the test so that you will have a record of any tasks that you performed incorrectly. A passing grade is 75 percent or higher. If you pass, you will receive a certificate in the mail within two to four weeks. If you do not pass, you can study and practice the skills that you missed and then schedule to retake the test at a later date.

Tips for Successfully Completing the Test

The following tips and suggestions are the result of feedback received from many individuals who have taken one or more MOS tests:

- Make sure that you are thoroughly prepared. If you have extensively used the application for which you are being tested, you might feel confident that you are prepared for the test. However, the test might include questions that involve tasks that you rarely or never perform when you use the application at your place of business, at school, or at home. You must be knowledgeable in all the MOS objectives for the test that you will take.

- Read each exam question carefully. An exam question might include several tasks that you are to perform. A partially correct response to a test question is counted as an incorrect response. In the example question on the previous page, you might apply bold formatting and move the words at your convenience to the correct location, but forget to center the first paragraph. This would count as an incorrect response and would result in a lower test score.

- You are allowed to use the application's Help system, but relying on the Help system too much will slow you down and possibly prevent you from completing the test within the allotted time. Use the Help system only when necessary.

- Keep track of your time. The test does not display the amount of time that you have left, so you need to keep track of the time yourself by monitoring your start time and the required end time on your watch or a clock in the testing center (if there is one). The test program displays the number of items that you have completed along with the total number of test items (for example, "35 of 40 items have been completed"). Use this information to gauge your pace.

- If you skip a question, you cannot return to it later. You should skip a question only if you are certain that you cannot complete the tasks correctly.

- Don't worry if the testing software crashes while you are taking the exam. The test software is set up to handle this situation. Find your test administrator and tell him or her what happened. The administrator will work through the steps required to restart the test. When the test restarts, it will allow you to continue where you left off. You will have the same amount of time remaining to complete the test as you did when the software crashed.

- As soon as you are finished reading a question and you click in the application window, a condensed version of the instruction is displayed in a corner of the screen. If you are unsure whether you have completed all tasks stated in the test question, click the Instructions button on the test information bar at the bottom of the screen and then reread the question. Close the instruction window when you are finished. Do this as often as necessary to ensure you have read the question correctly and that you have completed all the tasks stated in the question.

If You Do Not Pass the Test

If you do not pass, you can use the assessment printout as a guide to practice the items that you missed. There is no limit to the number of times that you can retake a test; however, you must pay the fee each time that you take the test. When you retake the test, expect to see some of the same test items on the subsequent test; the test software randomly generates the test items from a master test bank before you begin the test. Also expect to see several questions that did not appear on the previous test.

Microsoft e-Learning Library

Microsoft Learning is pleased to offer, in combination with our new *Microsoft Official Academic Course* for *Microsoft Office System 2003 Edition*, in-depth access to our powerful e-Learning tool, the Microsoft® e-Learning Library Version 2 (MELL 2) Desktop Edition for Office System 2003. The MELL Version 2 Desktop Edition for Office System 2003 will help instructors and students alike increase their skill and comfort level with Microsoft software and technologies—as well as help students develop the skills they need to succeed in today's competitive job market.

MELL Features

The MELL Version 2 Desktop Edition for Office System 2003 product included with this *Microsoft Official Academic Course* features:

- Fully customizable learning environments that help instructors pre-assess student's skill levels and direct them to the tasks that are appropriate to their needs.
- High-quality, browser-based training and reinforcement that offers students a familiar environment in which to acquire new skills.
- A powerful search tool that quickly scans a full library of learning materials and provides snappy answers to specific questions.
- Interactive exercises and focused lessons on specific subjects to help instructors direct their students quickly to exactly the content they need to know.
- Reliable, in-depth content, engaging simulations, automated support tools, and memorable on-screen demonstrations.
- An after hours and after class reference and reinforcement tool that students can take with them and use in their working lives.

Additionally, MELL Version 2 Desktop Edition for Office System 2003 fits easily into an existing lab and includes:

- Training solutions that are compatible with all existing software and hardware infrastructures.
- An enhanced learning environment that works without a separate learning management system (LMS) and runs in any SCORM-compliant LMS.
- The ability to send and receive shortcut links via e-mail to relevant help topics, which facilitates the learning experience in a classroom setting and encourages peer-to-peer learning.

Instructors who are preparing students for the MCSE/MCSA or MCAD credential can also use MELL 2 IT Professional Edition and MELL 2 Developer Edition to help students develop the skills they need to succeed in today's competitive job market. Both editions provide outstanding training and reference materials designed to help users achieve professional certification while learning real-world skills. Check out www.microsoft.com/mspress/business for more information on these additional MELL products.

Focused Students, Mastering Tasks

The MELL Version 2 Desktop Edition for Office System 2003 helps focus students on the tasks they need to know and helps them master those tasks through a combination of the following:

- Assessments that help determine the lessons that will require focus in the classroom or lab.
- Realistic simulations that mirror the actual software without requiring that it already be installed—making it ideal for students who may not have access to the latest Microsoft products outside of the classroom and labs.
- Within the simulation, the ability for a student to follow each step on his or her own, have the computer perform the step, or any combination of the two.

The MELL Version 2 Desktop Edition for Office System 2003 provides deep premium content that allows and encourages students to go beyond basic tasks and achieve proficiency and effectiveness—in class and eventually in the workplace. This depth is reflected in the fact that our desktop training titles are certified by the Microsoft Office Specialist Program.

The MELL Assessment Feature

MELL Version 2 Desktop Edition for Office System 2003 includes a skill assessment designed to help instructors identify topics and features that might warrant coverage during lecture or lab meetings. The skill assessment gives instructors an opportunity to see how much students already know about the topics covered in this course, which in turn allows instructors to devote meeting time to topics with which students are unfamiliar.

To use the assessment feature, follow these steps (note that the illustrations are specific to the Excel Core course, but the steps apply to all of the courses):

1 Insert the Microsoft Official Academic Course companion CD that accompanies this textbook into your CD drive.

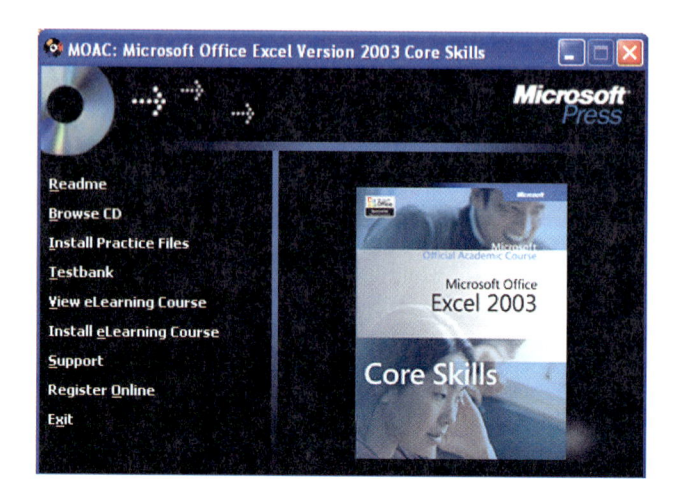

2 From the menu, select "View e-Learning Course."

3 Click on the training course you are interested in via the left navigation pane.

4 Click on "Pre-Assessment" within any core training topic on the accompanying MELL Version 2 Desktop Edition for Office System 2003 CD-ROM.

5 Click on "Take the Pre-Assessment."

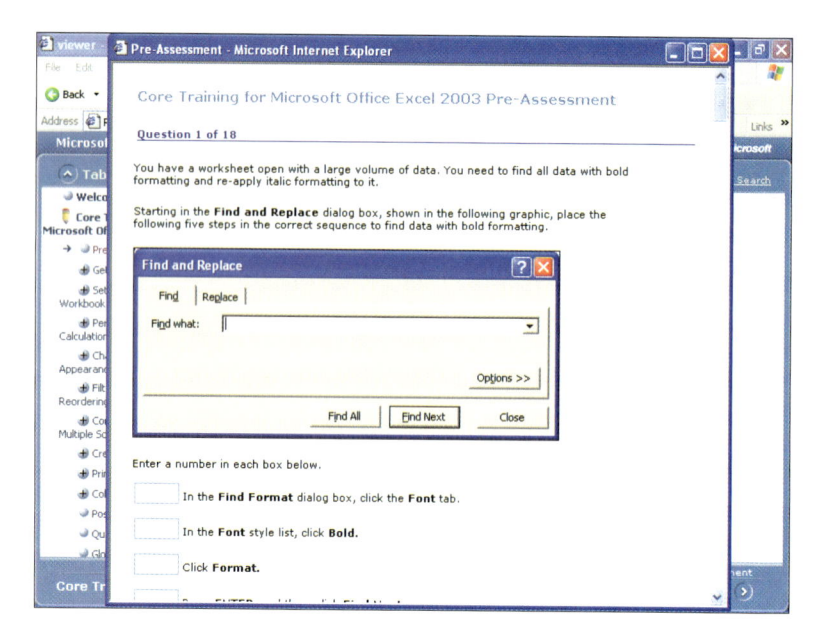

6 Input some correct answers and, if you choose, some incorrect answers as you move through the Pre-Assessment.

7 Click on "Show My Score" at the bottom of the Skills Assessment.

Microsoft e-Learning Library xxix

8 The "Show My Score" box details all the correct and incorrect answers and also provides correct answers for all the incorrect responses.

9 Additionally, the resultant table also provides a basic learning plan, directing you to areas you need to master while acknowledging the skills you already possess.

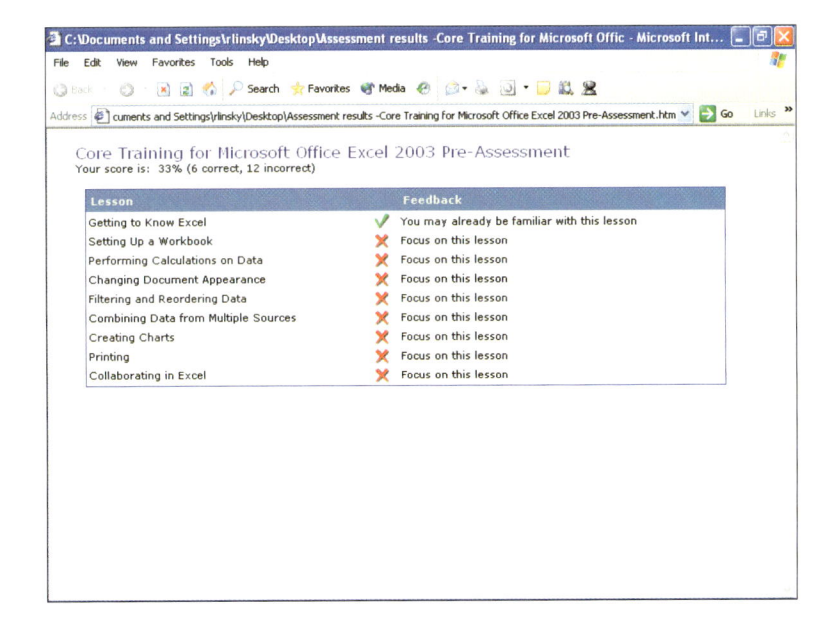

10 Click on either the "Print" or "Save" button to print or save to disk your Pre-Assessment results for future reference.

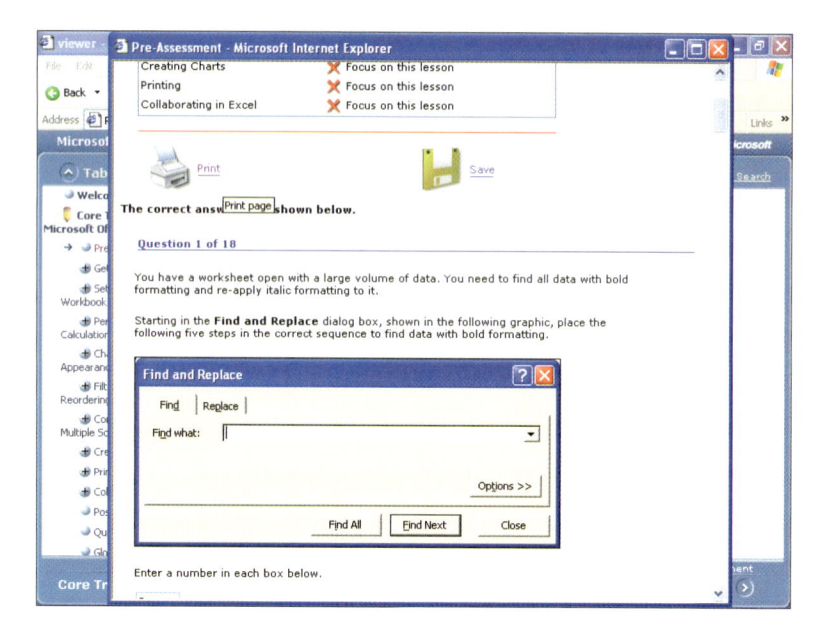

11 You are now ready to begin your interactive learning experience with MELL Version 2 Desktop Edition for Office System 2003!

LESSON 1

Introduction to Outlook

After completing this lesson, you will be able to:
- ✔ *Start Outlook.*
- ✔ *Navigate within Outlook.*
- ✔ *Use the Office Assistant.*

KEY TERMS
- Folder List
- folder
- item
- Office Assistant
- Navigation pane
- profile
- Reading pane
- shortcut

Managing work-related data often means recording and tracking information on paper stored in several different places. For example, a businessperson might record appointments and meetings in a day planner, while keeping phone numbers and addresses in a card file. Brief reminders were jotted down on small sticky notes. Other important business information was stored in files and folders in a desk drawer or filing cabinet.

Although many people have grown accustomed to these organizational approaches, Microsoft Office Outlook 2003 provides a better way to store, track, and integrate business and personal information. With Outlook, you can store and access important information in a single location on a personal computer. For example, you can use Outlook's electronic calendar to record meetings and appointment dates and times. Outlook can even sound an alarm or display a reminder on your computer screen when you have an appointment. You can record brief reminders to yourself on Outlook notes, which resemble sticky notes, and these notes can be displayed on your screen at any time for easy reference. You can use Outlook to record your daily or weekly tasks and check them off as you complete them. Outlook has an address book in which you can record phone numbers, addresses, e-mail addresses, and other information about your business and personal contacts. You can even view Web sites directly from Outlook, as well as open other Microsoft Office System documents. The power of Outlook lies in knowing how to use all of its capabilities to organize information efficiently.

Outlook 2003 has several improvements since the previous version. The most obvious change is the interface. The new interface simplifies navigation and dramatically improves the ease of reading messages.

In this lesson, you will tour many of the elements of Outlook to become familiar with it. You will start Outlook and view different folders, which are containers for programs and files. You will also use the new Navigation pane to display the contents of the selected folder or file. The new Reading pane provides a larger vertical area for displaying and reading messages. Finally, you will learn how to use the Help system in Outlook to find answers to your questions about using Outlook as a powerful tool to organize your data.

FIGURE 1-1

Outlook icon

Microsoft Office Outlook 2003

Starting Outlook

> **THE BOTTOM LINE**
>
> Microsoft Office Outlook 2003 requires a profile that includes all the information required to access your e-mail accounts and send messages. You establish this profile when you first sart Outlook.

As with all Microsoft Office System programs, there are several different ways to open Outlook. One method is to click the Start button on the Windows taskbar, point to All Programs, point to Microsoft Office, and click Microsoft Office Outlook 2003. This option is always available, even if you are using another Microsoft Office System program.

> **TROUBLESHOOTING**
>
> Be sure that you can see the Start menu and a clear area on your desktop before you start the process of adding the Outlook icon to your desktop.

You can also add the Outlook icon to your desktop, and then simply double-click the icon to start Outlook. Using the icon is faster and easier than using the Start button on the Windows taskbar. To add an Outlook icon to your desktop, click the Start button on the Windows taskbar, point to All Programs, point to Microsoft Office, hold down the Ctrl key, and drag the Microsoft Office Outlook 2003 icon onto your desktop. This process adds the icon to your desktop without removing it from the Start menu.

When you start Outlook, you are asked to select a profile. The Outlook **profile** is a set of data required to enable Outlook to access your e-mail accounts and address book. It includes the name of your e-mail account, the servers used to send and receive e-mail, and your passwords.

> **TROUBLESHOOTING**
>
> See the Appendix for more information about setting up a profile.

Lesson 1 Introduction to Outlook 3

Start Microsoft Outlook:

In this exercise, you start Microsoft Office Outlook 2003.

1 **On the Windows taskbar, click the Start button, point to All Programs, point to Microsoft Office, and click Microsoft Office Outlook 2003.**

Outlook starts. The available Outlook profiles are listed.

ANOTHER METHOD

Double-click the Outlook icon on your desktop.

FIGURE 1-2

Outlook profiles

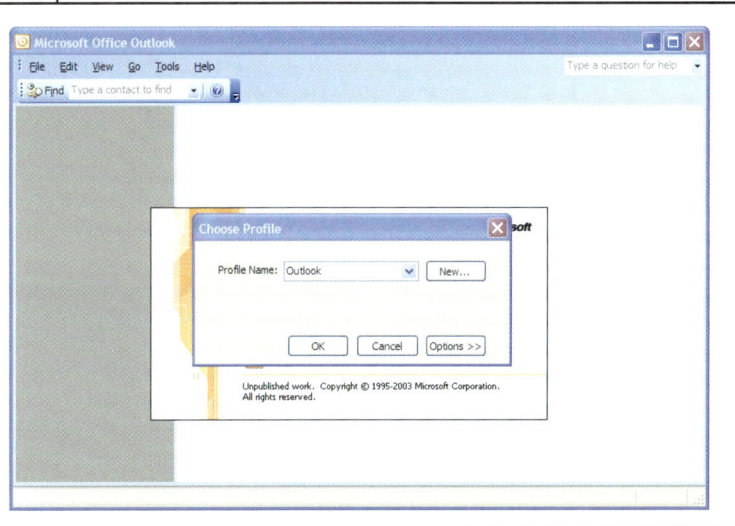

2 **If necessary, select your Outlook profile. Click the OK button.**

The main Outlook window is displayed, placing all of Outlook's functionality at your fingertips.

TROUBLESHOOTING

If you are opening Outlook for the first time, the Office Assistant (the animated paper clip character) might be displayed. To close the Office Assistant, right-click the paper clip, and click Close on the shortcut menu that appears. You will learn more about the Office Assistant later in this lesson.

3 **If necessary, click the Maximize button in the upper-right corner of the Outlook window.**

The Outlook window expands to fill the entire screen. This enables you to view the Outlook application at its best, providing a clear view of the information available in Outlook.

◆ **Keep Outlook open for the next exercise.**

Lesson 1 Introduction to Outlook

QUICK CHECK

Q: What is the purpose of the Maximize button?

A: The Maximize button expands the window to fill the entire screen.

QUICK REFERENCE ▼

Start Outlook

1. On the Windows taskbar, click the Start button.
2. Point to All Programs.
3. Point to Microsoft Office.
4. Click Microsoft Office Outlook 2003.
5. Select your profile and click OK.
6. If necessary, click the Maximize button.

Navigating Within Outlook

THE BOTTOM LINE

Microsoft Office Outlook 2003 has a new interface that enables you to save and access information quickly.

Now that you have opened the Outlook application, you can examine each element in the Outlook window. The Outlook window contains buttons, icons, menu commands, and other elements that enable you to navigate within Outlook and use Outlook effectively. The contents of this window change as you click buttons and icons and choose options. The table on the following page describes the basic functions of the elements displayed in the Outlook window.

TROUBLESHOOTING

If you used a previous version of Outlook, you will notice significant differences in the appearance of the Outlook window.

FIGURE 1-3

Outlook window

Element	Description
Title bar	Identifies the application currently running (in this case, Outlook) and the active Outlook folder.
Menu bar	Lists the names of the menus available in the current Outlook window. A menu displays a list of commands the application can perform.
Standard toolbar	Displays buttons that enable you to quickly access commonly used commands for the application.
Navigation pane	Provides access to the contents of folders that are available in Outlook, such as the Inbox and Calendar. The **Navigation pane** replaces the Outlook bar used in previous versions. To hide or display the Navigation pane, open the View menu and click Navigation pane. You will learn how to use the Navigation pane later in this lesson.
Item	Information displayed in Outlook. For example, in the Inbox, each message is an **item**; in Contacts, the contact record (phone and address information about an individual) is an item.
Status Bar	As you switch to different Outlook folders, the Status bar displays the number of items that are in a specific folder. For example, when you open Contacts, the Status bar displays the number of contacts in the folder.
Reading pane	A section of the Inbox window that displays the text of the selected message. The **Reading pane** can be moved, but the default location is the right side of the window. This provides the most vertical space to read longer messages without needing to scroll the text.

QUICK CHECK

Q: What is the purpose of the Navigation pane?

A: It provides access to the contents of folders that are available in Outlook.

Using Personalized Menus

THE BOTTOM LINE

Personalized menus provide fast access to the commands you use frequently.

Like other Microsoft Office System applications, Outlook has a default feature that enables you to personalize your menus. The first time you open a menu in Outlook, you see a short menu that displays the commands that are most frequently used by Outlook users. You also see two small arrows at the bottom of the menu. These arrows are used to expand the menu to display more options. You can expand the menu in two ways: click the arrows at the bottom of the menu or wait a few seconds for the menu to expand on its own. When you click a command on the expanded menu, Outlook immediately displays this command on the short menu. Outlook continues to adapt. Over time, if you stop using this command, it is removed from the short menu. The command will be displayed on the expanded menu.

6   **Lesson 1**   Introduction to Outlook

TIP

If you prefer to see the expanded menus instead of the short menus, open the Tools menu, click Customize, click the Options tab, select the Always Show Full Menus check box, and click Close.

Outlook 2003 includes a new menu. The Go menu contains a link to each of the main Outlook folders. This simply provides another way to move around in the Outlook application. Like the other menus, the short menu contains your most selections.

Use Outlook menus:

With Outlook open, you will now learn to use the Outlook menus.

TROUBLESHOOTING

Your short menu may display more commands than the samples in this exercise.

FIGURE 1-4

Short Tools menu

1 **On the menu bar, click Tools.**

The short Tools menu is displayed. The short Tools menu contains the options used most frequently by the majority of Outlook users. All of the menu options are not displayed.

2 **Click anywhere outside the menu.**

The menu closes. The focus shifts to the location you clicked.

3 **On the menu bar, click Tools.**

The short Tools menu is displayed. Again, only the most frequently used commands are displayed.

4 **Click the double arrows at the bottom of the short Tools menu.**

The expanded Tools menu is displayed. All commands available on the Tools menu are available for your use.

ANOTHER METHOD

To display the expanded menu, open the short menu and wait several seconds.

QUICK CHECK

Q: What is the meaning of the double arrows at the bottom of an open menu?

A: The double arrows indicate that additional options are available.

◆ Keep Outlook open for the next exercise.

QUICK REFERENCE ▼

To expand a short menu

1 Click the desired menu.

2 Click the double arrows at the bottom of the menu.

Using the Navigation Pane

> **THE BOTTOM LINE**
>
> The new Navigation pane contains buttons that provide one-click access to the standard Outlook folders.

You have used menus in the Outlook window to access commands and information. However, the Navigation pane provides faster access to most Outlook folders and items. It contains buttons that represent the components available in Outlook, such as the Mail, Calendar, and Contacts folders. When you click one of the buttons, the contents of the folder are displayed. For example, if you click the Calendar button, the content of the Calendar folder—a calendar containing your appointments—is displayed.

FIGURE 1-5

Navigation pane

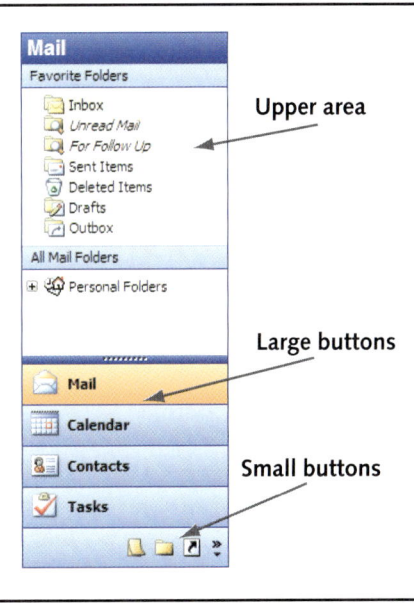

Buttons are displayed in the lower area of the Navigation pane. The buttons used frequently are large. Additional buttons are smaller. The content of the upper area of the Navigation pane depends on the button you select.

Outlook uses the term **folder** to describe how Outlook's functions and common items are divided within Outlook. For example, the Inbox folder contains e-mail messages that you have received and enables you to create messages within the Inbox folder. The Tasks folder contains a list of activities that you need to perform and enables you to create tasks. You cannot create a task in the Inbox folder or create a message in the Tasks folder. When you view the folders in Outlook, you'll notice that the appearance and options differ in each folder. For that reason, you can think of each folder as a separate program within Outlook, even though the functions work together without a seam.

> **TIP**
>
> Even though the Inbox, Contacts, Tasks, and other Outlook features are called "folders" in this book, you will sometimes see them referred to by name alone (for example, "the Inbox") rather than by name and identifier (for example, "the Inbox folder").

The Outlook folders directly accessed by the buttons are described in the following table.

Folder	Description
Mail	Displays the folders used to send and receive e-mail messages
Calendar	Displays a calendar and appointment book to track your schedule
Contacts	Stores the names, phone numbers, addresses, and other information about the people with whom you communicate
Tasks	Displays a to-do list of your personal and business tasks
Notes	Stores information on electronic sticky notes, such as ideas, grocery lists, or directions
Folder List	Displays a list of available folders; can be used to move items from one folder to another folder, create folders within folders, and much more (If your organization uses Microsoft Exchange Server, you might also see public folders that can be accessed by other network users.)
Shortcuts	Enables you to add links to additional files and folders that can be accessed by your computer
Journal	Displays a history of your Microsoft Office activities in a timeline format

Use the Navigation pane

You will now use the Navigation pane to view different Outlook folders.

1 **If necessary, on the Navigation pane, click the Mail button.**

The contents of the Mail folder are displayed. You will learn how to use the Inbox to send and receive e-mail messages in the next lesson.

Lesson 1 Introduction to Outlook   9

FIGURE 1-6

Mail folder

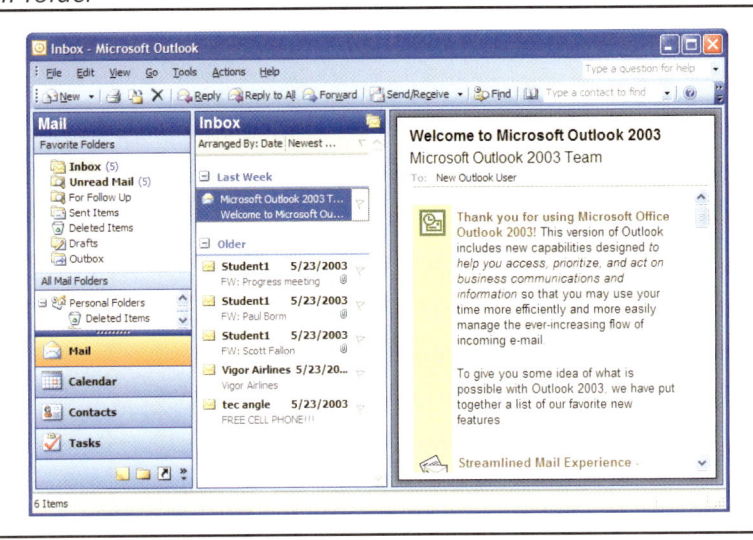

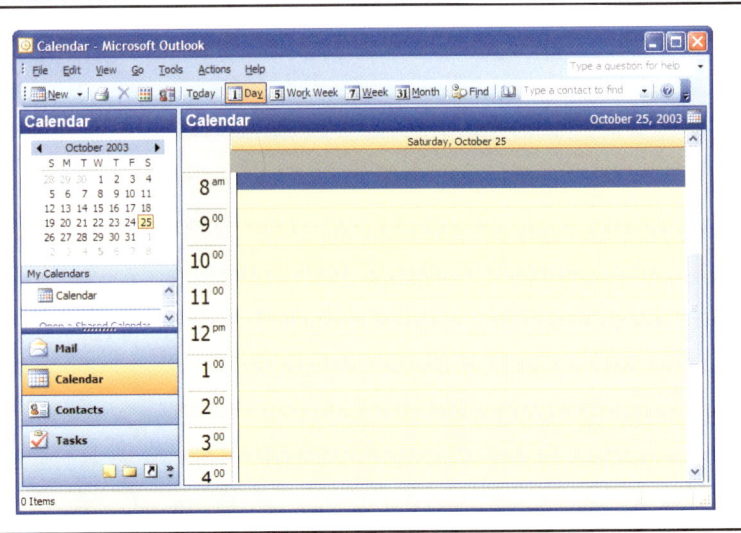

2. **On the Navigation pane, click the Calendar shortcut.**

   The contents of the Calendar folder are displayed. You will learn how to use the Calendar in Lesson 5, "Using the Calendar."

   FIGURE 1-7

   Calendar folder

10   Lesson 1 Introduction to Outlook

3 **On the Navigation pane, click the Contacts shortcut.**

The contents of the Contacts folder are displayed. You will learn how to create and edit contacts in Lesson 4, "Using Contacts."

FIGURE 1-8

Contacts folder

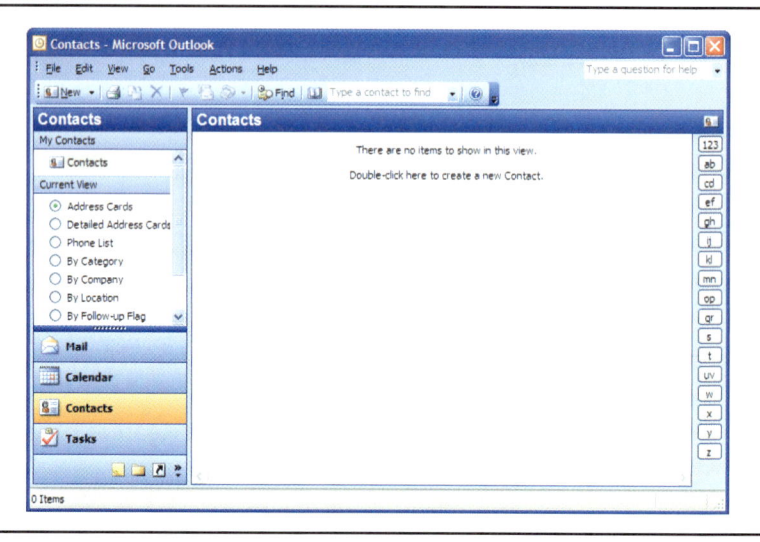

4 **On the Navigation pane, click the Tasks shortcut.**

The contents of the Tasks folder are displayed. You will learn how to create and edit tasks in Lesson 6, "Using Tasks."

FIGURE 1-9

Tasks folder

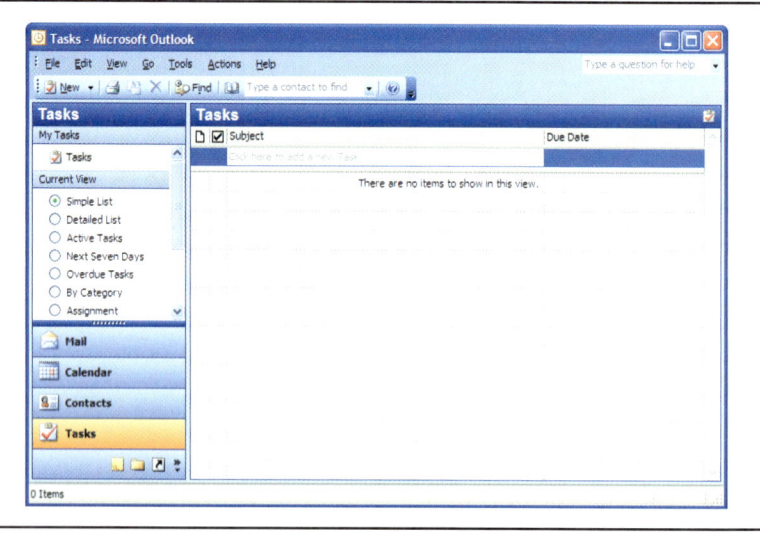

TROUBLESHOOTING

The remaining shortcuts in the Navigation pane are small buttons.

Lesson 1 Introduction to Outlook 11

5 **On the Navigation pane, click the Notes shortcut.**

The contents of the Notes folder are displayed. You will learn how to create and edit Notes in Lesson 7, "Using Notes."

FIGURE 1-10

Notes folder

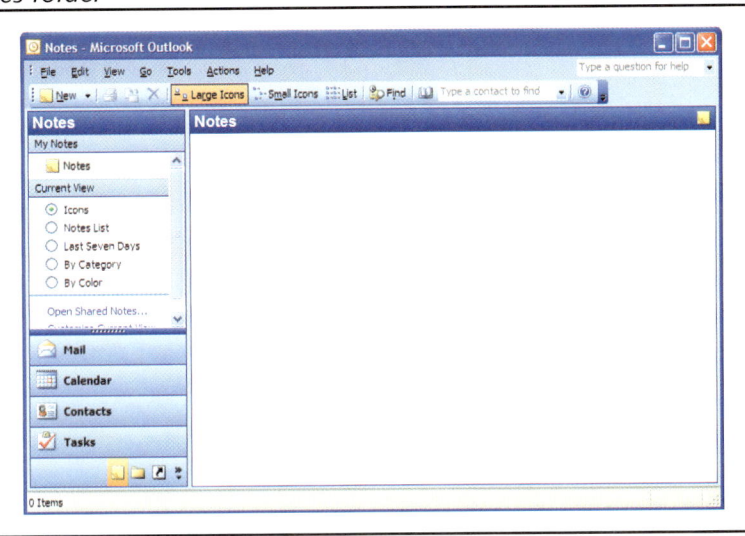

TROUBLESHOOTING

The information displayed on the right side of the window may not change when you select a different button. For example, the right side of the window doesn't change when you click the Folder List button.

6 **On the Navigation pane, click the Folder List button.**

The folders you can access are listed in the upper area of the Navigation pane.

FIGURE 1-11

Folder list

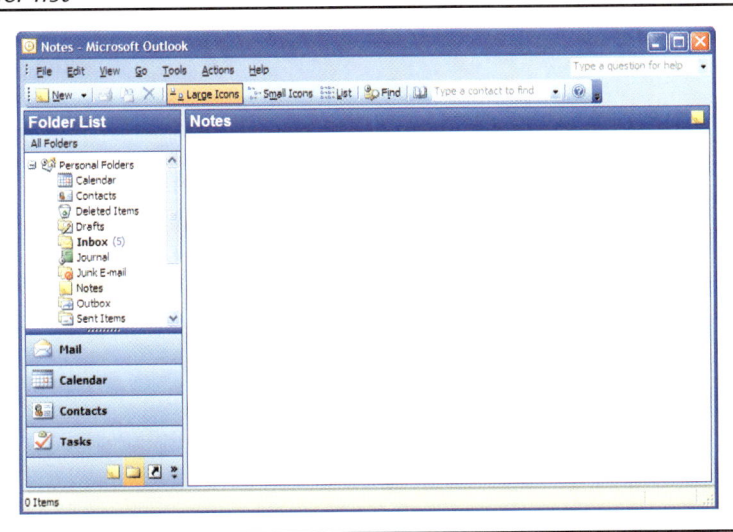

7 **On the Navigation pane, click the Shortcuts button.**

This area enables you to add new groups and **shortcuts**, creating links to additional folders and documents.

ANOTHER METHOD

Use the Folder List to access each folder.

FIGURE 1-12

Shortcuts

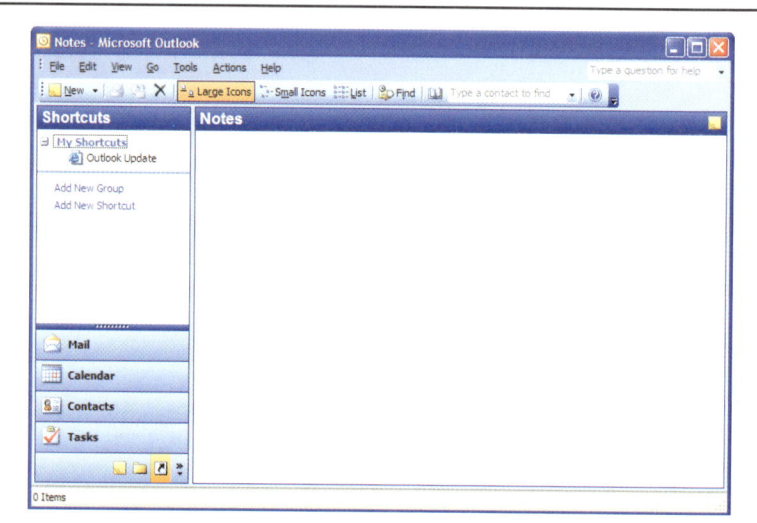

[screenshot of Outlook Notes window with Shortcuts pane showing My Shortcuts, Outlook Update, Add New Group, Add New Shortcut]

QUICK CHECK

Q: Identify the standard buttons displayed in the Navigation pane.

A: The standard buttons are the Mail, Calendar, Contacts, Tasks, Notes, Folder List, and Shortcuts.

◆ Keep Outlook open for the next exercise.

QUICK REFERENCE ▼

Use the Navigation pane

Click a button to access a specific folder.

Using the Folder List

THE BOTTOM LINE

Improvements in the Folder List have increased its usefulness and provided fast access to Outlook folders.

You can also view Outlook folders and their contents by using the **Folder List**. The Navigation pane displays buttons that provide access to frequently used folders. The Folder List displays additional folders available in Outlook, including folders such as Drafts and Sent Items used to store draft copies of e-mail messages you compose and copies of e-mail messages you send to other recipients.

The Folder List displays each folder as a small icon followed by the name of the folder. When you click a folder's icon, the contents of the folder are displayed. For example, if you click the Contacts shortcut in the Folder

Lesson 1 Introduction to Outlook 13

List, Outlook displays the contents of the Contacts folder, enabling you to view contact records.

Use the Folder List to display folders:

Now that you know how to use the Navigation pane, you will learn to use the Folder List to display Outlook folders.

1 Click the Folder List button on the Navigation pane.

The Folder List is displayed.

2 In the Folder List, click Inbox.

The contents of the Inbox folder are displayed on the right side of the window. The Folder List is still displayed.

FIGURE 1-13
Folder List and Inbox

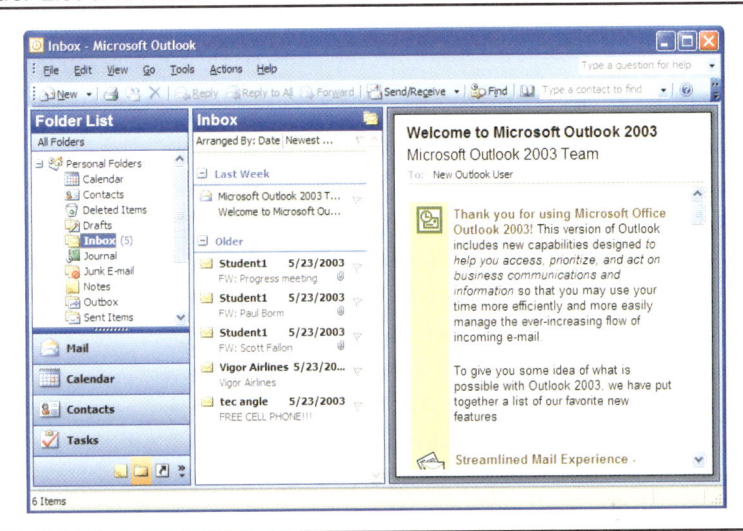

3 In the Folder List, click Tasks.

Outlook displays the contents of the Tasks folder. The Folder List is still displayed.

◆ Keep Outlook open for the next exercise.

QUICK CHECK

Q: How do you display the Folder List?

A: **Click the Folder List button on the Navigation pane.**

ANOTHER METHOD

Use the buttons in the Navigation pane to access each folder.

QUICK REFERENCE ▼

Display a folder using the Folder List

1 Click the Folder List button on the Navigation pane.

2 Click the name of the Outlook folder that you want to display.

Using the Office Assistant

> **THE BOTTOM LINE**
>
> The Office Assistant lets you use normal phrasing and key words to search for information in Outlook Help.

Outlook, like all Microsoft Office System applications, includes an extensive Help system that you can use to learn more about features and options available in Outlook. The **Office Assistant** is an animated character that provides helpful information about Outlook topics. By default, the Office Assistant appears as an animated paper clip named Clippit. However, you can choose to display the Office Assistant as an animated dog, cat, or any one of several other characters.

Help is readily available in Outlook. To view help when the Office Assistant is displayed, click the Office Assistant and type your question in the displayed box. Use your language of choice to phrase your request—for example, in Standard English, you might write, "How do you send a message?" or "What is in the Journal?" You can simply type a few words, such as "send message" or "Journal," to view information related to those topics. The Office Assistant interprets your request and displays topics that match one or more words in your request. Click the topic that most closely matches your request.

> **CHECK THIS OUT** ▼
>
> **Office Assistant**
> To change the Office Assistant, right-click the Office Assistant and click Choose Assistant. Click Next to view the various animations available and click OK when you find one that you like. All available animations may not be saved onto your hard drive during installation, so you may need to insert the Microsoft Office (or Microsoft Outlook) CD-ROM to install a new animation.

Use the Office Assistant:

In this exercise, you display the Office Assistant and use it to view help on an Outlook topic. You will then hide the Office Assistant to complete the exercise.

1 On the menu bar, click Help and click Show the Office Assistant.

The Office Assistant is displayed.

> **ANOTHER METHOD**
>
> Click the Microsoft Outlook Help button on the Standard Toolbar to access Outlook Help.

FIGURE 1-14

Office Assistant

2 Click the Assistant.

A box that asks you to type a question and click the Search button is displayed.

Lesson 1 Introduction to Outlook   15

3 Type *How do I send a message?* and click the Search button.

The Office Assistant displays Help topics that are relevant to the question you asked.

FIGURE 1-15

Help topics

TROUBLESHOOTING

Additional search results are available if Outlook is online when the search is performed.

4 Click the Send and Receive Messages option.

An Outlook Help window is displayed that explains how to send messages.

5 In the upper-right corner of the Help window, click the Close button.

The Outlook Help window closes.

6 In the upper-right corner of the task pane, click the Close button.

The task pane containing the search results is closed.

7 Right-click the Office Assistant and click Hide.

The Office Assistant disappears.

TIP

Keep the Office Assistant hidden unless you are using Microsoft Outlook Help.

- On the Navigation Bar, click the Mail button.
- If you are continuing to other lessons, keep Outlook open.
- If you are not continuing to the next lesson, close Outlook.

QUICK REFERENCE ▼

Use the Office Assistant

1 Open the Help menu and select the option Show the Office Assistant.
2 Click the Assistant, type a question, and click the Search button.
3 In the list of displayed topics, click the topic that most closely matches your help request.

Hide the Office Assistant

1 Right-click the Office Assistant.
2 Click Hide.

Key Points

✔ *The Outlook 2003 window provides a number of ways to navigate through the main Outlook components.*
✔ *You can use the Navigation pane and the Folder List to display different Outlook folders.*
✔ *The Office Assistant can be used to view more information about Outlook.*

Quick Quiz

True/False

T F 1. You can enter additional commands to personalize Outlook menus.
T F 2. Microsoft Outlook Help is the last option on every expanded Outlook menu.
T F 3. You can start Outlook from an icon on your desktop.
T F 4. Deleted Items is a small button on the Navigation pane.
T F 5. The Reading pane enables you to read information from Outlook Help.

Multiple Choice

1. To place a command on a short menu, _____.
   a. use the command once.
   b. don't use the command at all.
   c. use the command frequently.
   d. click the double-arrows at the bottom of the short menu.

2. To view your schedule, click the button labeled _____.
   a. Contacts.
   b. Schedule.
   c. Tasks.
   d. Calendar.

3. To access any Outlook folder, use the _____.
   a. Folder List.
   b. short menus.
   c. expanded menus.
   d. Outlook Help.

4. Each individual e-mail message you receive is a(n) _____.
   a. folder.
   b. item.
   c. attachment.
   d. shortcut.

5. Outlook Help will provide answers if you use the search field to _____.
   a. enter complete sentences that identify the information you need.
   b. enter key words.
   c. ask a question.
   d. all of the above.

Short Answer

1. What are the main functions in Outlook?
2. How do you use the Office Assistant to view help topics in Outlook?
3. How is the appearance of a command on a short menu determined?
4. Identify two ways to display an expanded menu.
5. List two ways to display an Outlook folder such as the Inbox.

On Your Own

Exercise 1

Display the View menu and display the expanded View menu. When you open the expanded View menu, move your mouse pointer across different menus on the Menu bar to view the results.

Exercise 2

Use the Folder List to display the contents of the Contacts folder and the Tasks folder. Use the Office Assistant to find out how to hide the Navigation pane. Hide the Navigation pane and redisplay it.

One Step Further

Exercise 1

Use the Navigation pane to display the Inbox, Calendar, Contacts, Tasks, and Notes. Observe the differences in the Standard toolbar as you select each shortcut in the Outlook Shortcuts group.

Exercise 2

Make a list of folders on your hard drive or network that you would like to access through Outlook to work more efficiently.

Exercise 3

Display the Office Assistant. Type **new message** in the box and view the available help topics.

LESSON 2

Using E-Mail in Outlook

After completing this lesson, you will be able to:

✔ Compose, address, and send messages.
✔ Format the body of a message.
✔ Attach a file to a message.
✔ Check for e-mail messages.
✔ View messages.
✔ Read messages.
✔ Reply to and forward messages.
✔ Print messages.
✔ Find messages.
✔ Recall messages.
✔ Delete messages.

KEY TERMS

- arrangement
- attachment
- AutoPreview
- Deleted Items folder
- Drafts
- e-mail
- file
- flag
- forward
- icon
- Inbox
- interoffice mail
- mail queue
- message header
- Microsoft Exchange Server
- Outbox
- recall
- reply
- Sent Items folder

Gone are the days when the telephone was the main way to communicate with other people immediately and postal mail was the chief way to send letters and documents to others. Today, e-mail enables you to communicate and share information with others in a way that is faster and more versatile than methods that were available in the past. **E-mail** refers to any communication that is sent or received via computers, either over the Internet or through a messaging program used with an organization's internal network, or intranet.

Creating, sending, receiving, and reading e-mail messages are the activities that you will probably perform most frequently with Microsoft Outlook. E-mail provides a fast way to send and receive messages, files, and documents such as reports, worksheets, and pictures.

In this lesson, you will learn how to create, address, format, and send an e-mail message. You will learn how to attach a file; check for and read messages; and reply to and forward messages you receive. You will learn how to flag messages with a reminder to yourself or to the recipient to follow up on the message. You will also learn how to print, find, and recall messages that you've sent. You will learn how to save e-mail messages that you aren't ready to send in Drafts, a folder that stores incomplete messages. Finally, you will learn how to delete messages.

> **IMPORTANT**
>
> Before you can use the practice files in this lesson, you need to install them from the companion CD for this book to their default location. For additional information on how to find and open files used in this book, see the "Using the CD-ROM" section at the beginning of this book.

To complete the exercises in this lesson, you will need to use the files named Map and Syllabus in the Outlook Practice folder that is located on your hard disk.

> **IMPORTANT**
>
> To complete some of the exercises in this lesson, you will need to exchange e-mail messages with a class partner. If you don't have a class partner or you are performing the exercises alone, you can send the message to yourself. Simply enter your own e-mail address instead of a class partner's address.

Composing, Addressing, and Sending Messages

Creating New Messages

> **THE BOTTOM LINE**
>
> Sending an e-mail message is similar to sending any type of correspondence. Outlook provides the tools for you to accomplish exactly what you need with your message.

If you've used other e-mail programs, you'll probably find that creating and sending messages is similar in Outlook. To create a new mail message, click the New button when you are in the **Inbox** folder. The message you create can be any length and contain any information. The following illustration displays the window used to create an e-mail message.

> **TROUBLESHOOTING**
>
> Your toolbars may be placed in different positions than the toolbars in these images.

Figure 2-1

Message window

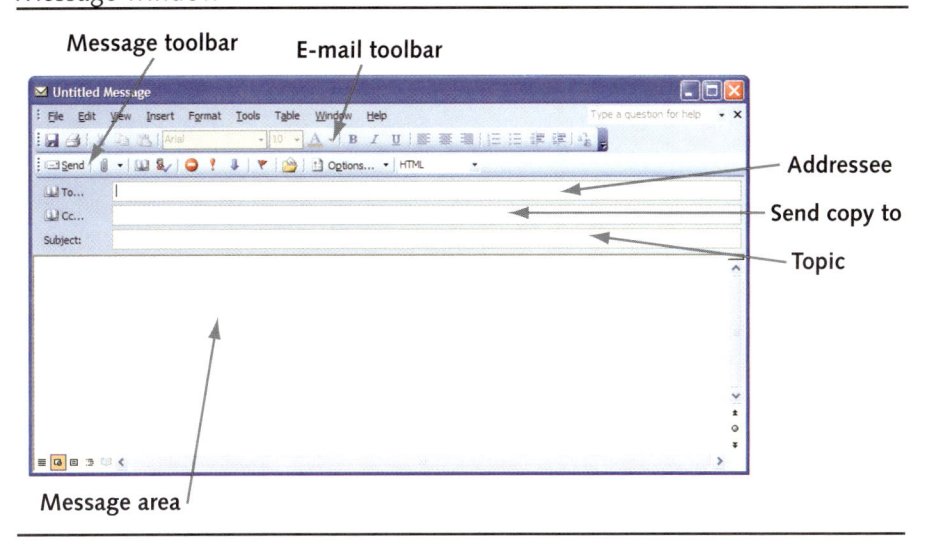

- Message toolbar
- E-mail toolbar
- Addressee
- Send copy to
- Topic
- Message area

Just as you must address an envelope before mailing it, you must also provide at least one e-mail address in the To box of your message. E-mail can be addressed to any number of recipients and the message is sent to all recipients simultaneously. To send a message to multiple recipients, type a semicolon after each recipient's e-mail address in the To box. After you type one or more e-mail addresses, enter the subject of your message, type the message, and click the Send button to send the message. Typically, your e-mail message arrives in the recipient's Inbox within seconds after you send it.

It is easy to address an e-mail message if you have sent a message to the same recipient before or the recipient's e-mail address is stored in Outlook's address book. The AutoComplete addressing function automatically completes the address as you start to type it. If the address Outlook suggests is correct, press the Tab key to enter the complete address. If Outlook finds several matches, it presents a list of possible matches. Use the arrow keys to select the correct entry and press the Enter key.

Below the To button is the Cc button. Cc is an acronym for carbon copy, referring to the days of printed letters when copies were made by using carbon paper. The copy contains the same content sent to the recipient identified in the To box. However, a copy of a message is sent to others for information purposes only; the Cc recipients are not required to take any action.

The Cc function is optional: You can send a message without sending any copies. However, there are times when it is valuable to be able to copy a message to others. To send a copy, simply enter the individual's e-mail address in the Cc box. To send a copy to multiple recipients, type a semicolon after each recipient's e-mail address. When the Cc recipient receives the message, his or her address appears in the message header as a Cc.

The subject of the message is usually a brief description of the information in the message. All of the message recipients will see the message header when the message arrives in their Inboxes. A **message header** includes the name of the sender, the subject of the message, and the date and time when the message was sent. This information enables recipients to quickly identify the purpose of the e-mail message without opening the message.

22 Lesson 2 Using E-Mail in Outlook

> **IMPORTANT**
>
> - Microsoft Office Outlook 2003 supports several types of Internet e-mail accounts. Account types include POP3, IMAP, and HTTP.
> - Post Office Protocol 3 (POP3)—Common type of e-mail account provided by an ISP (Internet Service Provider). To receive messages, you connect to an e-mail server and download messages to your local computer.
> - Internet Message Access Protocol (IMAP)—Messages are stored on the e-mail server. When you connect to an e-mail server, you read the headers and select the messages to download to your local computer.
> - Hypertext Transfer Protocol (HTTP)—Messages are stored, retrieved, and displayed as Web pages. MSN Hotmail, a free, Web-based e-mail service offered by Microsoft, provides HTTP accounts.

◆ Be sure to start Outlook before beginning this exercise.

Compose and send a message

now that you have learned the basics of working within Outlook, you will compose a message and send it to your class partner.

1 If necessary, click the Mail button and click the Inbox folder. Click the New Mail Message button on the Standard toolbar.

A message window is displayed. The message and all the information necessary to deliver the message are entered in this window.

> **ANOTHER METHOD**
>
> You can create a new e-mail message from any folder. Open the File menu, point to New, and click Mail Message to display a new message window.

2 In the To box, type the e-mail address of your class partner or type your e-mail address if you are working alone.

This identifies the recipient who will receive the message.

> **TROUBLESHOOTING**
>
> Your To box will contain your class partner's e-mail address.

3 Press Tab twice.

The insertion point skips through the Cc box and moves to the Subject box.

4 Type Picnic Reminder and press Enter.

The subject is entered and the insertion point moves to the message area.

Lesson 2 Using E-Mail in Outlook   23

5 Type Just a reminder… Our 5th annual Fun in the Sun picnic is on Saturday, June 6th.

Your message window contains all the necessary information.

Figure 2-2

Message ready to be sent

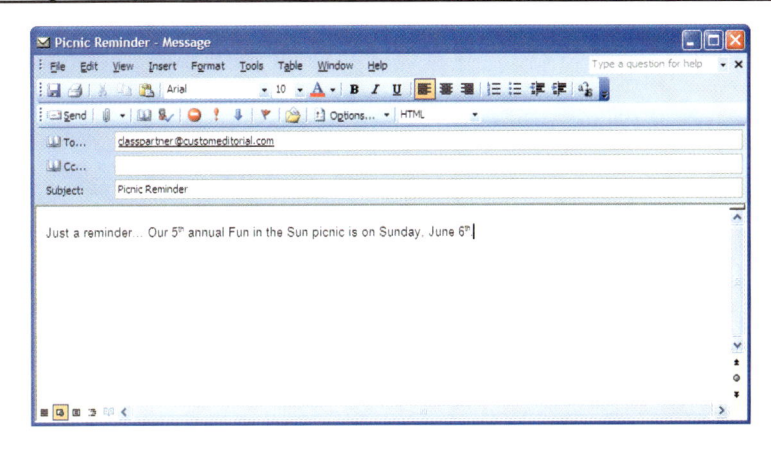

> **TROUBLESHOOTING**
>
> If the server is down or if there is a problem with the connection to the Internet, messages are placed in the **Outbox** until a connection is established.

6 On the Message toolbar in the message window, click the Send button.

The message is sent to the recipient.

> **IMPORTANT**
>
> Although you clicked the Send button, the message has not necessarily been sent over the Internet (or over the intranet) yet. By default, Outlook connects to your server (Workgroup, Corporate, or Internet service provider) to send and receive e-mail every 10 minutes. Messages that have been sent but have not yet made it to the server are stored in your Outbox. To send and receive e-mail immediately, click the Send/Receive button on the standard toolbar in the Mail folder. This action connects your computer to your server, sends all e-mail messages in the Outbox, and retrieves any messages that the server has for you. To avoid delays while performing the exercises in this book, click the Send/Receive button immediately after you click the Send button.

◆ Keep Outlook open for the next exercise.

QUICK CHECK

Q: What is the maximum length of a message sent in Outlook?

A: There is no limit.

QUICK REFERENCE ▼

Compose and send a message

1 In the Inbox, click the New Mail Message button on the Standard toolbar.

2 In the To text box, type an e-mail address.

3 Press Tab and type another e-mail address in the Cc box, if necessary.

4 Press Tab, type the message description in the Subject text box, and press Enter.

5 Type your message and click the Send button.

Formatting a Message

Formatting Messages

THE BOTTOM LINE

Microsoft Word is the default e-mail editor. Its formatting power can be used to enhance a message sent in Outlook.

Looks aren't everything, but a message that looks good makes a positive impact on the recipient. Microsoft Outlook uses Microsoft Word as the default e-mail editor, placing the power of Word's formatting options at your fingertips. The toolbar has been redesigned to group the Word functions that apply to e-mail. A few clicks of the mouse can apply formatting that highlights important information or gives your message a bit of flash to make it stand out in the crowd of messages that fill many Inboxes.

The Formatting buttons on the toolbar are familiar if you use Microsoft Word. They enable you to apply formats that create the image you want to present. Color the name of your product. Make the dates of a conference bold so recipients can see them at a glance. Highlight the important numbers in a sales report. Make your point with a bulleted list. Your options are endless.

Figure 2-3

E-mail toolbar

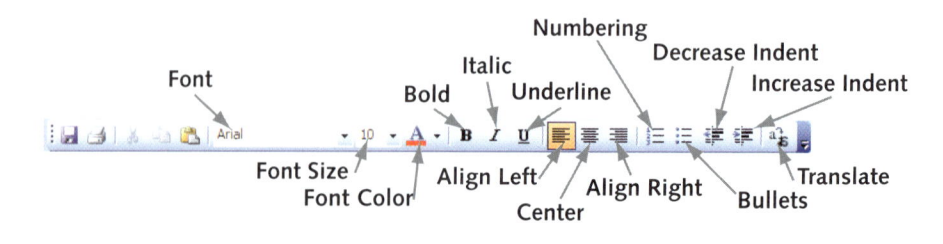

QUICK CHECK

Q: What application is used to format e-mail messages?

A: Microsoft Word is the default editor.

Applying formats is easy. Type the body of the e-mail message in the message area. Select the text you want to format. Click the appropriate button on the toolbar. The selected text immediately takes the new format.

You can include a Web site address in an e-mail message. When a recipient clicks the Web address, it automatically starts the default Web browser and displays the Web site. Including a Web site address in the message is helpful because the recipient does not need to leave the message to open a Web browser and type the Web site address to access the site. To include a Web site address in a message, just type it in the message. Outlook automatically formats the address (or URL, an acronym for Uniform Resource Locator) as a link to a Web page—for example, www.microsoft.com.

Flagging Messages

Flagging Messages for Follow-Up

> **THE BOTTOM LINE**
>
> You can use flags to alert a recipient to important messages or remind yourself to perform some action.

Sometimes it's necessary to remind yourself or notify recipients of the importance of a message that you are sending. Perhaps you sent a message about an event with a specific deadline or asked for input on a particular topic. You can **flag** the message to remind yourself to follow up on an issue or you can flag an outgoing message with a request for someone else to follow up with a reply.

When you create a new message, click the Message Flag button on the New Message toolbar in the message window. A dialog box is displayed that enables you to identify the reason you flagged the message, such as requesting a reply, requesting follow-up action, and stating that no response is necessary. You also can set the due date for the follow-up action. When a recipient receives a message with a flag, the purpose of the flag is displayed at the top of the message. If a date was set, that date appears as well. The message appears in the recipient's Inbox with either a red flag, indicating that action still needs to be taken, or a gray flag, indicating that the request is complete.

Figure 2-4

Flag for Follow Up dialog box

You can also flag messages you receive in your Inbox. Quick Flags is a new feature in Outlook 2003. Click the shaded flag **icon** to the right of the messages in your Inbox to flag the message. Click the flag icon a second time to mark the item as completed. Right-click the icon to clear the flag or change the color of the flag.

QUICK REFERENCE ▼
Flag a message to be sent

1. Create an e-mail message.
2. On the Standard toolbar in the message window, click the Message Flag button.
3. Select your options and click OK.

Flag a message you received

1. Click on an e-mail message in your Inbox.
2. Click the flag icon next to the message.

QUICK CHECK

Q: Can you flag messages after you receive them?

A: Quick Flags is a new feature that enables you to flag messages you receive.

Setting Message Priority

Changing Message Settings and Delivery Options

THE BOTTOM LINE

Outlook enables you to identify high-priority messages for the recipients.

You can also specify the priority for a message. When you mark a message as High priority, the message header appears in the recipient's Inbox with a red exclamation point, indicating that the message is important. You want the recipient to reply to or read the message as soon as possible. When you mark a message as Low priority, a blue, downward-pointing arrow appears in the message header, indicating that the message is not important. The recipient can reply to or read the message when it is convenient.

QUICK REFERENCE ▼
Set message priority

- On the Standard toolbar in the message window, click the Importance: High button.

or

- On the Standard toolbar in the message window, click the Importance: Low button.

QUICK CHECK

Q: How can you identify a high-priority message?

A: Mark the message with the Importance: High flag.

Saving Drafts

> **THE BOTTOM LINE**
>
> If you are interrupted before you can send a message, Outlook automatically saves your working draft.

If you are interrupted while composing a message, you can save it in your **Drafts** folder. You can complete and send the message later. You can create a draft of a message in two ways:

- In the top-right corner of the message window, click the Close button. Outlook will ask if you want to save the message. Click Yes to save the message without sending it.

or

- On the E-mail toolbar in the message window, click the Save button and click the Close button in the top-right corner of the message window.

QUICK CHECK

Q: Where are messages saved if you exit before sending the message?

A: The messages are saved in the Drafts folder.

QUICK REFERENCE ▼

Retrieve a draft:

1. Display the Folder List and click the Drafts folder.
2. Double-click the message to open it.
3. Complete or edit the message and send it just as you normally would.

Attaching a File to a Message

> **THE BOTTOM LINE**
>
> Outlook items and other files can be attached to a message and sent to a recipient.

Attaching Files to Messages

In today's fast-paced workplaces, you need to be able to get information to several people in a short amount of time. As an example, the sales manager at Adventure Works, an outdoor vacation resort, likes to distribute Microsoft Excel sales forecast workbooks to other managers at the resort. Rather than distributing printed copies or retyping the contents of these documents into an e-mail message, the sales manager can make the workbook file an **attachment**—an external document included as part of a message—and send the message and the attachment to all recipients at one time.

An attachment can be a file, a document stored on a disk, or another Outlook item. A **file** can be any type of document, such as a Microsoft Word document, an Excel spreadsheet, or a picture. An item is an Outlook object, such as a contact, task, or note. You will learn how to create and use these and other Outlook items later in this course.

> **TIP**
>
> The appearance of the icon depends on the file type of the attachment. For example, the icon for an attached Word file is the same icon that represents Word files in Windows Explorer. The icon for an attached Excel file is the same icon that represents Excel files in Windows Explorer.

The selected attachment appears in a new field, the Attach box, located below the Subject box. The attachment is displayed as an icon, or graphic representation of the attached file. The name and size of the file are also displayed. When you send the message, the message recipient can double-click the icon to open and view the file or item.

To attach a file to a message, compose the message just as you normally would and click the Insert File button on the New Message toolbar in the message window. Navigate to the folder that contains the file, click the file name, and click the Insert File button. Repeat this procedure to attach multiple files to a message.

To attach an Outlook item to a message, click the down arrow next to the Insert File button on the New Message toolbar. Select Insert Item to display the Insert Item dialog box. In the Look In list, click the folder name for the type of Outlook item, such as a contact, that you want to attach. In the Items list in the bottom pane, click the item that you want to attach and click OK. The icon representing the attached Outlook item is displayed in the Attach box.

Figure 2-5

Insert Item dialog box

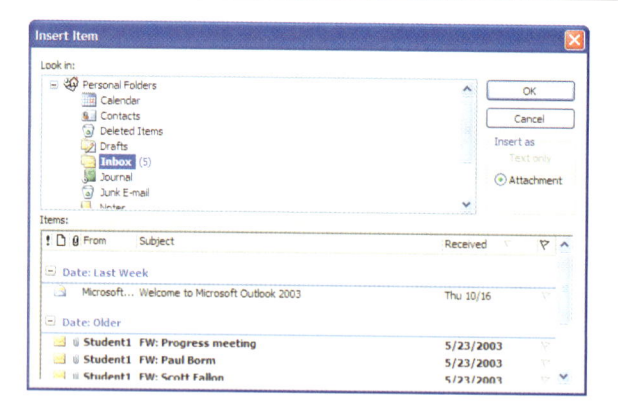

Send a message with an attachment

You will now practice many of the concepts you have learned. You will compose a message, attach a picture to the message, and send the message and file attachment to the recipient.

1 On the Mail toolbar, click the New Mail Message button.

A message window is displayed.

2 In the To box, type the e-mail address of the recipient.

3 Press Tab twice and type **Fun in the Sun Picnic Invitation** in the Subject box.

Lesson 2 Using E-Mail in Outlook   29

4. Press Enter. In the message area, type **Hope to see you at the picnic on June 6th at 1:00 P.M. For directions to Cherry Creek Park, please see the attached map. See you there!**

5. On the New Message toolbar in the message window, click the Insert File button.

   The Insert Item dialog box is displayed.

6. Click the Look in down arrow and navigate to the Outlook Practice folder on your hard disk.

   The items in the Outlook Practice folder are displayed.

   Figure 2-6
   Insert File dialog box

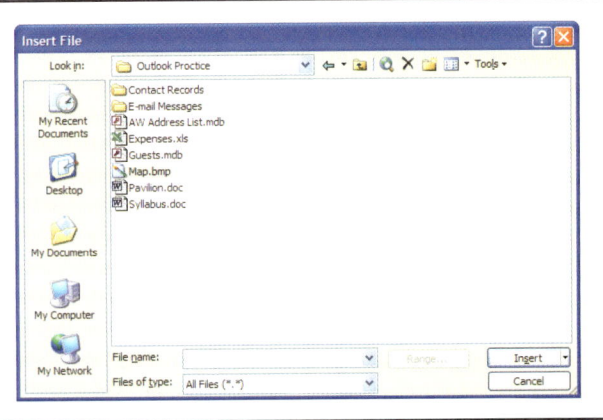

TROUBLESHOOTING

If you send an e-mail attachment to someone who connects to the Internet using a slow modem (33.6 Kbps or slower), you should limit the attachment size to 300 KB or less. Messages with large attachments can take a long time for the recipient's e-mail program to receive. A small pane may be displayed, asking if you want to resize the attachment (decrease its size) to send it faster. If the pane is not displayed, click the Attachment Options button.

7. Double-click the Map file to attach it to your e-mail message.

   Outlook attaches the Map file to the e-mail message and the Insert File dialog box closes. Your screen should look similar to the following.

   Figure 2-7
   New message with attachment

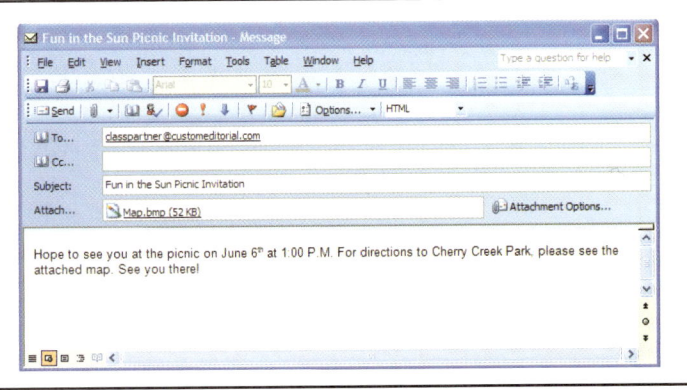

8 On the New Message toolbar in the message window, click the Send button.

The message is sent to the recipient.

◆ Keep Outlook open for the next exercise.

QUICK REFERENCE ▼
Attach a file to a message

1 Compose and address a message.
2 On the New Message toolbar in the message window, click the Insert File button.
3 Click the Look In down arrow and navigate to your file.
4 Double-click the file to attach it to the e-mail message.
5 On the New Message toolbar in the message window, click the Send button.

QUICK CHECK

Q: Can an Outlook item be sent as an attachment?

A: An Outlook item can be attached to an e-mail message.

Checking for E-Mail Messages

THE BOTTOM LINE
Messages are sent and received at regular intervals (intervals that you can adjust) and when you click the Send/Receive button.

Just as Outlook sends e-mail every 10 minutes, Outlook automatically checks for new mail every 10 minutes. Later in this course, you will learn how to change this setting to a longer or shorter interval. You can manually check for messages at any time. Simply click the Send/Receive button on the toolbar in the Mail folder. Any messages that are on the mail server are sent to your Inbox.

IMPORTANT
Interoffice mail—e-mail sent over a local area network (LAN) or to a **Microsoft Exchange Server** post office—is usually sent almost instantaneously. However, when you send e-mail to someone outside of your LAN or Exchange Server, you send the message over the Internet. Your Internet service provider's mail server places incoming messages in a mail queue. The **mail queue** is a list of messages received by a mail server organized in the order in which the messages are received. In turn, messages are sent to recipients in the order in which the server received them. Sometimes, this means you have to wait a few minutes to receive an Internet mail message that was sent to you.

Check for e-mail messages

Now that you have sent messages, it's time to check for incoming e-mail messages.

1 **If necessary, click the Mail button in the Navigation pane and select the Inbox folder.**

The contents of the Inbox folder are displayed. It contains the message headers for messages that you've already received.

ANOTHER METHOD

If you are using Exchange Server to send and receive e-mail messages, or if you have multiple e-mail accounts, point to Send/Receive on the Tools menu and click the account that you want to send to and receive from.

Figure 2-8

Message headers in the Inbox

2 **On the Standard mail toolbar, click the Send/Receive button.**

A progress bar indicating that Outlook is sending and receiving messages is displayed briefly before new message headers appear in the middle pane. The messages were created and sent in previous exercises by you or your class partner.

◆ Keep Outlook open for the next exercise.

QUICK REFERENCE ▼

Check for e-mail messages

1 If necessary, on the Navigation pane, click the Mail button and the Inbox folder.

2 On the Standard mail toolbar, click the Send/Receive button.

QUICK CHECK

Q: When does Outlook check for new messages?

A: Outlook checks for messages every 10 minutes and when you click the Send/Receive button.

View Messages

Viewing and Printing Messages

> **THE BOTTOM LINE**
>
> Outlook lets you arrange messages in a variety of predefined views which make it easier to find specific items you are looking for or to sort your messages.

You can gather some important information about the messages that arrive in your Inbox without actually reading the messages. The message header tells you who sent the message, the time the message arrived, and the subject of the message.

AutoPreview provides additional information. The message header for each message is displayed above a sample of the message's content. Up to three lines of each message is displayed. This enables you to scan for important messages and read a message without opening it in a separate window. AutoPreview is useful if you receive dozens of e-mail messages each day and want to scan through them quickly to determine which messages to read first. You can quickly spot junk e-mail messages that have deceptive headers.

A new feature in Outlook 2003, known as **arrangements**, enables you to view messages in 13 different ways. Each arrangement focuses on a different characteristic of the messages in your Inbox. For example, you can base your arrangement on the date the message was received or the individual who sent the message. By default, messages are arranged by the date they were received. The most recent message is displayed at the top of the list. However, one or more of the standard views may help you find information received in a specific message or group of messages. The following table describes the standard views.

Arrangement	Result
Date	Messages are grouped by the date they are received. This is the default arrangement.
Conversation	Messages are grouped by the subject of the message. By default, only flagged messages and messages you haven't read are displayed in the group.
From	Messages are grouped by the name in the From line of each message.
To	Messages are grouped by the name in the To line of each message.
Folder	Messages are grouped by the folder where they are stored. This arrangement is only available when you are viewing search results.
Size	Messages are grouped by the size of each message.
Subject	Messages are grouped alphabetically by the text in the Subject line of each message.
Type	Messages are grouped by the type of message. Types include meeting requests, task requests, and so on.
Flag	Messages are grouped by the color of the flag you assigned to the message. Messages flagged by the sender are not included in the groups of flagged messages.

Arrangement	Result
Attachments	Messages with attachments are placed in one group. Messages without attachments are placed in a second group.
E-mail account	If you have more than one e-mail account, messages are grouped by the e-mail account that received the message.
Importance	Messages are grouped by the importance assigned to each message. Groups are high, normal, and low importance.
Categories	Messages assigned to a specific category are placed with messages in the same category. You can add categories to the Master Category List or modify existing categories.

Besides using arrangements, you can also sort messages by any column. Simply click the column heading above the list of messages.

TROUBLESHOOTING

The Reading pane was turned off in this figure to display the column headings available in the Inbox.

Figure 2-9

Messages grouped by the From column

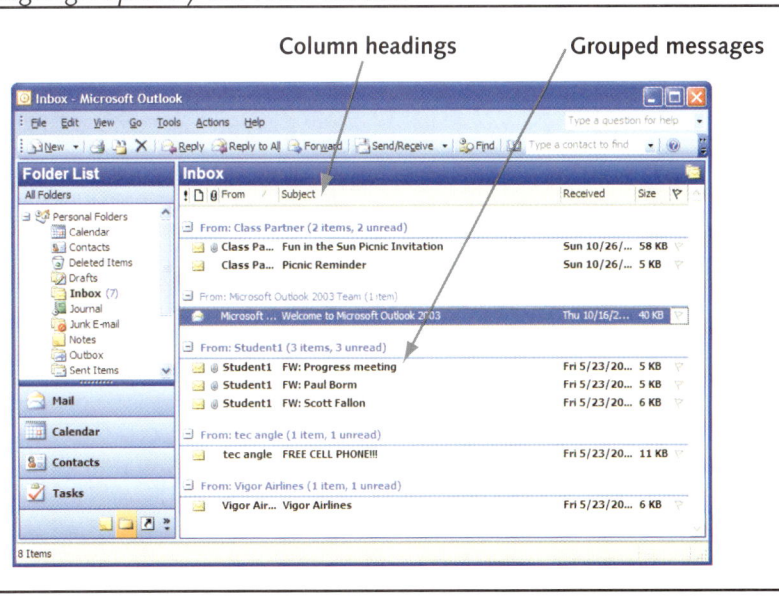

Messages that you have read are shown with an open envelope icon to the left of the message header; unread messages appear with a closed envelope icon. To read the body of a message in the Reading pane, click the message header in the Inbox. Double-click a message header to open the message in a separate window.

Select an arrangement

Since you have sent and received messages, you now select an arrangement to group mail messages.

1 **If necessary, click the Mail button in the Navigation pane and select the Inbox folder.**

The contents of the Inbox folder are displayed. It contains the message headers for messages that you've already received.

34 **Lesson 2** Using E-Mail in Outlook

2 Open the View menu. Point at the Arrange By option. Click on Attachments.

ANOTHER METHOD

Click the Sort by: Attachments column heading.

Messages with attachments are grouped in the upper area. Messages without attachments are grouped in the lower area.

TROUBLESHOOTING

The Reading pane was turned off in this figure to display the arrangement and message headers.

Figure 2-10

Messages arranged by attachments

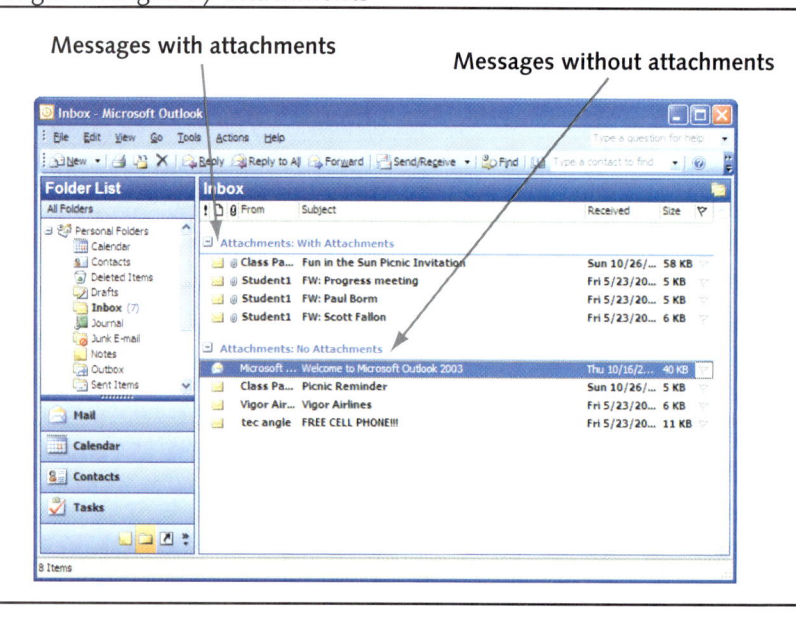

◆ Keep Outlook open for the next exercise.

QUICK REFERENCE ▼

Select an arrangement for e-mail messages

1 If necessary, on the Navigation pane, click the Mail button and the Inbox folder.

2 Open the View menu, point at the Arrange By option, and click on an arrangement.

Sort e-mail messages by column heading

1 If necessary, navigate to a mail folder.

2 Click on one of the column headings.

QUICK CHECK

Q: What is an arrangement?

A: An arrangement is a method of viewing messages.

Lesson 2 Using E-Mail in Outlook   35

Reading Messages

Viewing and Printing Messages

> **THE BOTTOM LINE**
>
> The Reading pane displays the content of an e-mail message. This allows you to get a quick glance at a message witout opening it.

Outlook 2003 incorporates several improvements that make it easier to read your e-mail messages. Many of the changes are visible the first time you open your Inbox. The new Reading pane is one of the obvious improvements. The Reading pane is designed for the way you read. By default, it is placed on the right side of the Outlook window. Like a sheet of paper, it is taller rather than wider. This enables you to read long messages without using the scroll bars or opening a separate window. Open attachments directly from the Reading pane, rather than opening them from a separate viewing window.

Read e-mail messages

Now you will read the e-mail messages that your class partner sent to you.

1 Click the Fun in the Sun message header.

The message is displayed in the Reading pane. The message header is displayed above the message. The name and size of the attachment are clearly identified. The icon representing the attachment tells you which application can be used to view the attachment. Images can usually be viewed by the Windows Picture and Fax Viewer. This eliminates your need for the application used to create the image.

Figure 2-11

Message displayed in the Reading pane

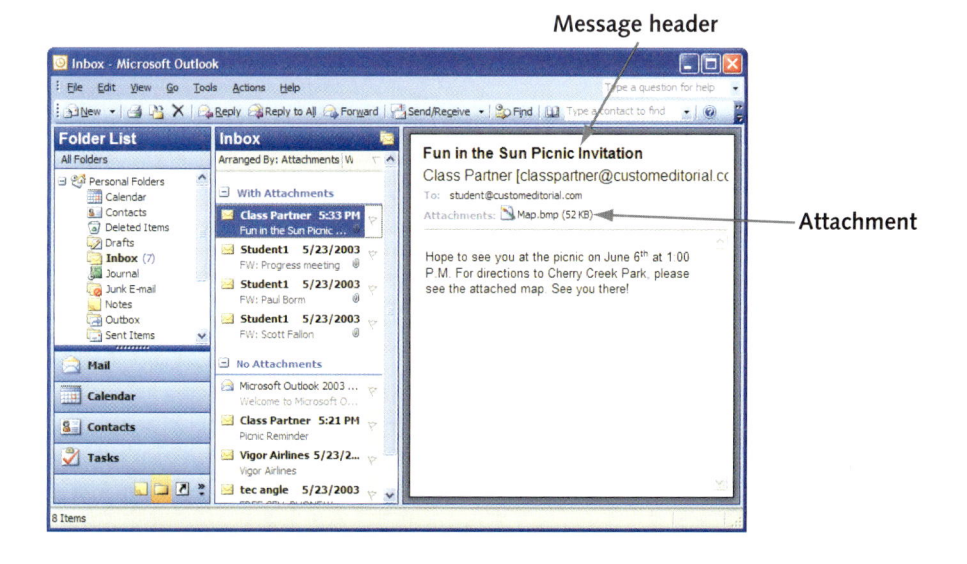

36 Lesson 2 Using E-Mail in Outlook

> **TROUBLESHOOTING**
>
> Be sure to single-click the Picnic Reminder message in Step 1. Double-clicking the message has a different result.

2 **Double-click the Fun in the Sun Picnic Invitation message header.**

The message is displayed in a separate window. Notice the attachment icon in the message.

Figure 2-12

Message displayed in a separate window

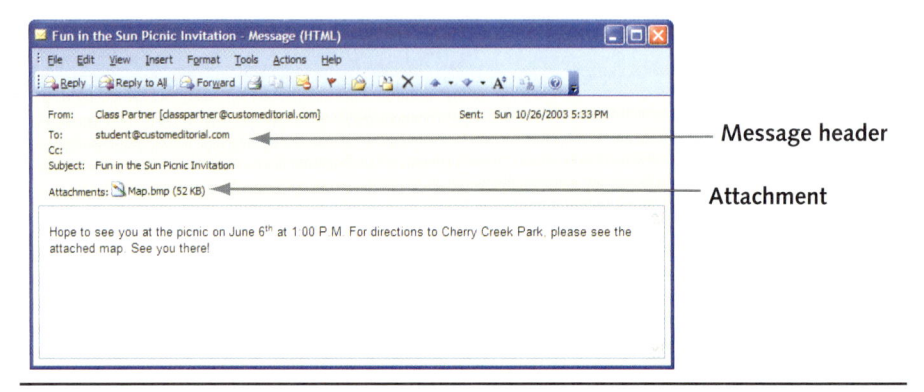

3 **Double-click the Map attachment icon in the message window.**

> **ANOTHER METHOD**
>
> You can also open the attachment from the Reading pane. In the message header, double-click the icon that represents the attachment.

The map is displayed in a separate window by the application your computer uses to view graphics.

Figure 2-13

Attachment displayed in a separate window

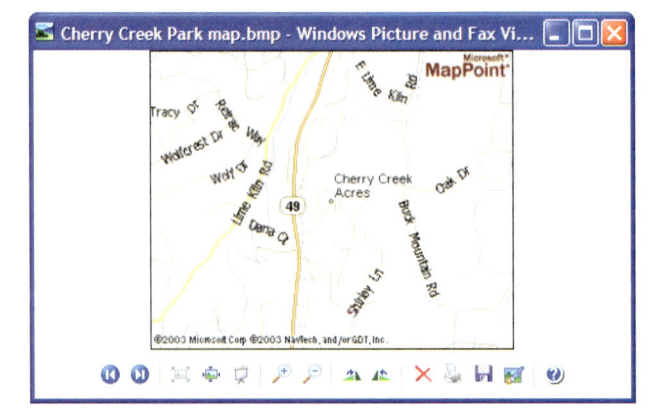

4 **In the top-right corner of the window that contains the map, click the Close button.**

The application closes.

Lesson 2 Using E-Mail in Outlook 37

5 In the top-right corner of the message window, click the Close button.

The message closes.

◆ Arrange the content of the Inbox by date.

◆ Keep Outlook open for the next exercise.

QUICK REFERENCE ▼

Read e-mail messages and messages with attachments

1 In the Inbox, click the message header of the message to display it in the Reading pane.

2 Double-click the attachment icon in the message (if one is included) to read the attachment.

> **QUICK CHECK**
>
> Q: Is the message header displayed in the Reading pane?
>
> A: **The message header is displayed in the Reading pane.**

Replying to and Forwarding Messages

THE BOTTOM LINE

Outlook enables you to respond to messages you receive and share the information in a message with additional recipients.

Responding to Messages

If you receive an advertisement via postal mail, you might read it or discard it. If you receive a letter from a friend sent via postal mail, you might respond by writing and sending a reply to your friend.

E-mail is similar. Sometimes, you'll read an e-mail message without replying to the message. At other times, you'll reply to e-mail messages sent by friends or co-workers. A **reply** sends a copy of the original message and additional text that you type, if any. The recipient sees the text RE: and the original subject in the message header. When you reply to a message, your response is automatically addressed to the sender. If the original message was sent to you and several other recipients, you can choose to reply to the sender or the sender and all the other recipients.

After you receive an e-mail message, you might decide that the information contained in the message will be useful to others. If so, you can **forward** the message to other recipients. Forwarding a message lets you send a message to individuals who were not originally on the recipient list. Select the message and click the Forward button on the Standard toolbar in the Inbox folder, type the e-mail addresses of the additional recipients in the To box, and click the Send button. You can also type additional information at the beginning of the forwarded message before you send it.

Respond to a message

As are typical actions, you will now reply to the message that you receive and forward the message to another individual.

38 **Lesson 2** Using E-Mail in Outlook

> **TIP**
>
> You need the e-mail address of someone in your class other than your class partner to complete this exercise. If another e-mail address isn't available, use your own address. Replies and forwarded messages will be sent to your address.

1 **In the Inbox, verify that the Fun in the Sun Picnic Invitation message header is selected.**

The message content is displayed in the Reading pane.

2 **On the standard mail toolbar, click the Reply button.**

A reply window containing the original message is displayed. The insertion point is already in the message area.

3 **In the message area, type Yes, I will attend the picnic.**

The text you add is included in the reply.

4 **On the New Message toolbar in the message window, click the Send button.**

The reply is sent to your class partner.

5 **On the standard mail toolbar, click the Send/Receive button.**

A reply from your class partner arrives in the Inbox.

Figure 2-14

Reply from your Class Partner

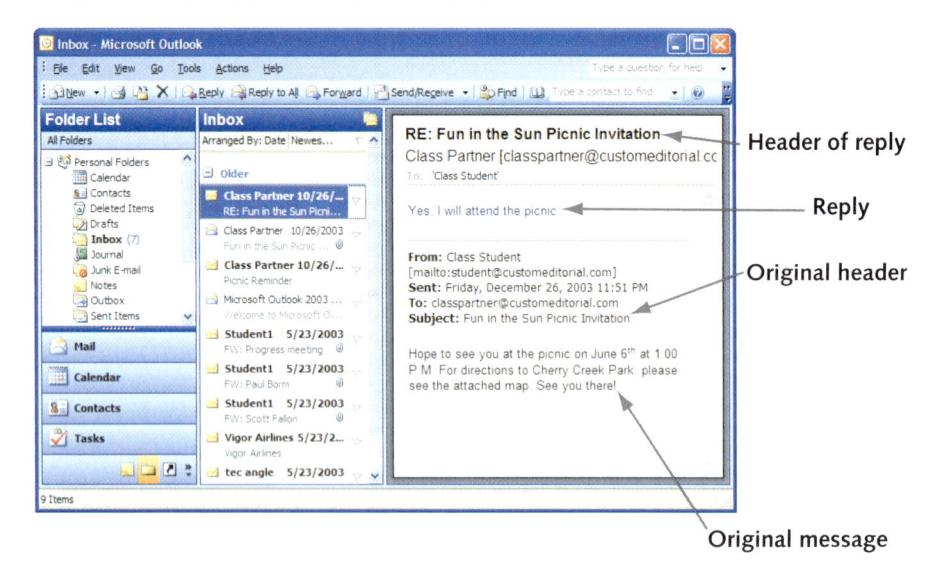

6 **In the Inbox, click the original Fun in the Sun Picnic Invitation message header again.**

The message is displayed in the Reading pane.

7 **Click the Forward button on the toolbar.**

A forward window opens with the original message displayed.

Lesson 2 Using E-Mail in Outlook 39

8 In the To box, type an e-mail address for a class member other than your class partner.

The message will be forwarded to this recipient.

> **TIP**
>
> When you forward a message you can add new text in the message area before you send it.

9 On the New Message toolbar in the message window, click the Send button.

The message is forwarded to a class member.

10 On the standard mail toolbar, click the Send/Receive button.

A forwarded message from a class member arrives in the Inbox.

Figure 2-15

Forwarded message

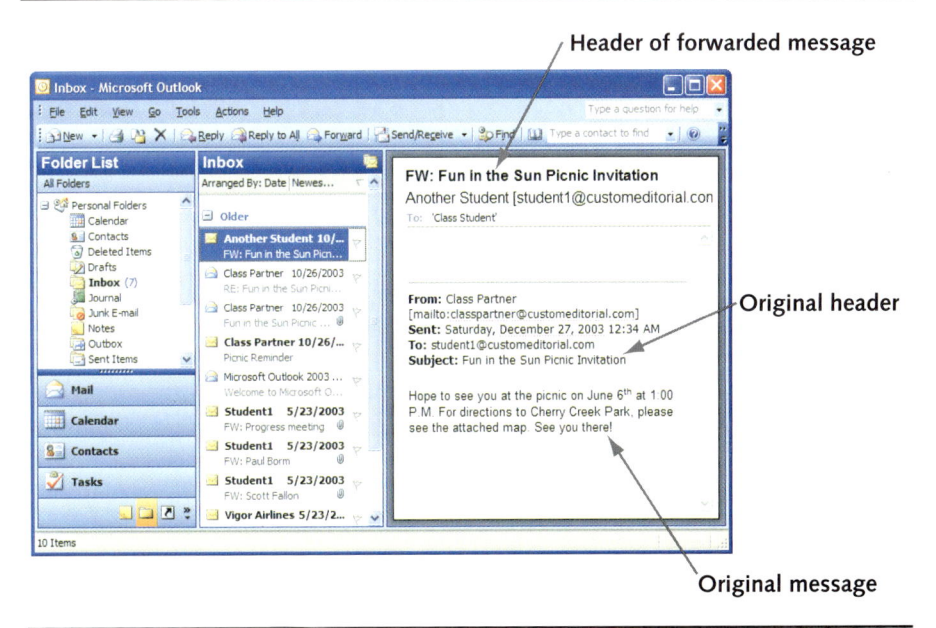

- Header of forwarded message
- Original header
- Original message

QUICK CHECK

Q: How do you add text to a reply?

A: Click in the message area and enter the text.

> **ANOTHER METHOD**
>
> You can also reply to or forward a message by clicking Reply or Forward on the Actions menu.

◆ Keep Outlook open for the next exercise.

QUICK REFERENCE ▼

Reply to a message

1. Click the message header for the message to which you want to reply.
2. On the standard mail toolbar, click the Reply button.
3. Type your message.
4. On the New Message toolbar in the message window, click the Send button.

Forward a message

1. In the Inbox, click the message header for the message that you want to forward.
2. On the standard mail toolbar, click the Forward button.
3. In the To box, type an e-mail address.
4. On the New Message toolbar in the message window, click the Send button.

Printing Messages

Viewing and Printing Messages

THE BOTTOM LINE

Though much work can be done electronically, there are times when you need printed documnets. With Outlook, you can print messages and attachments.

It's often convenient to print a copy of a message so you can read the message when you are not at your computer or so you can give the printed message to somebody who does not have access to e-mail. For example, Adventure Works employees found it useful to print a copy of a message that provided directions to the company picnic so they could follow the directions to get to the park.

TROUBLESHOOTING

When printing an attachment, Outlook might display an alert box warning you of the possible danger of viruses hidden within attached messages. Click the Print button in the message box to continue the printing process.

You can also print message attachments if the application used to create the attachment is installed on your computer. You can print an attachment by opening the attachment and using the Print command of the program that opens the attachment. You can also right-click the attachment icon in the message window and click Print on the shortcut menu. The attachment is printed by the default printer for your computer.

Outlook includes several options for printing e-mail messages when you are in the Inbox folder. Messages can be printed in Table style or Memo style. If you print using the Table style, the document contains a list of messages in a table format that resembles the Inbox; the message headers that are currently in your Inbox are listed under column headings, such as From, Subject, and Received. If you print using the Memo style, the document contains your name at the top of the page, information about the selected message (who the message was from, when the message was sent, who the message was sent to, and the subject of the message); the actual message is printed last.

TROUBLESHOOTING

Print Preview isn't available for HTML formatted items.

Select Page Setup on the File menu to open the Page Setup dialog box. This enables you to preview the page style, the size of the columns and rows (if you selected the Table style), and the fonts in which the message will be printed. Click the Paper tab in the Print Setup dialog box to change the paper type and select a page style. Paper options include letter, legal, and A4. Page styles include the Day-Timer and Franklin Day Planner styles.

Print an e-mail message and attachment

In this exercise, you print an e-mail message in the Memo style and set up Outlook to print an e-mail message and its attachment.

1 In the Inbox, click the Picnic Reminder message header.

The Picnic Reminder message header is selected.

2 On the standard mail toolbar, click the Print button.

One copy of the e-mail message is printed.

3 Click the original Fun in the Sun Picnic Invitation message header.

The Picnic Reminder message header is selected again.

4 On the File menu, click Print.

The Print dialog box is displayed. The options in the dialog box will be different if you choose Table Style.

TROUBLESHOOTING

The appearance of the Print dialog box and the printing process are based on your printer. Your options may differ from those illustrated.

Figure 2-16
Print dialog box

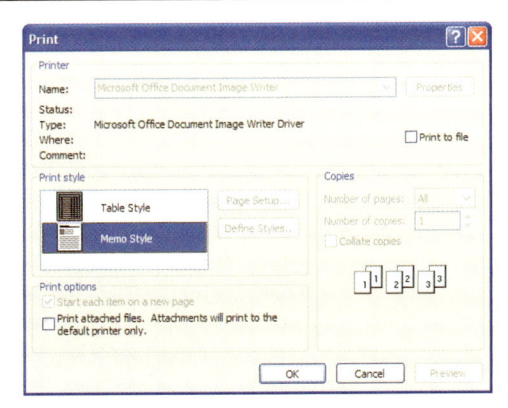

5 In the Print Options section of the dialog box, select the Print Attached Files check box, and click OK.

Outlook prints the e-mail message in the Memo style and prints the attachment.

◆ Keep Outlook open for the next exercise.

QUICK REFERENCE ▼

Print a message

1 In the Inbox, click the message header for the message that you want to print.

2 On the standard mail toolbar, click the Print button.

Print a message with an attachment

1 In the Inbox, click the message header for the message that you want to print.

2 On the File menu, click Print.

3 In the Print Options section in the Print dialog box, select the Print Attached Files check box and click OK.

QUICK CHECK

Q: What are the two layouts for printing messages?

A: Messages can be printed in table or memo format.

Finding Messages

Finding and Categorizing Messages

THE BOTTOM LINE

One of Outlook's many features lets you search messages for a specific word or phrase.

If you send and receive a lot of messages on a regular basis, your Inbox and **Sent Items folder** might contain dozens or even hundreds of messages. At some point, you might need to track down a specific message sent to a recipient or a message received from a particular e-mail address. For example, one of the new employees at Adventure Works said he didn't receive directions to the picnic. The sender opened the Sent Items folder and searched for a key word or phrase (such as picnic directions) that she knew was contained in the message. She forwarded the message to the employee who had not received the directions.

Find message

In this exercise, you find the messages that contain the word *directions*.

1 On the standard mail toolbar, click the Find button.

A small pane is displayed that enables you to enter search criteria.

2 In the Look For box, type directions.

This defines the text to be found in the messages.

Lesson 2 Using E-Mail in Outlook   43

3 Select the location or mail folders to be searched.

This defines the folder to be searched.

4 Click the Find Now button.

The results are displayed. The messages containing *directions* should be the only messages listed.

Figure 2-17

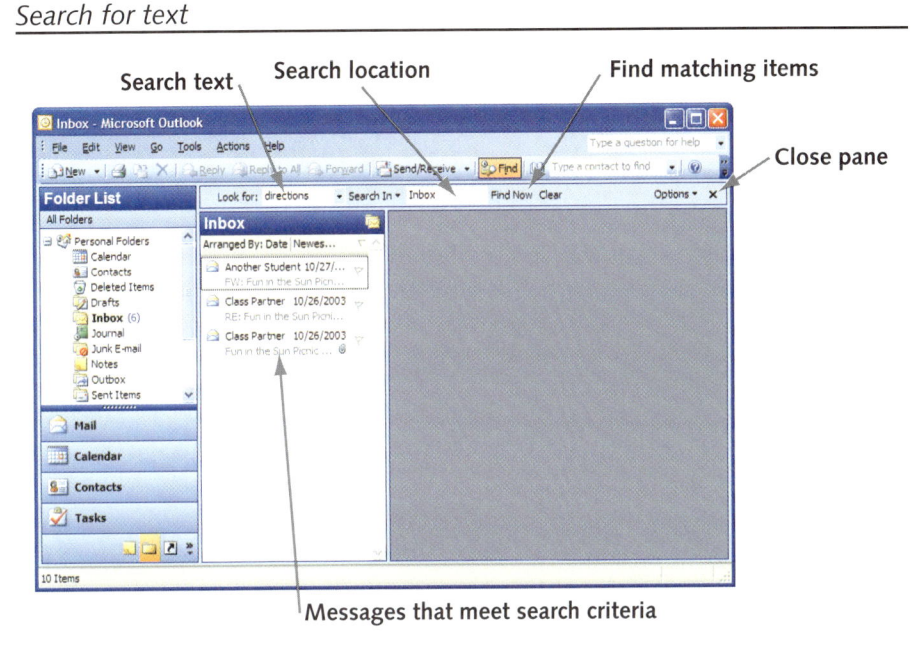

Search for text

5 Click the Close button in the small search pane.

The pane closes.

◆ Keep Outlook open for the next exercise.

QUICK CHECK

Q: Why would you use the search feature?

A: It enables you to find messages that contain specific text.

QUICK REFERENCE ▼

Find a message

1 On the standard mail toolbar, click the Find button.

2 In the Look For and Search In boxes, type the search criteria.

3 Click the Find Now button.

Recalling Messages

THE BOTTOM LINE

There may be occasions when, after you have sent a message, you realize that you need to make a correction to that message. With Outlook, you can retrieve messages before they are read and substitute a different message to issue a correction.

If you are connected to a network that uses Microsoft Exchange Server, you can **recall** a message and send an updated message. Use this feature to reissue information that might have been sent incorrectly the first time or to retrieve messages sent to the wrong recipient. For example, the recreation director at Adventure Works sent a message to the planning team announcing an upcoming event and accidentally typed the wrong price for attending the event. He recalled the message, made the correction to the date, and sent the corrected message.

To be recalled, a message must meet four criteria. The recipient must be logged on to the network. The recipient must use Microsoft Outlook. The message must be in the recipient's Inbox. The message must be unread.

Recall a message

To recall a message, take these steps:

1 **Open the Sent Items folder.**

Messages you sent are listed.

2 **Double-click the message to be recalled.**

The message opens in a separate window.

3 **Click Recall This Message on the Actions menu.**

The Recall This Message dialog box is displayed.

Figure 2-18

Recall This Message dialog box

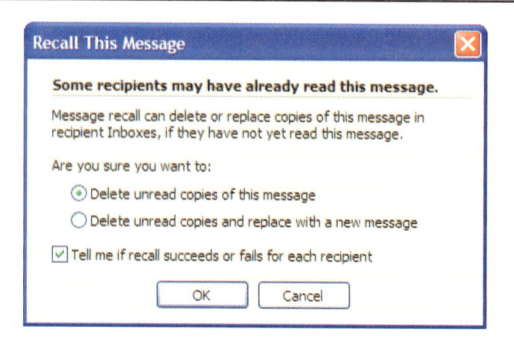

4 **Choose to delete the unread messages or delete the unread messages and send a replacement message.**

Select one of the options to deal with the message.

5 Click OK to recall the message.

All copies of the sent message that meet the recall criteria are recalled. If the option is selected, a replacement message is sent.

◆ Keep Outlook open for the next exercise.

QUICK REFERENCE ▼
Recall a message

1 Open the Sent Items folder.
2 Double-click the message header for the message that you want to recall.
3 On the Actions menu, click Recall This Message.
4 Click OK.

> **QUICK CHECK**
>
> Q: What are the criteria for recalling a message?
>
> A: The recipient must be logged on to the network. The recipient must use Microsoft Outlook. The message must be in the recipient's Inbox. The message must be unread.

Deleting Messages

> **THE BOTTOM LINE**
>
> When a message is no longer needed, it can be deleted. The two-step process used to delete messages prevents you from accidentally deleting critical information.

After reading new messages, you can leave them in the Inbox. However, you will find that over time your Inbox can become cluttered if you don't organize or remove messages regularly. You can choose to delete any outdated e-mail messages by clicking the message header and then clicking the Delete button on the standard mail toolbar or pressing the Delete key.

> **TIP**
>
> To select multiple message headers that are displayed together, click the first message header, hold down the Shift key, and click the last message header. To select multiple message headers that are not displayed together, click the first message header, hold down the Ctrl key, and click each additional message header.

When you delete messages, they are not permanently removed from Outlook. Instead, they are placed in the **Deleted Items folder** until you decide to empty it. This safeguard makes it possible to restore your messages if you accidentally delete them or realize that you still need certain deleted messages.

Delete messages

Since you are done with the Picnic Reminder message, you will delete this message from the Inbox and then empty the Deleted Items folder.

1 In the Inbox, click the Picnic Reminder message header.

The message is selected. The content is displayed in the Reading pane.

2 On the standard mail toolbar, click the Delete button.

The message moves to the Deleted Items folder.

TIP

To restore a deleted message, drag the message from the Deleted Items folder to the Inbox shortcut on the Outlook bar.

3 **In the Folder List, click Deleted Items.**

The Deleted Items folder opens, displaying the message that you deleted.

4 **Click the message.**

The message is selected.

5 **Press Delete.**

An alert box asks you to confirm the deletion.

ANOTHER METHOD

You can also delete all messages in the Deleted Items folder by clicking Empty "Deleted Items" Folder on the Tools menu.

6 **Click Yes.**

The items are removed from the Deleted Items folder and permanently deleted.

◆ If you are continuing to the next lesson, keep Outlook open.

◆ If you are not continuing to the next lesson, close Outlook.

QUICK CHECK

Q: Where is a message placed after it is deleted from the Inbox?

A: It is placed in the Deleted Items folder.

QUICK REFERENCE ▼

Delete a message

1 In the Inbox, click the message header for the message that you want to delete.

2 On the standard mail toolbar, click the Delete button.

Empty the Deleted Items folder

1 In the Folder List, click Deleted Items.

2 Select the message or messages that you want to delete.

3 Press Delete and click Yes.

Key Points

✔ *You can use Outlook to read an electronic message.*
✔ *Outlook provides the tools to reply to and forward messages.*
✔ *You can include an attachment in an e-mail message.*
✔ *Messages received and sent can be sorted and searched.*
✔ *Messages which are no longer needed can be deleted.*
✔ *Outlook items can be moved between folders.*

Quick Quiz

True/False

T F 1. Messages can be recovered from the Deleted Items folder.
T F 2. Message headers are not displayed in the Reading pane.
T F 3. Double-click a message header to display the message in the Reading pane.
T F 4. Only graphics can be sent as attachments.
T F 5. A message cannot be longer than 1,500 characters.

Multiple Choice

1. To permanently delete a message, _____.
   a. press the Delete key
   b. empty the Deleted Items folder
   c. click the Delete button
   d. select the Delete command from the Edit menu

2. Attachments can include _____.
   a. graphics
   b. Excel files
   c. Outlook items
   d. all of the above

3. Messages in the Sent Items directory have been _____.
   a. sent to other recipients
   b. received from other users
   c. stored because they are incomplete
   d. forwarded to you by other users

4. To be recalled, a message must be _____.
   a. incomplete
   b. deleted
   c. unread
   d. all of the above

5. A(n) _____ is sent to the person who sent the original message.
   a. forwarded message
   b. attachment
   c. reply
   d. draft

Short Answer

1. How do you manually check for messages in Outlook without waiting for messages to be sent or received at the preset interval?
2. What are the steps you take to create an e-mail message?
3. What happens to a message when you delete it from your Inbox?
4. What information is contained in the header of a message?
5. How do you read an e-mail message?

6. How do you save a message without sending it so that you can complete or edit the message later?
7. What is the Inbox?
8. What can you insert into an Outlook e-mail message?
9. What is the value of AutoPreview?

On Your Own

Exercise 1

The training director at Adventure Works must send an Outlook 2003 class announcement to those who signed up for the class. The date, time, and location of the class should be included in the message. Use the date, time, and location for your Outlook class to provide this information. A syllabus for the class must be sent as an attachment. You can find the syllabus in the Outlook Practice folder on your hard disk.

Send the class announcement with the syllabus—and include a flag—to your partner, to another member of your class, and to yourself. When you receive the message, print the syllabus.

Exercise 2

After you sent the class announcement, you discovered that the location of the class has changed. Notify the recipients that the location of the class has changed. After you've completed this task, delete the message.

One Step Further

Exercise 1

Create a message describing the benefits of using Outlook 2003. Use the Formatting toolbar to create visual interest. Set a flag to request a reply in 10 days. Send the message.

Exercise 2

Move the messages you sent about the picnic from the Sent Items folder to the Deleted Items folder. Delete the messages.

Exercise 3

A co-worker complains that it takes several minutes for his mail messages to be sent and he frequently experiences a delay in receiving messages. Use Microsoft Outlook Help to explain the delay in sending and receiving mail. Describe how he can fix the problem.

LESSON 3
Customizing E-Mail

After completing this lesson, you will be able to:

✔ *Specify e-mail options.*
✔ *Customize the appearance of e-mail messages.*
✔ *Use stationery.*
✔ *Add a signature to an e-mail message.*
✔ *Sort messages.*
✔ *Filter a view.*
✔ *Create folders.*
✔ *Move messages between folders.*
✔ *Organize the Inbox by using colors.*
✔ *Filter junk e-mail messages.*
✔ *Archive messages.*

KEY TERMS

- archive
- filter
- formatted text
- HTML
- junk e-mail
- Plain Text
- Rich Text
- rule
- signature
- sort
- stationery

As the popularity of the Internet increases, it is easy to become overwhelmed with e-mail messages from friends, family, and co-workers. You can make your e-mail more manageable by identifying, prioritizing, and storing the messages that you receive. If you use e-mail regularly and you receive a dozen messages or more per day, over time it can become difficult to find a particular message in an Inbox that contains hundreds of received messages. However, if you customize and organize the e-mail messages you send and receive, locating the right information is a simple process.

You can easily customize e-mail messages in Microsoft Office Outlook 2003 by applying specific options to your message. Available options include attaching a level of importance or sensitivity to a message, automatically sending replies to others, and saving sent messages to a specified folder. You can also set options that delay the delivery of a message. (For example, you can compose a birthday greeting to a friend but not have it sent until the recipient's birthday.) Another option makes a message invalid after a specified date. Other options include receiving notification when an e-mail message is read by the recipient, linking a message to a contact, and assigning a message to a category.

You can also customize e-mail messages by changing their appearance. In older e-mail programs, you were restricted to sending messages using only plain text, without text-formatting, color, or graphics capabilities. Most of today's programs include many of these capabilities. Using Microsoft Outlook, you can enhance your e-mail messages by placing images in the background, adding borders, using different fonts and colors, and formatting text. You can further customize your e-mail messages by adding a personalized signature, which is inserted at the end of an e-mail message. In a signature, you might include information such as your title, phone number, and e-mail address. You can also include graphics, such as your organization's logo.

Organizing messages in your Inbox is another way to manage your e-mail. It is easier to find a specific message and reduces the clutter in your Inbox. You can organize messages by moving them to different folders, deleting messages you no longer need, and color-coding your messages. For example, you can move unwanted e-mail messages from advertisers to the Deleted Items folder, or remove old messages from the Inbox by placing them in a storage folder or deleting them.

In this lesson, you will learn how to customize outgoing messages by adding options, backgrounds, images, borders, and a personal signature. You will also learn how to use a filter to temporarily limit displayed items that meet specific conditions, such as unread messages, messages flagged for attention, or messages with attachments. You will organize your Inbox by adding color to message headers so that you can identify particular senders, junk e-mail messages, or adult content. You will also learn how to create folders to organize and store messages by specific topics or projects. In addition, you will learn how to sort and store messages that are important to you.

> **IMPORTANT**
>
> To complete some of the exercises in this lesson, you will need to exchange e-mail messages with a class partner. If you don't have a class partner or you are performing the exercises alone, you can send the message to yourself. Simply enter your own e-mail address instead of a class partner's address.

Specifying E-Mail Options

> **THE BOTTOM LINE**
>
> With Outlook you can set options that alert recipients about the content of your messages.

Several options enable you to specify how messages are sent and where they are stored. For example, you can alert recipients that your e-mail message is more important than normal messages or inform recipients that the message contains sensitive information. You can set Outlook to forward a reply to other people or save your sent message in a particular folder. You can select the day and time that the message is sent and alert the recipient when the message is no longer relevant.

To select options for an e-mail message, open a new message window. Click the Options button on the New Message toolbar in the message window. The Message Options dialog box is displayed.

FIGURE 3-1

Message Options dialog box

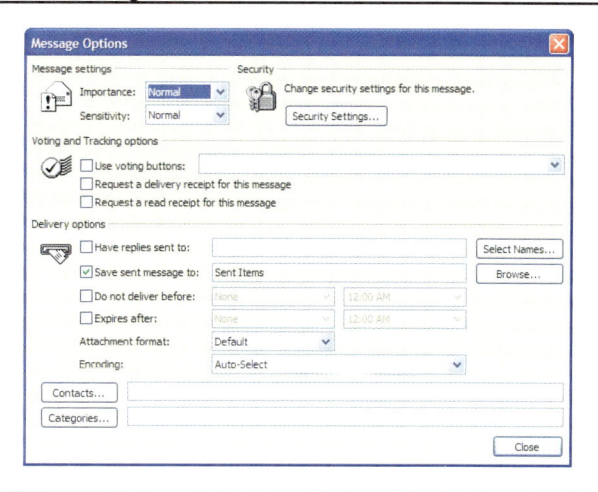

[Screenshot of Message Options dialog box showing Message settings (Importance, Sensitivity), Security, Voting and Tracking options, and Delivery options]

The e-mail options in the Message Options dialog box are explained in the following table. These selections are applied to the message you are currently creating.

Option	Description
Importance	Mark an e-mail message to be of high or low importance. When an e-mail message marked with high importance is received in Outlook, the message header displays a red exclamation point in the Importance column of the message header. A message of low importance displays a blue down arrow in the Importance column of the message header. All other e-mail messages are considered to be of normal importance and no icon will be displayed in the Importance column when they are received.
Sensitivity	Recommend how the recipient should regard the e-mail message. You can mark messages as normal, personal, private, or confidential. A warning appears at the top of personal, private, and confidential messages, stating the sensitivity of the e-mail message. Sensitivity *doesn't restrict access* to the message and shouldn't be considered a form of security.
Security Settings	Assign additional security measures, such as encryption and a digital signature, to the message.
Use Voting Buttons	Enable recipients to vote by selecting one of several choices. Use the standard button names or assign custom names to the buttons. This option requires Microsoft Exchange Server.
Request A Delivery Receipt For This Message	Select this option to receive notification when the message is delivered to the recipient's Inbox.
Request A Read Receipt For This Message	Select this option to receive notification when the recipient has read the message. When the recipient opens the message, an alert box asks if Outlook can notify the sender that he or she

(continued)

52 Lesson 3 Customizing E-Mail

(continued)

Option	Description
	read the message. If the recipient agrees, Outlook sends an e-mail message to the sender, stating when the message was read.
Have Replies Sent To	Message replies are automatically sent to the specified e-mail addresses. For example, if you send a message that requests more information about a particular topic, you can specify that the reply be sent to others who would also benefit from the information.
Save Sent Message To	When you send an e-mail message, a copy of the message is automatically saved in the Sent Items folder. Select this option to save a copy of the sent message in a folder that you specify.
Do Not Deliver Before	Delay delivery of an e-mail message until a later date or time. For example, on Monday, the marketing director at Adventure Works scheduled a meeting for Friday morning. When she scheduled the meeting, she created a message to be delivered on Thursday morning that included attached documents for attendees to review before the meeting.
Expires After	Some messages expire; they become invalid after a specific date. Include expiration dates for time-sensitive messages, such as invitations and deadlines. An expired message is dimmed or crossed out in the recipient's Inbox after the message has expired. An expired message that has not been read is dimmed, but the message can still be opened. Expired messages that have been read have a line through them to indicate that they have expired. Messages expire at the preset time of 5:00 P.M. (the end of the business day). To change the preset time, delete it and enter a new time.
Attachment Format	Attachments stored on your computer can be mapped to and readable on the Internet. Default uses the most common format for the attachment.
Encoding	Select this option to use mappings from the Windows character sets to alter Internet format for different languages.
Contacts	Select this option to link contacts to e-mail messages. For example, link the contact for the customer service manager to an e-mail message sent from a satisfied customer.
Categories	Select this option to assign the message to a category. Categorizing messages makes it easier to find and group related messages.

◆ Be sure to start Outlook before beginning this exercise.

Lesson 3 Customizing E-Mail 53

Specify e-mail options

As we begin the exercises for this lesson, you create a new message, mark the message as high priority, and send it to your class partner. Then you create another message, mark it as confidential, and send it to your class partner.

1 If necessary, open the Inbox folder.

The contents of the Inbox folder are displayed.

2 On the standard mail toolbar, click the New Mail Message button.

A message window is displayed.

3 On the New Message toolbar in the message window, click the Options button.

The Message Options dialog box is displayed.

TROUBLESHOOTING

If you send the e-mail message to a recipient who also uses Outlook, any flags or other settings that you specified are displayed in the recipient's message. Flags and other settings might not be displayed in the message if the recipient uses an e-mail program other than Outlook.

4 In the Message settings section, click the Importance down arrow, and click High.

5 Click the Close button.

The Message Options dialog box closes.

6 In the To box, type your class partner's e-mail address and press the Tab key twice.

ANOTHER METHOD

Because you have sent messages to your class partner several times, Outlook might display your class partner's address when you start to type it. Press Enter to accept the address in the field.

The insertion point moves to the Subject box.

7 In the Subject box, type Health Insurance Files and press Enter.

The insertion point moves to the message area.

8 Type Review all health insurance files for inaccuracies.

54 Lesson 3 Customizing E-Mail

FIGURE 3-2

Important message ready to be sent

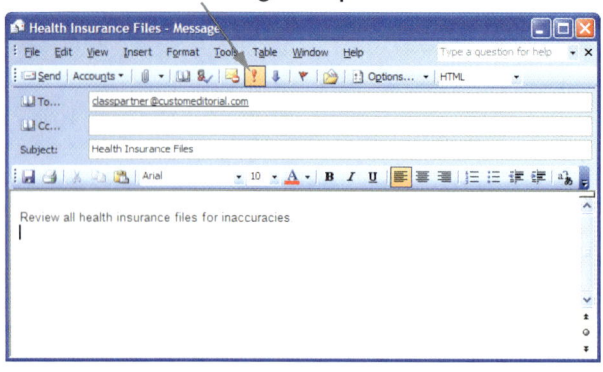

[Screenshot: Health Insurance Files message window with "This new message is important" label pointing to the importance indicator. To: classpartner@customeditorial.com; Subject: Health Insurance Files; Body: Review all health insurance files for inaccuracies]

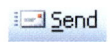

9 On the New Message toolbar in the message window, click the Send button.

The message is sent to your class partner.

10 On the standard mail toolbar, click the New Mail Message button.

A message window is displayed.

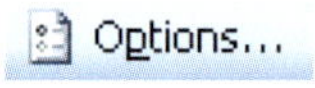

11 On the Message toolbar in the message window, click the Options button.

The Message Options dialog box is displayed.

12 In the Message settings section, click the Sensitivity down arrow, click Confidential, and click the Close button.

The Message Options dialog box closes.

FIGURE 3-3

Confidential message option

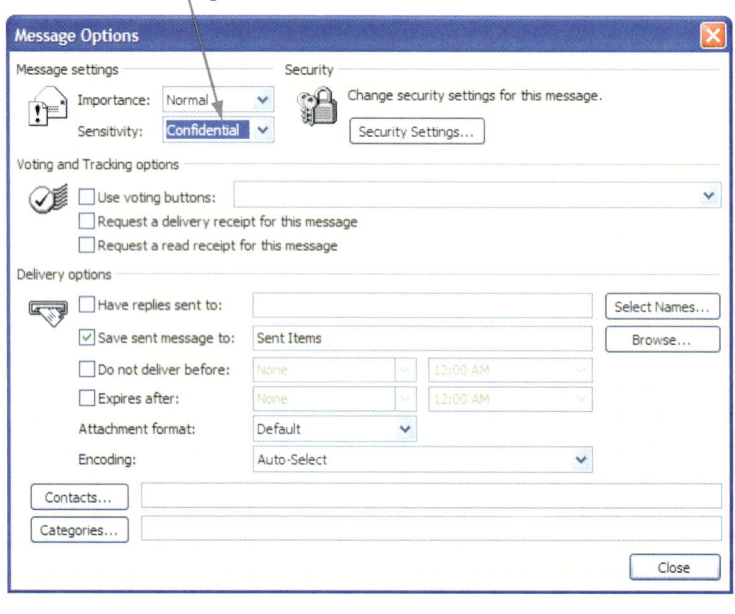

[Screenshot: Message Options dialog box with "This new message is confidential." label pointing to the Sensitivity field set to Confidential. Shows Message settings (Importance: Normal, Sensitivity: Confidential), Security, Voting and Tracking options, Delivery options (Save sent message to: Sent Items, Attachment format: Default, Encoding: Auto-Select), Contacts, Categories, and Close button.]

Lesson 3 Customizing E-Mail   55

13 **In the To box, type your class partner's e-mail address, and press Tab twice.**

The insertion point moves to the Subject box.

14 **In the Subject box, type Paycheck, and press Enter.**

The insertion point moves to the message area.

15 **Type Look for a $500 bonus in your next paycheck.**

16 **On the New Message toolbar in the message window, click the Send button.**

The message is sent to your class partner.

FIGURE 3-4

Confidential message ready to be sent

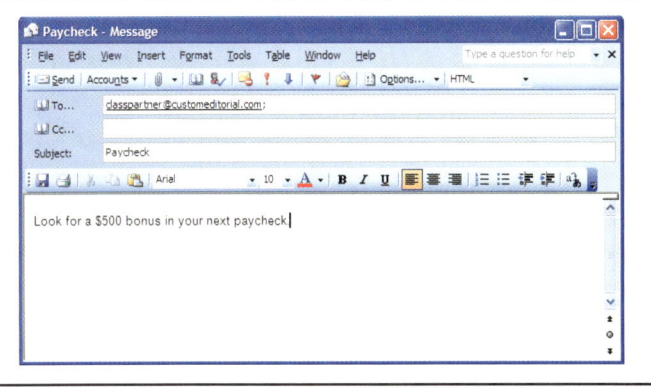

17 **On the standard mail toolbar, click the Send/Receive button. Click the high-priority message header.**

Two messages from your class partner arrive in the Inbox. Notice that a red exclamation point is displayed to the left of the Health Insurance Files message header. The content of the high-priority message is displayed in the Reading pane.

FIGURE 3-5

High-priority message received

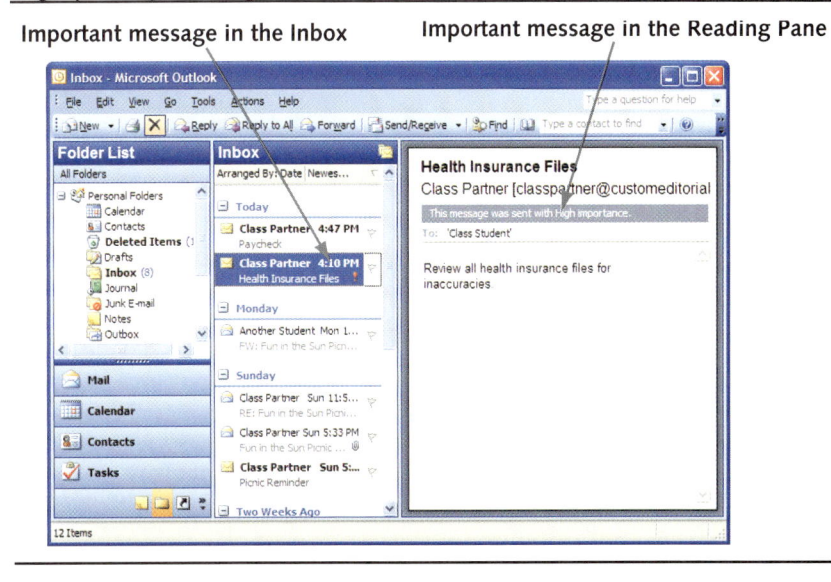

18 Click the message Paycheck.

The message is displayed in the Reading pane. Notice that the comment at the top of the message window states that the message is confidential.

FIGURE 3-6

Confidential message received

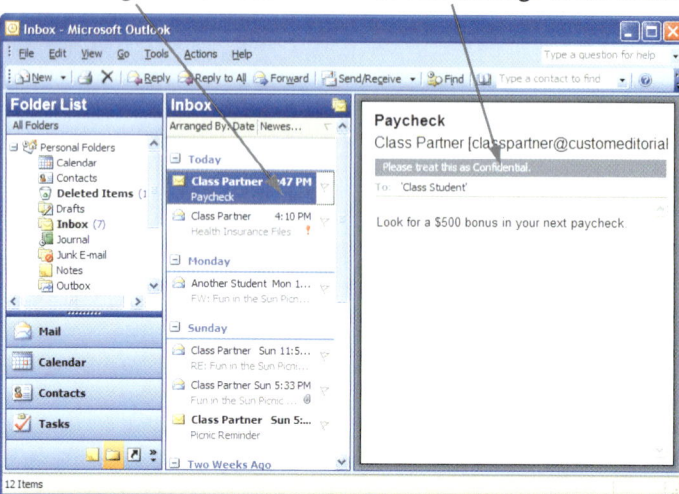

Confidential message in the Inbox   Confidential message in the Reading Pane

QUICK CHECK

Q: Does Outlook enforce confidentiality if you create a message identified as confidential?

A: Outlook can't enforce confidentiality.

◆ Keep Outlook open for the next exercise.

QUICK REFERENCE ▼

Specify e-mail options

1 On the standard mail toolbar, click the New Mail Message button.
2 On the New Message toolbar in the message window, click Options.
3 Select the options for the current message.
4 Click the Close button.

Customizing the Appearance of E-Mail Messages

Formatting Messages

THE BOTTOM LINE

You can send e-mail messages in HTML, Rich Text, or Plain Text. Formatting options are available in HTML and Rich Text.

In older e-mail programs, you were limited to sending e-mail messages in plain text that used only a few fonts. With Outlook, you can send e-mail messages with graphical backgrounds and formatted text. **Formatted text** appears in different sizes, colors, styles, and alignments. You can use these formatting options to customize a message for a particular event or recipient. For example, an e-mail invitation to a corporate shareholders' meeting requires a neutral background with a formal font, but an e-mail invitation to a birthday party needs a colorful background with text in a larger, more ornate font.

Outlook includes three message formats for sending and receiving messages: HTML, Rich Text, and Plain Text:

1. **HTML** is an acronym for Hypertext Markup Language, which is the formatting language used by Web browsers to format and display Web pages. Use HTML if you want to use text formatting, numbering, bullets, alignment, horizontal lines, backgrounds, animated graphics, pictures, and entire Web pages. Not all e-mail programs can display HTML formatting.

2. **Rich Text** is a standard method of formatting text with tags that can be understood by most word processors and newer e-mail programs. Use Rich Text if you want to use text formatting, bullets, and alignment. Rich Text can't support the extensive Web capabilities of the HTML format such as animated graphics and Web pages. Not all e-mail programs can display Rich Text formatting.

3. **Plain Text** is generic text that can be read by any e-mail program. Use Plain Text when you do not want to include any formatting in your messages. Plain Text is the safest option because all e-mail programs can read text in this format.

Specify one of the three message formats as a default format that is used for all your messages. However, you can always switch to another message format for an individual message. Outlook uses the format of a received message as the format for your reply message. For example, if you reply to a message sent to you in plain text, Outlook creates a reply in plain text format. This reduces the chance that your reply will use formatting or graphics that can't be displayed correctly by the correspondent's e-mail program.

> **TIP**
>
> When you click a reply or forward option in the E-Mail Options dialog box, a preview of the reply or forwarded message appears to the right of the selected option.

You can also change how your replies and forwarded messages are formatted and how the original text is included in the message, if at all. Use the On replies and forwards section of the E-Mail Options dialog box to change the appearance of replies and forwards.

The following table identifies the reply and forward options.

Option	Description
Do Not Include Original Message	The message consists of your response only; the original message does not appear with the reply. This option is useful if you want to send short replies to a recipient who will have no difficulty understanding your response. This option is not available when forwarding a message, because you want the original message text to be displayed.
Attach Original Message	The original message is included as an attachment to the reply or forwarded message.

Lesson 3 Customizing E-Mail

Option	Description
Include Original Message Text	The text of the original message is included below your comments in the reply or forwarded message. This is the default option.
Include And Indent Original Message Text	The text of the original message is indented under your comments. This option helps you distinguish the text of the original message from the text you add.
Prefix Each Line Of The Original Text	The text of the original message is included in the reply or forwarded message. You can select the special character, usually a ">", that is inserted before each line of the original text.

Change the format of a message

You will now change the format of your replies so that the text of the original message is sent as an attachment and your outgoing e-mail messages are sent in Rich Text format. Then you create an e-mail message, send it to your class partner, reply to a message from your class partner, and view a reply to your message.

1 On the Tools menu, click Options.

The Options dialog box is displayed.

FIGURE 3-7

Options dialog box

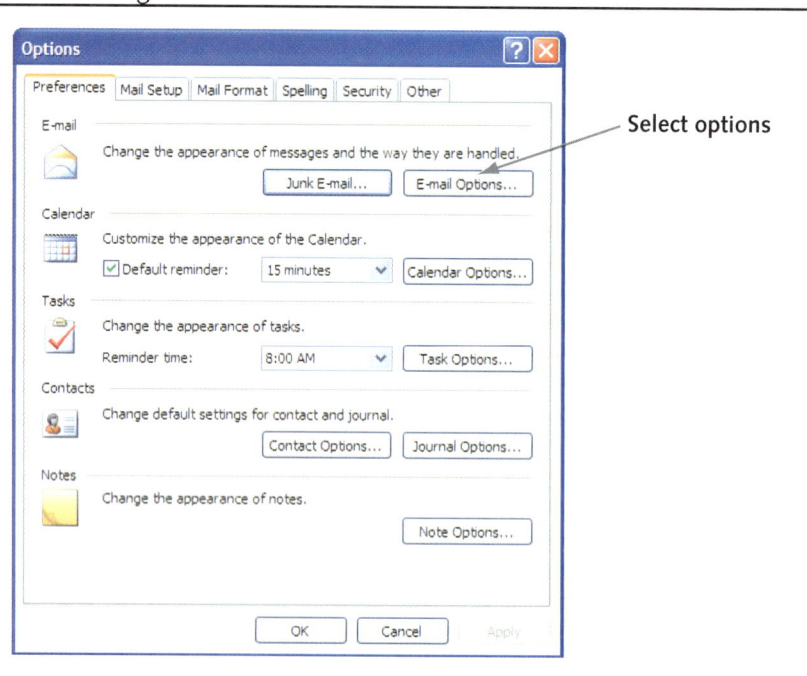

Select options

2 Click the E-Mail Options button.

The E-Mail Options dialog box is displayed.

3 In the On Replies And Forwards section, click the When Replying To A Message down arrow, click Attach Original Message, and then click OK.

The options are changed and the E-Mail Options dialog box closes.

Lesson 3 Customizing E-Mail 59

FIGURE 3-8

E-Mail Options dialog box

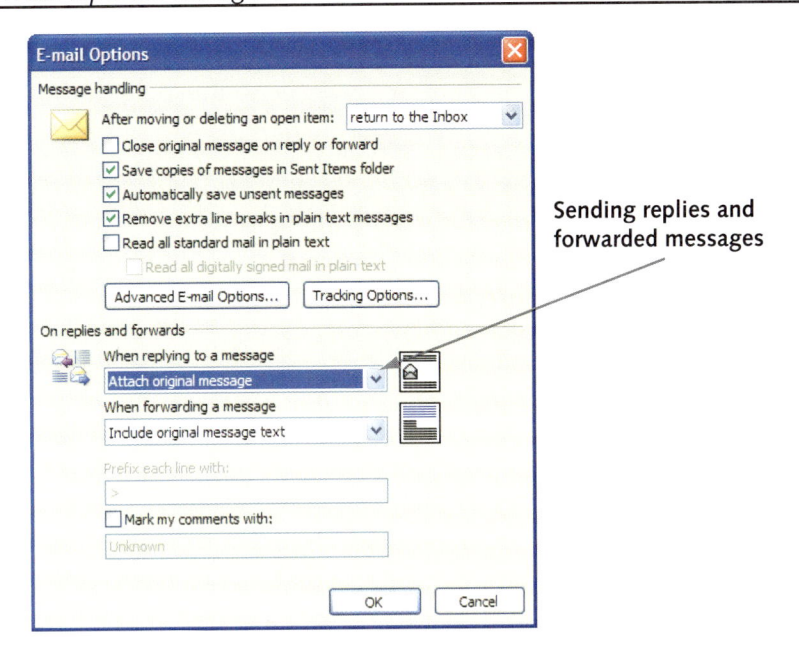

Sending replies and forwarded messages

4 In the Options dialog box, click the Mail Format tab.

5 In the Message Format section, click the Compose In This Message Format down arrow, click Rich Text, and click OK.

The format options are changed and the Options dialog box closes.

FIGURE 3-9

Format of outgoing messages

Select the format of messages you send

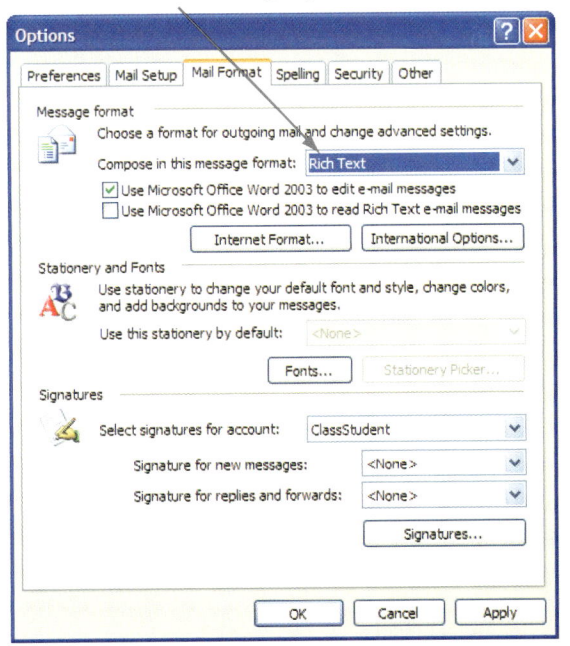

60 **Lesson 3** Customizing E-Mail

6 On the standard mail toolbar, click the New Mail Message button.

A message window is displayed.

7 In the To box, type your class partner's e-mail address, and press Tab twice.

The insertion point moves to the Subject box.

8 Type Going Away Party and press Enter.

The insertion point moves to the message area.

9 In the message area, type Please come to the AW pavilion for Frank's going away party. RSVP and select the text.

The selected text is highlighted.

TROUBLESHOOTING

If you don't see the Monotype Corsiva font in the list, choose another font that appeals to you.

10 On the E-mail toolbar in the message window, click the Font down arrow, scroll down, and click Monotype Corsiva.

The font Monotype Corsiva is displayed in the Font box and the selected text is modified.

11 On the Formatting toolbar in the message window, click the Font Size down arrow, and click 20.

The font size is set to 20 points and the selected text is modified.

12 On the Formatting toolbar in the message window, click the Font Color button, and select the Dark Red square (first square in the second row). Click to deselect the text.

The font color is set to dark red and the selected text is modified.

FIGURE 3-10

Formatted text in an outgoing message

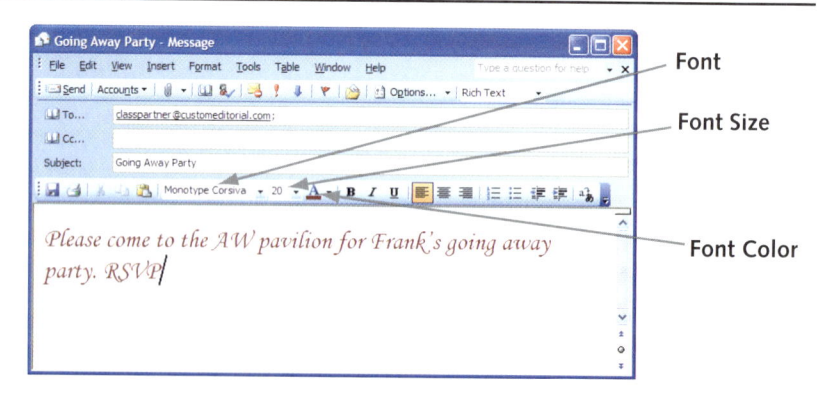

13 On the New Message toolbar in the message window, click the Send button.

The message is sent to your class partner.

14 On the standard mail toolbar in the Inbox folder, click the Send/Receive button.

A message from your class partner arrives in your Inbox.

Lesson 3 Customizing E-Mail   61

15 In the Inbox, click the message Going Away Party sent by your class partner.

The message is displayed in the Reading pane.

16 On the standard mail toolbar, click the Reply button.

A reply window appears. Notice that the original Going Away Party message is now an attachment.

17 In the message area, type **I will be there.** Click the Send button on the Message toolbar in the reply window.

The reply is sent to your class partner and the reply window closes.

FIGURE 3-11

Reply ready to be sent

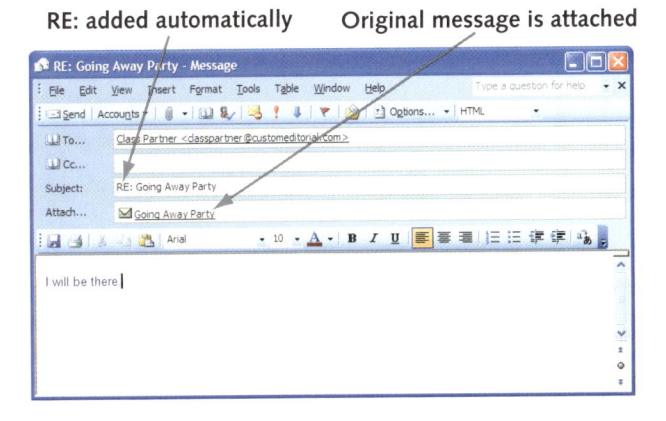

18 On the Standard toolbar, click the Send/Receive button. Delete the original invitation.

Your reply is sent and a message from your class partner arrives in the Inbox.

FIGURE 3-12

Reply arrives with attached original

QUICK CHECK

Q: What is Rich Text?

A: Rich Text is a standard method of formatting text with tags that can be understood by most word processors and newer e-mail programs.

62 Lesson 3 Customizing E-Mail

◆ Keep Outlook open for the next exercise.

QUICK REFERENCE ▼

Change message format

1. On the Tools menu, click Options.
2. Click the E-Mail Options button.
3. In the On replies and forwards section, choose an option and click OK.
4. In the Options dialog box, click the Mail Format tab.
5. In the Message format section, click the Compose in this message format down arrow, click a format, and click OK.

Using Stationery

Formatting Messages

THE BOTTOM LINE

Use stationery to add graphics that accent your message or create an image for your business.

When recipients receive a message from you, they normally see the message text on a white background. However, with Outlook, you can send e-mail messages that use color and images to create interest and catch the recipient's attention. Outlook stationery is like an electronic version of paper stationery. **Stationery** has predefined images, backgrounds, and borders that you can add to special e-mail messages like invitations or thank you notes.

TROUBLESHOOTING

All stationery designs are not installed when you install Outlook. If you select a design that isn't available on your computer, use the Microsoft Outlook or Microsoft Office CD-ROM to install additional stationery.

Other stationery designs are appropriate for business use. Outlook offers a variety of standard stationery designs. To send a decorative e-mail message, try the Ivy design, which has an ivy border on the left side of a message and room for your text. You can edit any text that is part of a design or you can create your own text.

CHECK THIS OUT ▼

Fun With Stationery
You can send birthday greetings to friends, family, or customers via e-mail. To make the e-mail messages appear festive, type *Happy Birthday* in large, colorful letters and use a cheerful stationery design in the body of the message.

Use stationery

In this exercise, you use stationery to customize a birthday party invitation and send the message to your class partner. You also view an invitation that you receive from your class partner.

1. On the Actions menu, point to New Mail Message Using, and click More Stationery.

The Select a Stationery dialog box appears.

Lesson 3 Customizing E-Mail 63

FIGURE 3-13
Select Stationery dialog box

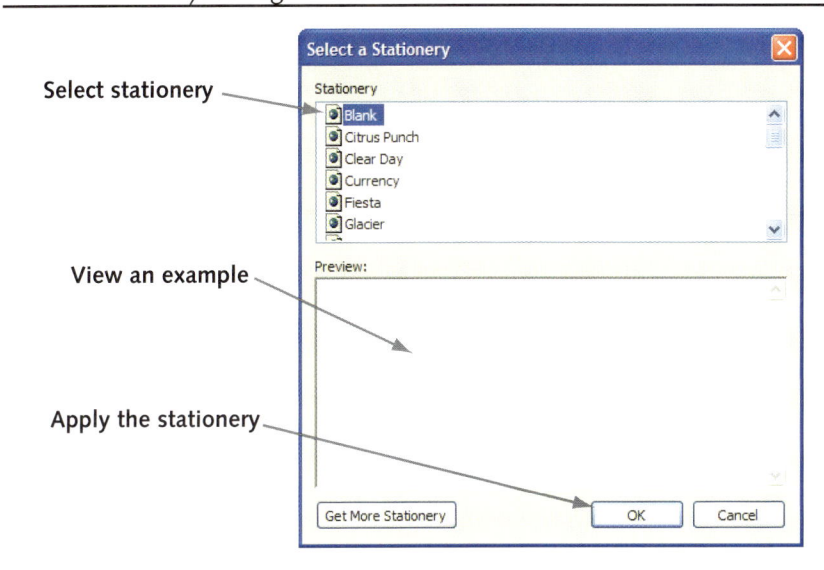

- Select stationery
- View an example
- Apply the stationery

ANOTHER METHOD
Additional stationery is available on your Outlook CD. You can also create your own stationery and make it available to other users.

2 **Scroll down the Stationery list and click Fiesta.**

A sample of the stationery is displayed in the Preview box.

3 **Click OK.**

The new message window uses the Fiesta stationery in the message area.

FIGURE 3-14
New message using selected stationery

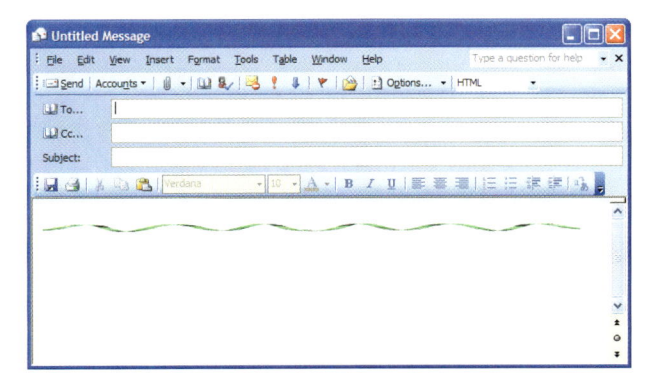

4 **In the To box, type your partner's e-mail address and press Tab twice.**

The insertion point moves to the Subject box.

5 **In the Subject box, type Mike's Birthday and press Enter.**

The insertion point moves to the message area.

64 **Lesson 3** Customizing E-Mail

6 In the message area, move the cursor to the end of the message, press Enter twice, and type A party to celebrate Mike's birthday! Press Enter. Type Saturday, June 6th! Press Enter. Type 1:00 P.M. Press Enter. Type Cherry Creek Park.

Notice the changes in the background, the graphics, the font, and the text alignment. These graphic elements and text characteristics are defined by the stationery.

FIGURE 3-15

Message using selected stationery ready to send

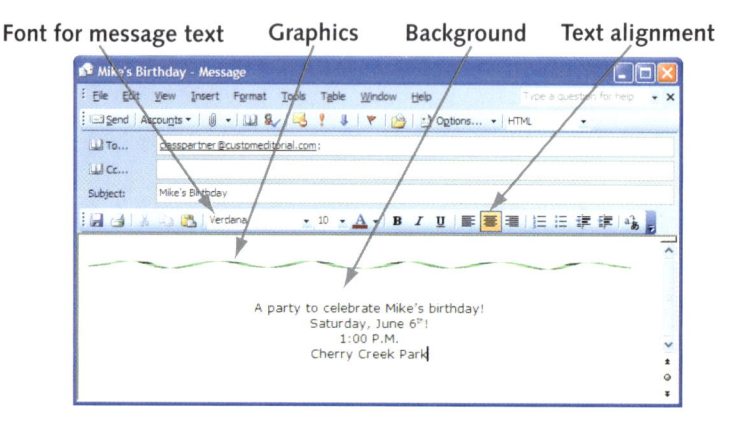

7 On the New Message toolbar in the message window, click the Send button.

The message is sent to your class partner.

8 On the standard mail toolbar, click the Send/Receive button.

A message from your class partner arrives in the Inbox.

9 Double-click the Mike's Birthday message header.

The message window opens. Notice the stationery background.

FIGURE 3-16

Message using selected stationery received

QUICK CHECK

Q: Why would you use stationery?

A: It can accent and compliment your message.

◆ In the top-right corner of the message window, click the Close button.

◆ Keep Outlook open for the next exercise.

> **QUICK REFERENCE** ▼
>
> **Use stationery**
>
> 1. On the Actions menu, point to New Mail Message Using, and click More Stationery.
> 2. Select the stationery you want and click OK.

Adding a Signature to an E-Mail Message

> **THE BOTTOM LINE**
>
> Add a signature that provides standard information in every e-mail message you send. A signature can include your name, title, and contact information.

Adding Signatures to Messages

Many people include contact information at the end of each message they send. Rather than typing this information every time, create a **signature** that Outlook adds to the end of all messages you send. Signatures usually include your name and e-mail address. You can include information such as a phone or fax number and your title. Company logos and other graphics can also be added to a signature. Select colors and fonts to create a unique and expressive signature. For example, one of the managers at Adventure Works ends her e-mail messages with a business signature, which includes her name, title, business name, phone number, and the Adventure Works logo.

> **TROUBLESHOOTING**
>
> If your signature contains colors or fonts, and you change the format of your message to Plain Text, the appearance of your signature also changes.

Create as many signatures as you need. In addition to a business signature, create a personal signature that includes your nickname or a favorite quote. Create a simple signature for messages sent in Plain Text format and create a more complex signature with a logo for messages sent in HTML or Rich Text format. Set up Outlook to automatically insert a signature in the message area or select which signature you want to use in a message. To select a signature in a new message window, open the Insert menu, point to the AutoText, point to the Signature option, and select the signature.

Outlook 2003 enables you to create and modify a unique signature for each Outlook account. These signatures are inserted when the related Outlook e-mail account is used. This is a handy feature for families that use the same Outlook application on the same computer, but use different e-mail accounts. Small businesses or organizations can also benefit when the registered user has several "jobs" within the organization. The user may send a public relations message from one e-mail account and order supplies from a second e-mail account.

Create a signature

You will now complete your message by creating a signature and using the signature when you send a message to your class partner.

1 **On the Tools menu, click Options.**

The Options dialog box appears.

2 **Click the Mail Format tab.**

3 **Click the Signatures button.**

The Create Signature dialog box is displayed.

FIGURE 3-17

Create Signature dialog box

TROUBLESHOOTING

Existing signatures may be listed in the Create Signature dialog box.

4 **Click the New button.**

The Create New Signature dialog box is displayed.

5 **In the first box, select the default text Untitled. Type class student signature.**

The name is assigned to the new signature.

Lesson 3 Customizing E-Mail 67

FIGURE 3-18

Create New Signature dialog box

ANOTHER METHOD

You can also choose to edit an existing signature. For example, you can include basic information in several signatures, but enter your title only in your business signature.

6 Verify that the Start with a blank signature option is selected and click the Next button.

The Edit Signature dialog box is displayed.

TIP

Later, you can use the Edit Signature dialog box to change the appearance of your signature. Select the text, click the Font or Paragraph button, and select formatting options.

7 Type your name and press Enter. Type Outlook Class. Click Finish and click OK in each dialog box to return to the Inbox.

When you create a new e-mail message, your signature is automatically placed in the message area.

TIP

In the Inbox, select Options from the Tools menu. Click the Mail Format tab. Your new class signature is selected in the Signature for new messages box. If you no longer want this signature to be placed in all new messages, select None or choose a different signature.

8 On the standard mail toolbar, click the New Mail Message button.

A message window is displayed. The class signature you created is already placed in the message area.

9 In the To box, type your class partner's e-mail address and press Tab twice.

The insertion point moves to the Subject box.

10 In the Subject box, type Outlook Class and press Enter. Type Are you enjoying the Outlook class?

The message containing the signature is ready to send.

11 On the New Message toolbar in the message window, click the Send button.

The message is sent to your class partner.

12 On the Standard toolbar, click the Send/Receive button.

A message from your class partner arrives in your Inbox.

TROUBLESHOOTING

Not all e-mail programs can display all the fonts that are available in Outlook or in your installation of Microsoft Windows. Similarly, if you receive a message that contains a font that you do not have installed, Outlook substitutes a font that is installed.

13 Click the **Outlook Class** message header.

The message is displayed in the Reading pane. Notice the sender's signature below the text.

FIGURE 3-19

Message with Class Partner's signature

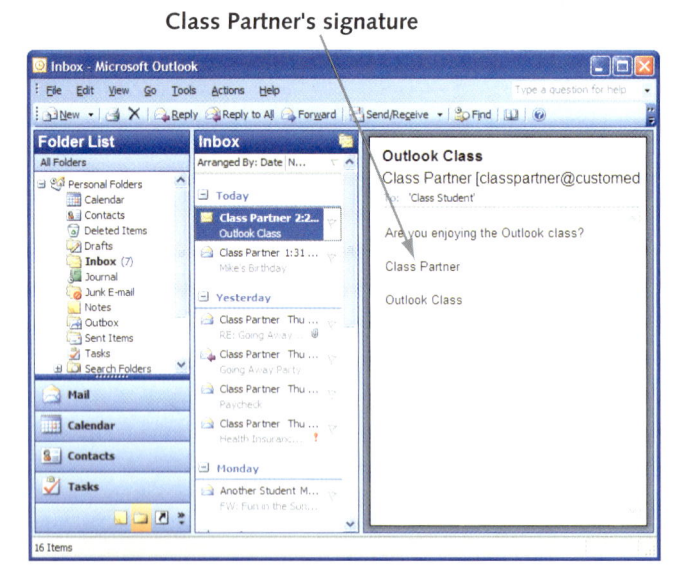

◆ Keep Outlook open for the next exercise.

Lesson 3 Customizing E-Mail 69

> **QUICK CHECK**
>
> Q: How many signatures can you create?
>
> A: There is no limit.

QUICK REFERENCE ▼

Create a signature

1. On the Tools menu, click Options.
2. Click the Mail Format tab.
3. Click the Signatures button.
4. Click the New button.
5. Type the name of your signature.
6. Verify that the Start with a blank signature option is selected.
7. Click the Next button.
8. Create your signature.
9. Click Finish and then click OK in each dialog box to return to the Inbox.

Sorting Messages

> **THE BOTTOM LINE**
>
> In Outlook, you can select an arrangement that displays messages in a specific sequence, making it easy to find a message or a group of messages.

Customizing How You View Messages

Arrangements, which you used in the previous lesson, present the messages in your Inbox in a specific order. You viewed messages by attachments, types, and so on. However, you may still want to view messages by a characteristic that isn't covered by one of the standard arrangements or sequence the messages by more than one criterion. Outlook enables you to **sort** messages, arranging the messages in your Inbox by the criteria you specify. When you sort in an arrangement, the messages remain in the same view; however, they are displayed in a different sequence or grouped by a specific characteristic.

> **TIP**
>
> Sorting does not remove messages from view. To temporarily remove messages from view, you must apply a filter. See "Filtering a View" in this lesson.

You can sort by four fields at the same time, thus performing a sort within a sort. When you perform a second sort on messages that have already been sorted, the second sort further organizes the list of sorted messages. For example, if you sort your Inbox by Subject in ascending order and then sort by Attachment in descending order, the Inbox will be sorted by Subject. Within the subjects, messages with an attachment will appear first.

70 **Lesson 3** Customizing E-Mail

Sort messages in your Inbox

Now that you have messages in your Inbox, you sort the list of messages by Attachment and by Subject. Then you clear the sort.

1 Open the View menu. Point to Arrange By. Point at Current View and click Customize Current View.

The Customize Views: Messages dialog box is displayed.

FIGURE 3-20

Customize Views: Messages dialog box

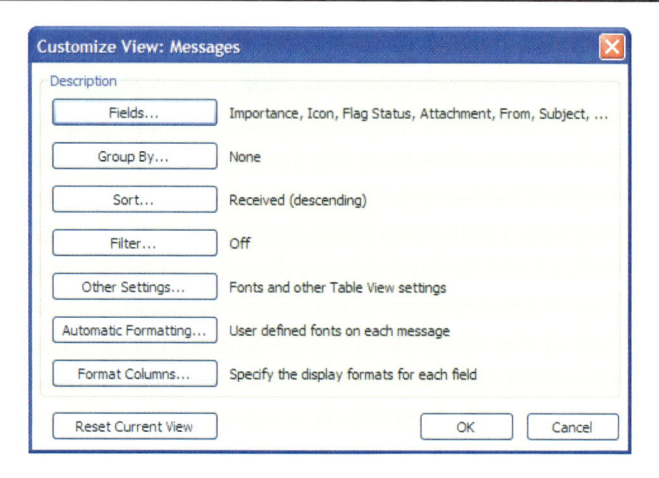

2 Click the Sort button.

The Sort dialog box is displayed.

FIGURE 3-21

Sort dialog box

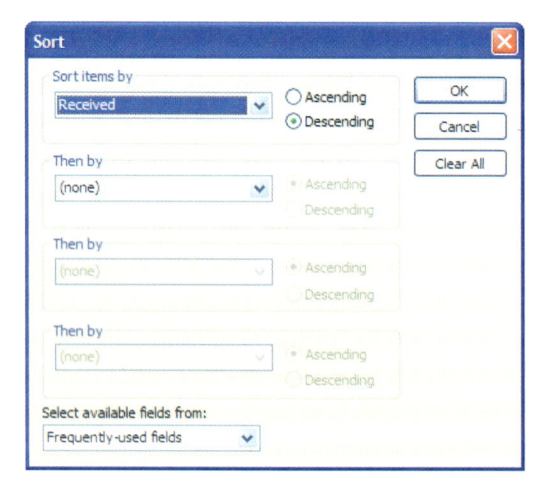

3 In the Sort Items By section, select Attachment, and verify that the Descending option is selected. Click OK twice.

The messages with attachments are displayed at the top of the message list.

Lesson 3 Customizing E-Mail 71

FIGURE 3-22

Messages sorted by attachments

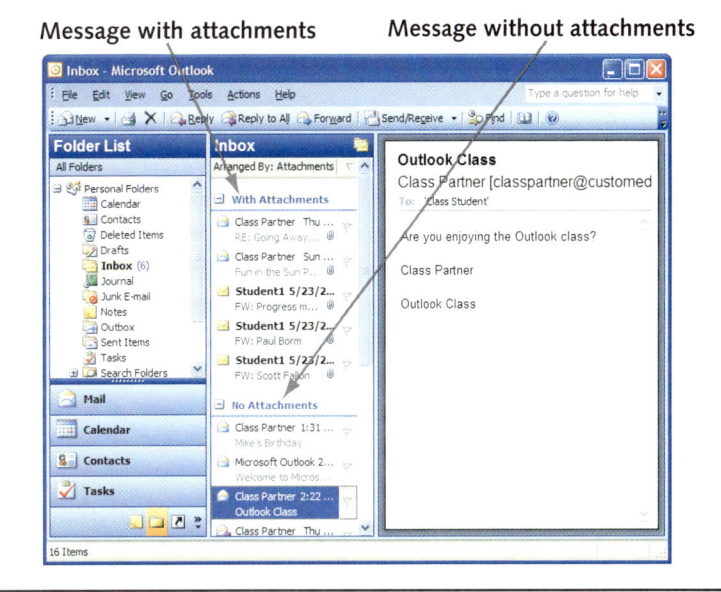

Message with attachments — Message without attachments

ANOTHER METHOD

You can also sort messages by clicking the column heading.

4 **Open the View menu. Point to Arrange By. Point at Current View and click Customize Current View.**

The Customize Views: Messages dialog box is displayed.

TIP

When messages are sorted in the Inbox, a small arrow appears in the associated column heading to indicate whether the messages are being sorted in ascending or descending order. The arrow points upward if messages are sorted in ascending order, and the arrow points downward if messages are sorted in descending order.

5 **Click the Sort button.**

The Sort dialog box is displayed. Notice that Attachment still appears in the Sort Items By box.

TROUBLESHOOTING

Outlook ignores the text FW: and RE: in the subject and uses the first letter that appears after the text FW: and RE: to sort by the subject.

6 **In the Then By section, click Subject. If necessary, click the Descending option and click OK twice.**

The messages with attachments still appear at the top of the message list and are sorted by subject in descending order (Z to A).

FIGURE 3-23

Sort criteria for messages in the Inbox

QUICK CHECK

Q: Are any sorted messages hidden from view?

A: No, the sequence of the messages is changed but messages are not hidden.

7 Open the View menu. Point to Arrange By. Point at Current View and click Customize Current View.

The Customize Views: Messages dialog box is displayed.

8 Click the Sort button.

The Sort dialog box is displayed.

9 Click the Clear All button.

The sort criteria are removed.

◆ Click OK twice to return to the Inbox.

◆ Keep Outlook open for the next exercise.

QUICK REFERENCE ▼

Sort messages

1 On the View menu, point to Arrange By.
2 Point at Current View and click Customize Current View.
3 Click the Sort button.
4 Select your options and click OK twice.

Filtering an Arrangement

Filtering Messages

THE BOTTOM LINE

You can further limit the messages you view by applying a filter to hide messages that don't meet your search criteria.

Apply a **filter** to display only items or files that meet certain conditions. For example, you could create a filter that displays only messages sent by a particular person or only messages that have a certain subject. Filtering makes it easier to find a particular message because messages that don't meet the conditions are not displayed. The more conditions you assign, the more specific your list of messages becomes.

A customer service representative at Adventure Works had dozens of messages in his Inbox and wanted to quickly find messages sent from his manager about a company picnic. He filtered his Inbox for messages that had the word picnic in the subject line and were sent from his manager. This action saved him the time and effort it would have taken to scroll through all his messages.

> **TIP**
>
> A filter is different from an arrangement because a filter hides messages from view that do not meet the conditions, while an arrangement simply rearranges the messages in a folder.

Use a filter with other methods of organizing messages. For example, after you sort the Inbox, filter the remaining e-mail messages. You can also filter messages as they arrive. For example, the training director at Adventure Works received numerous e-mail messages over the weekend regarding the results of a current training program. Some messages had instructor evaluations attached, and others did not. The training director wanted to reply to all the messages without evaluations first. To speed up the process, he applied the attachment arrangement and filtered messages containing the word *training*.

Messages use the Filter dialog box to apply a filter to a folder. To display the Filter dialog box, open the View menu. Point to Arrange By. Point at Current View and click Customize Current View. Click the Filter button. The Filter dialog box is divided into conditions that can be applied to filter a folder. The filter options are described in the following table.

FIGURE 3-24

Filter dialog box

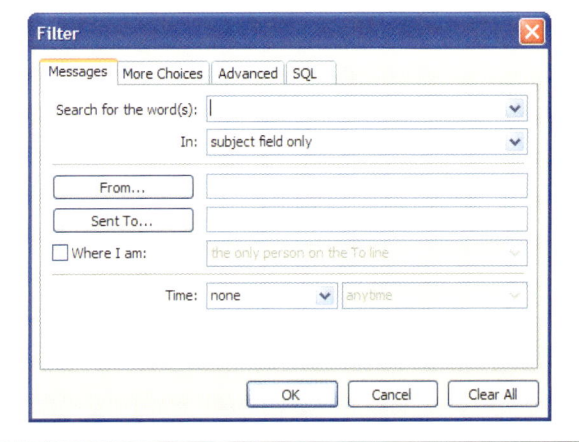

Condition	Description
Search for the word(s)	Filter the items in a folder by a specific word or words. By default, Outlook filters messages based on words in the subject field only, but you can filter according to words in the subject and message body as well as by frequently used text fields. Use this approach if you know a particular key word is unique to the messages you want to view. For example, if you want to view a message regarding a daily report, filter by the words *daily report* in the subject field.
From	This option filters messages by sender. Click the From button in the Filter dialog box to open the Select Names dialog box. Select the name or e-mail address of the person or persons to display after the filter is applied.
Sent To	This option filters messages by the recipient. Click the Sent To button in the Filter dialog box to open the Select Names dialog box. Select the name or e-mail address of the person or persons to display after the filter is applied.
Where I am	This option filters messages according to where your name or e-mail address appears in the message header. Filter messages in which you are the only person on the To line, messages in which you are on the To line with other people, or messages in which you are on the Cc line.
Time	This option filters messages by time. Use two boxes to select options. The first box contains options that establish an action to filter, such as messages received or sent. The second box contains options for setting the time criterion, such as yesterday or today. For example, you could filter a folder to search for messages sent this week or for messages received that have a due date of tomorrow.

You must remove a filter to show all the messages in the Inbox. To remove filters, click the Clear All button in the Filter dialog box.

Filter Messages

Now you apply a filter to display only messages that contain the word *birthday* in the subject or message body.

1 **Open the View menu. Point to Arrange By. Point at Current View and click Customize Current View.**

The Customize Views: Messages dialog box is displayed.

2 **Click the Filter button.**

The Filter dialog box is displayed.

3 **In the Search for the word(s) box, type birthday. Move to the In box. Select the option subject field and message body.**

This identifies the search text and the location to be searched.

Lesson 3 Customizing E-Mail 75

ANOTHER METHOD

You can also create a filter that searches only the subject if you know the message you want is titled appropriately.

FIGURE 3-25

Selected criteria for filter

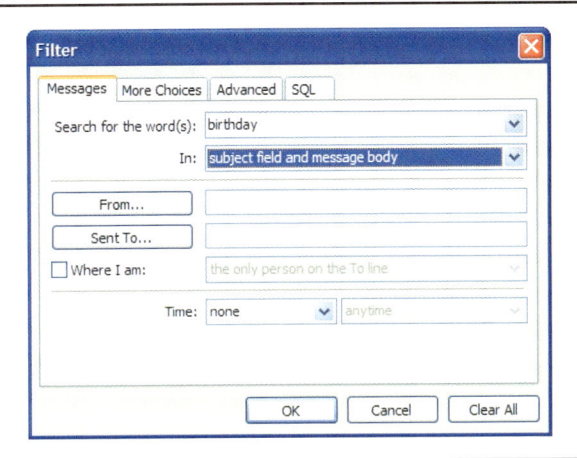

4 **Click OK twice.**

The filter is applied to the Inbox. Only messages containing the word *birthday* in the subject or message body are displayed.

FIGURE 3-26

Filtered messages

5 **Open the View menu. Point to Arrange By, point to Current View, and click Customize Current View.**

The Customize Views: Messages dialog box is displayed.

6 **Click the Filter button.**

The Filter dialog box is displayed.

QUICK CHECK

Q: Can you sort and filter messages?

A: Yes, messages can be sorted then filtered.

7 Click the Clear All button.

The Filter dialog box is cleared.

8 Click OK twice.

The filter is removed from the Inbox.

◆ Keep Outlook open for the next exercise.

QUICK REFERENCE ▼

Filter a view

1 On the View menu, point to Arrange By. Point at Current View and click Customize Current View.

2 Click the Filter button.

3 Select the filter options and click OK twice.

Creating Folders

Organizing Messages in Folders

THE BOTTOM LINE

You can use folders to organize messages and other Outlook items.

A folder organizes stored messages or other files and Outlook items. When you first start Outlook, several folders already exist, including the Inbox (where new e-mail messages appear), Sent Items (which contains copies of messages that you've already sent), Drafts (where unfinished messages are stored), and Deleted Items (which contains items that you deleted from other Outlook folders). You can create your own folders—such as folders for coworkers, managers, or projects—to organize messages more effectively.

When you create a folder, you must consider where the folder is to be placed. Most Outlook folders are located within one or more other folders. Display the Folder List to see which folders are inside other folders.

IMPORTANT

A folder created in Outlook must contain only a specific type of Outlook item—such as mail items only or contact items only. You identify the type of item that can be placed in the folder when you create the folder. *Any item moved to this folder is converted to that type of item, regardless of how the item was originally created.* For example, if you create a folder to hold mail items, and then move a task to the folder, a message window will appear with task information displayed in the subject and message area. The To box is empty, ready for you to address the message that contains information about the task and send it.

Lesson 3 Customizing E-Mail   77

Create a folder

You will now create a new folder named *Parties*, which will be used to store all messages that you receive about upcoming Adventure Works parties.

1 Open the File menu, point at the Folder option, and click New Folder.

The Create New Folder dialog box is displayed.

Figure 3-27

Create New Folder dialog box

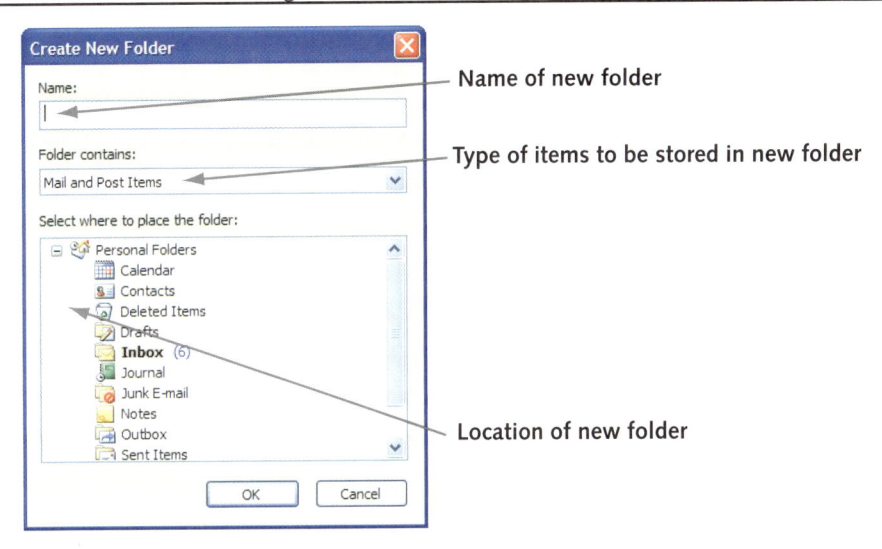

2 In the Name box, type **Parties**.

Notice that Mail and Post Items appear in the Folder contains box.

3 Verify that Inbox is selected as the location for the new folder and click OK.

The folder is created.

FIGURE 3-28

New folder created in the Inbox

ANOTHER METHOD

New Outlook folders can be created anywhere in the Folder List.

◆ Keep Outlook open for the next exercise.

78 | **Lesson 3** Customizing E-Mail

> **QUICK CHECK**
>
> **Q:** What limitations are associated with Outlook folders?
>
> **A:** All the items in an Outlook folder must be the same type of item.

Organizing Messages in Folders

QUICK REFERENCE ▼

Create folders

1. Open the File menu, point at the Folder option, and click New Folder.
2. In the Name box, type a folder name.
3. Select where the folder will be placed and click OK.

Moving Messages between Folders

THE BOTTOM LINE

Change a message into a different type of item by dragging it to a folder that contains the desired item type.

When you want to organize many Outlook items with similar subjects or content, you can group the items together in a folder for storage. You can also create additional folders within the original folder to further subdivide items more specifically. This system of organization can be helpful when you have a large project that requires many items dealing with many subjects. For example, the training director at Adventure Works has a folder for messages regarding training. This folder is further subdivided into folders for messages regarding each training class.

You can use four different methods to move a file from its current location to another folder: Drag the message from its current location to a different folder, click the Move To Folder button on the standard mail toolbar, use the Move Message option in the Organize pane, or create a rule to automatically move messages from one folder to another.

FIGURE 3-29

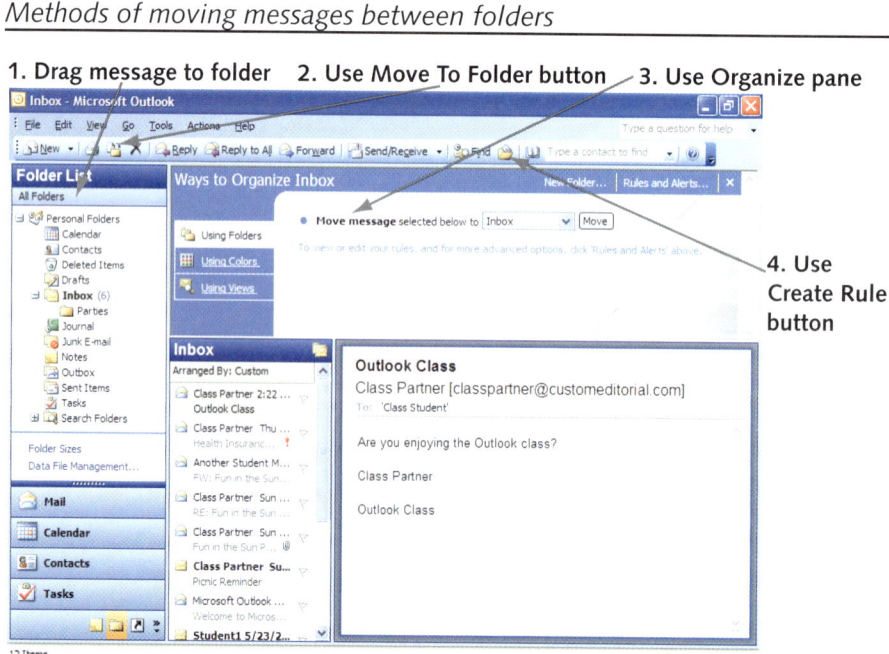

Methods of moving messages between folders

Lesson 3 Customizing E-Mail 79

You can manually move a selected message into a folder by dragging the message from the Inbox (or its current location) to the desired folder. Dragging is convenient if you want to move a message to a folder that is visible in the Outlook window. Messages can be dragged to folders on the Navigation pane and in the Folder List. For example, if you receive a message in your Inbox and want to move it to the Notes folder, drag the message header onto the Notes button in the Navigation pane or into the Notes folder in the Folder List.

Click a message header and click the Move To Folder button on the standard mail toolbar to open a menu of available folders. The list of folders on the menu changes to reflect folders based on the number of times they are selected. For example, if you frequently move messages to the Picnic folder but never move them to the Tasks folder, the Picnic folder is displayed on the menu, but the Tasks folder is not listed.

The Organize pane contains a Move Message option that moves selected messages to a folder. Like the Move To Folder button, select the message or messages and choose the folder from the Move Message list.

TIP

When you no longer want to use a rule, delete it.

You can also create a **rule** (a set of conditions, actions, and exceptions that perform a particular process) so that a message from a particular address is moved to a particular folder. Creating this rule is an easy way to organize messages if you always want to perform the same action. For example, the head chef of the Adventure Works frequently receives recipes from a friend. To help him stay organized, the chef created a rule so any e-mail messages he receives from this friend are moved to his Recipes folder. With this rule, the chef doesn't have to sort through his Inbox for new recipes; he can simply access any recipe messages in the Recipes folder.

Move messages

You will now move messages into the Parties folder, and create a rule that moves messages about parties to the Parties folder. Then you send a message to your class partner to test the rule. And, finally, you delete the rule.

1 **In the Inbox, select all messages sent in previous exercises about Mike's birthday party and the going away party.**

The messages are highlighted.

2 **Click the Move To Folder button on the standard mail toolbar.**

A short list of folders is displayed. The final option on the list is Move To Folder command.

TROUBLESHOOTING

If you move a message into the wrong folder, immediately after you've moved it you can click Undo Move on the Edit menu to move the message back to its previous location.

80 Lesson 3 Customizing E-Mail

3 **Click the Move To Folder command.**

The Move Items dialog box is displayed.

FIGURE 3-30

Move Items dialog box

4 **If necessary, click the plus sign (+) next to the Inbox.**

The Inbox expands to display the Parties folder.

5 **If necessary, click the Parties folder and click the OK button.**

The party messages are moved from the Inbox folder to the Parties folder.

FIGURE 3-31

Messages moved to the Parties folder

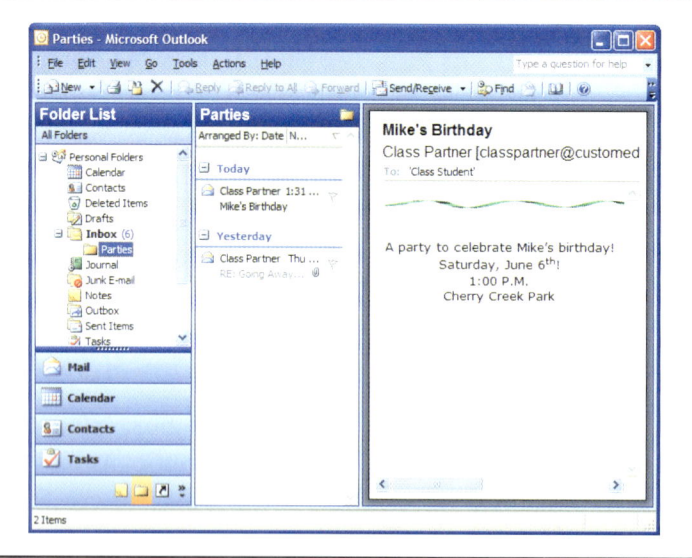

TROUBLESHOOTING

A message must be selected to activate the Create Rule button.

6 **Click one of the messages in the Parties folder and click the Create Rule button on the standard mail toolbar.**

The Create Rule dialog box is displayed. By default, it contains the characteristics of the selected message.

FIGURE 3-32

Create Rule dialog box

7 Delete the text in the Subject contains box. Type *party* in the field.

This specifies the conditions that must be met before the rule is enforced.

8 Click the Move E-Mail To Folder option, select Parties as the destination folder, and click the OK button.

This specifies the action that will be taken if the conditions to enforce the rule are met. An alert box is displayed. The new rule will be applied to incoming messages. The alert box also asks if you would like the rule to be applied to the current contents of this folder.

FIGURE 3-33

Rule to move specific messages to another folder

9 If necessary, click No so that the rule is not applied to the current contents of the folder.

The rule is created. New messages that arrive with the word *party* in the subject will be sent to the Parties folder.

ANOTHER METHOD

You can choose to apply the rule to the current contents, moving any existing messages that meet the criteria.

82 Lesson 3 Customizing E-Mail

10 On the standard mail toolbar, click the New Mail Message button.

A message window is displayed.

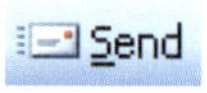

11 In the To box, type your class partner's e-mail address. In the Subject box, type *Party Test*, and in the message area, type *Is this message in the Parties folder?* On the New Message toolbar in the message window, click the Send button.

The word *party* in the subject line should meet the rule's criteria, causing the message to move to the Parties folder.

12 On the standard mail toolbar, click the Send/Receive button.

A message from your class partner arrives, and it is automatically moved to the Parties folder.

13 Open the Tools menu, and click the Rules And Alerts option.

The Rules And Alerts dialog box is displayed.

FIGURE 3-34

Rules And Alerts dialog box

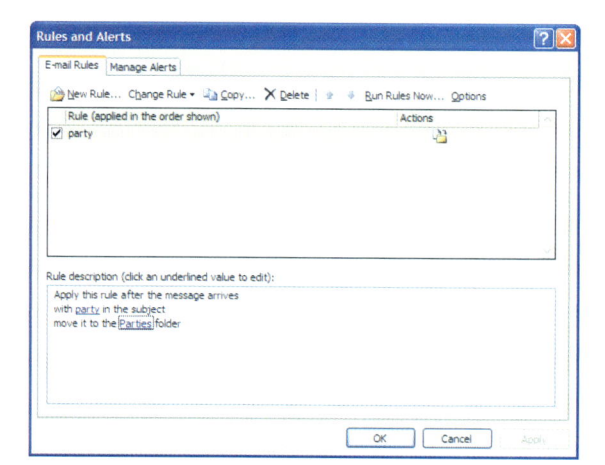

> **QUICK CHECK**
>
> **Q:** Can you manually move a message to another folder?
>
> **A:** Drag the message to the folder.

14 Click the party rule, click the Delete button, confirm the deletion in the alert box, and click OK.

The rule is deleted.

◆ Keep Outlook open for the next exercise.

QUICK REFERENCE ▼

Move messages between folders

1 Highlight the desired message.
2 Click the Move To Folder button on the standard mail toolbar.
3 Click the Move To Folder command.
4 Select the destination folder.
5 Click the OK button.

Color-Coding Message Headers

Managing Messages with Color

> **THE BOTTOM LINE**
>
> Messages that you send or receive can be color-coded. This helps you organize and find messages related to a specific individual or project.

You can create rules to color-code message headers that meet specific criteria. Organizing your Inbox by color helps you find specific messages when many messages are in your Inbox. For example, the training director at Adventure Works created a rule to color-code all message headers from the senior manager purple. When a purple message header arrives, the training director knows to give it special attention.

Color-coding your messages is a simple process using the Organize pane. Select the direction of the message (from or sent to), enter the e-mail address to be color-coded, and select the color. In the following exercise, all messages from Class Partner will be color-coded red. The result will be obvious when new messages from Class Partner arrive in the Inbox. When you choose to color-code messages sent to an individual, the color codes affect messages in the Sent folder. When you no longer want to use this color-code rule, apply automatic formatting.

Color-code message headers

In this exercise, you apply a red color code to the message headers from your class partner and then delete the rule.

1 Select a message in your Inbox that was sent from your class partner.

This provides the default information that is loaded into the rule before you specify any changes.

2 Open the Tools menu and select the Organize option.

The Organize pane is displayed.

FIGURE 3-35

Organize pane

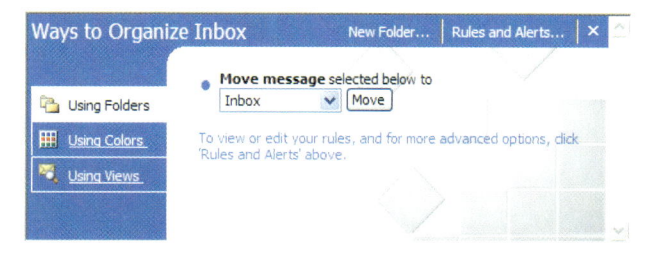

3 In the Organize pane, click the Using Colors option.

The Using Colors section of the Organize pane is displayed.

84 Lesson 3 Customizing E-Mail

4 **In the Organize pane, verify that the word from appears in the first Color Messages box. If necessary, enter your class partner's e-mail address, select Red in the third box, and click the Apply Color button.**

Messages received from your class partner are color-coded in red. Any future messages that your class partner sends will also be color-coded in red.

FIGURE 3-36

Color-code messages

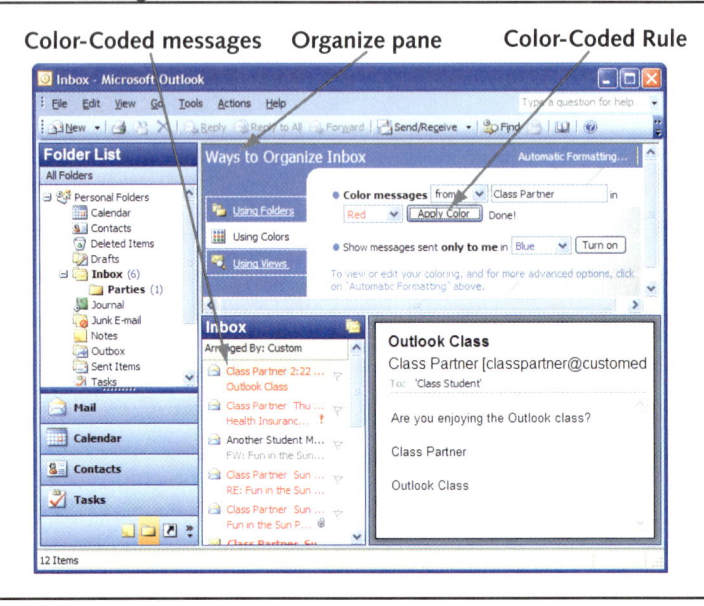

5 **In the top of the Organize pane, click the Automatic Formatting button.**

The Automatic Formatting dialog box is displayed.

FIGURE 3-37

Automatic Formatting dialog box

QUICK CHECK

Q: How do you apply color codes to messages?

A: Create a rule to color-code the messages.

ANOTHER METHOD

If you don't want to delete the rule, clear the check box to the left of the rule. The rule still exists, but is no longer being applied. Select the check box and click the Add button at any time to activate the rule.

6 In the Rules For This View list, click the rule **Mail received from [class partner]** to select it, click the Delete button, and click OK.

The rule to color-code messages from Student is no longer applied.

◆ Keep Outlook open for the next exercise.

QUICK REFERENCE ▼

Color-code message headers

1 Select a message.
2 Open the Tools menu and select the Organize option.
3 Click the Using Colors option.
4 Select your color options.
5 Click the Apply Color button.

Filtering Junk E-Mail Messages

Filtering Messages

THE BOTTOM LINE

For obvious reasons, you want to limit junk e-mail that arrives in your Inbox. Outlook's new detection method reduces junk e-mail. You can reduce junk e-mail further by creating a list of safe senders and a list of blocked senders.

Junk e-mail (unsolicited and unwanted e-mail, also known as spam) is an annoying problem for many Internet users. Junk e-mail can fill an Inbox with dozens, even hundreds, of advertisements, chain e-mails, and other nuisances. Unfortunately, many individuals and companies use junk e-mail as a major marketing tool because it is so inexpensive. Another form of junk e-mail is unsolicited messages with adult content that might be offensive or inappropriate for some people.

Microsoft Office Outlook 2003 incorporates new technology to reduce the amount of junk e-mail that finds its way into your Inbox. Rather than relying on a list of words and phrases that are common to junk e-mail, each message is evaluated separately. Based on factors such as the time the message was sent and the general content of the message, Outlook determines the probability that the message is junk e-mail.

Additionally, Outlook uses three lists to filter e-mail from specific e-mail addresses and domain names. This enables you to receive messages from any users in a specific domain, such as your employer or professional organization. You can also approve individual senders such as friends or family members. These filters provide control over the messages that can be delivered to your Inbox.

Filter List	Characteristics
Safe Senders List	Domain names and addresses that you want to receive e-mail messages from. By default, addresses in Outlook's address book and contacts are included in this list.
Safe Recipients List	Mailing lists and other subscriptions you belong to and want to receive e-mail messages from. This includes domain names and specific addresses.
Blocked Senders List	Domain names and addresses you do not want to receive e-mail from. This includes domain names and specific addresses.

An additional feature, Automatic Picture Download, can be turned off. This blocks the download of graphics and HTML content from unknown senders. HTML content and graphics sent by domain names and addresses on your Safe Senders List and Safe Recipients List are not blocked. To receive all HTML content in your messages, open the Tools menu, click Options, and click the Security tab. In the Download Pictures area, click the option Change Automatic Download Settings. Enable the option Don't Download Pictures Or Other Content Automatically In HTML E-mail.

You can add new junk e-mail addresses to the filter at any time. If a junk e-mail message arrives in your Inbox, right-click the message and click Junk E-mail on the shortcut menu.

You can also add new junk e-mail addresses to the filter in the Organize pane. Specify the color used to identify junk e-mail message headers. When you receive these messages, you will recognize the color and you can delete the messages without reading them.

Apply Junk E-Mail message filter

You will now customize your Junk E-Mail filter by adding a domain to the Safe Senders List and adding specific addresses to the Blocked Senders List.

1 Right-click on any message from your class partner.

A shortcut menu is displayed.

2 Point at Junk E-mail and click the option Add Sender's Domain To Safe Senders List.

All messages from this domain will arrive in your Inbox.

3 Right-click the message from Vigor Airlines.

The shortcut menu is displayed.

ANOTHER METHOD

You can add a domain name to the blocked senders list, but you may block messages you would rather receive if you block a popular domain such as Yahoo!.

Lesson 3 Customizing E-Mail   87

4 **Point at Junk E-mail and click the option Add Sender To Blocked Senders List.**

Future messages from this Vigor Airlines address won't arrive in your Inbox. The message currently in your Inbox from Vigor Airlines is color-coded and moved to the Junk E-mail folder.

5 **Right-click the message from Tec Angle.**

The shortcut menu is displayed.

6 **Point at Junk E-mail and click the option Add Sender To Blocked Senders List.**

Future messages from this Tec Angle address won't arrive in your Inbox. The message currently in your Inbox from Tec Angle is color-coded and moved to the Junk E-mail folder.

7 **Right-click any message, point at Junk E-mail and click Junk E-mail Options. Click on each tab in the Junk E-mail Options window.**

Examine the current settings. By default, the level of junk e-mail protection is set to Low. As you use Outlook and fill in your safe lists, you might want to increase the protection level.

FIGURE 3-38

Junk e-mail settings

> **QUICK CHECK**
>
> Q: What is junk e-mail?
>
> A: **Junk e-mail is unsolicited and unwanted e-mail, also known as spam.**

◆ Keep Outlook open for the next exercise.

QUICK REFERENCE ▼

Set junk e-mail options

1 Right-click any message.

2 Point at Junk E-mail and click Junk E-mail Options.

3 Change any settings.

4 Click the Apply button to apply the changes.

5 Click the OK button to return to the Inbox.

Archiving Messages

> **THE BOTTOM LINE**
>
> To reduce clutter in your mail folders, you can store old or outdated messages in a separate area.

When you install and begin to run Outlook, your folders are empty (except for one welcome message from Microsoft in your Inbox). After a few months, that condition changes drastically. You could have hundreds of e-mail messages in your Inbox and Sent Items folders if you don't move or delete messages periodically. If you keep all your messages in their original folders and you don't like to permanently delete e-mail messages, take advantage of Outlook's archive feature.

> **TROUBLESHOOTING**
>
> You can restore archived messages to your Inbox at any time.

Use the Outlook Archive feature to store old (you determine what length of time is considered "old") Inbox and Sent Items content within a single, compressed file stored on your hard disk, leaving only the most current information. When you archive outdated messages in a folder, they are removed from your Outlook folder and copied to a .pst file on your hard drive. Archiving merely helps to remove the clutter from your Outlook folders.

By default, Outlook will prompt you to archive messages in your folders at regular intervals. Outlook will not archive messages unless you click OK when prompted. If you don't specify AutoArchive settings for a folder, Global AutoArchive settings are used. To view the settings, select Options from the Tools menu. Click the tab labeled Other. Click the AutoArchive button to view information about archiving.

Mailbox Cleanup is a message management tool. It enables you to find and delete old items or items larger than a specific size, start the AutoArchive function, and empty your Deleted Items folder.

You can instruct Outlook to AutoArchive your Outlook folders for you or you can choose to archive the folders manually. Outlook archives items that are older than the time you specify.

Archive messages

You will now examine the AutoArchive settings.

Lesson 3 Customizing E-Mail   89

1 On the Tools menu, select Options.

The Options dialog box is displayed.

2 Click the Other tab.

Additional options are displayed.

3 Click the AutoArchive button.

The AutoArchive settings are displayed.

FIGURE 3-39

AutoArchive settings

QUICK CHECK

Q: How old should messages be before they are archived?

A: **You determine what length of time is considered old.**

◆ If you are continuing to the next lesson, keep Outlook open.

◆ If you are not continuing to the next lesson, close Outlook.

QUICK REFERENCE ▼

Set archive options

1 On the Tools menu, select Options.

2 Click the Other tab.

3 Click the AutoArchive button.

4 Make any changes.

5 Click OK twice to return to the Inbox.

Key Points

✔ *Outlook lets you customize your e-mail messages and organize your Inbox.*
✔ *You can use importance, sensitivity, and delivery options to inform recipients how they should handle the message.*
✔ *The appearance of your e-mail messages can be customized by creating them in Plain Text, Rich Text, and HTML formats.*
✔ *With Outlook you can create messages with stationery that compliments the message content.*
✔ *Signatures can be created that provide standard information at the end of every message you compose.*
✔ *You can set viewing options and sort and filter the Inbox.*
✔ *Outlook lets you create a folder and move messages between folders.*
✔ *Your Inbox can be organized by color-coding messages and filtering junk e-mail.*
✔ *Old messages can be archived so they do not clutter your Inbox.*

Quick Quiz

True/False

T   F   1. Formatted messages can be created in Plain Text.
T   F   2. You can have only one signature for each Outlook profile.
T   F   3. A list of sorted messages displays only messages that fit the sort criteria.
T   F   4. Confidential messages cannot be forwarded to other recipients.
T   F   5. You can color-code messages from a specific user.

Multiple Choice

1. Archived messages are _____.
   a. placed at the bottom of the mailbox
   b. deleted from your computer
   c. stored in a separate file
   d. color-coded

2. Messages from an address on your Safe Senders List are _____.
   a. placed in your Inbox
   b. placed in the Junk E-mail folder
   c. deleted before they arrive in your Inbox
   d. color-coded

3. Sorted messages are _____.
   a. displayed in a specific sequence
   b. hidden if they don't match the sort criteria
   c. moved to a different folder
   d. color-coded

4. An important message is identified by _____.
   a. an arrow
   b. an exclamation point
   c. a filter
   d. a color code

5. A design used to accent a message is _____.
   a. a signature
   b. an archive
   c. stationery
   d. a color code

Short Answer

1. How do you assign high-importance status to a message?
2. What does a filter do?
3. What is one way to distinguish messages from a specific person?
4. What is a signature in an e-mail message?
5. How can you store outdated messages?
6. What can you use to format a message with a predefined design?
7. What levels of importance does Outlook let you set for a message?
8. Where in Outlook do you filter junk e-mail?

On Your Own

Exercise 1

The new marketing director at Adventure Works needs to set up his e-mail workspace. First, create two folders for the new projects—Pool and Tennis Courts—starting next week. Place these folders in the Inbox folder.

Next, set up a business signature to include his name (Peters, James), title (marketing director), and phone number (555-555-0154). Set this signature as the default signature. Finally, the director has little time for junk e-mail, so set up the filters to identify and delete junk e-mail.

Exercise 2

The general manager of Adventure Works wants to invite a new member of the staff to a managers' meeting. Send an e-mail message to someone@example.com using appropriate stationery announcing the managers' meeting at 3:00 P.M. on Tuesday, in the dining room. Indicate that the message is important.

One Step Further

Exercise 1

Create a message that informs your customers that you have a new product. Use text and graphics to interest the customers in the new product.

Exercise 2

Create three new folders. Use rules and color codes to automatically help you organize messages from individuals you know will correspond with you regularly.

Exercise 3

Locate the Outlook file used to filter junk e-mail. Add several additional phrases to the list.

LESSON 4

Using Contacts

After completing this lesson, you will be able to:

✔ Open the Contacts folder.
✔ Create and edit contacts.
✔ Create multiple contact records for people at the same company.
✔ Delete and restore contacts.
✔ Use folders, views, and categories.
✔ Assign items to a category.
✔ Modify the Outlook Master Category List.
✔ Sort contacts.
✔ Send e-mail from the Address Book and the Contacts folder.
✔ Send and receive contact information by e-mail.
✔ Create a letter for a contact by using the Letter Wizard.

KEY TERMS

- Address Book
- Address Cards
- category
- contact
- contact record
- Contacts folder
- Master Category List
- vCard

To communicate efficiently with personal and business associates, many people keep important phone and fax numbers, addresses, and other relevant information in an address book or a business card holder. The tools in Microsoft Outlook help you create and organize contact information on your computer. In Outlook, a **contact** is a collection of information about a person or a company. Contact information is stored in the **Contacts folder**, which is essentially an electronic organizer that you can use to create, view, sort, and edit contact information. Contacts are integrated with other components of Outlook and other Microsoft Office System programs so that name, address, and phone information is available for use with other Outlook folders and Office programs.

Efficiency is one of the chief values of the Contacts folder. Each time you create a new contact, the name, e-mail address, and phone numbers are added to your Address Book. When you compose an e-mail message, use the Address Book to insert the appropriate e-mail address in the To or Cc box—you don't have to manually type the addresses.

In this lesson, you learn how to create, edit, and delete contacts. You also learn how to sort contacts and organize them by using folders and views. In addition, you learn how to use the Address Book and Contacts to send e-mail messages as well as how to send contact information as a vCard, or a virtual business card. At the end of this lesson, you learn how to compose and send letters in Microsoft Word by using contact information from Outlook.

94 Lesson 4 Using Contacts

> **IMPORTANT**
>
> Before you can use the practice files in this lesson, you need to install them from the companion CD for this book to their default location. For additional information on how to find and open files used in this book, see the "Using the CD-ROM" section at the beginning of this book.

The practice file Eric_Lang is required to complete the exercises in this lesson.

> **IMPORTANT**
>
> To complete some of the exercises in this lesson, you will need to exchange e-mail messages with a class partner. If you don't have a class partner or you are performing the exercises alone, you can send the message to yourself. Simply enter your own e-mail address instead of a class partner's address.

Viewing Contacts

> **THE BOTTOM LINE**
>
> Contact records can contain a variety of useful information about the people you know.

Creating and Updating Contact Information

Click the Contacts button in the Navigation pane or open the Go menu and click the Contacts option to view the contents of the Contacts folder. Outlook provides several formats for viewing contact information. Contacts are displayed in the Address Cards view by default. From the **Address Cards** view, you can see a contact's title bar, a follow-up flag (if one is present), a mailing address, and the associated company. You can also see four fields that hold telephone and fax information, and up to three of the contact's e-mail addresses.

Figure 4-1

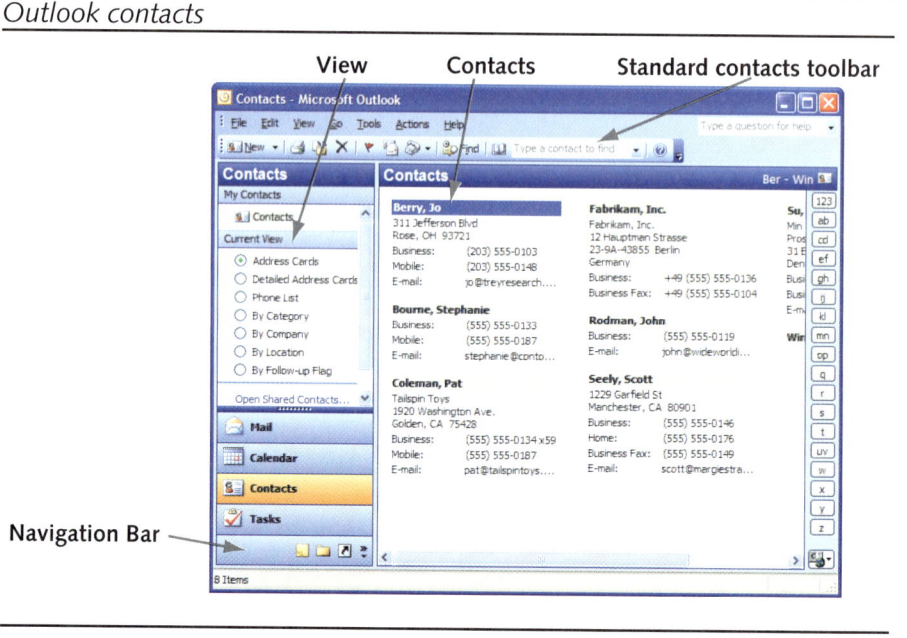

Outlook contacts

Lesson 4 Using Contacts 95

> **TROUBLESHOOTING**
>
> The Financial Information tab is not present for every contact.

Double-click the contact to view more detailed information in the contact window. It contains a menu bar, a Standard toolbar, and six tabs—General, Financial Information, Details, Activities, Certificates, and All Fields. The General tab contains the most frequently used information. Use the Details tab to add more information about contacts.

Figure 4-2

General information about the contact

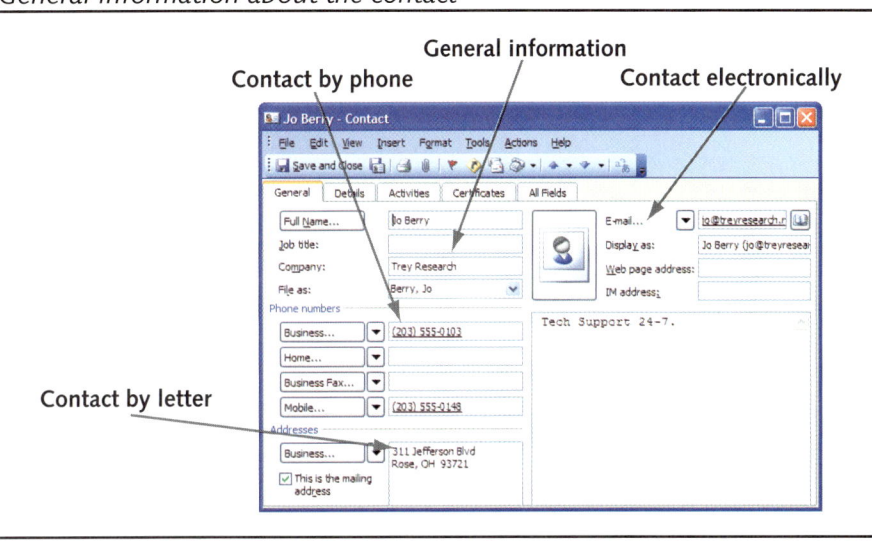

View contact information from any Outlook folder. On the Tools menu, point at Find, and click Advanced Find. Select Contacts in the Look For box. In the Search For The Words box, type the first few letters of the contact's name and click the Find Now button. The contact will be displayed in the bottom pane of the Advanced Find window. Double-click the contact to view information in the contact window.

Figure 4-3

Find a contact

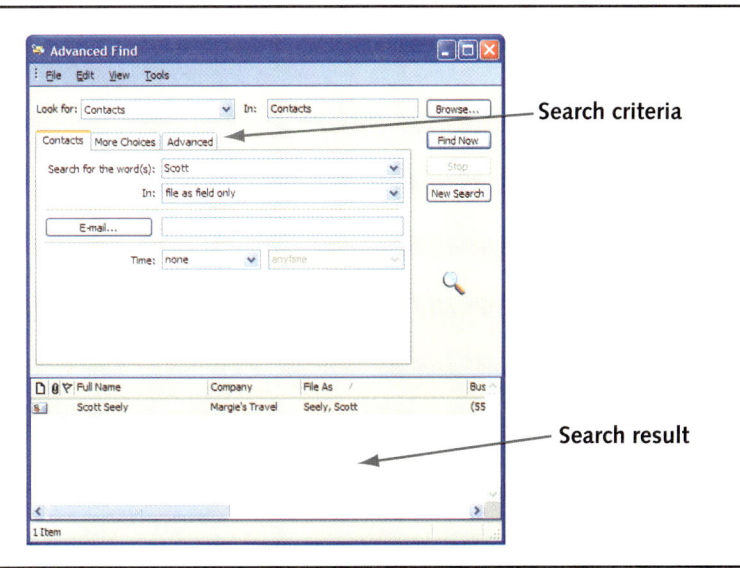

The General tab is displayed when you open a contact window. The General tab contains all the information that appears about the contact in the Address Cards view, as well as a box for a Web page address, an area for notes, links to other contacts, and assigned Outlook categories. When you create a new contact, you must enter at least a full name, a company name, or an e-mail address. (Only one of these is required so that the contact can be sorted properly.) All other entries are optional. If you enter an e-mail address but don't include a full name or company name, Outlook suggests that you provide one of these names before you save the contact.

The Details tab contains more specific information about the contact—the contact's office, department, profession, manager's name, assistant's name, the contact's nickname, spouse's name, and the contact's birthday and anniversary. All entries on the Details tab are optional.

Figure 4-4

Contact Details

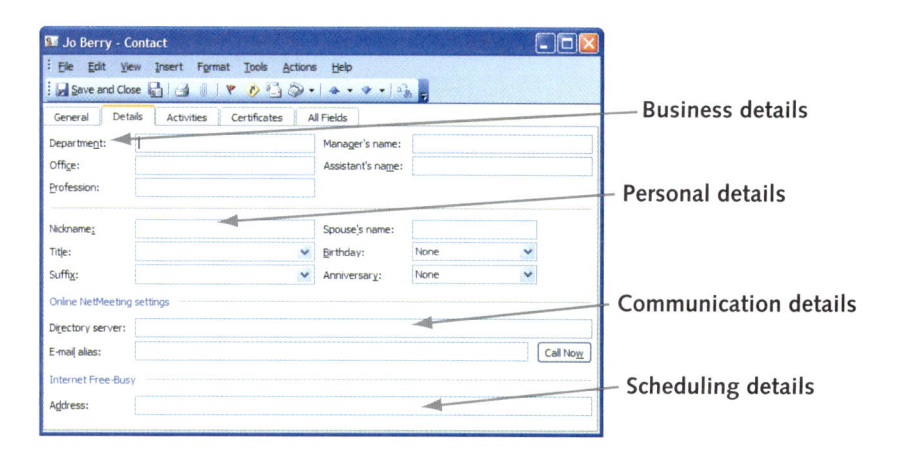

To close a contact window, click the Save And Close button or click the Close button in the top-right corner of the contact window.

◆ **Be sure to start Outlook before beginning this exercise.**

View contact information

You begin this lesson by viewing contact information.

1 **On the Navigation pane, click the Contacts button.**

ANOTHER METHOD

Open the Go menu and select Contacts.

The contents of the Contacts folder are displayed.

2 **Double-click the title bar of the Fabrikam, Inc. contact.**

The Fabrikam, Inc. contact window opens. Information on the General tab is displayed.

Lesson 4 Using Contacts   97

Figure 4-5

General information about Fabrikam

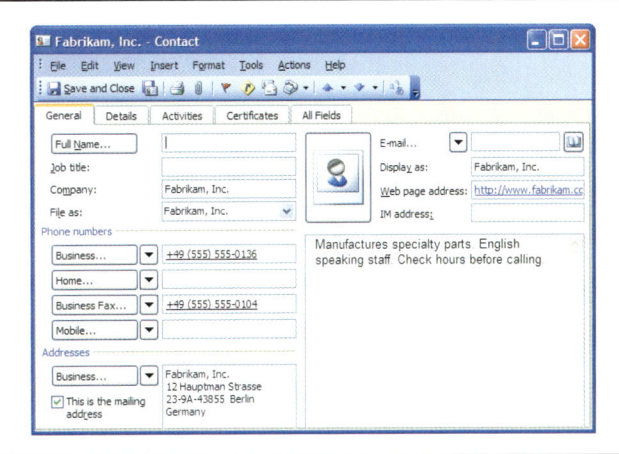

CHECK THIS OUT ▼

Outlook's Mapping Feature
When you want directions to a contact's home or business, use Outlook's mapping feature. Double-click the contact record. Under the Address button, click the down arrow to select the type of address (business, home, or other) that you want to find on a map. Then, on the Standard toolbar in the contact window, click the Display Map of Address button. If your computer is connected to the Internet, your Web browser opens to display a street map provided by the Microsoft Expedia Web site.

3 Click the Details tab.

The Details tab is displayed. Entering detailed information for any contact is optional. There is no information in the Details section for this contact.

Figure 4-6

Details have not been entered about Fabrikam

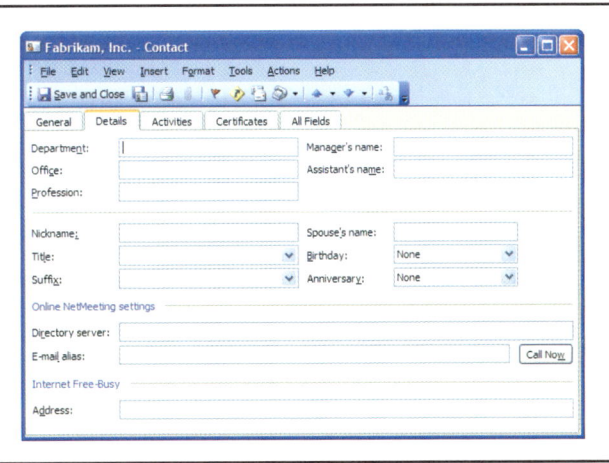

4 Click the General tab.

The General tab is displayed.

5 In the top-right corner of the contact window, click the Close button.

The contact window closes.

◆ Keep Outlook open for the next exercise.

QUICK REFERENCE ▼

View a contact

1 On the Navigation pane, click the Contacts button.

2 Double-click the contact record.

QUICK CHECK

Q: Where are the required fields for a contact record?

A: **They are located on the General tab.**

Creating and Editing a New Contact

> **THE BOTTOM LINE**
>
> You should keep your contact records up to date by creating new records and editing existing contact records.

Creating and Updating Contact Information

Creating a contact is simply a matter of typing information in boxes in the contact window. Each box represents a field, or a single item of contact information, such as an individual's name, a company's name, or a phone number. All the used fields form a **contact record**. On the standard contacts toolbar, click the New Contact button to display a blank contact window. To enter information in a box (field), click the box and type the information. To move to the next box, press Tab or click in the next box.

When you create a contact for a company rather than a specific person at the company, enter the company name in the Company box and leave the Full Name box blank. Outlook interprets any information in the Full Name box as an individual's name. It attempts to store the contact by name, placing the last name first. For example, if you create a contact for Adventure Works, enter Adventure Works in the Company box. If you type Adventure Works in the Full Name box, the contact is stored as Works, Adventure.

Figure 4-7

Enter the name of a company

Because some people have multiple phone numbers, addresses, and e-mail addresses, the Address, Phone, and E-Mail boxes can have multiple entries. To enter more than one number, address, or e-mail address, click the arrow next to the box to display a list of entry descriptions. Select the mix of fields that works for your contact.

Figure 4-8

Select the type of information you store

As you enter contact information, click the most appropriate entry description and enter the information in the box. For example, a customer service representative at Adventure Works is entering information for a contact who has both a pager and a mobile phone. In the first box, the representative selects Pager and types the pager number. In the next box, the representative selects Mobile and types the mobile phone number.

You can also store a contact's Web page address in the contact window. Unlike e-mail addresses, you can store only one Web page address at a time.

If you open a contact window for an existing contact and close Outlook, the contact window remains open so you can continue to view or modify the contact information.

To help you remember which contacts are related to certain activities, link the contact record to activities—such as tasks or e-mail messages. To link an activity, display the contact window, open the Actions menu, point to Link, and click Items. In the Look In list on the dialog box, click a folder that contains the activity that you want to link to the contact. In the Items list, click an item, such as an appointment, and click OK. You can see the linked activities on the contact's Activities tab.

Contact records in Microsoft Office Outlook 2003 can contain more than text. Include a photograph or other image in the contact record. On the General tab, click the large box next to the e-mail and Web page address. Browse to locate and select a graphic for the contact record. The image is automatically resized to fit into the box.

When you finish entering or modifying information for a contact, click the Save And Close button on the Standard toolbar in the contact window to save the information as a contact record and close the contact window.

Create Contact Records

Now that you have explored the Contact options, you will create three contact records.

1 On the standard contacts toolbar, click the New Contact button.

ANOTHER METHOD

Open the File menu, point at New, and click Contact.

A contact window is displayed. The insertion point is positioned in the Full Name box.

TROUBLESHOOTING

When you type a name in the Full Name box and move to a different box, the window's title bar replaces Untitled with the contact's name.

2 In the Full Name box, type Eric Lang and press Tab.

The insertion point moves to the Job Title box. Outlook automatically inserts Lang, Eric in the File As box.

3 Type **Director** and press Tab.

The insertion point moves to the Company box.

4 Type **Coho Vineyard**.

> **TIP**
>
> You don't need to type spaces or hyphens in a phone number. Outlook automatically formats phone numbers for you.

5 Click in the Business box and type **5555550142**.

6 Click the Mobile down arrow.

A list of fields is displayed. Notice that Business has a check mark next to it because you already entered a phone number in the Business field.

7 Click Pager.

The label for the field changes to Pager.

8 In the Pager box, type **5555550143**. Click in the Address box, type **4567 Coolidge St.** and press Enter. Type **Cherry Hills, NY 09472**.

The address is entered into the record.

9 Click the Add Contact Picture box. Navigate to the Outlook Practice folder and select the Eric_Lang file. Click the OK button.

The picture of Eric Lang is placed in the contact record.

10 Click in the E-Mail box. Type **eric@cohovineyard.com** and press Tab.

A line is displayed under the e-mail address and the Display as box is filled with the contact's name and e-mail address. This identifies how the contact's name is displayed in the To box when you send the contact an e-mail message.

11 Click in the Display As box if necessary. Delete the e-mail address, leaving Eric's first and last name.

When you use Outlook's e-mail function to send a message, Eric's first and last name are displayed in the To field. The e-mail address is not displayed. This feature makes your e-mail messages look more "friendly" and less "technical."

> **ANOTHER METHOD**
>
> If your computer is connected to the Internet, click the Web address to open your Web browser and access the site directly from the contact window.

12 Click in the Web Page Address box. Type **www.cohovineyard.com** and click in the Notes box.

A Web page link is created and the insertion point is placed in the Notes box.

13 Type **Eric is a mountain bike enthusiast.**

Figure 4-9

General information about Eric Lang

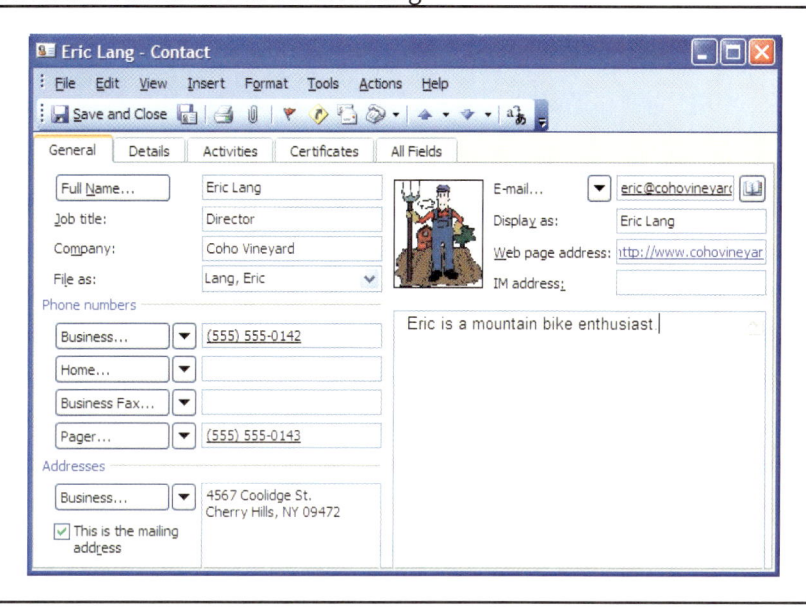

[Screenshot of Eric Lang - Contact window showing General tab with fields: Full Name: Eric Lang; Job title: Director; Company: Coho Vineyard; File as: Lang, Eric; Business phone: (555) 555-0142; Pager: (555) 555-0143; Business address: 4567 Coolidge St. Cherry Hills, NY 09472; E-mail: eric@cohovineyard; Display as: Eric Lang; Web page address: http://www.cohovineyar; Notes: Eric is a mountain bike enthusiast]

14 On the Standard toolbar in the contact window, click the Save And New button.

The contact record is saved and a blank contact window is displayed. This saves a step when you are entering several new contacts at the same time.

TROUBLESHOOTING

The exercises in this lesson use the contact information entered for you and your class partner. To perform these exercises alone, create contact records for you and a fictional class partner. Enter your e-mail address for both contact records. This enables you to complete the exercises by using only your e-mail address. However, your Inbox will not look the same as the samples in this lesson because messages for your class partner will also be in your Inbox.

15 Add a new record using your contact information. Type your name in the Full Name box and the e-mail address used for this class in the E-mail box. Press the Tab key.

Do not include personal information such as home phone or address. You will add this information later.

16 On the Standard toolbar in the contact window, click the Save And New button.

A contact record containing your information is saved.

17 Add a new record using your class partner's contact information. Type your class partner's name in the Full Name box and your class partner's e-mail address in the E-mail box.

Do not include personal information such as home phone or address. You will add this information later.

> **QUICK CHECK**
>
> **Q:** How many Web addresses can each contact record have?
>
> **A:** Each contact record can have one Web address.

18 On the Standard toolbar in the contact window, click the Save And Close button.

The contact is saved. The three contacts that you've added are displayed in the Contacts folder.

◆ Keep Outlook open for the next exercise.

QUICK REFERENCE ▼

Create a contact

1 On the standard contacts toolbar, click the New Contact button.
2 Enter contact information.
3 Click the Save And Close button.

Creating Multiple Contacts for the Same Company

Creating and Updating Contact Information

> **THE BOTTOM LINE**
>
> You can simplify the process of entering a second contact at the same company by creating a record that inherits information from the original record.

When entering multiple contacts for different people at the same company, you don't have to type company information for each new contact. Click an existing contact for the company, open the Actions menu, and click New Contact From Same Company. A new contact window is displayed. The company name, address, business phone, and business fax number are automatically inserted. Simply enter new information about the individual, such as the person's name and home phone number.

> **TIP**
>
> To store a copy of several selections at the same time and paste the items in different locations in a contact record or in different folders, use the Office Clipboard. The difference between the Office Clipboard and the general Windows Clipboard is the ability to collect and paste several items at the same time. The Windows clipboard stores only one item. If you copy or cut an item, it replaces the existing content of the Windows Clipboard. With the Office Clipboard, however, you can copy and store up to 24 items at the same time and select which stored item you want to paste. To use the Office Clipboard, open the Edit menu and select the Office Clipboard option.

Lesson 4 Using Contacts 103

Create another record for contact with the same company

Now you will create a new record for a contact who works at the same company as an existing contact.

TIP

You can change any information inherited from the original record.

1 **In the Contacts folder, click the contact record for Eric Lang that you created in the previous exercise.**

The contact is selected.

TROUBLESHOOTING

Outlook does not automatically add the same e-mail address for employees at the same company because most employees have different e-mail addresses. Simply type an e-mail address in the appropriate box.

2 **Open the Actions menu and select the option New Contact From Same Company.**

A new contact window is displayed. It contains the same company name, address, business phone number, and Web page address as the contact record for Eric Lang.

Figure 4-10

Inherited data for a new contact from a company in an existing record

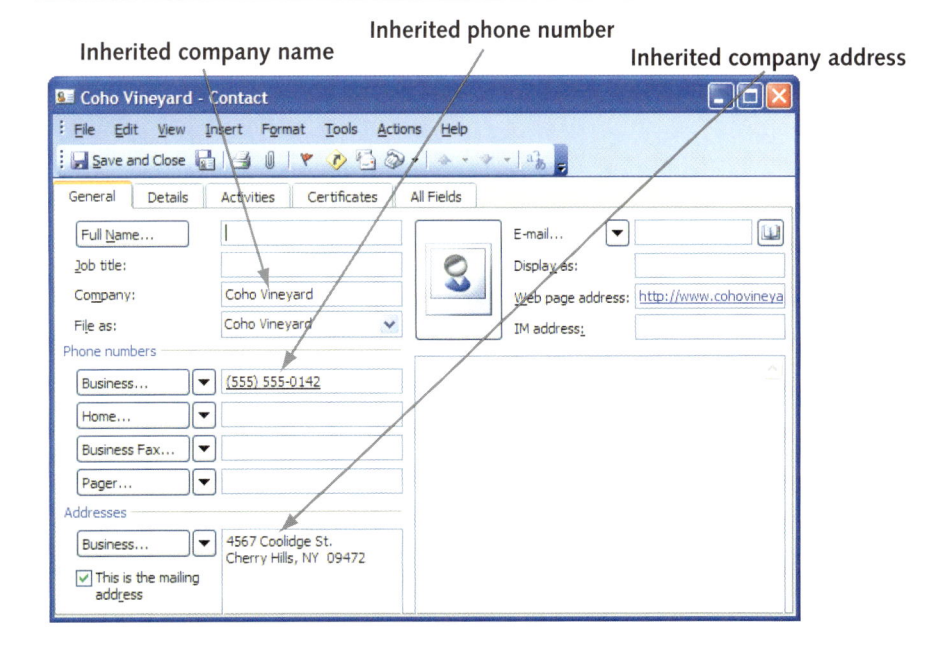

TROUBLESHOOTING

Change the Pager field to a Mobile field to enter a mobile phone number.

Lesson 4 Using Contacts

3 Type the following contact information in the appropriate boxes:
Full Name   Wendy Wheeler
Job Title   Sales Representative
Mobile   5555550110
E-Mail   wendy@cohovineyard.com

4 Remove the e-mail address from the Display As field.

This makes the address on any e-mails appear friendlier and less technical.

Figure 4-11

General data entered for a new contact from a company in an existing record

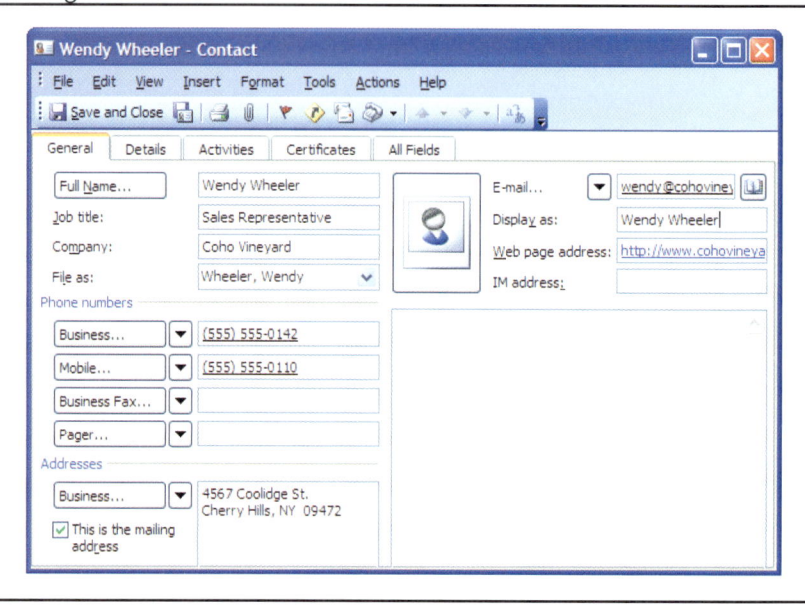

5 Click the Details tab.

The Details tab is displayed.

6 If necessary, click in the Department box and type Sales.

This entry specifies a different department for Wendy.

7 On the standard contacts toolbar in the contact window, click the Save And Close button.

The information about Wendy Wheeler is saved as a new contact and the record is displayed in the Contacts folder.

◆ Keep Outlook open for the next exercise.

QUICK REFERENCE ▼

Create multiple contacts for the same company

1 Select a record.
2 Open the Actions menu and select the option New Contact From Same Company.
3 Enter or modify any contact information.
4 Click the Save And Close button.

QUICK CHECK

Q: Why isn't the e-mail address inherited from the original contact record?

A: Most employees working for the same business have different e-mail addresses.

Lesson 4 Using Contacts 105

Deleting and Restoring Contacts

Organizing Contact Information

> **THE BOTTOM LINE**
>
> In Outlook, contacts are not really deleted until the Deleted Items folder is emptied. This provides a safety net in case you accidentally delete a contact.

Just as it is important to clean up your e-mail folders by deleting old messages occasionally, it's important to remove outdated contacts. If you no longer do business with a particular company or an employee leaves your company, delete the corresponding contact records in Outlook. Deleting old or unwanted contact records helps you find and organize the contacts you use regularly.

The Deleted Items folder can be set to empty—permanently delete—all items in the folder when you exit Outlook. To set the Deleted Items folder to be emptied when you exit Outlook, open the Tools menu, click Options, and click the Other tab. Select the Empty The Deleted Items Folder Upon Exiting check box, click Apply, and click OK.

Figure 4-12

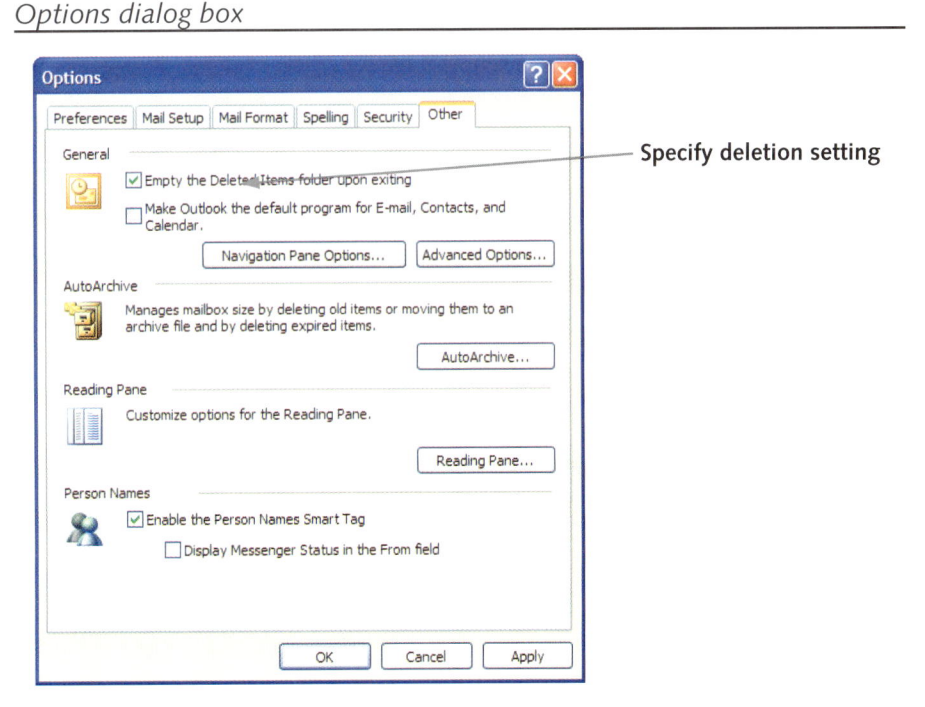

Options dialog box

When you delete a contact, Outlook doesn't ask for confirmation. Outlook simply moves the contact to the Deleted Items folder. The contact is not permanently deleted when you do this; you can open the Deleted Items folder and double-click the contact. However, if you delete a contact from the Deleted Items folder or you empty the contents of the Deleted Items folder, the contact is permanently deleted.

If the last step you performed was to delete a contact record, you can quickly restore the record. Open the Edit menu and select the Undo option.

You can restore a deleted contact if you haven't emptied the Deleted Items folder since the item was deleted. To return a deleted contact to the Contacts folder, drag the contact from the Deleted Items folder onto the Contacts button on the Navigation pane.

Delete and restore a contact

As practice, in this exercise, you delete and restore a contact.

1 Click the Min Su contact record.

The contact record is selected.

2 On the standard contacts toolbar, click the Delete button.

The record is moved to the Deleted Items folder.

3 On the Navigation pane, click the Folder List button.

The folders are displayed.

4 Click the Deleted Items folder.

The contact record is in the Deleted Items folder.

Figure 4-13

Deleted contact record

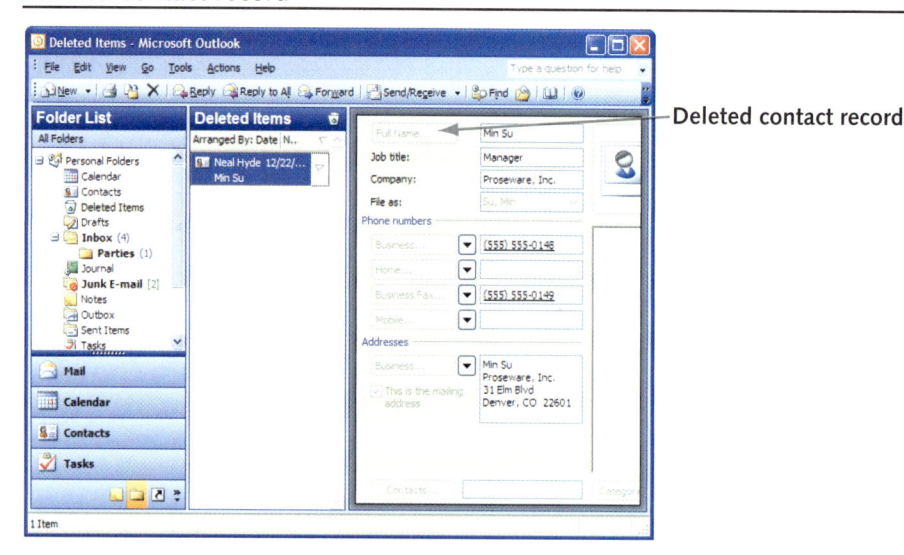

5 Drag the Min Su contact to the Contacts button on the Navigation pane.

The Min Su contact moves to the Contacts folder.

ANOTHER METHOD

Open the Edit menu and select the Undo option.

6 On the Navigation pane, click the Contacts button.

The contents of the Contacts folder are displayed. The Min Su contact record has been restored to the Contacts folder.

◆ **Keep Outlook open for the next exercise.**

QUICK CHECK

Q: How do you restore a contact?

A: Drag it to the Contacts folder.

QUICK REFERENCE ▼

Delete a contact

1. Select a record.
2. Click the Delete button.

Restore a deleted contact

1. Select a record in the Deleted Items folder.
2. Drag the record to the Contacts folder.

Using Folders to Organize Contacts

THE BOTTOM LINE

Create folders to hold contact records that are related by a common characteristic.

You can use folders to organize your contacts just as you used folders to organize your e-mail messages. Create new folders to meet your needs and organize your contacts more efficiently. For example, Adventure Works uses many different contractors to perform maintenance at the resort. The office manager decided to move all the contact information for these contractors into a folder named Maintenance so she can easily locate a particular contractor without looking through her long list of contacts.

Create a folder and move a contact

So far we have worked within the folders that are available within Outlook. Now you will create a folder and move a contact into it.

1. **Open the Tools menu and click the Organize command.**

   The Organize pane is displayed.

2. **In the Organize pane, click the Using Folders link.**

   The Using Folders section of the Organize pane is displayed.

3. **In the top-right corner of the Organize pane, click the New Folder button.**

   The Create New Folder dialog box is displayed.

ANOTHER METHOD

Create a new folder in the Folder List.

4. **In the Name box, type Personal.**

   This identifies the content of the folder.

Figure 4-14

Create a new contact folder

5. **In the Folder Contains box, verify that Contact Items is displayed and click OK.**

    The Personal folder is added to the Contacts folders listed on the left.

6. **Click the Wingtip Toys contact record in the Contacts pane.**

    The contact record is selected.

7. **In the Organize pane, click the Move button.**

    The Wingtip Toys contact moves to the Personal folder.

8. **Click the Personal folder listed on the left.**

    The contact Wingtip Toys is displayed in the Personal folder.

Figure 4-15

Move a contact into the new folder

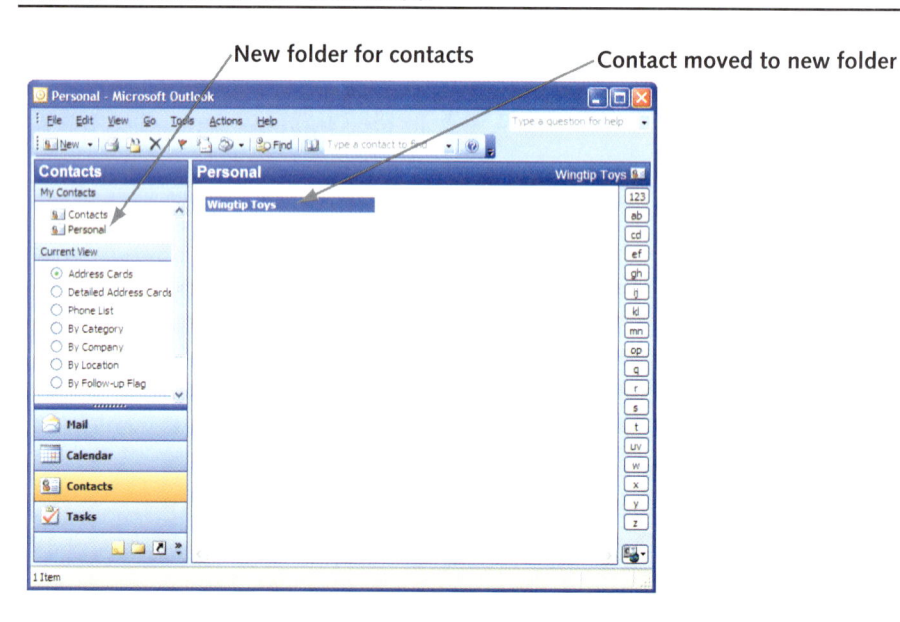

Lesson 4 Using Contacts 109

9 **Click the Contacts folder.**

The contents of the Contacts folder are displayed.

> ### TROUBLESHOOTING
>
> Occasionally, a file may not be displayed in the expected location. A filter may be applied to the folder. To clear the filter, open the View menu, point at the Arrange option, point at the Current View option, and select the Customize Current View option to display the dialog box. Click the Filter button to display the Filter dialog box. Click the Clear All button to remove all filters for the selected folder and click the OK button in each dialog box to return to the main window.

◆ Keep Outlook open for the next exercise.

QUICK REFERENCE ▼

Create a folder

1 Open the Tools menu and click the Organize command.
2 In the Organize pane, click the Using Folders link.
3 In the top-right corner of the Organize pane, click the New Folder button.
4 Name the folder and click the OK button.

Move a contact record to a folder

1 Select the record.
2 Select the folder in the Organize pane.
3 Click the Move button.

QUICK CHECK

Q: Why would you add new folders?

A: **Folders are a valuable organizational tool.**

Using Views to Organize Contacts

Organizing Contact Information

> ### THE BOTTOM LINE
>
> Displaying contact records in a selected Outlook view makes it simple to find a specific contact record.

Like e-mail messages, contact records can appear in several different views, or groups, which can help you find contacts faster and easier. For example, if you are looking for a particular contact and you know the contact's company, you could group your contact records by Company to search more effectively.

> ### ANOTHER METHOD
>
> To use views to organize contacts, open the Tools menu and click the Organize option. In the Organize pane, click the Using Views option, and select a view in the Change Your View box.

In the Address Cards (the default view) and Detailed Address Cards views, contacts are displayed as cards, similar to business cards in a card file. In all other views, contacts are displayed in a table format with columns and rows. Each contact is displayed in a row, separated by columns that correspond to fields in the contact, such as Company and Business Phone. The contents of the columns change to reflect the contents of the selected view. When contacts are displayed in tables, the contacts are divided into groups with expandable gray bars that summarize the contents of each group. For example, when you display your contacts in the By Location view, you see several gray bars that display the text Country/Region: (location) ([number] items). If you had four contacts located in the United States and two in the United Kingdom, you see two gray bars that display the text Country/Region: United States of America (4 items) and Country/Region: United Kingdom (2 items). To see the contacts, click the plus sign (+) located at the left end of the bar. To hide the contacts, click the minus sign (–) located at the left end of the bar. The following table details each view.

View	Description
Address Cards	Contacts appear similar to business cards. They are arranged in alphabetical order.
Detailed Address Cards	The view resembles the Address Cards view, but it displays more information.
Phone List	Contacts are arranged in rows and columns; most telephone fields are displayed. As the name suggests, this view makes it easy to find a contact's telephone number.
By Category	Contacts are grouped by categories. Categorizing contacts emphasizes the characteristics the contacts have in common. (Learn about categories in the next section of this lesson.)
By Company	Contacts appear grouped by company. This view is useful for finding contacts based on the contents of the Company box. If you have several contacts employed by the same company, use this view to identify the job title and the department for each contact.
By Location	Contacts are grouped by Country/Region based on the content in the Address box. This view is useful when you have international contacts.
By Follow-Up Flag	Contacts are grouped by Follow-Up Flag. This view is useful when you have marked contacts for follow-up. For example, add a follow-up flag for a contact who requested additional information or registered for a conference.

Display contact records

Next you will experiment with displaying contact records in different views.

Lesson 4 Using Contacts   111

1 In the Current View area of the Navigation pane, select Detailed Address Cards.

ANOTHER METHOD

You can also change views through the menu. Open the View menu, point at Arrange By, point at Current View, and click an available view.

The Contacts view changes to display your contacts in Detailed Address Cards view.

Figure 4-16

Detailed address cards

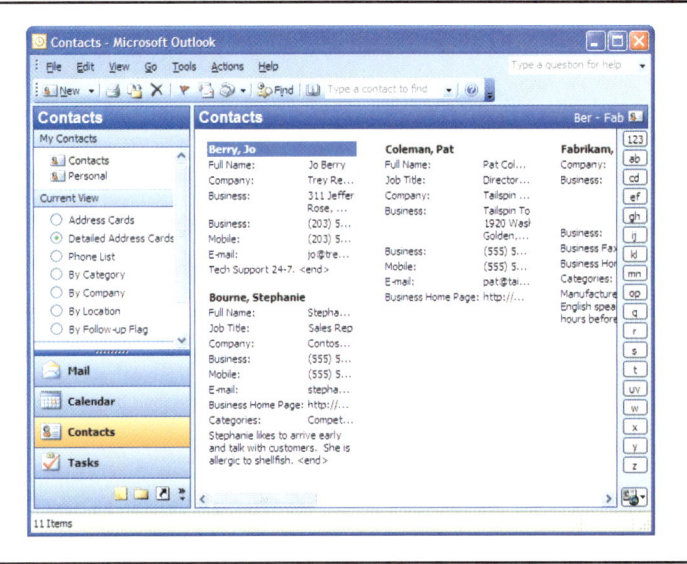

2 In the Current View area of the Navigation pane, select Phone List.

The Contacts view changes to list your contacts by name, company, and phone numbers.

Figure 4-17

View contacts by phone list

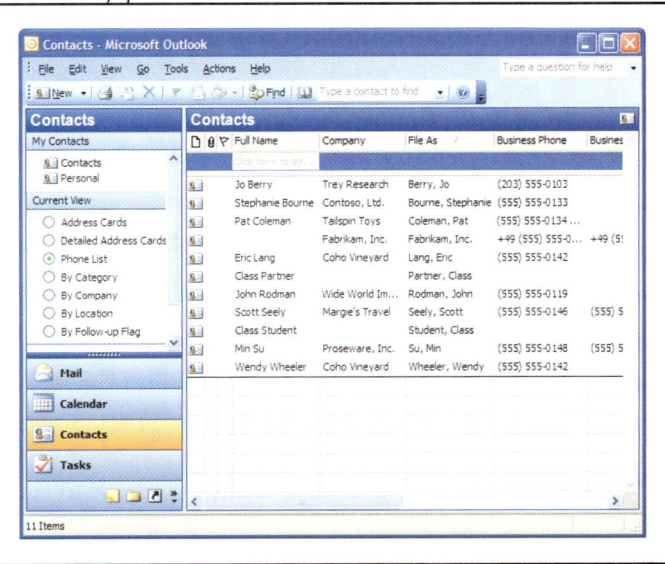

Lesson 4 Using Contacts

3 **In the Current View area of the Navigation pane, select By Category.**

The Contacts view changes to list your contacts by category. Each category is represented by a gray bar. Expand a bar to view the contact records it contains.

Figure 4-18

View contacts by category

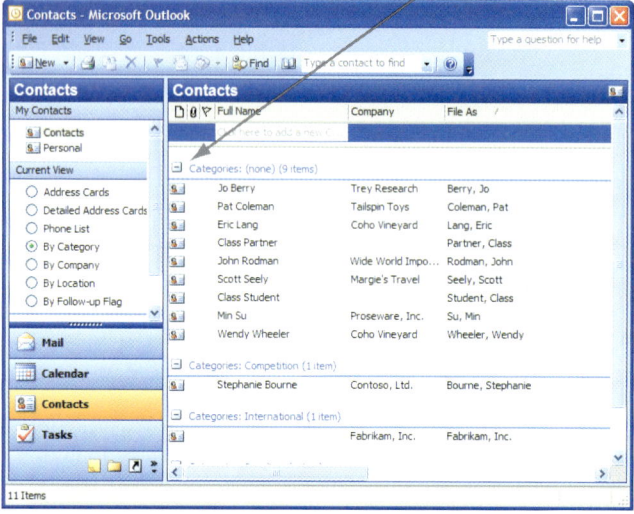

4 **In the Current View area of the Navigation pane, select By Company.**

The Contacts view changes to list your contacts in alphabetic sequence based on the name of the company. Contacts without a company are listed first.

Figure 4-19

View contacts by company

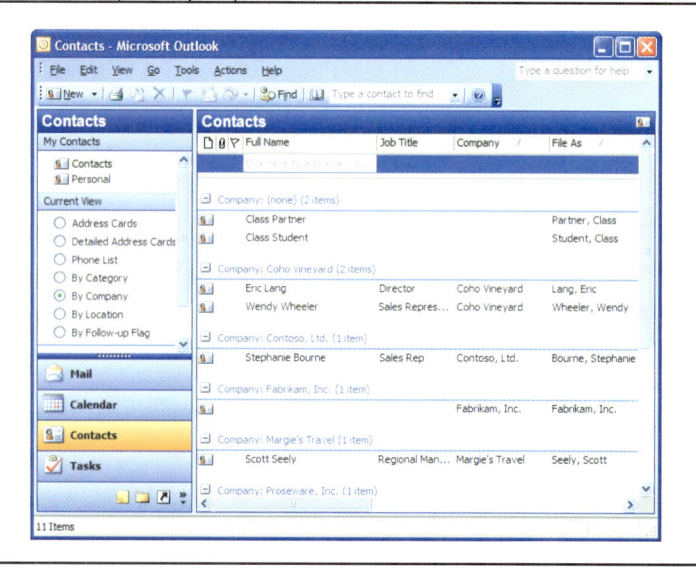

5 **In the Current View area of the Navigation pane, select By Location.**

The Contacts view changes to list your contacts by geographic location. Contacts that don't provide information for this category are listed first.

Figure 4-20

View contacts by location

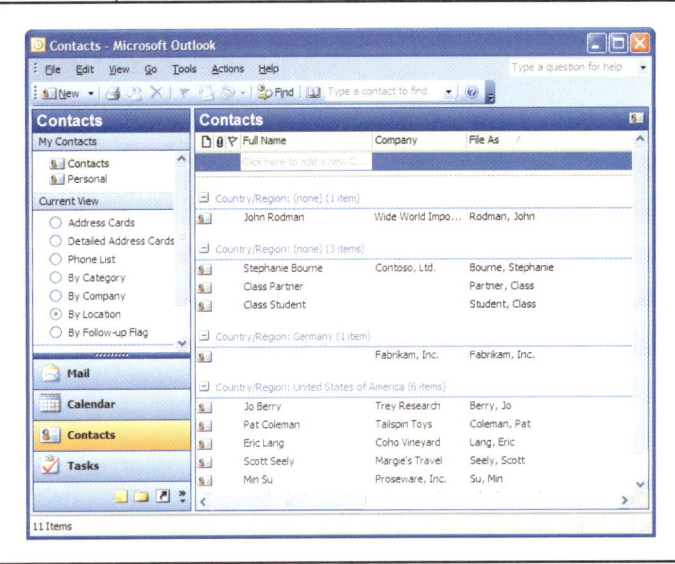

6. **In the Current View area of the Navigation pane, select By Follow-up Flag.**

    The Contacts view changes to list your contacts based on the follow-up flag currently assigned to the contact. All contacts don't have follow-up flags.

Figure 4-21

View contacts by follow-up flag

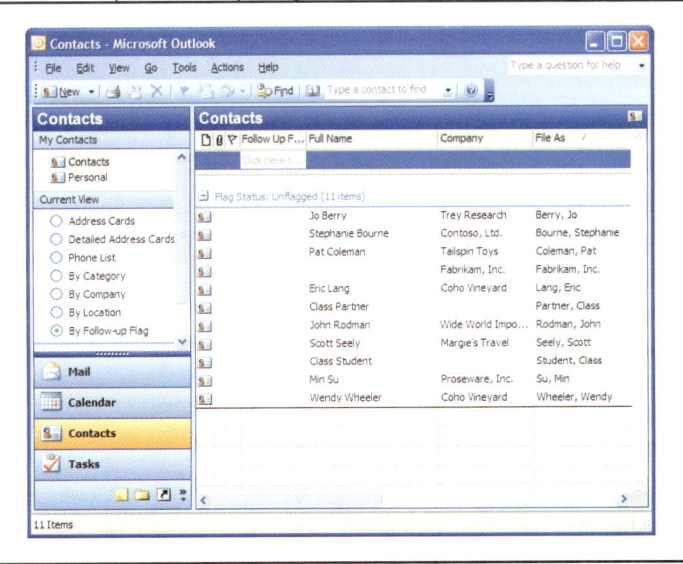

> **QUICK CHECK**
>
> Q: Can you change the method of viewing your contact records?
>
> A: **Yes, you can view contact records in several different arrangements.**

7. **In the Current View area of the Navigation pane, select Address Cards.**

    The Contacts view changes to display the default view of contacts as address cards.

◆ Keep Outlook open for the next exercise.

QUICK REFERENCE ▼

Display contact records

In the Current View of the Navigation pane, select a view.

Using Categories to Organize Contacts

Organizing Contact Information

THE BOTTOM LINE

You can organize contacts when you assign contact records to categories that describe an important characteristic of each record.

Outlook provides other approaches that you can use to organize and group contacts, including the use of categories. A **category** is a keyword or phrase associated with an Outlook item, such as a contact. A category is typically a brief description of the method used to group contacts. Categories are based on common characteristics, such as *business, personal,* and *customers*.

To assign a contact to a category, select the contact, and click the Using Categories link in the Organize pane. In the first line, select an existing category such as Holiday, Business, or International, and click the Add button. The contact is added to the selected category.

Assigning Items to a New Category

Finding and Categorizing Messages

THE BOTTOM LINE

If Outlook's existing categories don't meet your needs, you can create new categories.

Outlook provides dozens of ready-made category descriptions, but you can create more categories to meet your specific needs. For example, the operations manager at Adventure Works assigned the ready-made Outlook category Suppliers to all companies that sell products and services to the resort. When she needs a list of the resort's suppliers, she can view her Contacts folder by category. All contacts that have been assigned to the Suppliers category are displayed in a group. She could narrow the categorization further by creating custom categories for each department, such as Restaurant Suppliers, Business Office Suppliers, and Housekeeping Suppliers.

Lesson 4 Using Contacts 115

Figure 4-22

Organize contacts by categories

Assign contacts to an existing category — Create a new category

To create a new category, open the Organize pane and click the Using Categories link. In the second box, enter the name of the new category. Click the Create button to create the category. Assign any appropriate existing contacts to the new category.

Assign contacts to a new category

Since you have created contacts, you will create a new category, assign two contacts to the category, and then view your contacts by category.

1 Open the Tools menu and click the Organize command.

The Organize pane is displayed.

2 In the Organize pane, click the Using Categories link.

The Using Categories section of the Organize pane is displayed.

3 Click in the Create A New Category Called box, type Finance, and click the Create button.

The Finance category is created and Finance becomes the selected category in the upper box. This makes it easy to assign contacts to the category immediately.

Figure 4-23

New category

4 In the Contacts folder, click the John Rodman contact record.

The contact record is selected.

5 **In the Organize pane, click the Add button.**

The contact record is assigned to the new Finance category.

Figure 4-24

Record assigned to a new category

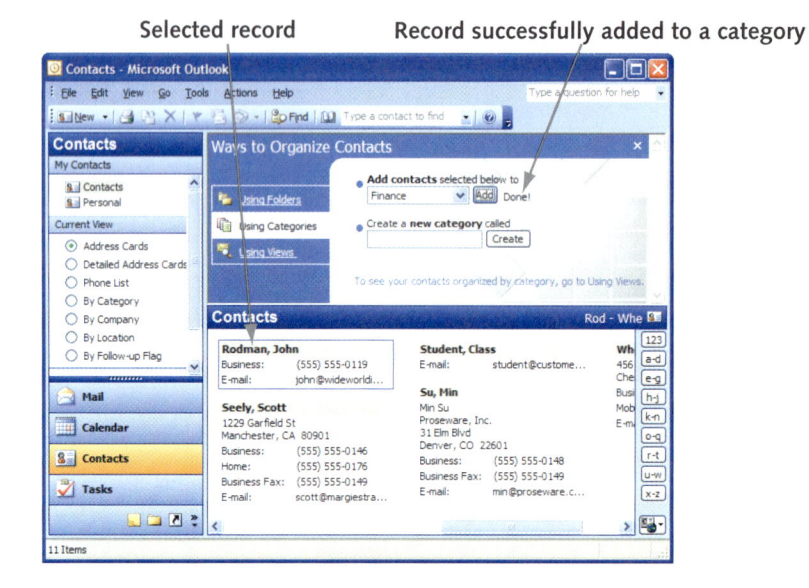

6 **In the Contacts folder, click the Scott Seely contact record.**

The contact record is selected.

7 **In the Organize pane, click the Add button.**

The contact record is assigned to the Finance category.

8 **In the Current View area of the Navigation pane, select By Category.**

Scott Seely and John Rodman are displayed as the contacts in the Finance category.

Figure 4-25

Records displayed by category

Lesson 4 Using Contacts 117

ANOTHER METHOD

In the Navigation pane, click the Address Cards option.

QUICK CHECK

Q: What is the basis for creating or using categories?

A: Categories are based on common characteristics.

9 If necessary, reopen the Organize pane. Select the Address Cards view.

The Contacts folder returns to the Address Cards view.

◆ Keep Outlook open for the next exercise.

QUICK REFERENCE ▼

Assign contacts to a new category

1 Open the Tools menu and click the Organize command.

2 In the Organize pane, click the Using Categories link.

3 Enter the category in the Create A New Category Called box and click the Create button.

4 Select a contact record and click the Add button in the Organize pane.

Assigning Items to Multiple Categories

Finding and Categorizing Messages

THE BOTTOM LINE

If you want to view a record for different reasons, you can assign a contact record to more than one category.

Relationships with contacts can be complex, so it's not unusual when a contact doesn't fit neatly into a single category. For example, Adventure Works hosts an international convention organized by a company in Mexico. The contact record for the convention organizer can be assigned to the International, Key Customer, or Business category—or to all three categories.

Over time, your relationship with each contact changes. Update category assignments as necessary to reflect a contact's current status.

Fortunately, you can assign contacts to more than one category. By assigning multiple categories to a contact, you make the contact record more accurately reflect your relationship to the contact and you enhance your ability to sort that contact by a particular category. However, don't assign a contact to more categories than necessary. The benefit of sorting contacts by category is undermined if a contact appears in almost every category.

To assign a contact to an additional category or change an existing category, select the contact, open the Edit menu, and select the Categories option. Select the appropriate check box to assign a category. Select a check box that already has a check mark in it to remove the contact from that category.

Lesson 4 Using Contacts

Assign a contact to multiple categories

Now you will assign the contact Scott Seely to two additional categories—Business and Supplier.

TIP

You can open a contact record from any view in the Contacts folder.

1 In the Contacts folder, click the contact record for Scott Seely.

The contact is selected.

ANOTHER METHOD

Double-click a contact to open it in a new window.

2 Open the Edit menu and select the Categories option.

The Categories dialog box is displayed. Scott Seely is already assigned to the Finance category.

Figure 4-26

Categories dialog box

3 In the Categories dialog box, select the Business check box and the Suppliers check box. Click OK.

The categories are added to the contact record.

4 In the Current View area of the Navigation pane, select By Category.

Scott Seely is listed in three categories. Notice that Fabrikam, Inc., is also listed in the Suppliers category.

Lesson 4 Using Contacts 119

Figure 4-27

Scott Seely assigned to multiple categories

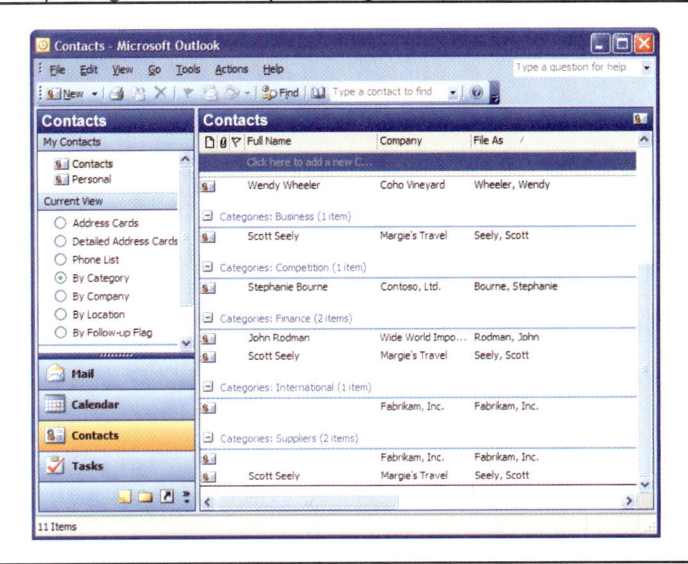

QUICK CHECK

Q: Why would you assign a contact to more than one category?

A: This makes it easier to find a contact.

5. If necessary, reopen the Organize pane. Select the Address Cards view.

The Contacts folder returns to the Address Cards view.

◆ Keep Outlook open for the next exercise.

QUICK REFERENCE ▼

Assign contacts to multiple categories

1. Select the record.
2. Open the Edit menu and select the Categories option.
3. Select the additional categories and click OK.

Modifying the Outlook Master Category List

THE BOTTOM LINE

You can modify the Master Category List as needed or reset the list to Outlook's original categories.

Outlook's ready-made list of categories is the **Master Category List**. It contains many useful categories, such as Hot Contacts, Holiday, and VIP, but you can add your own categories. In a previous exercise, you used the Organize pane to create a new category named Finance. Outlook automatically added that category to the Master Category List. You can open the Master Category List directly and add more custom categories to the list. In fact, you can customize the Master Category List in many ways, even deleting categories that you don't use. You can also reset the Master Category List to restore the default categories if you decide you want a fresh start.

Figure 4-28

Master Category List

TIP

Notice that the Finance category that you created in the previous exercise appears in the Master Category List.

Modify and reset the Master Category List

You will now work with the Master Category List. First you add a category to the Master Category List. Then you delete a category from the Master Category List. And, last, you reset the Master Category List to its original content.

1 **Open the Edit menu in the main Outlook window. Click Categories.**

ANOTHER METHOD

Right-click any contact record and click the Categories option.

The Categories dialog box is displayed.

2 **Click the Master Category List button.**

The Master Category List dialog box is displayed.

3 **In the New Category box, type Charities and click the Add button.**

Charities is added to the Master Category List.

4 **In the Master Category List, click Ideas and click the Delete button.**

Ideas is deleted from the Master Category List.

5 **Click the Reset button.**

An alert box states that the Master Category List will be reset to contain only the categories that were installed with Outlook and items assigned to deleted categories keep their assignments. In this case, the Finance and Charities categories will be deleted because neither category is part of the original Master Category List. However, the two contacts that have been assigned to the Finance category will retain their category assignments.

6 Click OK.

The Master Category List is reset. The custom Finance and Charities categories are deleted and the Ideas category is restored.

Figure 4-29

Reset Master Category List

7 Click OK twice.

The Master Category List dialog box closes and the Categories dialog box closes.

◆ Keep Outlook open for the next exercise.

QUICK REFERENCE ▼

Modify the Master Category List

1 Open the Edit menu in the main Outlook window. Click Categories.

2 Click the Master Category List button.

3 Make any needed changes and click OK twice.

QUICK CHECK

Q: Why would you edit the Master Categories List?

A: **Customizing the list makes it more useful.**

Sorting Contacts

THE BOTTOM LINE

Contact records can be sorted to find a specific record.

Sorting contacts can help you find a contact faster and easier. You can sort contacts in any view, in either ascending order (A to Z) or descending order (Z to A) by a specific field, or by a particular column header that appears at the top of the view's table, such as Company, Job Title, or Personal Home Page. When you sort in a view, the contacts remain in the same view; however, they are displayed in a different sequence.

Organizing Contact Information

> **TIP**
>
> Remember, a filter hides contacts that don't meet a set of criteria. When you use the Sort command, all contacts are displayed.

For example, the human resources manager at Adventure Works needed to find a contact but could only remember that the contact's first name was Kim. After she sorted her Contacts folder by First Name, the contacts were displayed in alphabetical order based on each contact's first name. She could have also used the Find button on the standard toolbar to search for Kim. However, because the Find feature looks for a match in the name, company, address, and categories fields, it might find matches that she definitely did not want. For example, Kimborough Museum of Science matched because Kim is part of the museum's name. Sorting by a particular column heading is often faster than the Find feature.

Add a second field to perform a sort within a sort. When you include a second field, the second sort narrows the first sort criterion even further. For example, you can sort contacts by Country/Region in ascending order and then sort by Business Address in ascending order. The contacts are sorted by Country/Region. Within the Country/Region groups, contacts are sorted by Business Address.

Sort contacts

To practice sorting you will sort the list of contacts in Phone List view by Business Phone number.

1 **In the Current View area of the Navigation pane, select Phone List.**

The Contacts view changes to list your contacts by name, company, and phone numbers.

2 **Open the Tools menu and select the Organize option.**

The Organize pane is displayed.

3 **In the Organize pane, click the Using Views link. Click the Customize Current View button.**

The Customize View dialog box is displayed.

Figure 4-30

Customize View dialog box

Lesson 4 Using Contacts 123

4 **Click the Sort button.**

The Sort dialog box is displayed.

ANOTHER METHOD

Many times, you can sort contacts for your needs by clicking a column heading.

5 **In the Sort Items By section, click Business Phone. Verify that the Ascending option is selected.**

Figure 4-31

Sort dialog box

6 **Click OK twice.**

The contents of the selected Contacts folder are sorted by Business Phone.

Figure 4-32

Sorted records

7 **In the Organize pane, click the Customize Current View button.**

The Customize View dialog box is displayed.

124 **Lesson 4** Using Contacts

8 Click the Sort button.

The Sort dialog box is displayed.

9 Click the Clear All button and click OK twice to close the dialog boxes.

The contents of the Contacts folder are no longer sorted by Business Phone.

10 In the Organize pane, select the Address Cards view.

The Contacts view is changed to Address Cards.

> **QUICK CHECK**
>
> Q: Why would you sort contact records?
>
> A: Sorting records makes it easier to find a specific contact record.

◆ Keep Outlook open for the next exercise.

QUICK REFERENCE ▼

Sort contact records

1 Select a view in the Navigation pane.
2 Open the Tools menu and select the Organize option.
3 In the Organize pane, click the Using Views link.
4 Click the Customize Current View button.
5 Click the Sort button.
6 Select the Sort criteria.
7 Click OK twice to return to the main Contacts folder.

Using the Address Book to Send E-Mail

Using Address Books

THE BOTTOM LINE

Outlook lets you use the Address Book in any Outlook folder to send an e-mail message.

When you create a new contact record, some of the information is copied to the **Address Book**, which stores names, e-mail addresses, and phone numbers. To open the Address Book from any folder in Outlook, click the Address Book button on the Standard toolbar.

Figure 4-33

Address Book

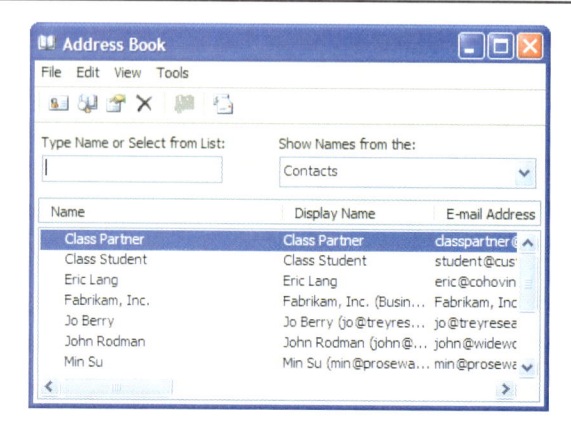

Lesson 4 Using Contacts

> **TROUBLESHOOTING**
>
> If your computer is set up for the Corporate or Workgroup e-mail service, your Address Book will look slightly different (and have different options) than the one discussed in this lesson.

Within the Address Book window is a toolbar and a list of contact information for each record in the Contacts folder. The toolbar contains six buttons—New Entry, Find Items, Properties, Delete, Add to Contacts, and New Message. The buttons are described in the following table.

Button	Description
New Entry	Add a new contact or a distribution list to the Address Book.
Find Items	Open the Find dialog box that enables you to search for names containing a specific sequence of letters.
Properties	Display the General tab of a contact record. You can add or edit contact information.
Delete	Permanently delete an entry from the address book.
Add to Contacts	The Address Book and Contacts list interact.
New Message	Open a blank e-mail message addressed to the selected contact.

If a contact has an e-mail address, you can send messages to the contact directly from the Address Book. You don't need to copy or manually type the e-mail address into the To box of a new message window.

Send mail from the Address Book

Now you will open the Address Book, select an e-mail address, and send an e-mail message through the Address Book.

> **TIP**
>
> The Address Book button is on the standard toolbar for each Outlook folder.

1 On the standard contacts toolbar, click the Address Book button.

The Address Book is displayed.

Figure 4-34

Address Book

2 Click your class partner's name and click the New Message button.

A new message window is displayed. Your class partner's address is in the To box.

Figure 4-35

Message sent from Address Book

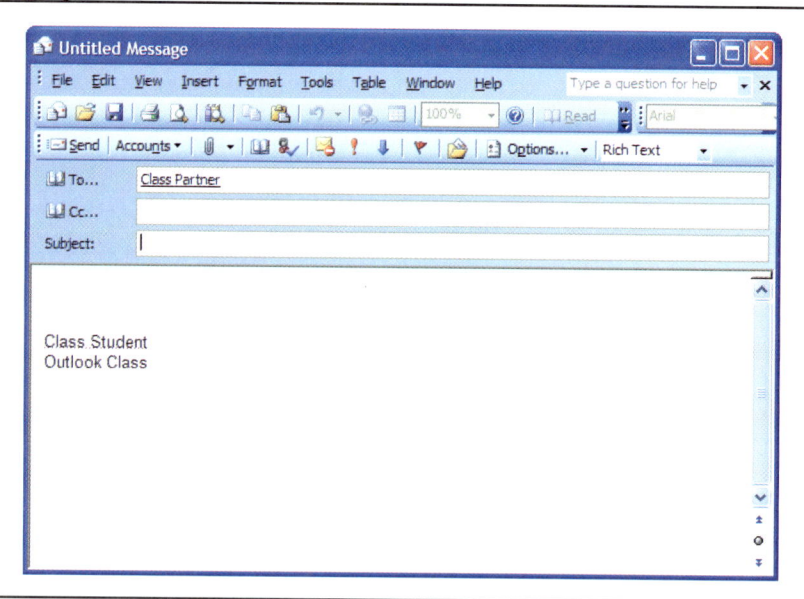

3 In the Subject box, type Address Book.

> **TIP**
>
> This message is not used in another part of the lesson. It is not necessary to send or receive the message.

4 Click in the message area and type You are in my address book. On the toolbar in the message window, click the Send button.

The message is sent to your class partner.

5 In the top-right corner of the Address Book, click the Close button.

QUICK CHECK

Q: Where can you open the Address Book?

A: The Address Book can be opened from the standard toolbar in each Outlook folder.

◆ Keep Outlook open for the next exercise.

QUICK REFERENCE ▼

Send e-mail using the Address Book

1. On the standard contacts toolbar, click the Address Book button.
2. Select a contact and click the New Message button.
3. Write the message and click the Send button.

Using Contacts to Send E-Mail

THE BOTTOM LINE

Just as you were able to send a message from the Address Book, you can also send a message to one of your contacts without moving to the Mail folder.

You can send e-mail directly from the Contacts folder without opening the Inbox folder first. To send an e-mail message to a contact from the Contacts folder, select the contact record in the Contacts folder. On the standard contacts toolbar, click the New Message To Contact button. A message window is displayed. The e-mail address of the selected contact is in the To box. You can type additional information in the e-mail message and click the Send button.

You can send e-mail messages from Contacts even when the recipient is not a contact. On the Standard toolbar, click the down arrow to the right of the New Contact button, and click Mail Message. A blank message window is displayed, enabling you to create and send a message to someone who isn't in your Contacts.

TIP

In a message window, click the Address Book button in the To field. This displays the Address Book and enables you to insert or add addressees to the message.

Send a message from a Contact folder

You will now send a message to your class partner directly from a contact window.

1. **In the Contacts folder, double-click your class partner's contact record.**

   Your class partner's contact record is displayed in a new window.

TIP

You can send a new message from the standard toolbar in any of the Outlook folders.

128 **Lesson 4** Using Contacts

2 On the Standard toolbar in the contact window, click the New Message To Contact button.

A message window is displayed. Your class partner's e-mail address is located in the To box. The insertion point is in the Subject box.

3 Type Outlook Class and press Enter.

The insertion point moves to the message area.

> **TIP**
>
> These messages are not used in another part of the lesson. It is not necessary to send or receive the messages.

4 Type How is the Outlook class going? Click the Send button.

The message is sent.

5 In the top-right corner of the contact window, click the Close button.

The contact window closes. Your class partner's contact record is still selected.

6 On the Navigation pane, click the Mail button. If necessary, go to the Inbox.

Messages you have received are displayed.

7 Click the Send/Receive button.

The message sent by your class partner is received.

Figure 4-36

Message sent from Contacts folder

◆ Keep Outlook open for the next exercise.

> **QUICK CHECK**
>
> **Q:** Can you send a message to someone who isn't one of your contact records?
>
> **A:** You can send a message to someone who isn't one of your contact records.

QUICK REFERENCE ▼

Send a message from a Contact folder

1. Double-click a contact record.
2. On the standard toolbar in the contact window, click the New Message To Contact button.
3. Type your message and click the Send button.

Sending and Receiving Contact Information via E-Mail

Sending and Receiving Contact Information

THE BOTTOM LINE

A vCard creates or updates a contact record without the recipient typing in the new information.

IMPORTANT

To use vCards in Outlook, you must have the VcViewer program installed and Outlook must be set up using the Internet Only configuration. If an alert box states that you do not have the VcViewer program installed, you can install it from the Outlook or Microsoft Office 2003 CD-ROM.

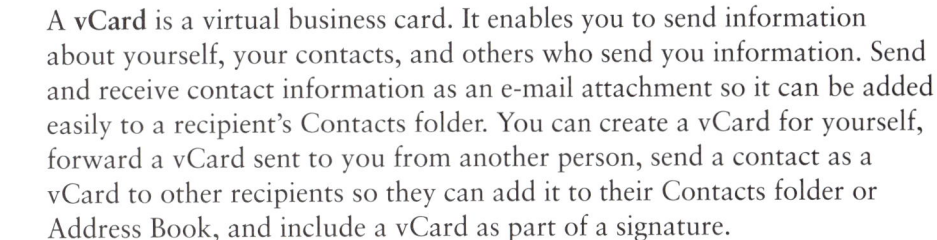

A **vCard** is a virtual business card. It enables you to send information about yourself, your contacts, and others who send you information. Send and receive contact information as an e-mail attachment so it can be added easily to a recipient's Contacts folder. You can create a vCard for yourself, forward a vCard sent to you from another person, send a contact as a vCard to other recipients so they can add it to their Contacts folder or Address Book, and include a vCard as part of a signature.

Sending a vCard

THE BOTTOM LINE

Sending a vCard ensures that others have current contact information for you.

Exchanging contact information using vCards is fast and convenient. If you send a text message containing contact information, the recipient must type it into Outlook as a new contact. It is much easier for the sender and the receiver to use vCards. You can send a vCard and the recipient can add it directly to his or her Contacts folder. For example, the head chef of Adventure Works attaches a vCard with his address and phone information to his signature. When he sends e-mail to other people, they receive the vCard and can easily add it to their Contacts folder. To send a vCard from Contacts, click the contact record you want to send, open the Actions menu, and select the Forward as vCard option. A new message window opens. The contact information is a vCard attached to the message. In the To box, type the recipient's e-mail address and click the Send button.

Use vCards

In this exercise, you forward your contact information as a vCard to a member of your class, make the vCard part of your signature, and send a message to a class member with a vCard as part of your signature.

> **TIP**
> A vCard can be sent as an attachment in a specific message or included in a signature that is automatically added to each message you compose.

1 **In the Contacts folder, double-click your contact record.**

Your contact window is displayed.

2 **In the Address box, type the address for your company, your home address, or a fictitious address.**

This provides additional contact information.

3 **On the standard contacts toolbar, click the Save And Close button.**

The contact window closes. Your contact record is still selected in the Contacts folder.

4 **Right-click your contact record and click Forward.**

A new message window is displayed with FW: [Your Name] in the Subject box. The vCard is located in the bottom of the message window as an attachment.

5 **Click the To button.**

The Select Names dialog box is displayed.

6 **In the Select Names dialog box, click your class partner's name, click the To button, and click OK.**

The Select Names dialog box closes and your class partner's name is displayed in the To box.

7 **On the toolbar in the message window, click the Send button.**

Your contact information is sent as a vCard.

8 **Open the Tools menu and click Options.**

The Options dialog box is displayed.

9 **Click the Mail Format tab, and click the Signatures button.**

The Create Signature dialog box is displayed.

Lesson 4 Using Contacts 131

10 **Verify that the signature you created in a previous lesson is selected and click the Edit button.**

The Edit Signature dialog box is displayed.

Figure 4-37

Edit Signature dialog box

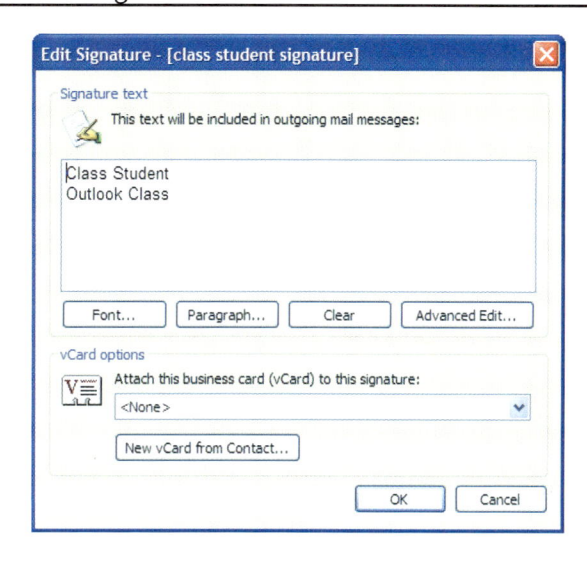

11 **At the bottom of the dialog box, click the New vCard From Contact button.**

The Select Contacts To Export As vCards dialog box is displayed.

Figure 4-38

Select Contacts To Export As vCards

12 **Click your name, click the Add button, and click OK.**

In the Edit Signature dialog box, notice that your name is displayed in the Attach This Business Card (vCard) To This Signature box.

13 Click OK three times to return to the Contacts folder.

Your contacts are displayed.

14 Click your class partner's contact record. On the standard toolbar, click the New Message To Contact button.

A new message window is displayed. Your class partner's e-mail address is located in the To box, your signature is displayed in the message area, and a vCard is attached to the message.

15 In the Subject box, type My new signature. In the message area, type Look at my new signature. and click the Send button on the Message toolbar.

The message is sent to your class partner.

> **TIP**
>
> You will view the message sent by your class partner in the next exercise.

◆ Keep Outlook open for the next exercise.

QUICK REFERENCE ▼

Send a vCard

1 Right-click a contact record and click Forward.

2 Address the message and click the Send button.

QUICK CHECK

Q: How can you automatically send a vCard with every message you send?

A: Make the vCard part of your signature.

Receiving a vCard

> **THE BOTTOM LINE**
>
> You can keep your contact records current by saving the vCards you

When you receive a vCard, it is displayed as an attachment to an e-mail message. Open it by double-clicking the vCard icon just like any other attachment. The vCard opens as a contact window. You can insert additional information, such as who sent you the card, or edit existing information. Click the Save And Close button to add the vCard to your Contacts folder.

If the vCard is a duplicate of an existing contact, an alert box is displayed. You can choose to add the contact as a second record or add updated information from the new contact to the existing contact.

Receive a vCard

In this exercise, you receive and save the vCard sent by your class partner.

> **TIP**
>
> A vCard can be received as an attachment or part of the sender's signature.

Lesson 4 Using Contacts 133

1 **Double-click the My New Signature message you received from your class partner in the previous exercise.**

A message window is displayed. The vCard is an attachment to the message.

Figure 4-39

Received vCard in signature of message sent by your class partner

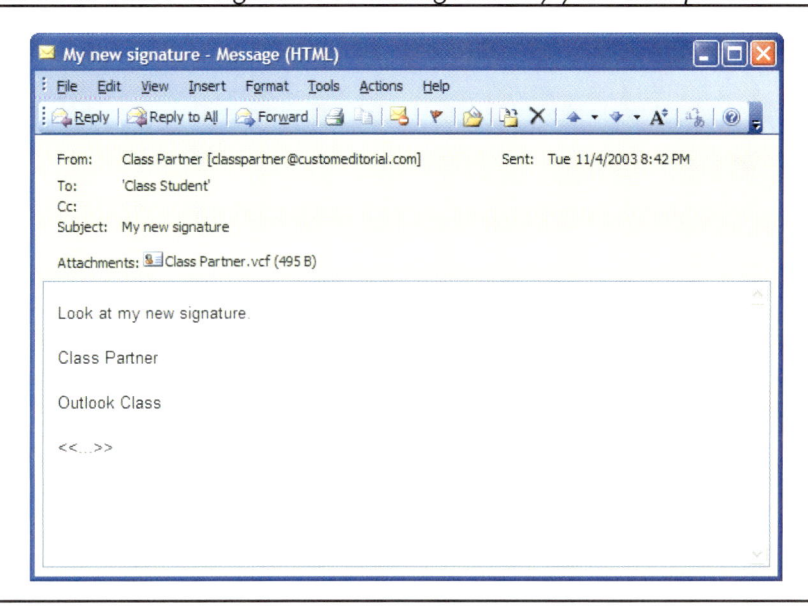

TROUBLESHOOTING

An alert box might be displayed. Continue to open the vCard.

2 **Double-click the vCard.**

The vCard is displayed as a contact record.

3 **Click the Save And Close button.**

An alert box indicates that this is a duplicate record.

Figure 4-40

Alert box for duplicate record

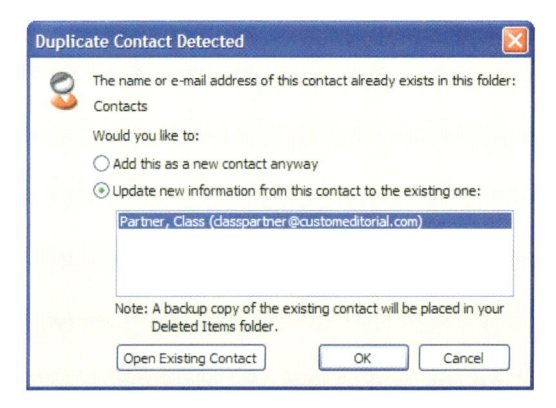

4 **Choose to update the existing record and click OK.**

Outlook saves the vCard as a contact record in the Contacts folder.

134 **Lesson 4** Using Contacts

5 **Close the message window. On the Navigation pane, click the Contacts button.**

The Contacts folder is displayed.

6 **In the Contacts folder, find your class partner's contact record and verify that the information in the vCard has been added to the contact record.**

The contact record has been modified.

QUICK CHECK

Q: What happens if you receive the same vCard twice?

A: You can update the contact record.

Figure 4-41

Updated contact information from vCard

Partner, Class
Suite 5
1104 Main Street
Smallville, MO 80909
E-mail: classpartner@cus...

◆ Keep Outlook open for the next exercise.

QUICK REFERENCE ▼

Receive a vCard

1 Double-click a message containing a vCard attachment.

2 Double-click the vCard.

3 Click the Save And Close button.

Creating a Letter for a Contact

THE BOTTOM LINE

With Microsoft Word's Letter Wizard you can create letters addressed to your contacts.

Outlook e-mail capabilities are integrated with all other Microsoft Office applications. This means you can initiate some activities directly in an Office application that you would otherwise have to do from within Outlook. For example, you can use your Address Book to create and send documents in Microsoft Word. After you create a document in Word, click the E-Mail button on Word's Standard toolbar to quickly send the document as an e-mail message.

Conversely, you can also initiate an e-mail message in letter format from within Outlook, which can launch Word so you can compose the body of the letter. You don't need to type the recipient's address in the letter if it already exists in a contact record.

For example, an administrative assistant at Adventure Works needs to write a letter to a client regarding his account. Instead of opening Word and typing the client's information in the upper-left corner of the letter, the assistant creates the letter from the contact record in Outlook, and the contact information is automatically added to the letter.

Lesson 4 Using Contacts 135

Although Outlook starts the letter-creation process, you actually create and compose the letter in Microsoft Word. The Letter Wizard dialog box is displayed in Word to walk you through the steps in the letter-creation process. In the first step, on the Letter Format tab, choose a letter format, including letterhead, page design, and letter style. In the second step, on the Recipient Info tab, select the recipient's name, mailing address, and a salutation. In the third step, on the Other Elements tab, select options concerning reference lines, mailing instructions, attentions, subjects, and courtesy copies. In the fourth and final step, on the Sender Info tab, select information about the person sending the letter (either yourself or someone else), and letter closing options. After the fourth step is finished, the Letter Wizard closes and you can type the body of the letter.

IMPORTANT

To complete the next exercise, you must have Microsoft Word installed on your computer.

Use the Letter Wizard

Now you will use the Letter Wizard to format and compose a letter to contact Scott Seely.

TROUBLESHOOTING

If the Office Assistant is displayed, right-click the Assistant and click Hide on the shortcut menu that is displayed.

1 In the Contacts folder, click the Scott Seely contact record. Open the Actions menu and select the New Letter To Contact option.

Word opens and the first dialog box of the Letter Wizard is displayed.

2 Complete the Letter Wizard and click the Finish button.

The Letter Wizard closes and the letter is displayed in Word. You can now add the body text to the letter.

TIP

Although you made many formatting decisions in the Letter Wizard, you can change the format after the letter is created.

3 Complete the letter by typing the following body text. Adventure Works is now taking bids for new signs. If you would like to obtain more information and place a bid, contact us at 555-555-0129.

4 Save the letter in the Outlook Practice folder on your hard disk as Letter to Scott Seely.

The letter is saved in the Outlook Practice folder.

◆ **Close Microsoft Word.**

Lesson 4 Using Contacts

QUICK CHECK

Q: Which application owns the Letter Wizard?

A: The Letter Wizard is part of Microsoft Word.

- If you are continuing to the next lesson, keep Outlook open.
- If you are not continuing to the next lesson, close Outlook.

QUICK REFERENCE ▼

Use the Letter Wizard

1. Select a contact record.
2. Open the Actions menu and select the New Letter To Contact option.
3. Complete the Letter Wizard and click the Finish button.
4. Complete and save the letter.

Key Points

- ✔ Contacts can be viewed, edited, deleted, and restored.
- ✔ You can create multiple contact records for people at the same company.
- ✔ In Outlook, you can sort and organize contacts using folders, views, and categories.
- ✔ The Outlook Master Category List can be modified.
- ✔ The Address Book as well as the contacts can be used to send e-mail messages directly. You do not need to be in the Mail folder.
- ✔ You can send and receive contact information as a vCard.
- ✔ Using Microsoft Word, you can create a letter to a contact.

True/False

T F 1. Contact records are deleted immediately when you click the Delete button.

T F 2. Every contact record should be assigned to every category.

T F 3. Sort contact records in some views by clicking a column heading.

T F 4. The Address Book contains only contact records for individuals who have received a letter from you.

T F 5. You can send a message to a contact from any Outlook folder.

Multiple Choice

1. Contacts can be assigned to _____ category(categories).
    a. one
    b. three
    c. every
    d. All of the above

2. When a vCard is received, it is a(n) _____.
    a. attachment
    b. part of the message body
    c. chore to type the new information
    d. All of the above

3. The _____ enables you to add an address to an e-mail message without typing it.
   a. Master Category List
   b. Address Book
   c. Letter Wizard
   d. All of the above

4. A deleted contact is _____.
   a. removed immediately
   b. stored until you enter a new contact record
   c. stored in the Deleted Items folder
   d. assigned to the Deleted category

5. Organize contacts by _____.
   a. assigning them to categories
   b. moving them to folders
   c. sorting them
   d. All of the above

Short Answer

1. How can the Address Book save you time in addressing a new message?
2. Can you add categories to the Master Category List? If so, how do you make the changes?
3. What is a category?
4. How do you enter multiple contacts for the same company?
5. What is a vCard?
6. What happens when you click the Save And New button after entering contact data?
7. For a contact record to be complete, which fields in the contact window are required?
8. In general, what is the purpose of the Contacts folder?
9. Where does a contact go when you delete it, and how do you permanently delete a contact?

On Your Own

Exercise 1

The new marketing director at Adventure Works needs to add two new contacts for the advertising agency of Contoso, Ltd. The members of the agency are Susan W. Eaton, President, and Eva Corets, Ad Consultant. The address for the company is 55 Pine Terrace, Suite 400, San Jose, CA 11111. Each contact is to be assigned to the Business and Strategies categories. The additional information the marketing director has for each person is the business phone, mobile phone, pager, and e-mail address.

Enter the following contact information for Susan W. Eaton:

Name	Susan W. Eaton
Job Title	President
Business Phone	555-555-0177
Pager	555-555-0132
Mobile Phone	555-555-0151
E-Mail Address	susan@contoso.com

Enter the following contact information for Eva Corets:

Name	Eva Corets
Job Title	Ad Consultant
Pager	555-555-0163
Mobile Phone	555-555-0184
E-Mail Address	eva@contoso.com

TROUBLESHOOTING

You must complete Exercise 1 before you can continue to Exercise 2.

Exercise 2

Compose a formal letter to the president of Contoso, Ltd. indicating what a pleasure it was to meet with her team and expressing confidence that the advertising campaign for Adventure Works is in good hands. Save or print the letter.

One Step Further

Exercise 1

Send two vCards to your class partner using the information you entered in the first exercise.

Exercise 2

Add the vCards you receive from your class partner to your Contacts folder.

Exercise 3

Assign the vCards you receive from your class partner to a category for suppliers. If necessary, create the category. Delete the vCards from your Contacts folder.

LESSON 5

Using the Calendar

After completing this lesson, you will be able to:

✔ *Navigate within the Calendar.*
✔ *Change Calendar views.*
✔ *Schedule appointments and events.*
✔ *Create recurring appointments.*
✔ *Set reminders.*
✔ *Edit appointments.*
✔ *Delete appointments.*
✔ *Organize appointments using categories and views.*
✔ *Plan meetings with others.*
✔ *Print a calendar.*
✔ *Save a calendar as a Web page.*
✔ *Integrate the Calendar with other Outlook components.*

KEY TERMS

- Appointment Area
- appointment
- Calendar
- Date Navigator
- event
- meeting
- recurring appointment
- TaskPad
- Work Week

For many busy businesspeople, there never seems to be enough time in the day to finish all their tasks. To keep track of all your day-to-day duties, meetings, and appointments, it is important to stay organized. To do this, you can jot down your appointments and other scheduling information in a day planner or enter the information into a palm-size computer. You can also use Microsoft Office Outlook 2003 to plan your day and your week. Because Outlook uses the full power of your computer, you can often take advantage of features not available with a day planner or a palm-size computer. For example, in Outlook, you can set an alarm to notify you of an upcoming appointment. You certainly can't expect your day planner to sound an alarm.

The Outlook Calendar is just as easy to use as the calendar hanging on your wall or buried on your desk. Use the Calendar, to set reminders, create a list of daily tasks to perform, change appointment times, and automatically mark meetings that occur on a regular basis (such as a weekly department meeting). You can print your daily, weekly, or monthly calendar and take it with you when you are away from your desk or your office, and you can make your schedule available to others over a network (via Microsoft Exchange Server) or over the Internet so co-workers can see when you are available for meetings.

In this lesson, you will learn how to navigate within the Calendar. You will use the Calendar to schedule and edit appointments and events. You will set reminders and plan meetings with others. Finally, you will print a copy of your calendar to take with you or distribute and you will see how the Calendar is integrated with other Outlook components.

> **IMPORTANT**
>
> To complete some of the exercises in this lesson, you will need to exchange e-mail messages with a class partner. If you don't have a class partner or you are performing the exercises alone, you can send the message to yourself. Simply enter your own e-mail address instead of a class partner's address.

Using the Outlook Calendar

Looking at Calendars in Different Ways

> **THE BOTTOM LINE**
>
> The Outlook Calendar can help you organize a busy schedule by tracking your appointments, meetings, and events.

Outlook places many features at your fingertips. The **Calendar** is a component of Outlook that can be used like a desk calendar or a day planner. In the Calendar, you can create information about activities that take place at scheduled times, called **appointments**. You can track and plan events, which are activities that occupy long periods of time, such as vacations or conventions. You can also schedule **meetings**, which are appointments that you invite or request others to attend.

Understanding Appointments and Meetings

Many people use the terms *appointment* and *meeting* interchangeably. In the Outlook Calendar, however, there is a clear distinction between an appointment and a meeting.

In the Outlook Calendar, an *appointment* is anything that is scheduled—a doctor's appointment, a business trip, a management meeting, a luncheon engagement, a racquetball game, and so on. A *meeting*, though, is a kind of appointment. Specifically, a meeting is an appointment in which you use the Outlook Calendar to request the attendance of other people. For example, if you plan a management meeting for two hours on Tuesday and use the Calendar to e-mail invitations to the other managers, Outlook considers this to be a meeting. If you plan the management meeting, use the telephone to call each manager to request his or her attendance, and then schedule the meeting time in the Outlook Calendar, Outlook does not consider this to be a meeting, just an appointment.

Therefore, if you schedule an activity, but don't use the Outlook Calendar to request the attendance of others, you are scheduling an appointment. If you use the Outlook Calendar to request the attendance of others at a scheduled activity, you are creating a type of appointment called a meeting. Even if you call something a meeting, Outlook might not.

Lesson 5 Using the Calendar 141

Navigating Within the Calendar

When you click the Calendar shortcut on the Outlook Bar, the Calendar opens and the Day view of your schedule appears by default. This view shows the Calendar divided into four sections—the **Appointment Area**, the **Date Navigator**, the Navigation pane, and the **TaskPad**.

Figure 5-1
Outlook Calendar window

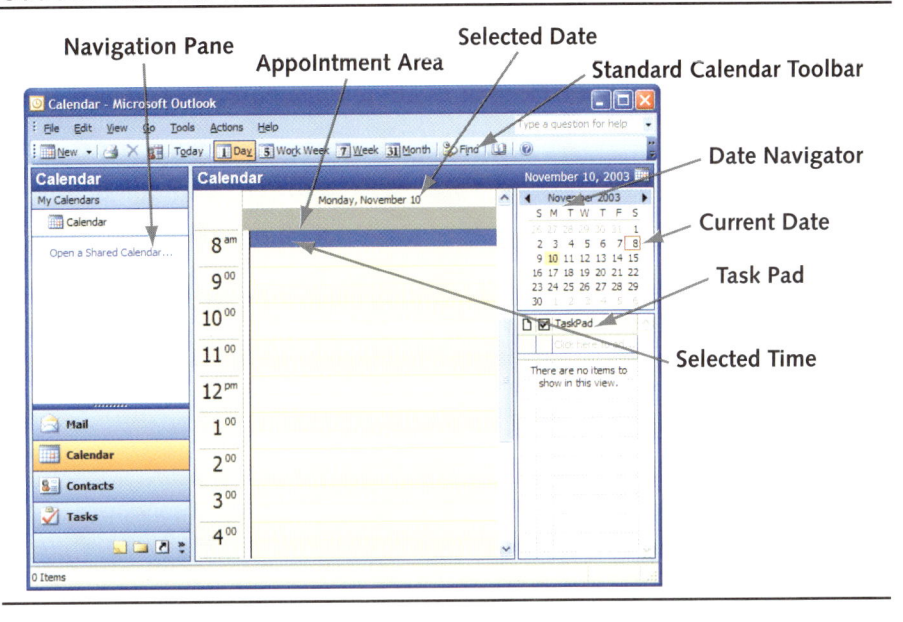

TIP

The selected date is displayed above the Appointment Area and shaded on the Date Navigator. The current date is outlined in the Date Navigator.

Section	Description
Appointment Area	The Appointment Area resembles a daily planner. Use the area to schedule activities, which can be displayed by day, work week, week, or month. By default, the workday starts at 8:00 A.M. and ends at 5:00 P.M. The time slots outside this workday period are shaded. Use the scroll bars to display entry lines for any time of the day or night.
Date Navigator	The Date Navigator displays a full-month calendar, regardless of the number of days displayed in the Appointment Area. It may be displayed on the Navigation pane on the left side of the Appointment Area or on the right side of the Appointment Area. Its location is determined by the presence or absence of the TaskPad. Scroll backward and forward through different months and years to find dates by using two different options. First, use the left or right arrows at the top of the Date Navigator to scroll backward and

(Continued)

(continued)

	forward through the months. Second, click and hold the name of the month to display a list of months and click a month in the list to display it in the Calendar. You can also click a different date in the Date Navigator to display the day in the Appointment Area.
Navigation pane	The Navigation pane enables you to move from one Outlook folder to another. It also may contain the Date Navigator, which enables you to move back and forth in time.
Task Pad	Use the TaskPad to record tasks that you want to accomplish. This function works directly with Outlook's Tasks folder.

◆ Be sure to start Outlook before beginning this exercise.

Navigate the Calendar

We begin this lesson by learning to navigate through the Calendar's Appointment Area and Date Navigator.

TROUBLESHOOTING

The first view displayed in this exercise may be different on your computer. Click the Day button and select TaskPad on the View menu to see the correct view.

1 On the Navigation pane, click the Calendar button.

The contents of the Calendar folder are displayed.

Figure 5-2

Outlook Calendar day view

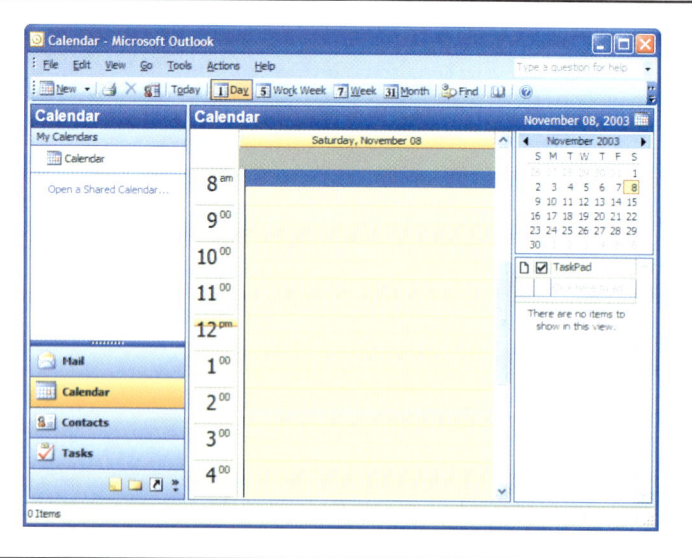

2 In the Appointment Area, drag the scroll bar to the top.

The Appointment Area is divided into 30-minute increments. Dark lines separate each hour. Light lines separate each half-hour. Only the start of each hour is labeled. The time slot between the hours (12:30, 1:30, etc.) isn't labeled. The day starts at 12:00 A.M.

3 Scroll to the bottom of the Appointment Area.

The day ends at 11:30 P.M.

4 In the Date Navigator, click tomorrow's date.

The Appointment Area displays tomorrow's date.

5 At the top of the Date Navigator, click the left arrow.

The previous month is displayed, but the date in the Appointment Area remains the same.

6 At the top of the Date Navigator, click and hold the right arrow on the month bar for a few seconds.

Time moves forward rapidly in the Date Navigator.

7 In the Date Navigator, click and hold the name of one of the currently displayed months.

A menu of months is displayed.

8 Move the pointer to the month at the top of the list and release the mouse button.

The Date Navigator displays the selected month.

9 On the Standard Calendar toolbar, click the Go To Today button.

The current day is displayed in the Appointment Area and the Date Navigator.

ANOTHER METHOD

You can quickly display a different date. Right-click in the Appointment Area, select the Go To Date option, click the Date down arrow, select a date, and click OK.

◆ Keep Outlook open for the next exercise.

QUICK REFERENCE ▼

Navigate through the Calendar

Use the Date Navigator to view different dates.

144 **Lesson 5** Using the Calendar

Changing the Calendar View

Looking at Calendars in Different Ways

> **THE BOTTOM LINE**
>
> Using standard views and arrangements helps you stay on top of your schedule.

Many personal planners show appointment and task information in a variety of ways. The Outlook Calendar also provides a variety of views. Although the default display in the Calendar is the Day view, you can change the view to display a **Work Week** (five business days), Week (seven days), or a Month.

Several standard arrangements are also available. Arrange your calendar by day/week/month, active appointments, events, annual events, recurring appointments, and category. To select an arrangement, open the View menu, point at Arrange By, point at Current View, and select a view.

The days of the work week are normally Monday through Friday, but you can change them to fit a different work schedule. Open the Tools menu and select Options. On the Preferences tab, click the Calendar Options button. In the Calendar Work Week section, select the check boxes of the days of the week that you want to display and click OK twice.

Change the Calendar view

Now that you are familiar with the default Calendar view you will now learn how to change the view of the Calendar.

1 On the Standard Calendar toolbar, click the Work Week button.

The five days of a standard work week are displayed in five columns.

Figure 5-3

Work week view

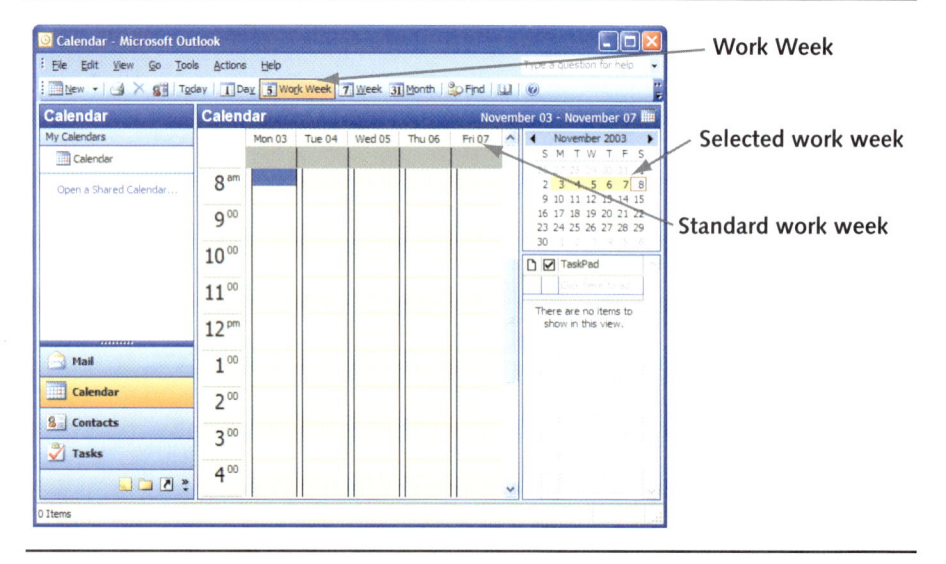

— Work Week
— Selected work week
— Standard work week

2 On the Standard Calendar toolbar, click the Week button.

The view changes to seven days.

Lesson 5 Using the Calendar 145

Figure 5-4

Week view

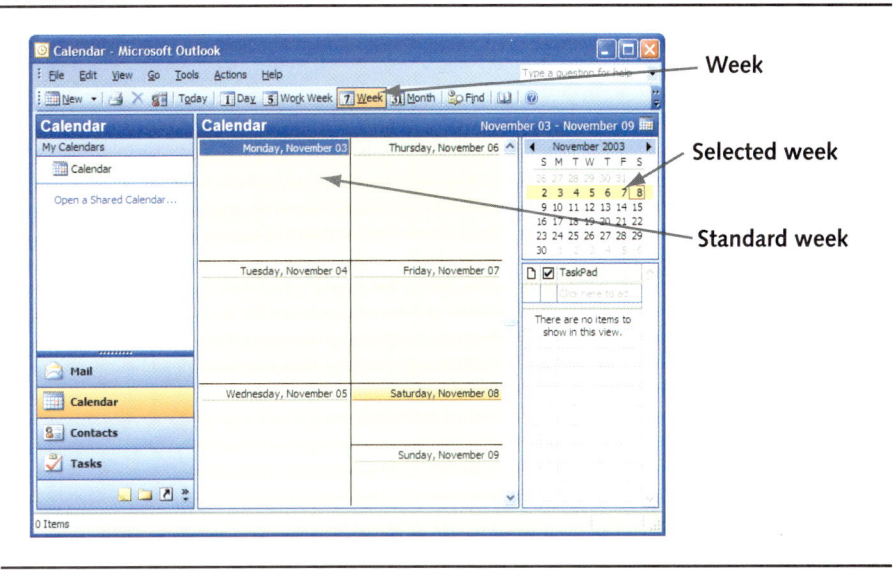

[Screenshot of Calendar Week view with labels: Week, Selected week, Standard week]

TIP

Days that are not part of the current month are shaded. You can still view activities entered for these days.

3 On the Standard Calendar toolbar, click the Month button.

The view changes to display a month.

Figure 5-5

Month view

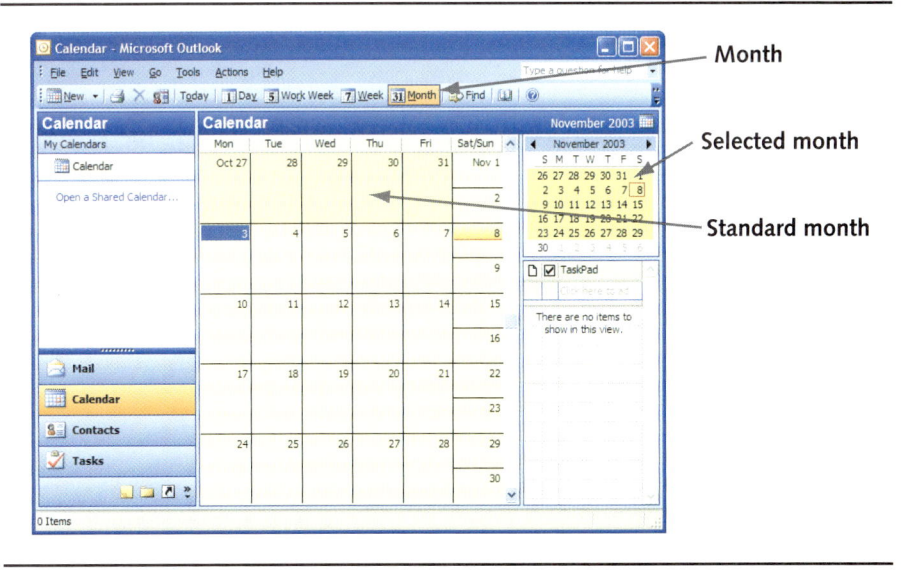

[Screenshot of Calendar Month view with labels: Month, Selected month, Standard month]

4 On the View menu, point at Arrange By, point at Current View, and click Active Appointments.

A list of active appointments is displayed. The list is empty if you haven't created appointments yet. Notice that the toolbar changes and a label appears above the list that tells you a filter has been applied.

146 **Lesson 5** Using the Calendar

Figure 5-6

Active appointments arrangement

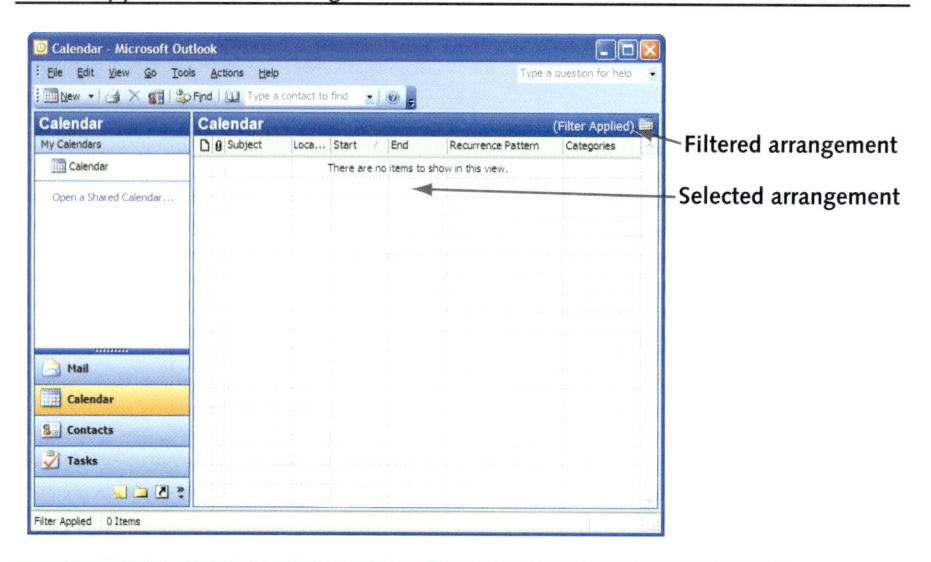

[Screenshot of Calendar - Microsoft Outlook window showing Filter Applied view with "Filtered arrangement" and "Selected arrangement" callouts]

5 On the View menu, point to Arrange By, point to Current View, and click Day/Week/Month.

The filter is removed. The standard calendar toolbar and the month view are displayed.

6 On the Standard Calendar toolbar, click the Day button.

The view returns to the day view.

◆ Keep Outlook open for the next exercise.

QUICK CHECK

Q: What is the difference between an appointment and a meeting?

A: You must use Outlook to invite others to a meeting.

QUICK REFERENCE ▼

View the Calendar

On the Navigation pane, click the Day, Week, or Month button.

Scheduling Appointments and Events

THE BOTTOM LINE

Scheduling appointments and events in Outlook helps you manage your time efficiently.

An appointment is an activity that takes place at a scheduled time that does not require you to request the attendance of other people. Examples of appointments include meeting with a sales representative, visiting a doctor, picking up your dry cleaning, or any other activity that can be scheduled. When you enter an appointment into the Calendar, the appointment is displayed in one slot. Because the slots are measured in increments of 30 minutes, by default, an appointment takes 30 minutes to perform.

However, you can increase the duration of an appointment by dragging the top or bottom border of the blue box that surrounds the appointment entry. For example, the marketing director at Adventure Works has a doctor's appointment Monday morning at 9:00 A.M. Her doctor always seems to run at least an hour behind schedule, so the marketing director wants to specify that the appointment end at 11:00 A.M. She scheduled the appointment time by clicking the bottom border of the 9:00 A.M. time slot in the Appointment Area and dragging the border down to the top of the 11:00 A.M. time slot.

Figure 5-7

Appointment scheduled in the Appointment Area

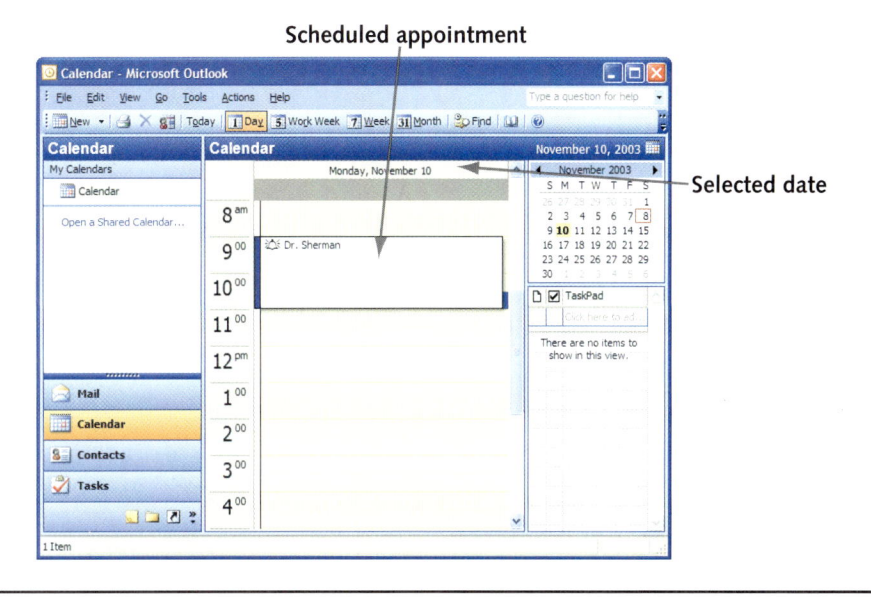

To add details to an appointment, double-click the scheduled time slot. The detailed appointment window is displayed. Enter the details that are necessary and use the Memo Area to enter notes about the appointment.

Figure 5-8

Appointment detail window

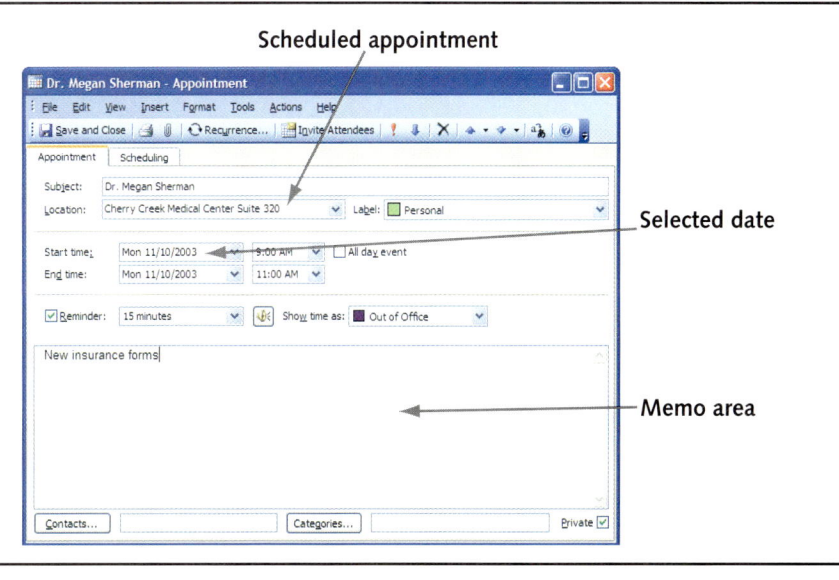

The following basic components are displayed in the window:

Component	Description
Subject	Change the topic or purpose of the appointment directly within the Appointment Area or change it in the Subject box.
Location	Use this box to identify where the appointment occurs. Outlook maintains a list of previously entered locations. Scroll through the Location box to select a previous appointment location.
Label	Assign a color to color-code appointments. This enables you to identify the type of appointment at a glance.
Start Time	Outlook uses the starting time in the Appointment Area by default. You can change the starting time in the appointment window.
End Time	Outlook automatically inserts the ending time in the Appointment Area. You can change the ending time in the appointment window.
Reminder	Use this field to specify when Outlook informs you about the meeting. The entry is based on the amount of time before the meeting. If you do not want a reminder, clear the Reminder check box.
Show Time As	Use this option to let others know that you are busy, free, or out of the office, or that the appointment is tentative.
Memo Area	Use the text area at the bottom of the dialog box to type any notes or additional reminders. If you add text to the memo area, you can see the text in the Calendar by opening the Preview pane.

You can also schedule a lengthy event in the Calendar. An **event** is a function that usually makes you unavailable for the entire day or for multiple days—such as a vacation, business trip, or an off-site seminar. Events are displayed in the Calendar as a banner at the top of the Appointment Area. You can schedule appointments and meetings during an event. For example, you could mark the next two days as an event because you will be attending a convention. You can still make appointment entries for different lectures and presentations that you will be attending during the convention. Double-click an event to open an event window, which is very similar to the appointment window.

Schedule an appointment

You will now create two appointments and one multiday event.

1 **In the Date Navigator, click the next workday.**

The Appointment Area displays the date.

TROUBLESHOOTING

A bell icon to the left of the appointment indicates that Outlook will remind you to attend the appointment. Setting reminders is discussed later in this lesson.

Lesson 5 Using the Calendar 149

2 **In the Appointment Area, click the 12:00 P.M. time slot.**

The 12:00 P.M. time slot is selected.

3 **Type** Lunch with caterer **and press Enter.**

The half-hour appointment is entered.

4 **Click in the 2:00 P.M. and type** Meeting with Picnic Planning Committee. **Press Enter.**

Two appointments for tomorrow are created.

5 **Select the bottom border of the 2:00 P.M. time slot and drag the mouse pointer down to the top of the 3:30 P.M. time slot.**

Three slots are selected, indicating an hour-and-a-half appointment.

Figure 5-9

Scheduled appointments

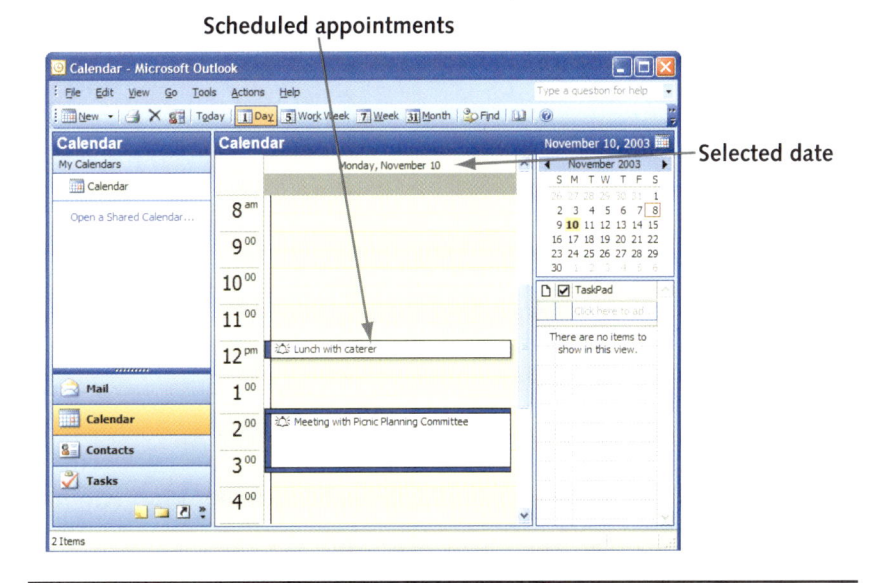

6 **In the Date Navigator, click Monday of the following week.**

The Appointment Area displays the Monday of the following week.

7 **On the Standard Calendar toolbar, click the New Appointment button.**

ANOTHER METHOD

Open the File menu, point at New, and click Appointment.

An appointment window is displayed. The insertion point is already in the Subject box.

8 **In the Subject box, type** Vacation **and press the Tab key.**

The insertion point moves to the Location box.

9 **In the Location box, type** Hawaii **and select the All Day Event check box.**

Notice that the window is now called Vacation - Event.

150   **Lesson 5**   Using the Calendar

10 **Click the End Time down arrow.**

A mini-calendar is displayed.

11 **In the mini-calendar, click a date two weeks from the shaded date.**

When you close the appointment window and return to the Calendar, it will display a two-week vacation.

12 **Click the Show Time As down arrow and select Out Of Office.**

Your Calendar indicates to others that you are out of the office for this two-week period.

13 **Select Personal in the Label box.**

The color you assign to an appointment indicates the type of appointment.

Figure 5-10

Vacation-Event window

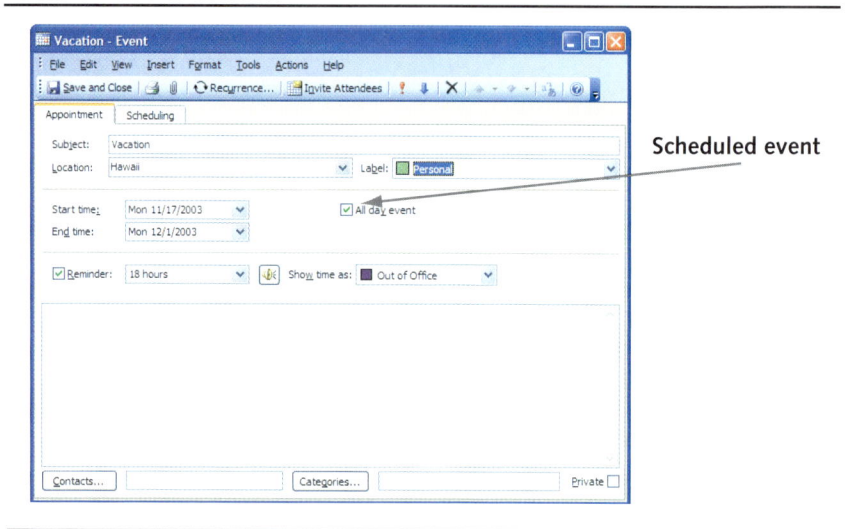

14 **On the Standard toolbar in the event window, click the Save And Close button.**

The window closes. The event, Vacation (Hawaii), is displayed at the top of the Appointment Area. In the Date Navigator, the vacation days are displayed in bold type.

Figure 5-11

Scheduled event

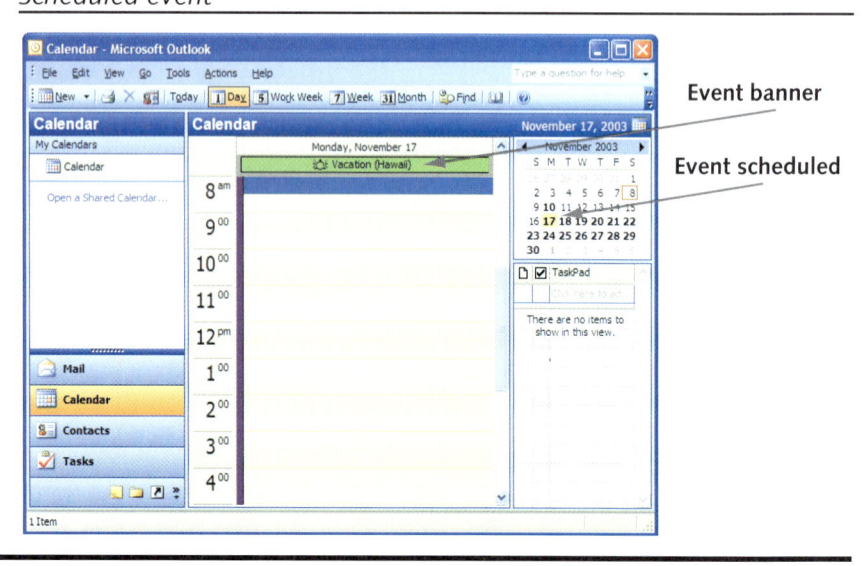

QUICK CHECK

Q: What is the difference between an appointment and an event?

A: An event lasts a day or more.

Scheduling Appointments and Events

◆ Keep Outlook open for the next exercise.

QUICK REFERENCE ▼

Schedule an appointment

1. Enter the appointment in the Appointment Area.
2. Drag the borders to set the appointment time.

Creating Recurring Appointments

THE BOTTOM LINE

You can create a recurring appointment to save time. Outlook enables you to schedule a regular appointment once rather than entering it every time it occurs.

Some meetings and appointments are held on a regular basis at the same time and on the same day each week. These appointments are referred to as **recurring appointments**. For example, the office manager at Adventure Works calls a supplier to place an order every Friday morning at 10:00 A.M. To remind herself of this task, she creates a recurring appointment in her calendar.

For daily appointments, you can specify whether they occur every day (Monday, Tuesday, Wednesday, Thursday, Friday, Saturday, and Sunday) or every weekday (Monday, Tuesday, Wednesday, Thursday, and Friday). For weekly appointments, you can specify the number of weeks that pass before repeating the appointment (every two weeks, for example), and the day of the week (such as every other Monday). For monthly appointments, you can specify the day of the month, and for yearly appointments, you can specify the day of the year.

Create a recurring appointment

Now you will create a recurring appointment.

1 In the Date Navigator, select the date that is four Tuesdays into the future.

The fourth Tuesday into the future is displayed in the Appointment Area.

TIP

When creating a recurring appointment in the Appointment Area, the date does not have to be on the same day of the week as the appointment. You can change the day of the week in the Appointment Recurrence dialog box.

2 In the Appointment Area, click the 8:00 A.M. time slot, type **Weekly sales meeting**, and press Enter.

The weekly sales meeting is entered as an appointment.

3 Drag the bottom border to the top of the 10:00 A.M. time slot.

Four slots are selected, indicating a two hour appointment.

4 Double-click the appointment.

The appointment window is displayed. The subject of the appointment is the same name that you just typed in the Appointment Area.

TIP

Recurring meetings, appointments, and events can be scheduled on multiple days in one week.

Recurrence...

5 On the toolbar in the appointment window, click the Recurrence button.

The Appointment Recurrence dialog box is displayed. Notice that the appointment time is the same time you specified in the Appointment Area.

Figure 5-12

Appointment Recurrence dialog box

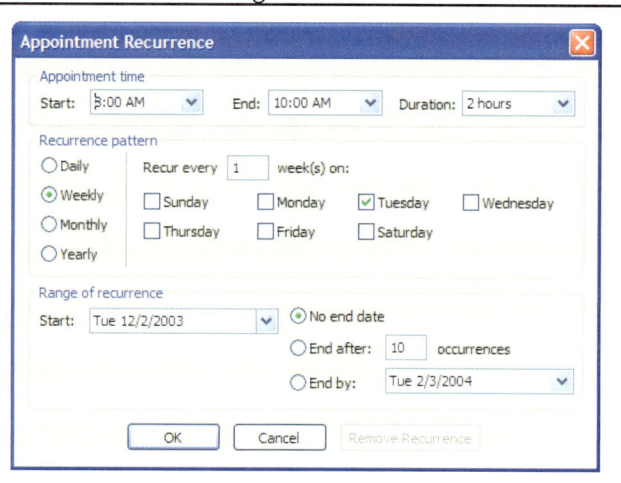

6 In the Recurrence Pattern section, click the Weekly option if necessary.

7 If necessary, select the Tuesday check box and clear the check boxes for all other days.

8 In the Range Of Recurrence section, click the End After option. In the End After box, double-click 10, and type 8.

The appointment recurs on Tuesdays for eight weeks.

TROUBLESHOOTING

If the recurring appointment conflicts with another appointment in the future, Outlook displays a warning. You can reschedule or cancel the appointment.

9 Click OK.

The dialog box closes and you can access the appointment window.

Lesson 5 Using the Calendar 153

10 Click in the Location box and type Adventure Works Pavilion.

The information for this appointment is complete.

Figure 5-13

Recurring appointment

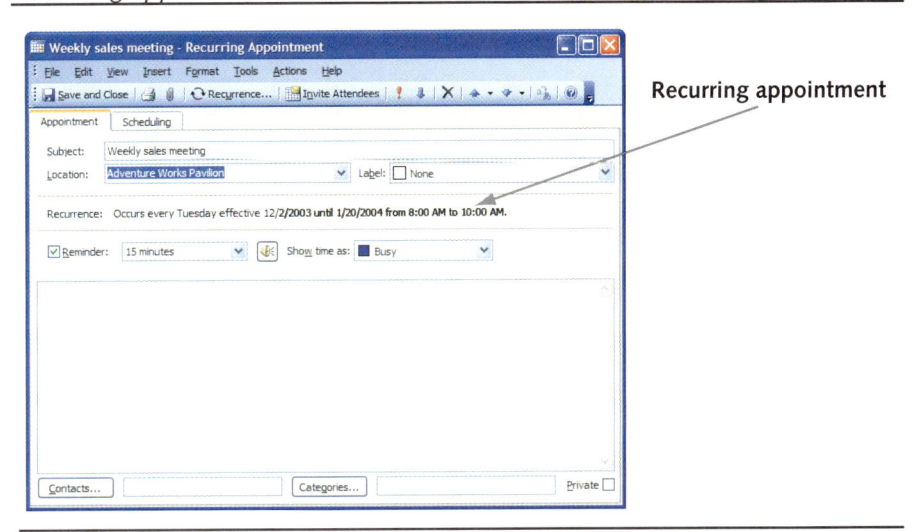

11 On the Standard toolbar in the appointment window, click the Save And Close button.

The recurring appointment is saved.

12 In the Date Navigator, click several Tuesdays into the future.

The recurring meeting message continues to appear in the Appointment Area.

13 On the Standard Calendar toolbar, click the Go To Today button.

Today's date is displayed in the Calendar.

ANOTHER METHOD

You can change an existing appointment into a recurring appointment. Double-click the existing appointment and click the Recurrence button on the Standard toolbar in the appointment window. Enter the recurrence information, click OK, and click the Save And Close button.

◆ Keep Outlook open for the next exercise.

QUICK REFERENCE ▼

Create a recurring appointment

1 Enter the appointment in the Appointment Area.
2 Double-click the appointment.
3 Click the Recurrence button.
4 Select the recurrence pattern.
5 Save the appointment.

QUICK CHECK

Q: Why would you schedule a recurring appointment?

A: The appointment happens at a regular interval

Setting Reminders

> **THE BOTTOM LINE**
>
> A visual reminder and a sound can ensure that you make it to meetings on time. Give yourself time to prepare by setting the reminder to announce the appointment 10 minutes or more before the scheduled time.

When you are extremely busy or preoccupied with a particular task, you can easily forget about an upcoming appointment. With Outlook, you can let the Calendar remind you. When you set up an appointment, you can choose to be reminded before the appointment occurs. If you choose this option, you can also select when the reminder is displayed before the appointment. The appointment is displayed with a bell next to its description, indicating that you will be reminded of the appointment. You can also choose a sound that will play (if any) when the reminder is displayed on the screen. The following reminder dialog box is displayed before the appointment begins.

Figure 5-14

Reminder

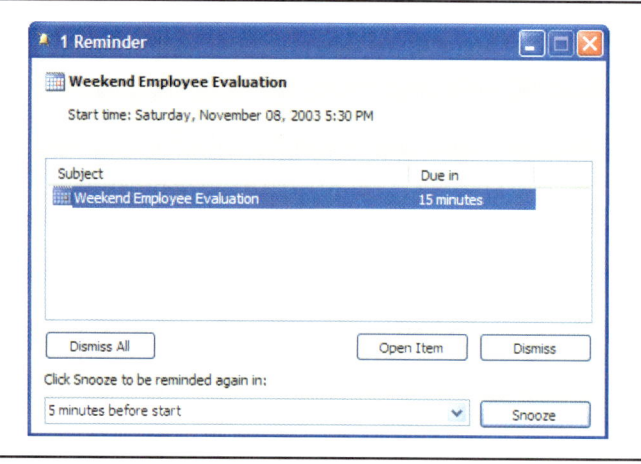

> **IMPORTANT**
>
> Outlook must be running to display the Reminder dialog box. If you are using a different program and Outlook is running, the Reminder dialog box is displayed on top of any open windows and documents.

Set a reminder

In this exercise, you set a reminder for the appointment *Meeting with Picnic Planning Committee* that you entered in a previous exercise.

1 **In the Date Navigator, click the next workday.**

The appointments for tomorrow are displayed.

Lesson 5 Using the Calendar 155

2 Double-click the appointment Meeting with Picnic Planning Committee.

The appointment window is displayed.

3 If necessary, select the Reminder check box. In the Reminder field, select 10 minutes.

Outlook will remind you that you have an appointment 10 minutes before the scheduled appointment.

Figure 5-15

Reminder dialog box

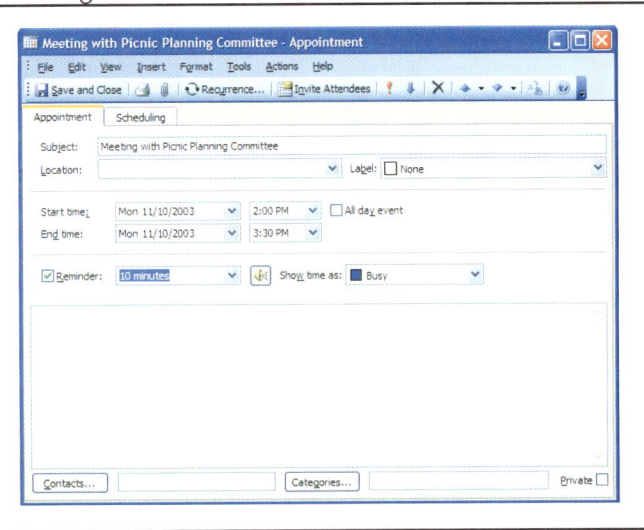

TROUBLESHOOTING

To hear the reminder sound, your computer must have a sound card and speakers that are turned on. Whether or not you have sound capabilities, Outlook still displays the Reminder dialog box.

4 On the Standard toolbar in the appointment window, click the Save And Close button.

The reminder is set.

◆ Keep Outlook open for the next exercise.

QUICK REFERENCE ▼

Set a reminder

1 Double-click the appointment.
2 Select the Reminder check box.
3 Select the time period in the Reminder field.
4 Save the appointment.

QUICK CHECK

Q: How is a reminder presented?

A: It displays a window and makes a sound.

Editing Appointments

Updating and Organizing Appointments

> **THE BOTTOM LINE**
>
> You change details about an appointment so your information is up to date.

In addition to setting reminders for appointments, you can add information about the appointment—such as who is involved or additional topics discussed—and you can attach files for reference or mark the appointment as private. You can also set the level of importance for an appointment. By default, the level of an appointment is Medium, but you can change this to High or Low. Use the appointment window or the Appointment Area to change appointment information—such as the start and end times or the location—at any time.

For example, when the marketing director at Adventure Works meets with clients, she jots down the attendees' names and the topics she wants to discuss in the memo area of her appointment window. If her appointment has to be rescheduled for later in the day, she changes the start and end times and sets a reminder.

Edit an appointment

You will edit the appointment *Lunch with caterer* created earlier in the lesson and change the date of the appointment.

1 **Double-click the appointment "Lunch with caterer."**

The appointment window is displayed.

2 **Click in the Location box and type Mom's Kitchen Cafe.**

The location will be added to the appointment information.

3 **Click the first Start Time down arrow.**

A mini-calendar is displayed.

4 **In the mini-calendar, click the day after the currently scheduled date.**

The date of the appointment will be changed.

5 **Click the Show Time as down arrow and click Out Of Office.**

Others who view your schedule will see that you are out of the office for the appointment.

6 **On the Standard toolbar in the appointment window, click the Importance: High button.**

The importance of the appointment is elevated.

7 **In the bottom-right corner of the window, select the Private check box.**

The appointment will be considered private. Others with access to this schedule can see that there is an appointment and that you will be out of the office, but they can't see any details.

Lesson 5 Using the Calendar 157

Figure 5-16

Edited appointment

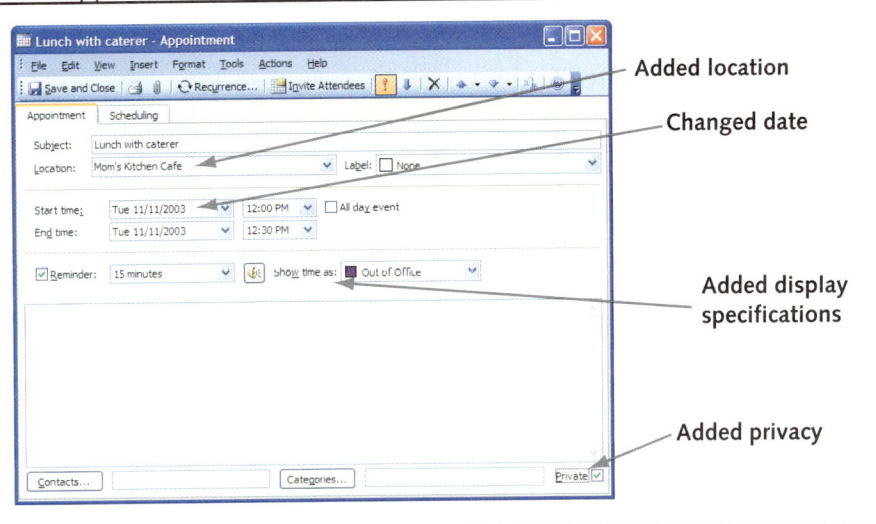

- Added location
- Changed date
- Added display specifications
- Added privacy

8. **On the Standard toolbar in the appointment window, click the Save And Close button.**

   The modifications are saved.

9. **On the Navigation Bar, click the day of the appointment.**

   The appointment is displayed on the schedule. The location of the appointment is displayed next to the subject. A key icon is displayed to the left of the subject, indicating that the appointment is private.

Figure 5-17

Additional information displayed in Appointment Area

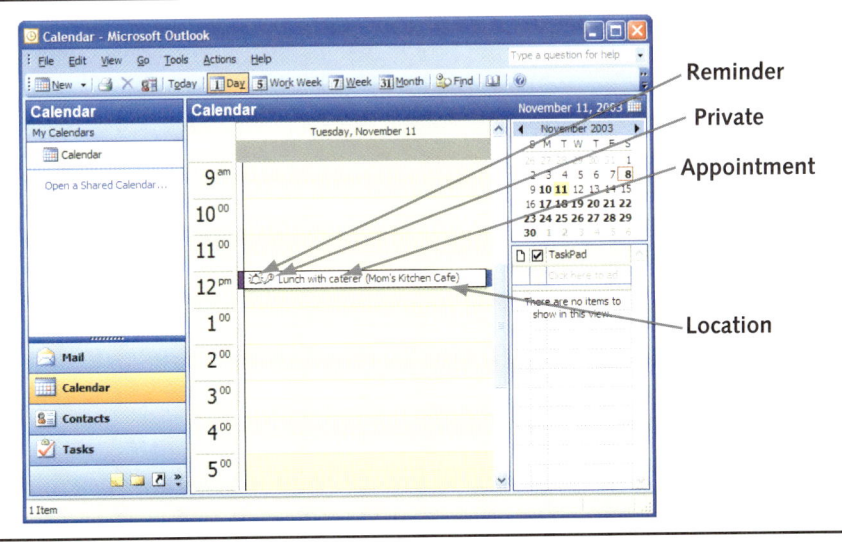

- Reminder
- Private
- Appointment
- Location

ANOTHER METHOD

Change the time or duration of an appointment in the Appointment Area by dragging an appointment from one time entry to another. In Month view, which displays multiple days, you can drag an appointment to a different day.

QUICK CHECK

Q: How do you edit an appointment?

A: Double-click the appointment, make the changes, and save the appointment again.

◆ Keep Outlook open for the next exercise.

QUICK REFERENCE ▼

Edit an appointment

1. Double-click the appointment.
2. Make any necessary changes.
3. Save the appointment.

Deleting Appointments

THE BOTTOM LINE

Keep your schedule clean and uncluttered by removing unnecessary appointments.

Updating and Organizing Appointments

If an appointment is cancelled or its occurrence has already passed, you can remove the appointment from the Calendar. When you delete an appointment, it is moved to the Deleted Items folder, like e-mail messages and contacts. The deleted appointments remain there until you empty the Deleted Items folder. You can restore an appointment from the Deleted Items folder by dragging it back into the Calendar folder.

IMPORTANT

When you try to delete a recurring appointment, Outlook will ask if you want to delete the current selected appointment or all occurrences of the appointment.

Delete and restore an appointment

Working with existing appointments, you delete a normal appointment and a recurring appointment, and restore an appointment.

1. **Click the appointment "Lunch with caterer."**

   The appointment is selected.

2. **On the Standard Calendar toolbar, click the Delete button.**

   The appointment moves to the Deleted Items folder.

3. **In the Date Navigator, click one of the Tuesdays that are displayed in bold (after the vacation days).**

   The recurring appointment for the selected date is displayed in the Appointment Area.

4. **Click anywhere on the appointment Weekly Sales Meeting. Click the Delete button.**

   An alert box is displayed, as shown in Figure 5-18. It asks if you want to delete the currently selected appointment or all occurrences. If you

Figure 5-18

Confirm Delete dialog box

select the Delete All Occurrences option, Outlook deletes every occurrence of the appointment Weekly sales meeting. The option to delete this one is already selected.

5 Click OK.

The selected appointment is deleted, but all other occurrences remain.

6 In the Navigation pane, click the Folder List button. When the folders are displayed, click the Deleted Items folder.

The contents of the Deleted Items folder are displayed.

7 Drag the appointment "Lunch with caterer" onto the Calendar button on the Navigation pane. Click the Calendar button.

The Calendar is displayed.

8 On the Date Navigator, click the original date for the lunch meeting with the caterer.

Notice that the appointment *Lunch with caterer* has returned to its original date and time.

ANOTHER METHOD

You can also right-click an appointment that is not currently selected and click Delete on the shortcut menu.

◆ Return to today's date.

◆ Keep Outlook open for the next exercise.

QUICK REFERENCE ▼

Delete an appointment

1 Click the appointment.

2 On the Standard Calendar toolbar, click the Delete button.

QUICK CHECK

Q: Where does a deleted appointment go?

A: A deleted appointment is stored in the Deleted Items folder until the folder is emptied.

Organizing Appointments by Using Categories

THE BOTTOM LINE

In Outlook, you can assign appointments to categories to track appointments by purpose, associated events, or other meaningful groups.

Like contacts, appointments can be organized by categories to view just the appointments you need to see. In the Using Categories section of the Organize pane, you can select one of the existing categories, such as Holiday, Business, or Gifts. You can also create your own categories and assign appointments or events to the new categories.

Looking at Calendars in Different Ways

Create and assign a category

Now will you create a category and assign a category to the appointment *Meeting with Picnic Planning Committee* that you entered in a previous exercise.

1 Open the Tools menu and click the Organize option.

The Organize pane is displayed.

Figure 5-19

Organize pane in the Calendar folder

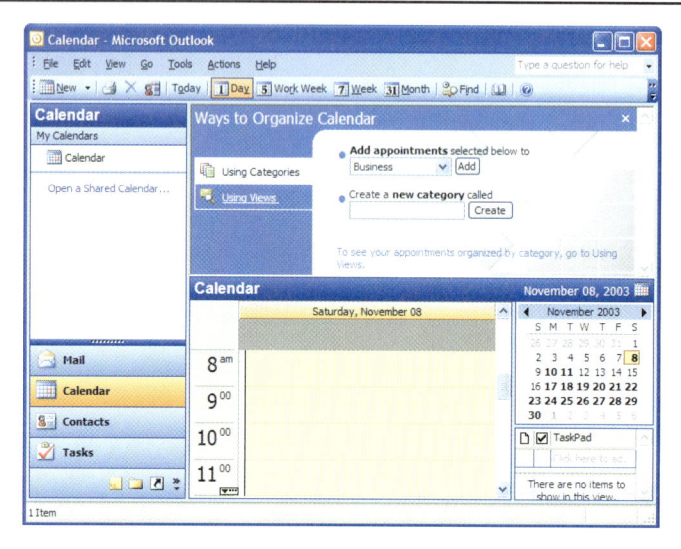

2 In the Organize pane, click in the Create A New Category Called box, type **Planning** and click the Create button.

The category, Planning, is created. It is displayed in the Add Appointments Selected Below To box in the Organize pane. This enables you to quickly add appointments to the new category. Later, you can use the category to locate an appointment.

3 In the Date Navigator, locate and click the appointment "Meeting with Picnic Planning Committee."

The appointment is selected.

4 In the Organize pane, click the Add button.

The appointment is assigned to the Planning category.

Figure 5-20

Appointment assigned to a category

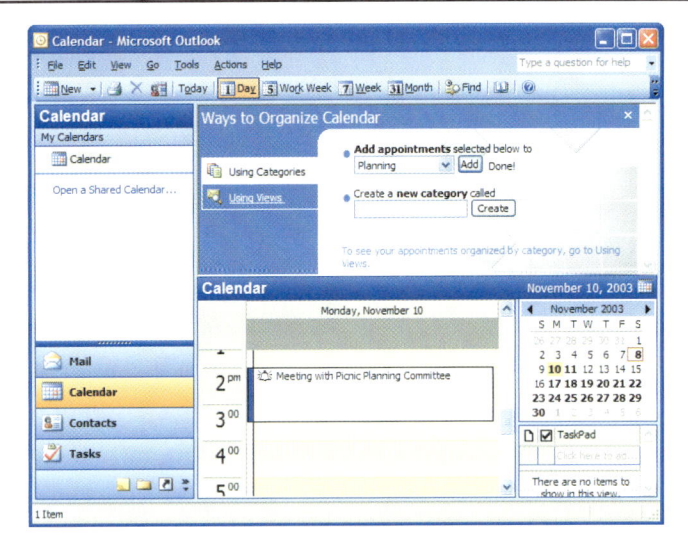

QUICK CHECK

Q: Why would you assign an appointment to a category?

A: **You can use the category to locate the appointment later.**

ANOTHER METHOD

Double-click any appointment. Enter the category in the Categories field and save the appointment.

◆ Keep Outlook and the Organize pane open for the next exercise.

QUICK REFERENCE ▼

Assign an appointment to a category

1. Open the Tools menu and click the Organize option.
2. In the Organize pane, elect an existing category or create a new category.
3. In the calendar, select the appointment.
4. In the Organize pane, click the Add button.

Looking at Calendars in Different Ways

Organizing Appointments by Using Arrangements

THE BOTTOM LINE

Outlook's Arrangements feature helps you keep track of appointments by displaying those that meet specific requirements.

You've already used the basic arrangements to view Calendar items. With Outlook, you can also determine which appointments are displayed in the Calendar so that you see only a specific type of appointment or only appoint-

162 Lesson 5 Using the Calendar

ments for a particular period. Arrangements include Active Appointments, Events, Annual Events, Recurring Appointments, and By Category. Changing the view in this manner enables you to quickly identify a particular type of appointment. For example, if you want to see only appointments that require a full day or multiple days, display the Calendar Events arrangement. If you've assigned appointments to different categories, view appointments by category so you can identify related appointments. To view a different arrangement, use the Organize pane or on the View menu, point at Arrange By, point at the Current View option and select the desired arrangement.

Display different Calendar views

Next you will use the Organize pane to display appointments in different arrangements.

1 **In the Organize pane, click the Using Views link.**

The Using Views section of the Organize pane is displayed.

Figure 5-21

Using Views option in the Organize pane

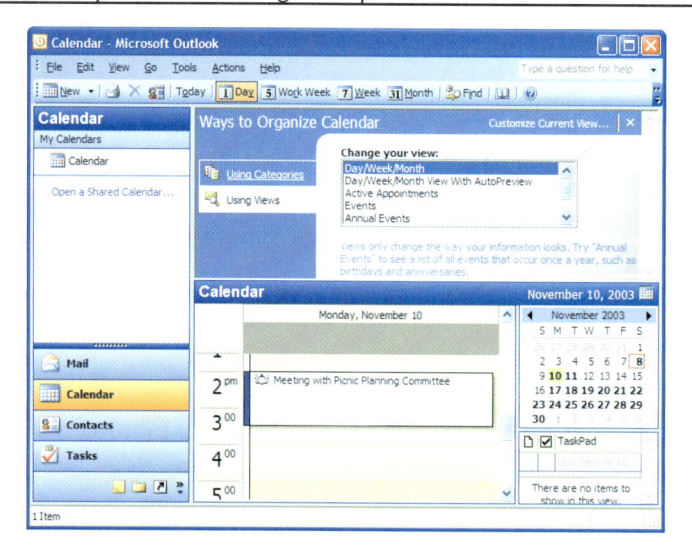

2 **In the Change Your View list, select By Category.**

The appointments are divided into categories displayed below the Organize pane. Each bar identifies the number of items in the category. The Planning category contains one item.

Lesson 5 Using the Calendar 163

Figure 5-22

View appointments by category

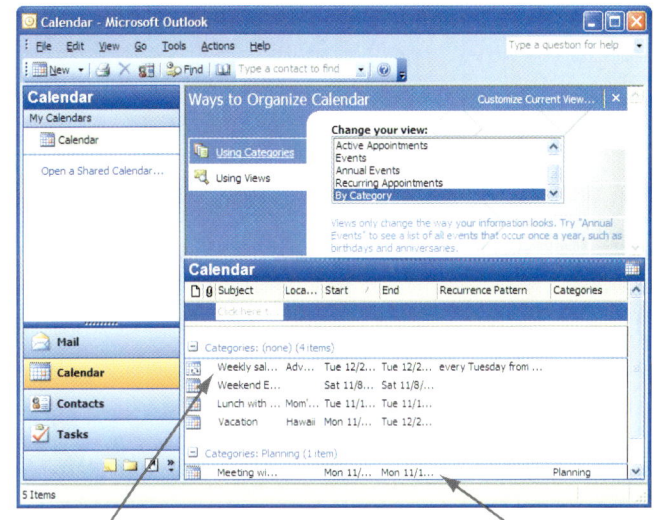

Appointments not assigned to a category

Appointments assigned to a category

> **TIP**
>
> If necessary, scroll to view the entire list of appointments.

3 **If necessary, click the plus sign (+) on the left side of the Planning gray bar.**

The appointment you added to the Planning category in the previous exercise is displayed.

4 **In the Organize pane, click Recurring Appointments in the Change Your View list.**

Only recurring appointments are displayed.

Figure 5-23

View recurring appointments

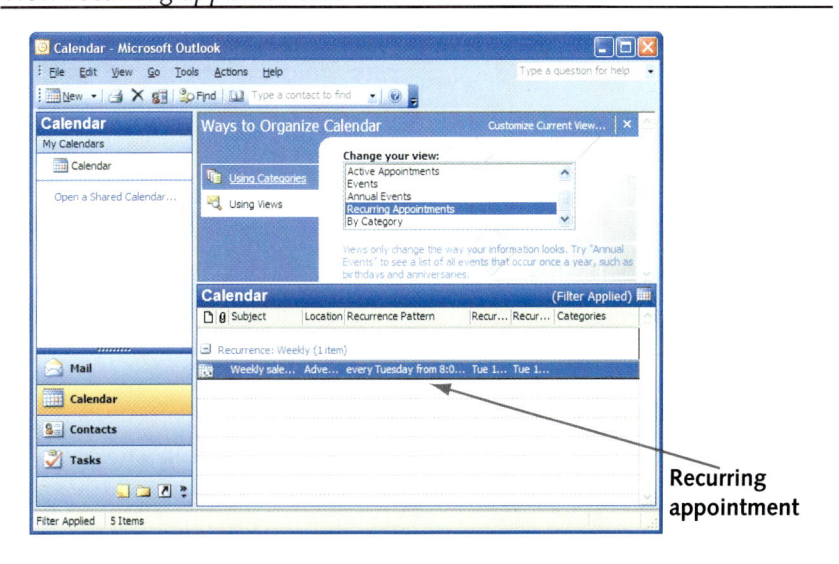

Recurring appointment

5 In the Change Your View list, click Active Appointments.

All upcoming appointments are displayed in table format.

Figure 5-24

View active appointments

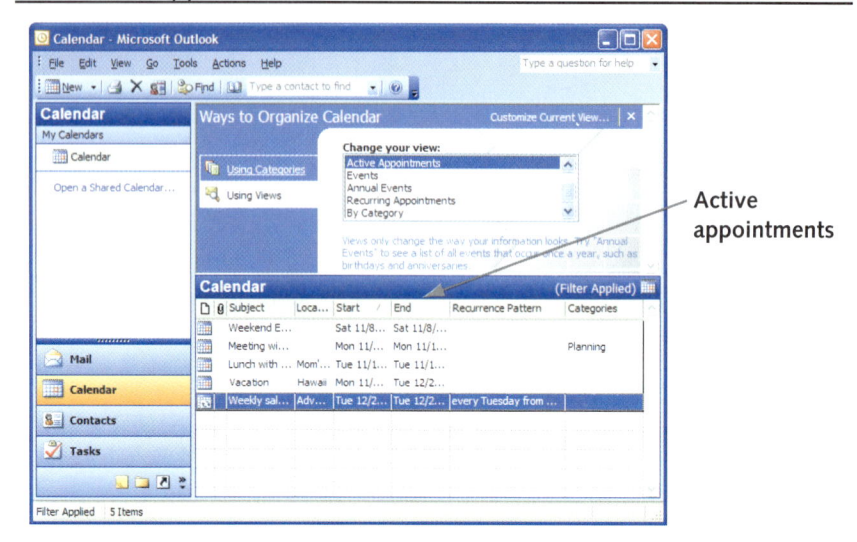

6 In the Change Your View list, click Day/Week/Month.

The view returns to the default Calendar view.

7 In the Tools menu, click the Organize option.

The Organize pane closes.

◆ Keep Outlook open for the next exercise.

QUICK CHECK

Q: What is the default view for Outlook's Calendar?

A: The Day/Week/Month arrangement is the default.

QUICK REFERENCE ▼

Display an arrangement

1 Open the Tools menu and click the Organize option.

2 Click Using Views in the Organize pane.

3 Select a view in the Change Your View list.

Planning Meetings

THE BOTTOM LINE

Planning meetings and gathering the participants into a single time and location can be difficult. Outlook's scheduling functions can help you match up available times, locations, and resources.

Scheduling Meetings

Arranging a time for a meeting can be difficult because you have to coordinate multiple schedules. You can play phone tag all day with your prospective meeting attendees, attempting to schedule them for a commonly available meeting time, or you can use the Outlook Calendar.

Sending a Meeting Request

Scheduling Meetings

When you set up a meeting in Outlook, you send each prospective attendee a meeting request. For each prospective attendee, you can specify that his or her attendance is required or optional. (If you specified that a particular attendee's attendance is required and he or she declines the invitation to attend the meeting, you need to reschedule it.) The meeting request is an e-mail message that tells people what the meeting is about, where it will be held, and when the meeting will take place.

> **IMPORTANT**
>
> In an Exchange Server environment, Outlook makes it easy to view co-workers' busy schedules and enable them to view your schedule. You can't see the actual appointments for other people on your network, but you can see the time periods that have been blocked off as busy for a particular employee. This approach helps to ensure that you have scheduled a meeting for a time that is available to all your prospective attendees. When you send your meeting requests via e-mail in this environment, you are more likely to receive acceptances from most or all of the prospective attendees.

Send a meeting request

To practice scheduling a meeting, you will create a meeting and invite your class partner to the meeting. In the next exercise you will respond to your partner's meeting request.

1 On the Date Navigator, click the last Monday of next month and click the 9:00 A.M. time slot.

The last Monday of next month is displayed in the Appointment Area.

2 On the Standard Calendar toolbar, click the down arrow to the right of the New Appointment button, and select the Meeting Request option.

The meeting window is displayed.

Figure 5-25

Meeting Request window

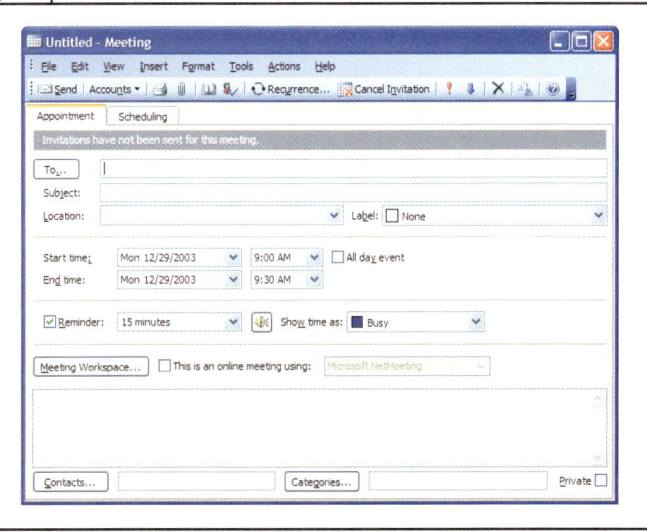

3 Click the To button.

The Select Attendees And Resources dialog box is displayed.

Figure 5-26

Select Attendees And Resources dialog box

TIP

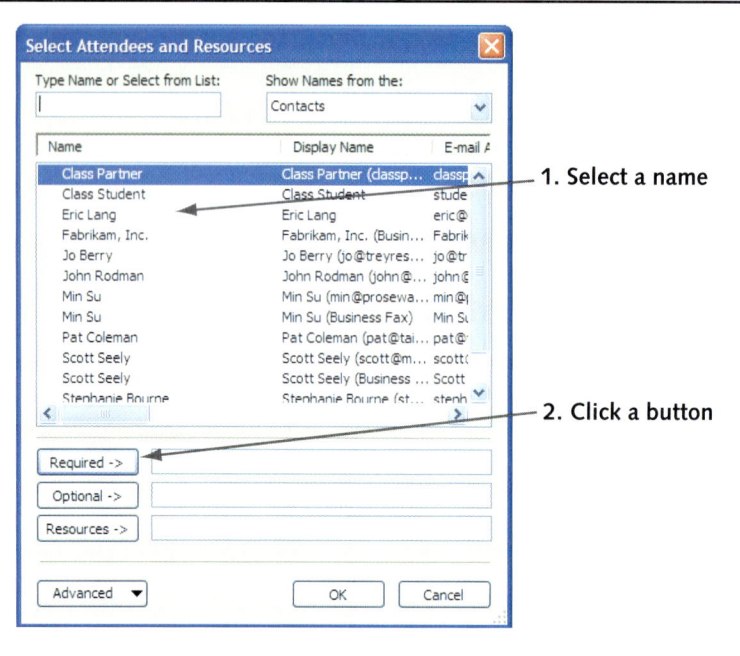

To invite attendees who are not required to attend a meeting, click the attendee and click the Optional button.

4 Select your class partner's name, click the Required button, and click OK.

The meeting window becomes active. Your class partner's name is now in the To box.

5 Click in the Subject box, type Client Review meeting, and press Tab.

The insertion point moves to the Location box.

6 In the Location box, type Conference Room 3.

The date, start time, and end time are already specified.

7 Click in the memo box and type I'm looking forward to discussing the project's requirements.

Lesson 5 Using the Calendar 167

Figure 5-27

Meeting request

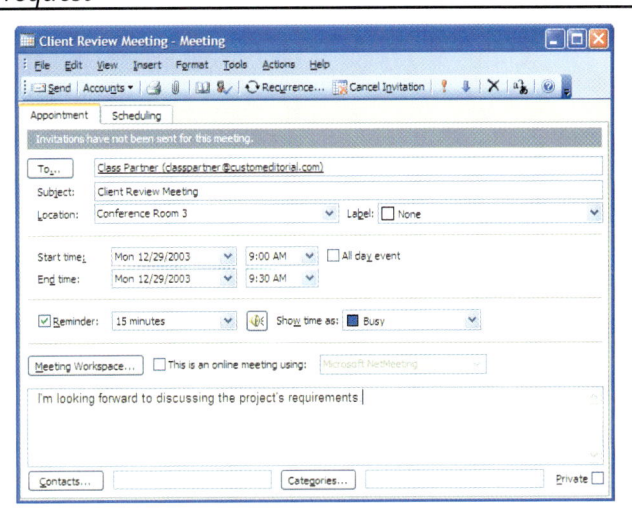

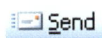

8 On the Standard toolbar in the meeting window, click the Send button.

The meeting request is sent to your class partner. The meeting is displayed in the Calendar with a bell icon (indicating that a reminder has been set) and an icon that resembles two heads (indicating that other people are invited to the meeting).

Figure 5-28

The meeting request has been sent

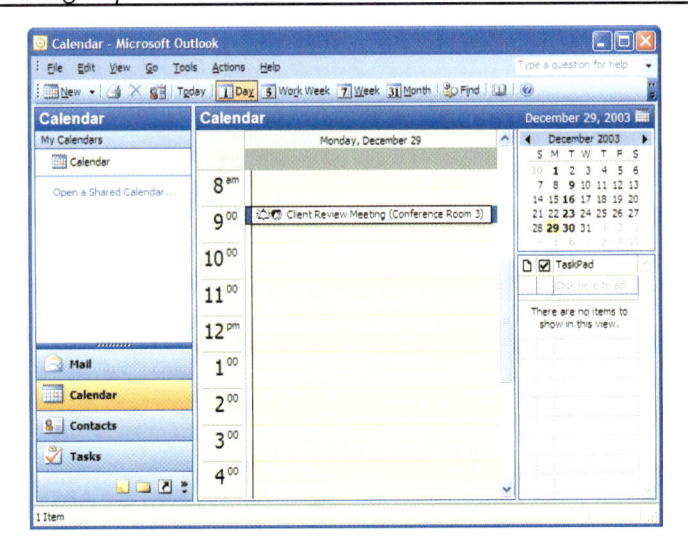

ANOTHER METHOD

If necessary, after a meeting has been set up in the Calendar, you can add and remove attendees. Double-click the meeting, open the Actions menu, and click Add Or Remove Attendees to display the Select Attendees And Resources dialog box. To delete an attendee, click the attendee in the Message Recipients list and press the Delete key. To add

> **ANOTHER METHOD (continued)**
>
> an attendee, click the attendee's name in the Name list and click the Required or Optional button. When you are finished, click OK and click the Save And Close button on the Standard toolbar. In the alert box, you can choose to send updates to attendees.

9 In the Appointment Area, click the meeting. On the Standard toolbar, click the Delete button.

An alert box is displayed, stating that attendees have not been notified that the meeting has been cancelled. You can either send a cancellation and delete the message or delete the meeting in your calendar without sending a cancellation.

10 Click the Delete without sending a cancellation option and click OK.

The meeting is deleted.

> **IMPORTANT**
>
> You deleted this message for training purposes. Normally, you would not delete a meeting you just organized (unless you made a mistake). You need to delete the meeting because you will receive a meeting request to attend this same meeting from your class partner. You need to have this time open so that Outlook will not find a scheduling conflict.

◆ Keep Outlook open for the next exercise.

QUICK REFERENCE ▼

Send a meeting request

1 On the Standard Calendar toolbar, click the down arrow to the right of the New Appointment button, and select the Meeting Request option.

2 Select the attendees and resources.

3 Identify the subject, location, and time of the meeting.

4 Click the Send button.

Responding to a Meeting Request

Responding to Meeting Requests

When somebody sends you a meeting request via e-mail, a message is displayed that includes buttons that you can use to accept, decline, tentatively accept the invitation, or propose a new time for the meeting. If you accept, the meeting is added to your calendar and an e-mail response accepting the invitation is sent to the meeting organizer. If you decline, you can choose to decline with or without a response. For example, you might want to decline, but let the person who sent the meeting request know when you are available. If you select the Tentative option, the meeting is added to your calendar, but your time for the meeting is classified as tentatively scheduled. Select the Tentative response if you think you can attend the meeting, but something more important may require your attention at that time.

Lesson 5 Using the Calendar 169

The last option for responding to a meeting request is Propose New Time. Select this option if you can't meet at the time selected by the sender requesting the meeting, but you can attend at a different time or date. For example, a co-worker requests a meeting for 1:00 PM tomorrow. However, you have a lunch meeting scheduled that you think could run a little long. Send a response to the meeting request that proposes the new meeting time of 2:00 PM.

Respond to a meeting request

In this exercise, you receive a meeting request from your class partner and propose a new time for the meeting.

1 Open the Go menu and click Mail. If necessary, click the Inbox in the Navigation pane.

The contents of the Inbox are displayed.

2 On the Standard Mail toolbar, click the Send/Receive button.

A meeting request from your class partner arrives in the Inbox.

3 Click the meeting request.

The meeting request opens in the Reading pane.

Figure 5-29

The meeting request has been received

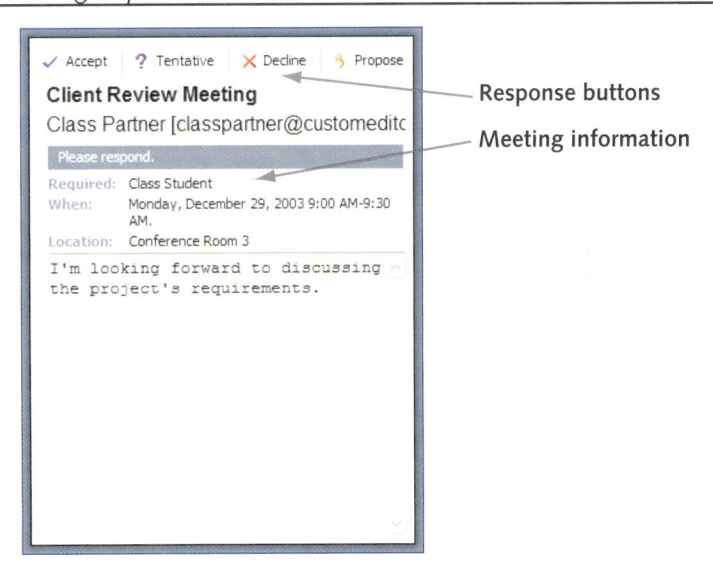

4 On the message, click the Propose button.

The Propose New Time dialog box is displayed.

TROUBLESHOOTING

A dialog box inviting you to join a Microsoft service that enables you to view calendars for other members may be displayed. Click Cancel in the dialog box to continue.

Figure 5-30

Propose New Time dialog box

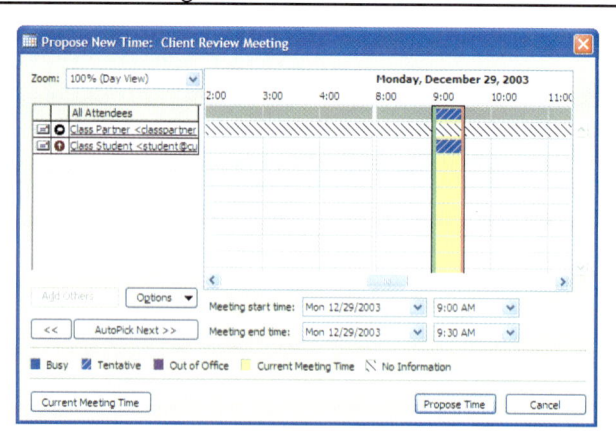

5. **Drag the borders of the current meeting time to the right to propose the new time of 10:00 A.M. to 10:30 A.M. Click the Propose Time button.**

   An e-mail response is created. It contains the current time and the proposed time. You can add text to the body of the e-mail.

Figure 5-31

New time proposed for meeting

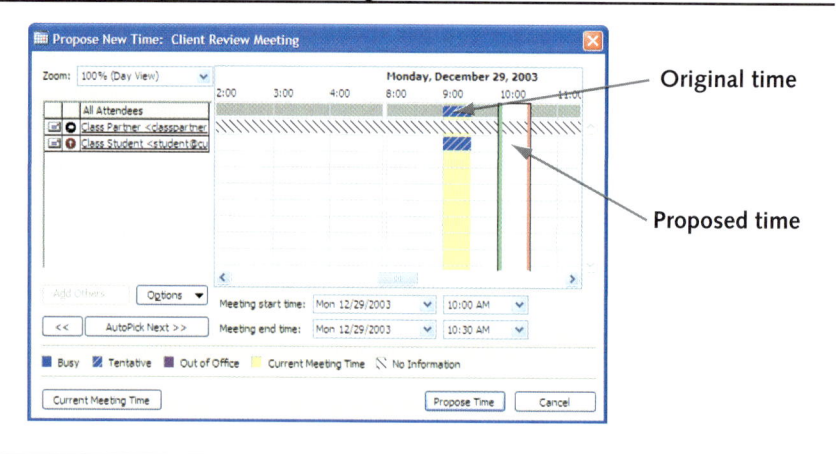

TROUBLESHOOTING

If you had accepted the meeting, your class partner would have received an e-mail with the subject Accepted: Client Review meeting. The meeting would be scheduled in your calendar.

6. **On the Message toolbar, click the Send button.**

   The e-mail containing the proposed time is sent to your class partner. Your response is considered to be a "tentative acceptance." Your class partner is responsible for rescheduling the meeting and sending a new meeting request.

Figure 5-32

Message proposing a new time for meeting

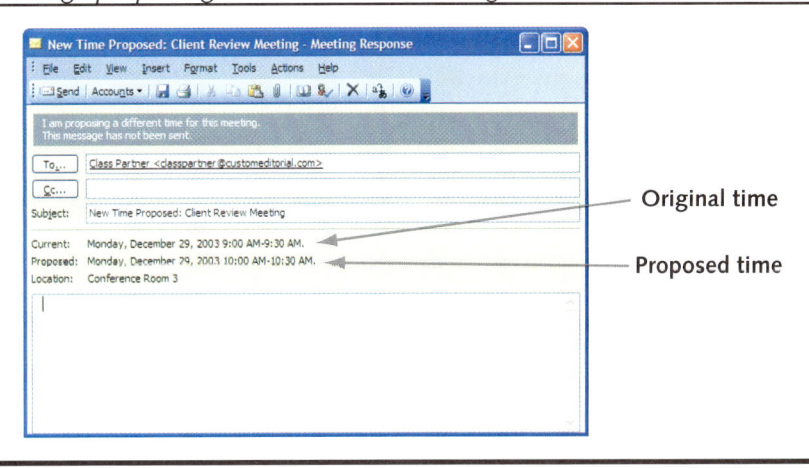

— Original time
— Proposed time

◆ Keep Outlook open for the next exercise.

QUICK REFERENCE ▼

Respond to a meeting request

1. In the Inbox, click the meeting request.
2. On the meeting request, click a button to accept, decline, or propose a new time.
3. If you propose a new time, drag the borders to the new time and click Propose Time. If you accept or decline the meeting, indicate in the alert box if you wish to include comments with your response.
4. Click the Send button.

Reserving Meeting Resources

Scheduling Meetings

In addition to inviting people to meetings, you can schedule resources, such as conference rooms, flip charts, or computers. For example, when the office manager at Adventure Works scheduled the budget review meeting for the president, she booked a large conference room and an overhead projector through Outlook.

To schedule a resource, the resource must have its own mailbox on your server. One person, usually the office manager, sets up and administers the mailbox for the resource. The resource is self-sufficient because it automatically accepts and rejects invitations. For example, if you attempt to reserve a conference room for a particular time period but somebody has already reserved the conference room, your meeting request will be rejected for the conference room resource.

To reserve a resource, invite it to the meeting, just as you would invite a person. In the Select Attendees And Resources dialog box, click the resource, and click the Resources button. The resource is added to your message list. If the resource you scheduled is free, the meeting is automatically entered in the resource's calendar so that no one else can reserve the same resource at the same time.

172 **Lesson 5** Using the Calendar

QUICK CHECK

Q: Why would you invite a conference room to a meeting?

A: **It reserves the resource for the meeting.**

QUICK REFERENCE ▼

Reserve meeting resources

1 On the Standard Calendar toolbar, click the down arrow to the right of the New Appointment button, and select the Meeting Request option.

2 Select the resources.

3 Identify the subject, location, and time of the meeting.

4 Click the Send button.

Printing Calendars

Printing Calendars

THE BOTTOM LINE

Print a calendar to take with you or distribute to others who can't access your schedule electronically.

Many people who use Outlook as their scheduling tool like to take a printed copy of their schedule with them when they leave their desk or their office. As you might expect, Outlook provides several printing options for your Calendar. Specifically, you can print different views of the Calendar, such as a daily, weekly, or monthly view. Use the Print dialog box to specify the range of days and style that you want to print. The Print dialog box includes five styles:

- Daily—The days that you specify will be printed. The printout contains one day per page.
- Weekly—The weeks that you specify will be printed. The printout contains one week per page.
- Monthly—The months that you specify will be printed. The printout contains one month per page.
- Tri-fold—The printout is divided into three columns. The first column contains a day view. The second column is the TaskPad. The third column is a week view.
- Calendar Details—Appointments, meetings, and events scheduled in the Calendar are described and listed under the day they occur.

The events coordinator at Adventure Works likes to attach a printout of a calendar in the Monthly Style to her newsletter. The calendar notifies readers of upcoming events at the resort.

Print a calendar

Sometimes, after you create appointments in your calendar, you need a printed copy of your schedule. In this exercise, you specify print options and print a two-month calendar in the Monthly Style.

1 **On the Standard Calendar toolbar, click the Print button.**

The Print dialog box is displayed.

Figure 5-33

Print dialog box

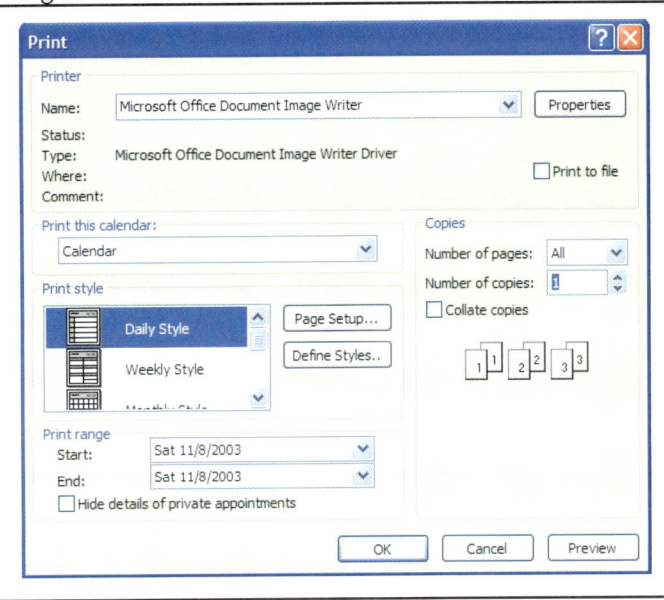

QUICK CHECK

Q: Can you print a calendar for a specific day?

A: You can specify the time period before you print a calendar.

2 In the Print Style section, click Monthly Style. In the Print Range section, click the Start down arrow.

A mini-calendar is displayed.

3 Click the first day of this month. Also in the Print Range section, click the End down arrow.

A mini-calendar is displayed.

4 Click the last day of next month and click OK.

The Print dialog box closes and a two-month calendar prints in the Monthly Style.

ANOTHER METHOD

You can also print the Calendar in a Day-Timer or a Franklin Day Planner format. In the Print dialog box, click the Page Setup button, click the Paper tab, and select the desired page size in the Size list.

◆ Keep Outlook open for the next exercise.

QUICK REFERENCE ▼

Print a calendar

1 On the Standard Calendar toolbar, click the Print button.

2 Select the printing options.

3 Click OK.

174 **Lesson 5** Using the Calendar

Saving a Calendar as a Web Page

Saving a Calendar as a Web Page

THE BOTTOM LINE

With Outlook you can create a calendar that can be viewed by others on the Internet or your intranet.

Save your calendar as a Web page so people can access your calendar via the Internet or a company intranet. When you save a calendar as a Web page, Outlook converts the calendar to HTML (Hypertext Markup Language) format. HTML is the formatting language that all Web browsers (such as Microsoft Internet Explorer) use to display text and graphics. A calendar can be placed on a Web site or it can remain in a file that others can download for later access. When you save a calendar as a Web page, you can specify the calendar time frame that you want to share, include appointment details, or add a background.

For example, the events coordinator at Adventure Works used to attach a copy of the monthly events calendar to the employee newsletter. However, after the company's intranet was established, she began to post the calendar to the company's Web site.

Save your Calendar

With a calendar created, you will now save your Calendar as a Web page.

1 On the File menu, click Save As Web Page.

The Save As Web Page dialog box is displayed.

2 In the Duration section, click the Start Date down arrow and click the first day of the current month. Click the End Date down arrow and click the last day of the current month.

This selects the time period for the calendar. Only the current month will be saved.

3 In the Calendar Title box, type your name (if necessary), press the spacebar, and type Class Calendar.

4 Click the Browse button.

The Calendar File Name dialog box is displayed.

5 Click the Save In down arrow, and navigate to the Outlook Practice folder.

You will store the calendar in this directory.

6 In the File Name box, type MyClassCalendar.

The HTML file will be named MyClassCalendar. Commonly, the name of the file may include your name and the time period covered by the calendar.

CHECK THIS OUT ▼

Sending Schedules
You can save a schedule as a Web page so you can send it as an attachment to a message.

IMPORTANT

Do not include any spaces when you name a Web page file. If the name of the file is part of a Web address (such as www.calendars.microsoft.com/MyClassCalendar.htm), the space will not be recognized and the file can't be viewed on the Web.

Lesson 5 Using the Calendar 175

7 **Click the Select button.**

The Save As Web Page dialog box becomes active.

Figure 5-34

Save As Web Page dialog box

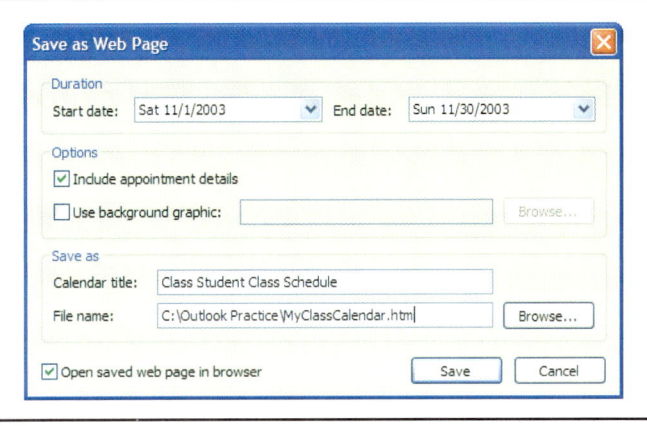

IMPORTANT

If Internet Explorer does not automatically display the Web calendar, you can manually open the calendar through Windows Explorer. Display Windows Explorer. Navigate to the location you selected to store the files. Many files were created as a result of saving the Web calendar. Double-click the main HTML file. Internet Explorer opens and displays the Web calendar.

8 **Click the Save button.**

The calendar is saved as a Web page that can be displayed in Internet Explorer. By default, the Web page is displayed immediately.

Figure 5-35

Calendar displayed as a Web page

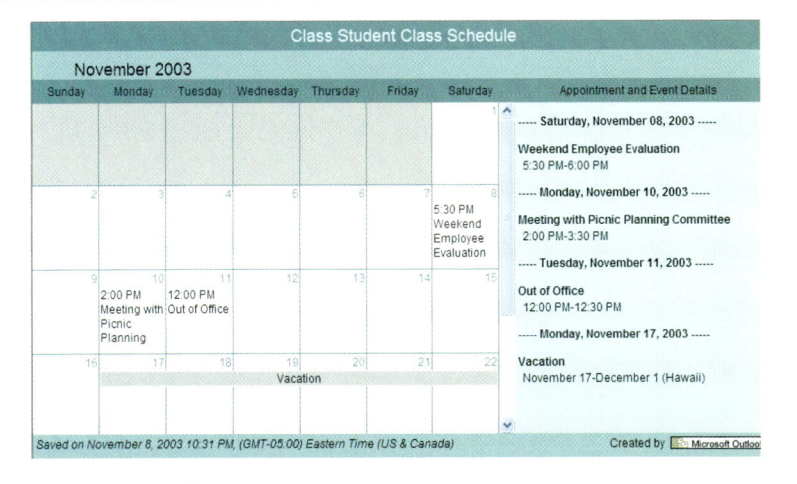

9 **In the top-right corner of the Internet Explorer window, click the Close button.**

QUICK CHECK

Q: In what format is a calendar saved to become a Web page?

A: **The calendar is saved in HTML format.**

QUICK REFERENCE ▼

Save a calendar as a Web page

1 On the File menu, click Save As Web Page.
2 Select the time period and enter a name for the Web page.
3 Select the file destination.
4 Save the file.

Integrating the Calendar with Other Outlook Components

Creating and Updating Tasks

THE BOTTOM LINE

Outlook's TaskPad lets you create tasks, keep track of their progress, and mark when they are complete.

The Calendar includes the Appointment Area, Date Navigator, and TaskPad. Use the Appointment Area and the Date Navigator to schedule appointments and meetings. Use the TaskPad to enter task descriptions, such as creating a weekly status report or listing phone calls that you need to make. Each row on the TaskPad indicates a separate task. The tasks in Calendar are also displayed in the Outlook Tasks folder, which you can access by clicking the Tasks button on the Navigation pane.

Create and complete a task

In this exercise, you create a task and mark it as completed.

1 In the TaskPad, click in the box that contains the text Click Here To Add A New Task.

The text is replaced with a blank line and an insertion point.

2 Type Call park about picnic and press Enter.

The task *Call park about picnic* is displayed in the task list.

Lesson 5 Using the Calendar 177

Figure 5-36

Task list

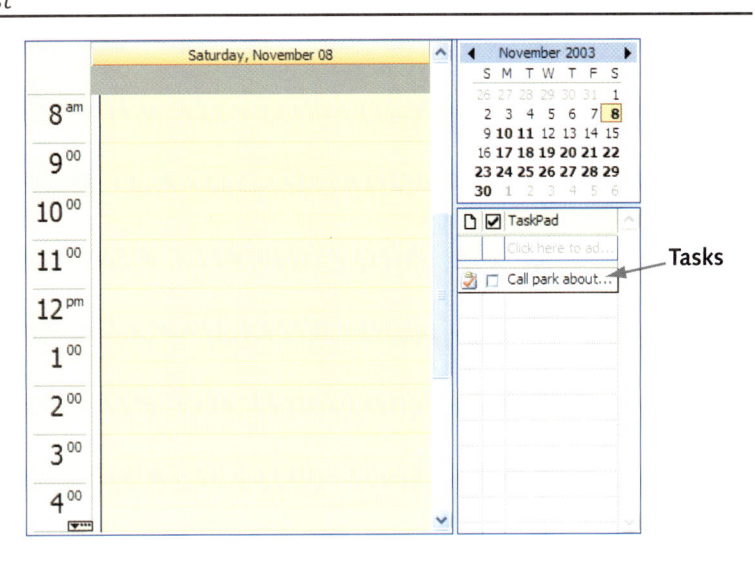

[Calendar view screenshot showing Saturday, November 08 with TaskPad on the right displaying "Call park about..." task — labeled Tasks]

3 **On the Navigation pane, click the Tasks button.**

The contents of the Tasks folder are displayed. The task *Call park about picnic* is displayed in the task list.

Figure 5-37

Tasks folder

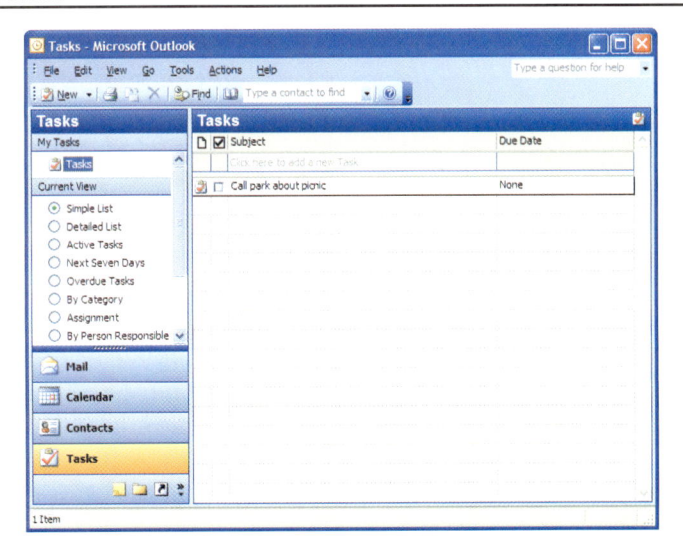

[Screenshot of Tasks - Microsoft Outlook window showing the Tasks folder with "Call park about picnic" task]

Figure 5-38

Task completed in the Calendar folder

[Screenshot of TaskPad showing "Call park about..." with strikeout]

4 **On the Navigation pane, click the Calendar button.**

The contents of the Calendar folder are displayed.

5 **In the TaskPad, select the check box to the left of the task.**

A check is displayed in the check box and the task has a strikeout line through it, as shown in Figure 5-38.

178 Lesson 5 Using the Calendar

6 On the Navigation pane, click the Tasks button.

The contents of the Tasks folder are displayed. The task *Call park about picnic* also has a line through it.

QUICK CHECK

Q: Can you mark a task as completed in the Calendar folder?

A: Yes, a task can be completed in the Calendar folder.

ANOTHER METHOD

Create a task in the Tasks folder and view it in the Calendar's TaskPad.

- On the Navigation pane, click the Calendar button.
- If you are continuing to the next lesson, Keep Outlook open.
- If you are not continuing to the next lesson, close Outlook..

QUICK REFERENCE ▼
Create and complete a task

1 In the TaskPad, click in the box that contains the text Click Here To Add A New Task.

2 Type the task and press Enter.

3 In the TaskPad, select the check box to the left of the task.

4 Save the file.

Key Points

- ✓ In Outlook, you can navigate through the Calendar, change views, and create and edit appointments and events.
- ✓ You can create recurring appointments and meetings as well as set reminders to yourself.
- ✓ Appointments and meetings can be organized by category and views.
- ✓ Through Outlook you can plan meetings with others and send meeting invitations by e-mail.
- ✓ Outlook lets you print a calendar and save the calendar as a Web page.
- ✓ The task list lets you keep track of items which you need to complete. As you accomplish the tasks you can mark them as complete.

Quick Quiz

True/False

T F 1. All tasks must be created in the Tasks folder.

T F 2. Appointments cannot be assigned to a category.

T F 3. Calendars can only be distributed to others by printing.

T F 4. The Date Navigator enables you to view a date six months in the future.

T F 5. Recurring appoints must be scheduled for the same day every week.

Multiple Choice

1. To view a different date, use the _____.
   a. Navigation pane
   b. Date Navigator
   c. TaskPad
   d. All of the above

2. Propose a new meeting time _____.
   a. every time you receive a meeting request
   b. by clicking the Accept button
   c. by clicking the Propose button in a meeting request
   d. All of the above

3. The Calendar enables you to _____.
   a. plan meetings
   b. set recurring appointments
   c. schedule appointments
   d. All of the above

4. A(n) _____ is a function that usually makes you unavailable for the entire day or for multiple days.
   a. recurring appointment
   b. meeting
   c. event
   d. appointment

5. Organize your calendar by _____.
   a. assigning appointments to categories
   b. saving it as a Web page
   c. printing it
   d. All of the above

Short Answer

1. How do you invite others to a meeting?
2. What is the Appointment Area?
3. Time slots in the Calendar are divided into what increment of time?
4. Can you change the Work Week view to include days other than Monday through Friday?
5. What is the Date Navigator?
6. In what styles can you print a calendar?
7. What are two ways you can view a calendar?
8. What is a recurring appointment?
9. How can you tell that you will be reminded of a meeting?
10. In addition to printing your calendar, how can you make it accessible to others?

On Your Own

Exercise 1

The marketing director at Adventure Works wants to get her team on board for the new ad campaign. She wants to schedule a weekly team meeting on Fridays from 10:00 A.M. until noon in Conference Room 2 for the next four months. At the meeting, they will discuss the progress and status of the ad campaign project. Schedule this as a meeting, invite any member of your class to attend, and indicate that this class member's attendance is required.

Exercise 2

The marketing director will be taking a vacation to Tahiti after the ad campaign project is underway—five months from now. She wants anyone who looks at her schedule to know that she is out of the office for the two weeks she is in Tahiti. Schedule this event for a two-week period five months from now.

One Step Further

Exercise 1

You have been placed in charge of the company picnic. Make a list of tasks you must perform before the picnic. Mark three of the tasks as completed.

Exercise 2

Your company recently announced a new intranet. Your supervisor requests that everyone in her department place their calendars on the intranet. Prepare your calendar and save it as a Web page.

Exercise 3

You will be conducting interviews for a new receptionist. Schedule the following appointments.

Monday	8:30 A.M.	Aaron Con
Monday	10:00 A.M.	Jim Hance
Tuesday	1:00 P.M.	Britta Simon
Tuesday	2:30 P.M.	Debra E. Keiser
Wednesday	9:00 A.M.	Bradley Beck

LESSON 6

Using Tasks

After completing this lesson, you will be able to:

✔ Create tasks in Outlook.
✔ Change the task view.
✔ Add task details.
✔ Sort tasks.
✔ Print a task list
✔ Organize tasks by using folders.
✔ Organize tasks by using categories.
✔ Assign tasks to others.
✔ Accept or decline tasks.
✔ Mark tasks as complete.
✔ Manually record a task in the Journal.
✔ Delete tasks.

KEY TERMS

- Journal
- owner
- ownership
- task
- task list
- Tasks folder

Sometimes, a project can be so big that it seems overwhelming. It can become difficult to keep track of everything you have to do each day. A to-do list is a great way to manage big projects and your daily activities. Seeing a list of the things you have to do helps you organize and prioritize more efficiently. Breaking a large project into smaller tasks makes it seem more manageable and ensures that you won't forget a critical step. Also, checking off the items creates a sense of accomplishment. For example, the marketing director at Adventure Works creates a daily list of things to do based on her current activities, special projects, and obligations to friends, family, and business associates.

The Microsoft Office Outlook 2003 task list provides a place for you to record a to-do list or track tasks required to complete a project. In Lesson 5, you saw the TaskPad that appears in the Calendar. When you make entries in the Calendar TaskPad, the entries are also recorded in the task list, which provides several options for organizing and viewing tasks that are not available in the Calendar TaskPad.

In this lesson, you will learn how to enter a **task**—a personal or work item to be completed. You will add details to a task, mark tasks as complete, and delete a task in the **Tasks folder**. You will sort and organize tasks by using folders and categories. Finally, you will learn how to assign tasks to others, accept or decline tasks assigned to you, mark tasks as complete, and manually record a task in the Journal.

> **IMPORTANT**
>
> To complete some of the exercises in this lesson, you will need to exchange e-mail messages with a class partner. If you don't have a class partner or you are performing the exercises alone, you can send the message to yourself. Simply enter your own e-mail address instead of a class partner's address.

Creating Tasks

> **THE BOTTOM LINE**
>
> With Outlook you can create a task list that can keep you on-track in completing any project.

Creating and Updating Tasks

Tasks can be as basic as a to-do list of personal errands, such as grocery shopping, picking the kids up at baseball practice, and going to doctor appointments. They can also be as elaborate as a list of milestones that need to be completed during a lengthy or complex work project. Breaking down a project into tasks helps you keep track of items that are accomplished and items that still need attention.

To create a **task list**, identify your priorities. Decide exactly what needs to be done and know the dates the task items are due. Some tasks are more important than others. If possible, the most important tasks should be completed first. Sometimes, the most difficult part of a task is deciding how to break it into smaller, more manageable steps or additional and more specific tasks. Finally, you can assign a due date. Although you do not need to give a task a due date, a due date keeps tasks in order and keeps you aware of deadlines.

Click the Tasks button on the Navigation pane to display the task list in the default view, called Simple List. The task list is divided into Subject and Due Date columns. Tasks that are overdue are displayed in red; tasks that you have completed appear with a strikeout line through them.

Lesson 6 Using Tasks 183

Figure 6-1

Outlook Tasks window

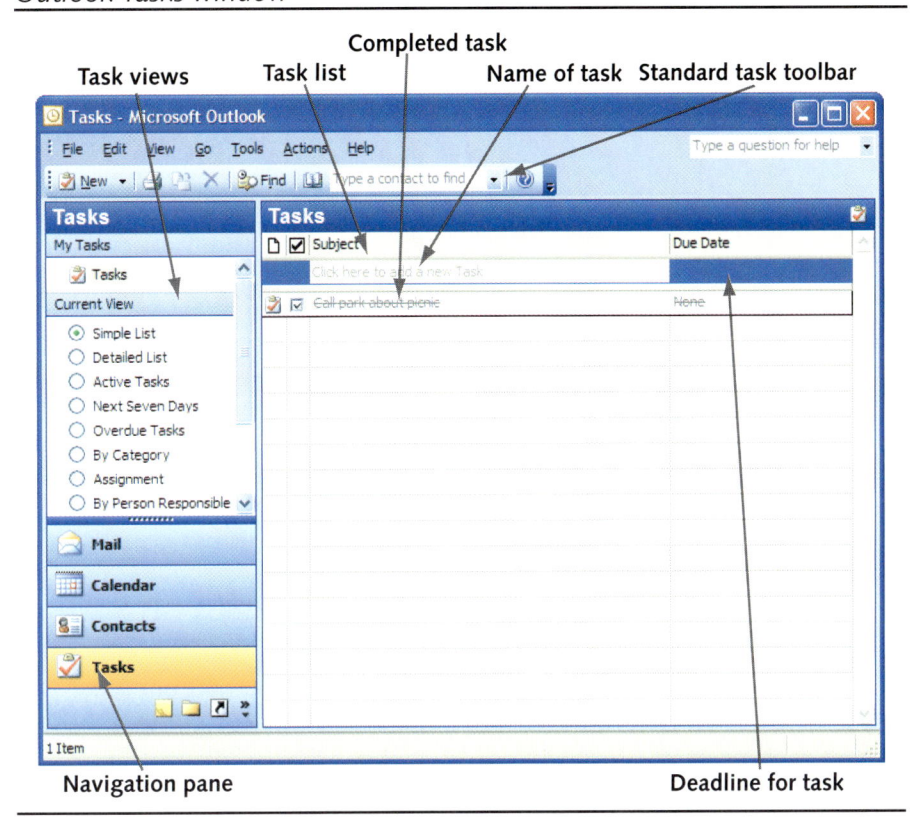

[Screenshot of Outlook Tasks window with labels: Task views, Task list, Completed task, Name of task, Standard task toolbar, Navigation pane, Deadline for task]

You can create a task in one of four ways—click the New Task button on the standard toolbar, type in the TaskPad window in the Calendar, type a task in the task list, or drag an item to the Tasks button on the Navigation pane.

◆ Be sure to start Outlook before you begin exercise.

Create tasks

We will begin the exercises in this lesson by creating four tasks using the task list.

1 On the Navigation pane, click the Tasks button.

The contents of the task folder are displayed.

2 Click in the box that contains the text "Click here to add a new Task." Type Call band to check availability for the picnic.

This will become the name of the task.

3 To the right of the task that you just created, click in the Due Date column.

The insertion point and a down arrow are displayed in the Due Date column.

TIP

To access other months, click the arrows to the right and left of the month.

184 **Lesson 6** Using Tasks

4 **Click the down arrow to display the mini-calendar.**

The current month and year are displayed and today's date is shaded.

5 **Click the Today button.**

Today's date is entered in the Due Date column.

6 **Press Enter.**

The new task is placed in the task list. The insertion point remains in the first row of the Subject column to add more tasks.

7 **Type** Make a dentist appointment for Emily. **Press Enter.**

The new task is placed in the task list and the insertion point remains in the first row of the Subject column. A due date is not assigned.

8 **Type** Call Cherry Creek Park to reserve sheltered picnic area. **To the right of the task, click in the Due Date column.**

The insertion point and a down arrow are displayed in the Due Date column.

9 **Click the down arrow to display the mini-calendar. Click the date four days from today. Press Enter.**

The date four days from today is placed in the Due Date column. The new task is placed in the task list and the insertion point remains in the first row of the Subject column.

10 **Type** Complete the Outlook class. **Press Enter.**

The new task is placed in the task list.

Figure 6-2

Tasks added to the task list

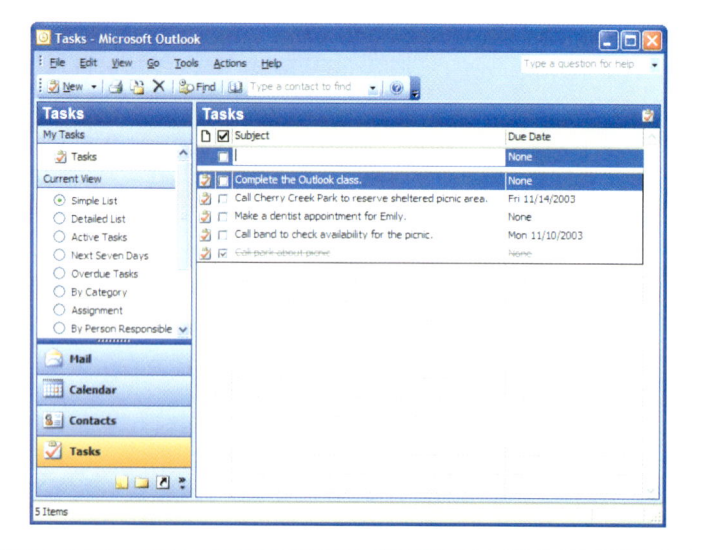

ANOTHER METHOD

Drag an item to the Tasks button on the Navigation pane.

Lesson 6 Using Tasks 185

QUICK CHECK

Q: How do you know that a task is overdue?

A: An overdue task is displayed in red.

◆ Keep Outlook open for the next exercise.

QUICK REFERENCE ▼

Create a task

1. On the Navigation pane, click the Tasks button.
2. Click in the box that contains the text "Click here to add a new Task."
3. Enter the name of the task.
4. Optionally, enter additional details.
5. Press Enter.

Changing Task Views

Organizing Tasks

THE BOTTOM LINE

When you use different views of your tasks it can help you focus your priorities.

As you learned in previous lessons, when you change the view of a folder, new criteria determine how items are displayed. The same is true for the task list. Different views can present your tasks in greater or more meaningful detail. For example, you might want to display only tasks that are due on a specific day. In the past, you had to use the View menu to change the view of the task list. The Navigation pane has streamlined this into a single click.

When you change the task list view, different columns are displayed. This makes it an excellent organization tool. Focus on tasks due today or this week. Improve your long-term planning by increasing your awareness of upcoming due dates.

You can change details about a task by clicking the appropriate column. If you click in the Importance, Due Date, Date Complete, or Status column, a down arrow is displayed. Click the down arrow to display a list of available options.

Change the task view

Continuing to work with the tasks we entered in the previous exercise, you will change the view of the task list several times.

1. **Click the Detailed List option in the Current View area of the Navigation pane.**

   This view contains information about the status, percent complete, and categories for each task.

186   **Lesson 6**   Using Tasks

Figure 6-3

Detailed task list contains additional information

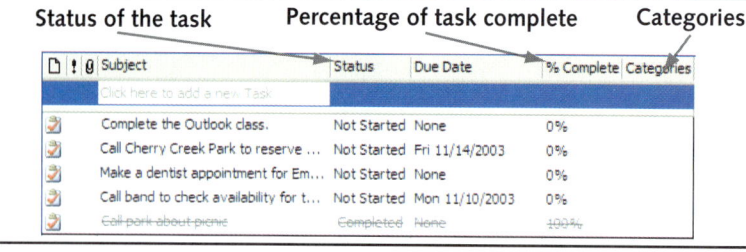

Status of the task   Percentage of task complete   Categories

2 Click the Next Seven Days option in the Current View area of the Navigation pane.

This view contains information about tasks that are due in the next seven days. Because this view applies a filter, tasks without a due date are not displayed.

Figure 6-4

Tasks due in the next seven days

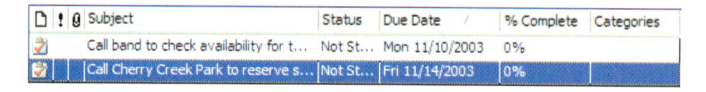

3 Click the Task Timeline option in the Current View area of the Navigation pane.

This view contains a unique look at the task list. Again, tasks without a due date are not displayed.

TROUBLESHOOTING

You might need to scroll to view both items.

Figure 6-5

Task timeline view

◆ Return to the Detailed List view for the next exercise.

ANOTHER METHOD

Open the View menu, point at Arrange By, point at Current View, and click one of the available views.

QUICK REFERENCE ▼

Change the task view

Click one of the view options in the Navigation pane.

QUICK CHECK

Q: Why is selecting a different view a good organization tool?

A: It enables you to focus on different columns of information.

Adding Task Details

Creating and Updating Tasks

THE BOTTOM LINE

When you include details such as due dates, status, and percent complete it can help you view and organize your task list in ways that will help you achieve your goals.

Often the Simple List view for the task list does not show all the columns you need for adding information about a more complicated task. For example, the marketing director at Adventure Works set up a task to create a project plan for the upcoming advertising campaign. Because this task is crucial to the project, it has a high priority and a definite due date. The marketing director created the task, assigned the task a high priority flag, assigned a due date, and assigned the task to a category.

When you want to add several details to a task, it's often easiest to use the task window or switch to the Detailed List view. The task window has two tabs—Task and Details. Most of the information that is displayed in the task list is on the Task tab. The Details tab contains boxes to add information regarding the actual hours of work needed to complete a task, data about mileage and billing, and information regarding any companies involved with the task.

Figure 6-6

Task window

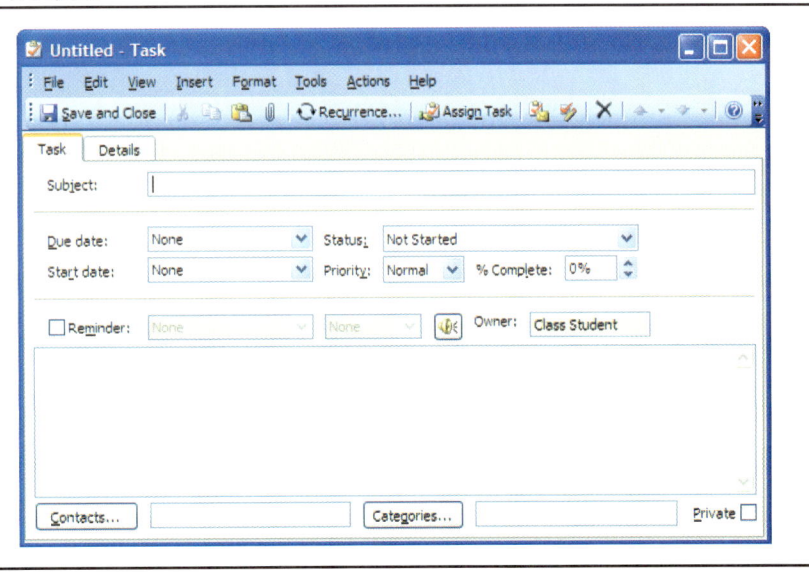

The task window is displayed when you double-click a task or click the New Task button. In the task window, the boxes on the Task tab correspond to the column headings displayed in the different task list views. The options you select in these boxes or the information you enter can be used as criteria for organizing your tasks. Some of the options on the Task tab are described in the following table.

188 Lesson 6 Using Tasks

Box/Button	Description
Subject	The text of the task is the Subject. You can change the task by editing it here.
Due date	Specify a deadline for completing the task.
Start date	Set a date for beginning the task.
Status	Mark a task's progress as Not Started, In Progress, Completed, Waiting On Someone Else, or Deferred.
Priority	Set the importance of the task to Low, Normal, or High.
% Complete	Indicate the amount of work done on a task. Enter any percentage from 0% to 100%. The task status changes to reflect the percentage.
Reminder	Identify the length of time between the reminder and the due date. If you don't want to be reminded, clear the Reminder check box. Click the appropriate down arrows to display a list of dates or times.
Owner	Identify the person responsible for the task. By default, the task creator is the task owner.
memo area	Use the text area at the bottom of the window to record notes or additional reminders.
Contacts	Click this button to display the Select Names dialog box and select contacts that you can link to this task.
Categories	Click this button to display the Categories dialog box and assign the task to a category.
Private	By selecting this check box, you can hide this task so others who have access to your schedule cannot see it.

> **TIP**
>
> Outlook understands natural language in most date boxes. For instance, in the Due Date or Start Date box, you can type *yesterday* to display yesterday's date, type *next Monday* to display next Monday's date, or type *one week from today* to display the date seven days from the current date. Be specific. If you type a vague expression like *soon* or *ASAP*, Outlook displays an error message. You can also enter a natural-language date in the Due Date column of the task list.

Add details to a task

Continuing to work with tasks, you now change the task view, create a new task with details, and add information to an existing task.

1 **Click the New Task button.**

The task window is displayed. The insertion point is already placed in the Subject box.

> **ANOTHER METHOD**
>
> You can also press Ctrl+N to display a new task window.

2 **In the Subject box, type Call Jen to arrange a birthday dinner for Dad.**

This becomes the name of the task.

3 **Click the Due Date down arrow.**

A mini-calendar is displayed.

4 **Click the date two days from today.**

The selected date is displayed in the Due Date box.

5 **Click the Status down arrow and click In Progress.**

In Progress is displayed in the Status box.

6 **Click the Priority down arrow and click High.**

High is displayed in the Priority box.

Figure 6-7

Task window with information

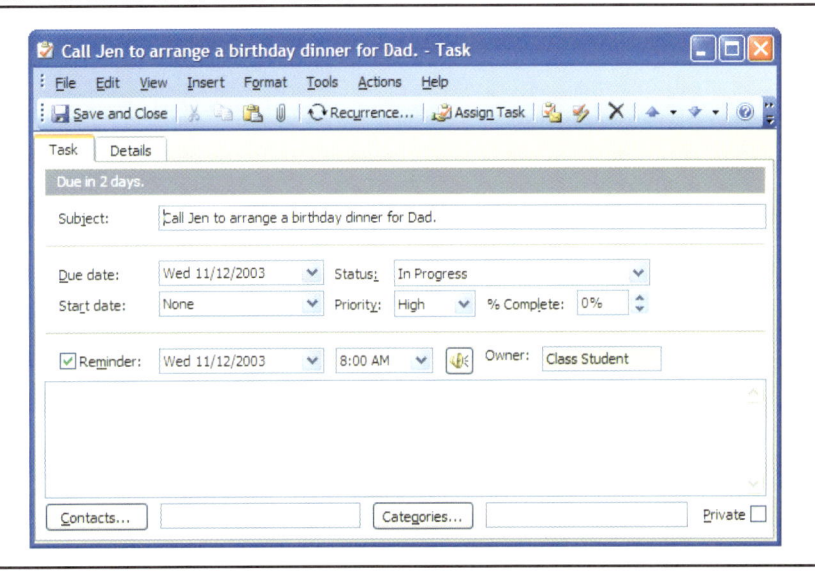

7 **On the Standard toolbar in the task window, click the Save And Close button.**

The task window closes, and the task is placed in the task list. Notice that an exclamation point appears in the Priority column, indicating that the task is high priority.

8 **Double-click the task "Call Cherry Creek Park to reserve sheltered picnic area."**

A task window is displayed. A note at the top of the task window indicates that the task is due in four days. The Subject box already contains the text you entered in the previous exercise.

9 **Click the Start Date down arrow and click tomorrow's date.**

Tomorrow's date is displayed in the Start Date box.

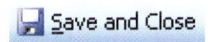

10 **On the Standard toolbar in the task window, click the Save And Close button.**

The task is updated.

11 **Click the Active Tasks view on the Navigation pane.**

The updated information is displayed.

Figure 6-8

Active Tasks view with updated information

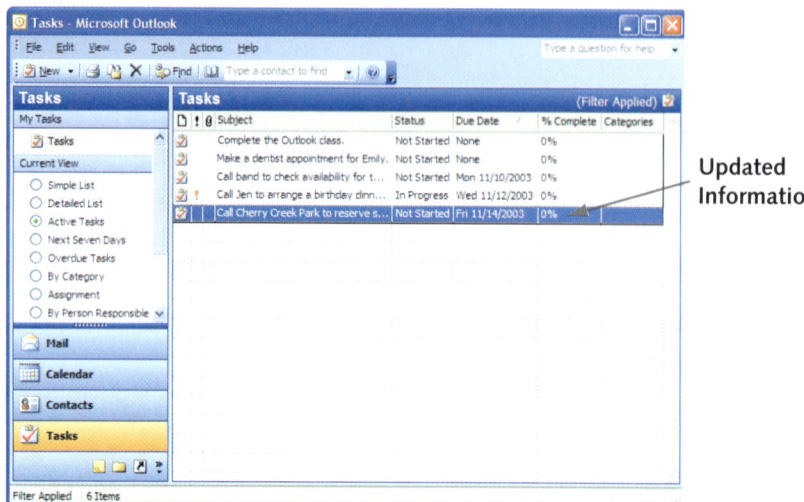

▶ Keep Outlook open for the next exercise.

QUICK CHECK

Q: What are the possible entries for the status of a task?

A: A task can be Not Started, In Progress, Completed, Waiting On Someone Else, or Deferred.

QUICK REFERENCE ▼

Add details to a task

1. Create a task or double-click an existing task.
2. Add new details to the task information.
3. Click the Save And Close button.

Sorting Tasks

THE BOTTOM LINE

In Outlook you can sort tasks when you focus on one or two characteristics of your tasks to select a sort sequence.

Organizing Tasks

You can sort tasks by a field in the task list, such as Status, Priority, or Due Date. For example, the marketing director at Adventure Works sorted her task list for the ad campaign by Due Date so she could plan her upcoming deadlines.

To sort the task list, click a column heading. The task list is sorted according to the contents of that column. Click the same column heading a second time to reverse the sort order. For example, if you click the Subject column heading, Outlook sorts tasks alphabetically from Z to A. If you click the Subject column heading again, Outlook sorts tasks alphabetically from A to Z.

Figure 6-9

Tasks sorted in alphabetic order

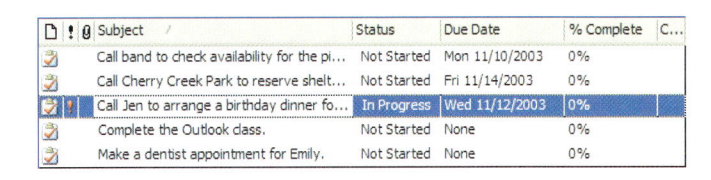

D	!	0	Subject	Status	Due Date	% Complete	C...
			Call band to check availability for the pi...	Not Started	Mon 11/10/2003	0%	
			Call Cherry Creek Park to reserve shelt...	Not Started	Fri 11/14/2003	0%	
	!		Call Jen to arrange a birthday dinner fo...	In Progress	Wed 11/12/2003	0%	
			Complete the Outlook class.	Not Started	None	0%	
			Make a dentist appointment for Emily.	Not Started	None	0%	

Figure 6-10

Tasks sorted in reverse alphabetic order

D	!	0	Subject	Status	Due Date	% Complete	C...
			Make a dentist appointment for Emily.	Not Started	None	0%	
			Complete the Outlook class.	Not Started	None	0%	
	!		Call Jen to arrange a birthday dinner fo...	In Progress	Wed 11/12/2003	0%	
			Call Cherry Creek Park to reserve shelt...	Not Started	Fri 11/14/2003	0%	
			Call band to check availability for the pi...	Not Started	Mon 11/10/2003	0%	

To quickly add or change a due date in the task list, click the task's Due Date box and click the down arrow that appears to the right of the column. Click a date or click the Today button to choose the current date.

Sort tasks

To practice sorting, in this exercise, you sort tasks by Due Date and by Status.

1 Click the Detailed List option on the Navigation pane.

The Detailed List view is displayed.

2 Click the Due Date column heading.

The tasks are sorted by due date. The due date the farthest in the future is displayed first. Tasks without a due date appear last.

3 Click the Due Date column heading again.

The tasks are sorted again by due date. The tasks without a due date appear first, and the due date the farthest in the future appears last.

4 Click the Status column heading.

The tasks are sorted by status. The tasks that have the Not Started status appear first, the In Progress tasks are displayed next, and the Completed tasks are listed last.

5 Click the Status column heading again.

The tasks are sorted by status again. The Completed tasks appear first, the In Progress tasks are displayed next, and the Not Started tasks are listed last.

6 Click the Subject column heading.

The tasks are sorted alphabetically.

Lesson 6 Using Tasks

> **QUICK CHECK**
>
> Q: What happens when you click a column heading?
>
> A: The task list is sorted by that criterion.

> **ANOTHER METHOD**
>
> To sort tasks, you can also right-click an empty area of the tasks list and select the Sort option from the displayed menu. Select the desired sort criteria in the Sort dialog box and click OK. This enables you to sort by more than a single criterion.

◆ Keep Outlook open for the next exercise.

> **QUICK REFERENCE ▼**
>
> **Sort tasks**
>
> Click a column heading.

Printing a Task List

Organizing Tasks

> **THE BOTTOM LINE**
>
> You can print your task list to make it portable, separating it from your computer.

You can print a task list to carry with you, distribute to co-workers, or hang on the refrigerator. For example, if you create a task list to identify the milestones of a project, you probably want to print a copy of the task list and bring it with you to the next project status meeting. To print a task list, click the Print button on the Standard toolbar to display the Print dialog box. Select the print style. You can click the Page Setup button to choose options, such as text formatting, different paper sizes, and types of paper. When you are finished selecting options, click OK.

Two print styles are available—Table Style and Memo Style. The Table Style option prints the task list in columns, similar to the way it appears in Outlook. The Memo Style option prints selected tasks in a two-column list. The name of the task is displayed in the left column and the due date is displayed in the right column. Additional information about the tasks, such as the subject, status, and percent complete, appears in paragraph form below the columns. If you've created several columns for a task list and they won't fit within the page margins, Memo Style might be a better printing option. When you select Memo Style, you can print tasks one after another or print each task on a separate page.

> **QUICK CHECK**
>
> Q: What print styles are available for a task list?
>
> A: A task list can be printed in table style and memo style.

Organizing Tasks by Using Folders

Organizing Tasks

THE BOTTOM LINE

As you can do with other features in Outlook, you can use folders to store related Outlook tasks.

If you work on several projects at the same time, it can be helpful to place the tasks for each project in a different folder. For example, the events coordinator at Adventure Works is planning a banquet. She created a folder called Banquet so she could have a centralized location for all the planning tasks related to the banquet.

Organize tasks by folders

Since you have a number of tasks related to the picnic, you create a folder and move the picnic tasks into it.

1 Open the Tools menu and click the Organize option.

The Organize pane is displayed.

2 Click the Using Folders link.

The Using Folders section of the Organize pane is displayed.

3 In the top-right corner of the Organize pane, click the New Folder button.

The Create New Folder dialog box is displayed. The insertion point is already located in the Name box.

4 Type *Picnic Tasks.* In the Select Where To Place The Folder box, verify that the Tasks folder is selected, and click OK.

The new folder is created.

Figure 6-11

Create New Folder dialog box

5 Click the task "Call Cherry Creek Park to reserve sheltered picnic area." Press and hold the Ctrl key and click the task "Call band to check availability for the picnic."

Both tasks are selected.

6 In the Organize pane, click the Move button.

ANOTHER METHOD

Drag the task to a different folder.

The tasks are moved to the Picnic Tasks folder.

Figure 6-12
Tasks have been moved to the Picnic Tasks folder

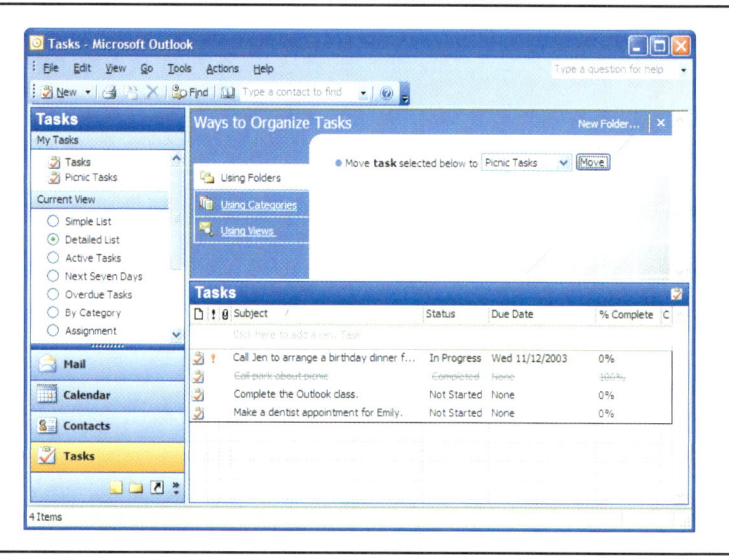

7 On the Navigation pane, click the Folder List button.

Folders are listed.

8 Click on the plus sign next to the Tasks folder in the folder list. Click the name of the folder you just created.

The tasks moved to the Picnic Tasks folder are displayed.

Figure 6-13

Contents of the Picnic Tasks

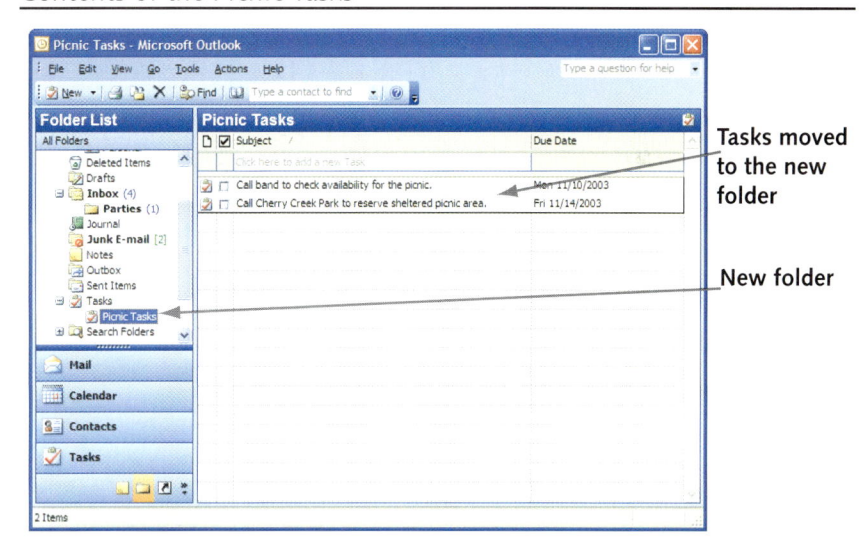

[Screenshot of Picnic Tasks - Microsoft Outlook window, showing Tasks moved to the new folder and the New folder labeled Picnic Tasks]

QUICK CHECK

Q: Can you create new folders to organize tasks?

A: Yes, you can create new folders to organize tasks efficiently.

◆ Keep Outlook open for the next exercise.

QUICK REFERENCE ▼

Organize tasks by folder

1. Open the Organize pane.
2. Click the Using Folders link.
3. Create a new folder or select an existing folder.
4. In the task list, select a task.
5. In the Organize pane, click the Move button.

Organizing Tasks by Using Categories

Organizing Tasks

THE BOTTOM LINE

Categories provide another means to sort tasks into related groups.

Categories have helped you organize many Outlook items. Categories can also be used to organize tasks. Categorizing tasks makes it easier to access specific related tasks. In the Using Categories section of the Organize pane, select one of the existing categories, such as Holiday, Business, or Gifts. You can also create your own category.

Assign a task to a category

You will now assign a task to a category and apply the By Category view to your task list.

1. Click the Tasks button on the Navigation pane and click the Tasks folder in the list of available folders.

The tasks in the Tasks folder are displayed.

196 **Lesson 6** Using Tasks

> **CHECK THIS OUT ▼**
>
> **Categories for Projects**
> You can create categories related to your work or home projects. Then assign tasks to these categories to track your progress.

Figure 6-14

Contents of the Tasks folder

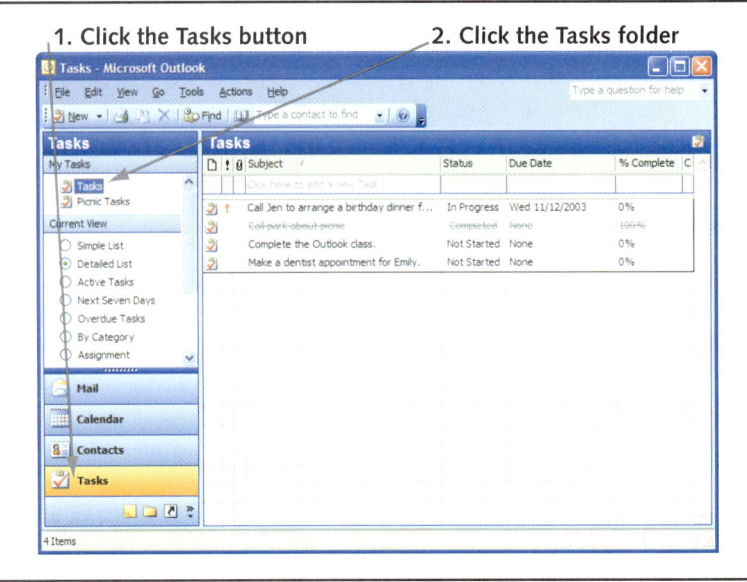

1. Click the Tasks button
2. Click the Tasks folder

2 Open the Tools menu and click the Organize option.

The Organize pane is displayed.

3 If necessary, click the Using Categories link.

The Using Categories section of the Organize pane is displayed.

4 Select the existing "Personal" category in the Add Tasks Selected Below To box.

The category is selected.

5 In the task list, click the task "Call Jen to arrange a birthday dinner for Dad" and click the Add button in the Organize pane.

The task is added to the Personal category. The text Personal is displayed in the Categories column of the task.

Figure 6-15

Task assigned to a category

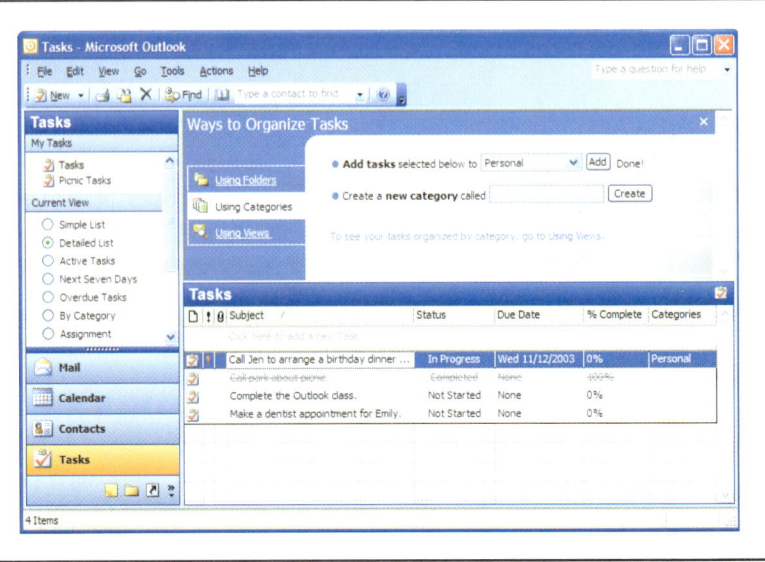

Lesson 6 Using Tasks 197

> **TIP**
>
> If necessary scroll the list of tasks to the right or drag the borders of the columns to resize the columns to display the categories.

6 In the Organize pane, click the Using Views link.

The Using Views section of the Organize pane is displayed.

7 In the Change Your View list, select By Category. If necessary, click the plus sign (+) to expand the categories.

The By Category view is displayed. Notice that there are two gray bars. One category is none. The other category is Personal. The Personal category contains the single task *Call Jen to arrange a birthday dinner for Dad*.

Figure 6-16

Task assigned to the Personal category

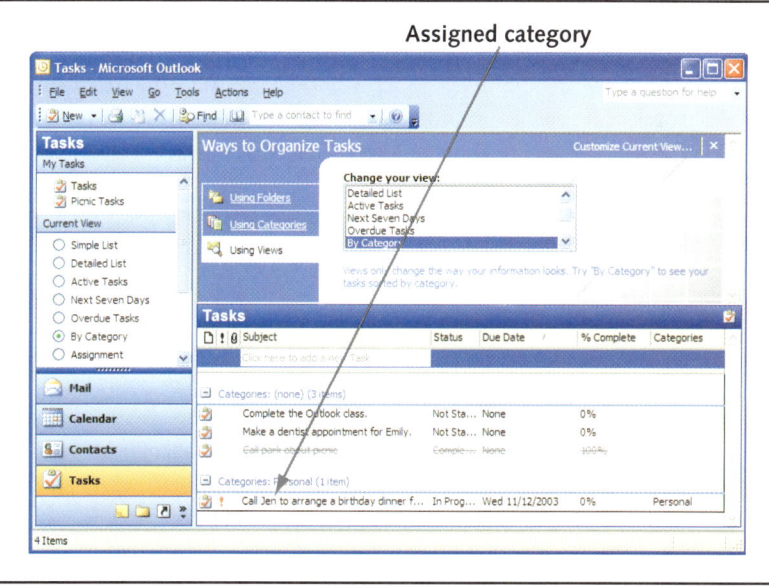

8 In the Organize pane, select Detailed List in the Change Your View box and click the Close button in the Organize pane.

The tasks are displayed in Detailed List view and the Organize pane is closed.

◆ Keep Outlook open for the next exercise.

QUICK REFERENCE ▼

Organize tasks by category

1 Open the Organize pane.
2 Click the Using Categories link.
3 Create a new category or select an existing category.
4 In the task list, select a task.
5 In the Organize pane, click the Move button.

QUICK CHECK

Q: Why would you assign tasks to categories?

A: **This makes it easier to access specific related tasks.**

Assigning Tasks to Others

Accepting, Declining, and Delegating Tasks

THE BOTTOM LINE

Often, particularly on large projects, it is necessary to divide tasks. With Outlook you can assign tasks to others. This allows you to manage each aspect of a project.

Many projects involve more than one person. In addition to setting up tasks for a project, you might also need to assign different tasks to various members of a team. In Outlook, you can easily assign a task to someone else. When you assign a task, you send that person a task request as an e-mail message generated by Outlook. The recipient can accept or decline the task.

When you create a task in your task list, you are the **owner** of the task. As the owner, you are the only person who can edit the task. If you assign the task to someone else and the recipient accepts the task, the **ownership** (the ability to make changes to the task) passes to the recipient. If you assign a task to someone and he or she accepts it, you can choose to keep an updated copy in your task list and receive status reports when the task is edited or completed.

Assign tasks

You will now create two tasks and assign them to your class partner.

1 On the standard tasks toolbar, click the New Task button.

ANOTHER METHOD

You can also open the Actions menu and click New Task Request to display a task request.

The task window is displayed. The insertion point is already in the Subject box.

TROUBLESHOOTING

The name of the brochure should not be the same as the brochure name used by your class partner. When you receive the task assignment in the next exercise, using the same brochure name would cause conflict.

2 Type Edit the [insert name here] brochure. Click the Priority down arrow and select High.

Notice that you are currently the owner of the task.

Figure 6-17

The creator of a task owns the task

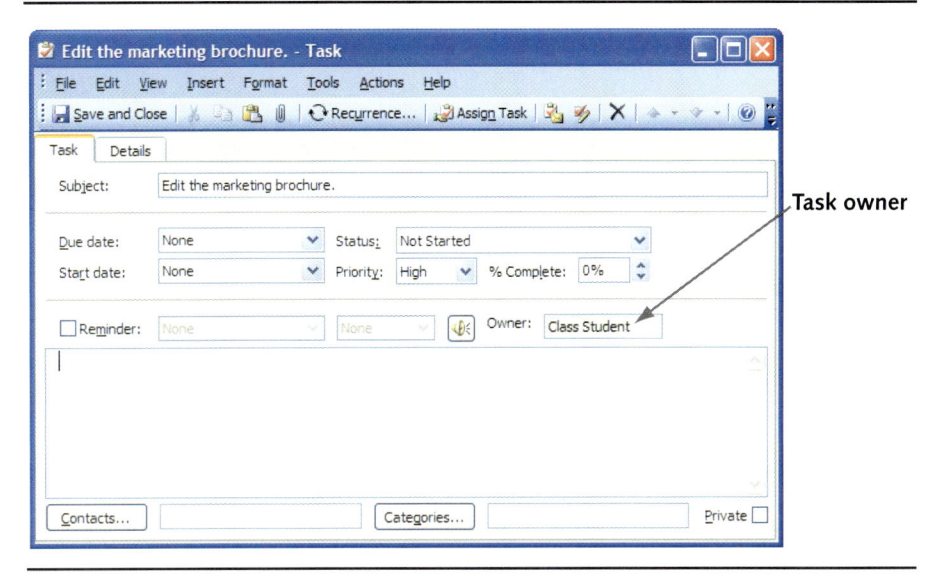

[Screenshot of task window with "Task owner" label pointing to "Class Student" in the Owner field]

3 **On the toolbar in the task window, click the Assign Task button.**

A task request window, which is similar to the task window, appears. A note at the top of the window indicates that the task request has not been sent yet.

4 **Click the To button.**

The Select Task Recipient dialog box is displayed.

5 **In the Select Task Recipient dialog box, click your class partner's name, and click OK.**

Your class partner's name is displayed in the Message Recipients box. The Select Task Recipient dialog box closes.

TROUBLESHOOTING

The addressee cannot be the same as the sender. If you don't have a class partner, use a second address entry for yourself that has a different e-mail address.

Figure 6-18

Task request to be sent

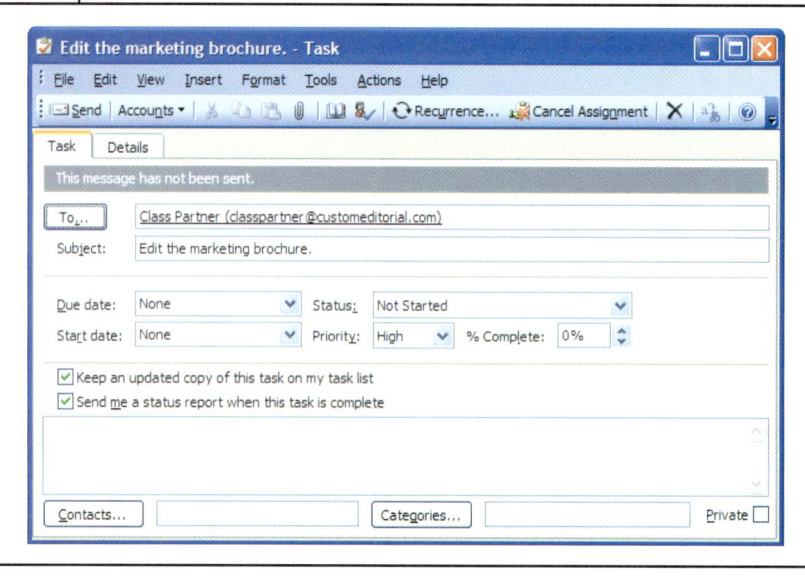

TROUBLESHOOTING

An alert box may be displayed when you assign a task. It states that the task reminder has been shut off because you are no longer the owner of the task. Click OK.

6 On the Standard toolbar in the task window, click the Send button.

The task is sent to your class partner.

7 On the Standard Tasks toolbar, click the New Task button.

The task window is displayed.

8 In the Subject box, type **Arrange printing for [insert name here] brochure.** Click the Due Date down arrow and click "Tuesday of next week."

This provides basic task information.

9 On the Standard toolbar in the task window, click the Assign Task button.

A task request window is displayed. A note at the top of the window indicates that the task request has not been sent yet and gives the number of days until the task is due.

10 Click the To button.

The Select Task Recipient dialog box is displayed.

11 In the Select Task Recipient dialog box, click your class partner's name and click the To button.

Your class partner's name is placed in the Message Recipients box.

12 Click OK.

The Select Task Recipient dialog box closes.

13 On the Standard toolbar in the task window, click the Send button.

The task is sent to your class partner.

◆ Keep Outlook open for the next exercise.

QUICK REFERENCE ▼
Assign a task

1. Create or select a task.
2. In the task request window, click the Assign Task button.
3. Click the To button, select the assignee, and click OK.
4. Click the Send button.

QUICK CHECK

Q: Who owns a task when it is created?

A: A task is owned by its creator when it is created.

Accepting or Declining Tasks

Accepting, Declining, and Delegating Tasks

THE BOTTOM LINE
To keep a project moving, accept or decline task requests when you receive them. Accepting a task request adds it to your task list. Declining a task returns it to the previous task owner.

Sending a task request does not mean that the recipient automatically agrees to perform the task. The recipient must respond to the message, either by accepting or declining it. If the recipient declines a task request, the sender can reassign the task to someone else. If the recipient accepts a task request, the recipient receives ownership of the task and the sender receives a message of acceptance. This process prevents tasks from falling between the cracks in large projects. For example, the marketing director at Adventure Works assigned a task related to the picnic to the head chef. Because the chef had prior obligations, he declined the task. After receiving the chef's reply, the marketing director assigned the task to the head chef's assistant, who accepted the task.

If you receive a task request, you become the temporary owner of the task until you decide what to do with it—to accept or decline the task. If you accept a task, you become the permanent owner of the task. If you decline a task, you return ownership of the task to the person who sent the task request.

A task request arrives in your Inbox as an e-mail message. Double-click the message to open the task request. To accept a task request, click the Accept button. To decline a task request, click the Decline button. Although it is not necessary, you can include a comment with your reply, such as providing a start time, asking questions, or stating a reason for declining the task. To reply without a comment, click the Send The Response Now option. To enter a comment before sending the reply, click the Edit The Response Before Sending button. Type your comment and click the Send button to send the response.

Respond to a task request

In the last exercise, your class partner sent you task requests. In this exercise, you accept a task request and send a response without comment to the original sender. You also decline a task request and send a response with a comment to the original sender.

1 On the Navigation pane, click the Mail button. If necessary click the Inbox folder.

The contents of the Inbox are displayed.

2 On the Standard toolbar, click the Send/Receive button.

Two task requests from your class partner arrive in the Inbox.

TROUBLESHOOTING

Depending on when your class partner sends task requests, you might need to click the Send/Receive button (in the Inbox) again to receive these task request messages.

3 In the Inbox, click the task request "Edit the [insert name here] brochure."

The task request is displayed in the Reading pane.

Figure 6-19

Task request received in the Inbox

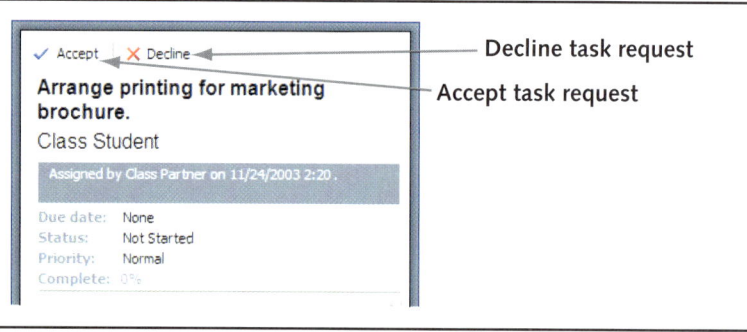

ANOTHER METHOD

You can also right-click the message header of a task request in the Inbox and click Accept to accept a task request or Decline to refuse the assignment.

Figure 6-20

Accepting a task request

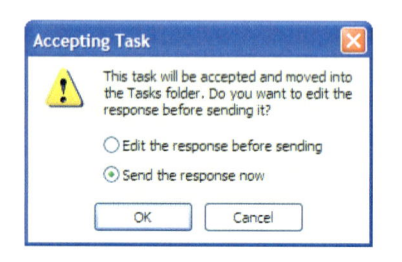

4 On the message in the Reading pane, click the Accept button.

An alert box is displayed. The Send The Response Now option is already selected.

5 Click OK.

The response is sent as an e-mail message. Notice that the task request, Edit [insert name here] brochure is no longer in the Inbox.

6 In your Inbox, click the task request "Arrange printing for [insert name here] brochure."

The task request is displayed in the Reading pane.

7 On the Standard toolbar in the task request window, click the Decline button.

An alert box is displayed. The Send The Response Now option is already selected.

Lesson 6 Using Tasks 203

8 **Click the Edit The Response Before Sending option and click OK.**

A task window is displayed. The insertion point is already in the memo area.

9 **In the memo area, type I'm sorry, but my schedule doesn't allow me to accept this task.**

You have provided a reason for declining the task.

Figure 6-21

Declining a task request

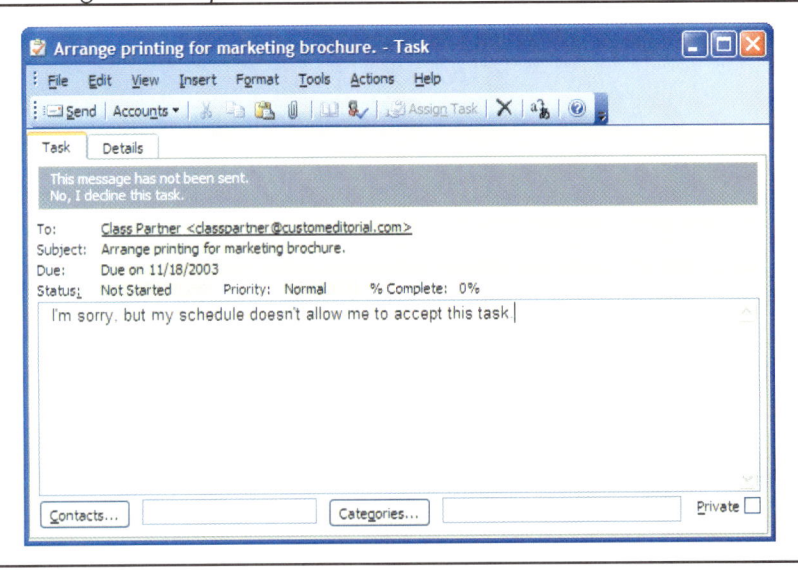

10 **On the Standard toolbar in the task window, click the Send button.**

The response to the task request is sent as an e-mail message.

11 **On the Standard toolbar in the Mail folder, click the Send/Receive button.**

Two responses from your class partner about the task requests you sent arrive in your Inbox. One message accepts a task and one message declines a task.

12 **On the Navigation pane, click the Tasks button.**

The contents of the Tasks folder are displayed. The task you accepted is displayed in the task list. The task you declined is not in your task list.

◆ Keep Outlook open for the next exercise.

QUICK CHECK

Q: Can a task be assigned automatically?

A: No, the task must be accepted by the new owner.

QUICK REFERENCE ▼

Accept or decline a task

1 Receive the task request.
2 View the task request in the Reading pane.
3 Click the Accept or Decline button.
4 If necessary, add a comment to the message and send the message.

Marking Tasks as Complete

Managing Tasks Assigned to You

THE BOTTOM LINE

Completed tasks remain in the task list to show progress, but they are marked so that you can tell which are completed and which remain to be done.

When you mark a task as complete, the task is listed with a strikeout line through it and the task no longer appears in the Active Tasks view. New tasks marked as complete remain in the task list. You can make a task that has been completed active again by changing its status. To mark a task as complete, double-click the task to display the task window, click the Status down arrow, and click Completed. If you click the Details tab, you can also enter a different completion date (other than the current date) and additional completion information (such as total number of hours worked).

Mark a task as complete

Now you mark a task as complete using the Details tab of the task window, mark a task as complete using the Status box of the task window, and mark a task as complete in the task list.

1 Double-click the task "Make a dentist appointment for Emily."

The task window is displayed.

2 Click the Details tab and click the Date Completed down arrow.

A mini-calendar is displayed.

TROUBLESHOOTING

Select today's date or any previous date to complete the task. You cannot use a date in the future.

3 Click the date for yesterday.

Yesterday's date is displayed in the Date Completed column.

4 On the toolbar in the task window, click the Save And Close button.

A line is placed through the task Make a dentist appointment for Emily.

5 In the Navigation pane, click the Picnic Tasks folder.

The contents of the Picnic Tasks folder are displayed.

6 Double-click the task "Call band to check availability for the picnic."

The task window opens.

7 Click the Status down arrow.

The Status list is displayed.

8 Click Completed.

The task is marked as complete.

Lesson 6 Using Tasks 205

Save and Close

9 On the Standard toolbar in the task window, click the Save And Close button.

The task is displayed with a line through it.

10 Right-click the task "Call Cherry Creek Park to reserve sheltered picnic area." Click the Mark Complete option.

ANOTHER METHOD

To mark a task as complete in the task list, right-click the task and click Mark Complete on the shortcut menu that appears. If the task list is displayed in Detailed List view, you can type 100 in the % Complete column for the task. In most views, you can simply click the checkbox in front of a task.

The task is displayed with a line through it.

Figure 6-22
Completed tasks

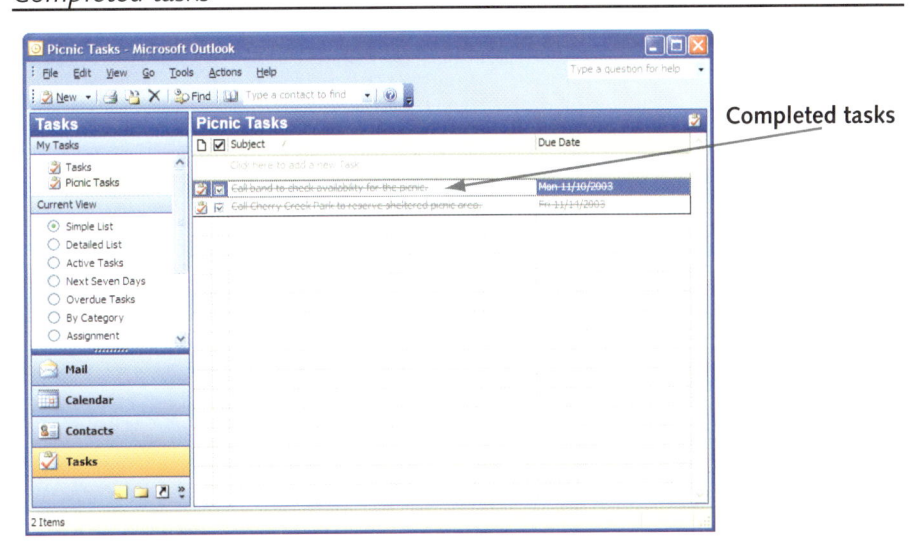

◆ Keep Outlook open for the next exercise.

QUICK REFERENCE ▼

Mark a task as complete

1 Double-click a task.
2 Click the Details tab.
3 Enter today's date or a previous date.
4 Click the Save And Close button.

QUICK CHECK

Q: How can you tell that a task has been completed?

A: A completed task has a strikeout line through it.

Manually Recording a Task in the Journal

THE BOTTOM LINE

Outlook's Journal helps you track the amount of time spent on each task.

Tracking Dealings with Contracts

The **Journal** is a folder in Outlook that displays information in a timeline format. The Journal can record when you create, use, and modify Microsoft Office System documents (such as Microsoft Excel, Access, Word, and PowerPoint). When the Journal tracks an Office document, it displays each document's type, name, date, the amount of time the document was open, and the path in which the document is stored on your computer. The document path is useful if you can't remember where you stored a document. Double-click any Office document or Outlook item recorded in the Journal to open the item.

To set the Journal to automatically track Office documents, open the Tools menu, click Options, and click the Journal Options button in the Options dialog box. In the Journal Options dialog box, select the check boxes next to the Office applications you want to track, and click OK twice.

Figure 6-23

Journal Options dialog box

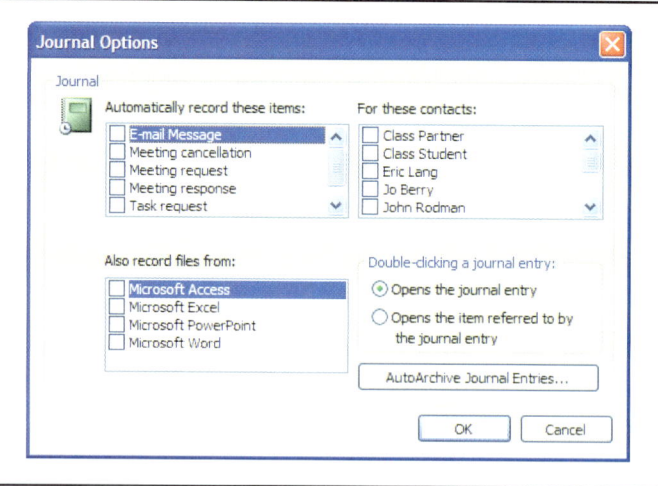

You can also use the Journal to track various Outlook activities, such as e-mails and tasks. To track an Outlook item, such as a task, you need to manually record it in the Journal.

For example, the marketing director at Adventure Works likes to record tasks in the Journal so she can have a record of the time she spends on a task. This information helps her schedule future projects and gives her a clear picture of where her time goes each week.

Lesson 6 Using Tasks 207

> **IMPORTANT**
>
> The Journal button may not be displayed in the Navigation pane. To display the Journal button, click the Configure Buttons icon at the bottom of the Navigation pane. Point at Add Or Remove Buttons, and click the Journal option. The Journal button will be added to the row of small buttons at the bottom of the Navigation pane.

Use the Journal

You will now work with the Journal. First you create a task and record it in the Journal. Then you access the task from within the Journal and update it.

1 In the Navigation pane, click the folder Picnic Tasks.

The tasks in the Picnic Tasks folder are displayed.

2 In the task list, click in the box that contains the text "Click here to add a new Task." Type Create brochures. Press Enter.

The new task is created.

3 Drag the new task to the Journal button on the Navigation pane.

A Journal entry window is displayed.

Figure 6-24

Journal entry for a task

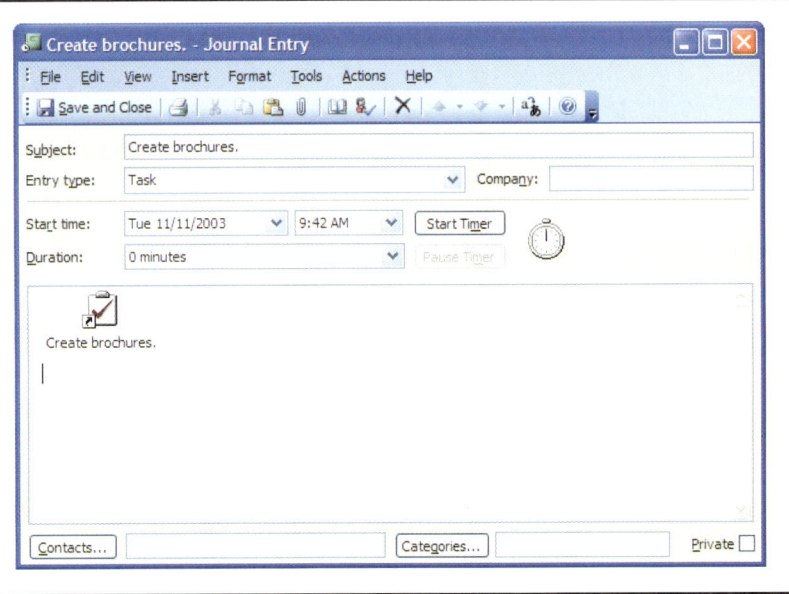

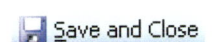

4 On the toolbar in the Journal entry window, click the Save And Close button.

The task will be tracked in the Journal.

5 In the Navigation pane, click the Journal button.

The contents of the Journal are displayed.

208　**Lesson 6**　Using Tasks

> **TROUBLESHOOTING**
>
> An alert box may be displayed that asks you to confirm that you want the Journal activated. Click Yes to continue, and click OK in the Journal Options dialog box.

6 If necessary, on the Standard toolbar, click the Day button and the By Type view.

The current day appears in the Journal. The task is displayed in the Journal under the time at which you created the task.

> **TROUBLESHOOTING**
>
> You might need to scroll to view the entry.

Figure 6-25

Journal view of the day

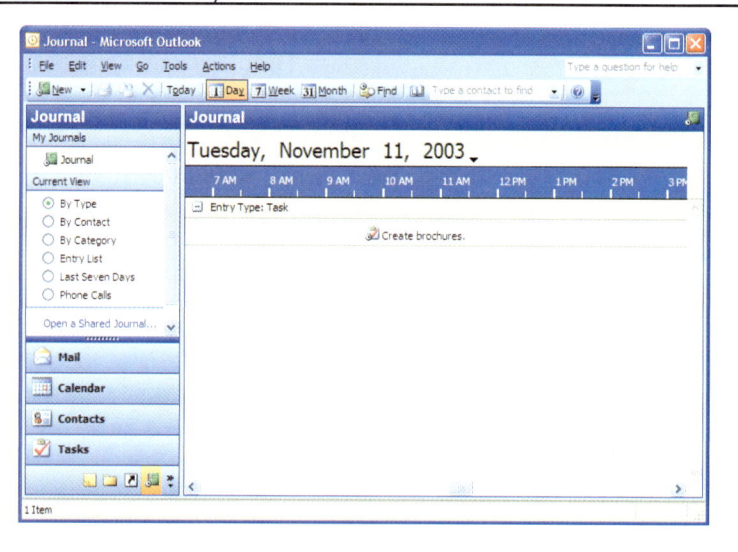

7 Right-click the task and click Open Item Referred To.

The task is displayed in a task window.

8 In the % Complete box, select the 0% and type 100. On the toolbar in the task window, click the Save And Close button.

The task is updated.

9 Click the Tasks button on the Navigation pane. If necessary, click the Picnic Tasks folder.

Notice that the task has been updated in the task list. It is marked as completed. A line has been placed through it.

Lesson 6 Using Tasks 209

QUICK CHECK

Q: What is the purpose of the Journal?

A: It can record when you create, use, and modify Microsoft Office System documents and various Outlook items.

Figure 6-26

The task is completed

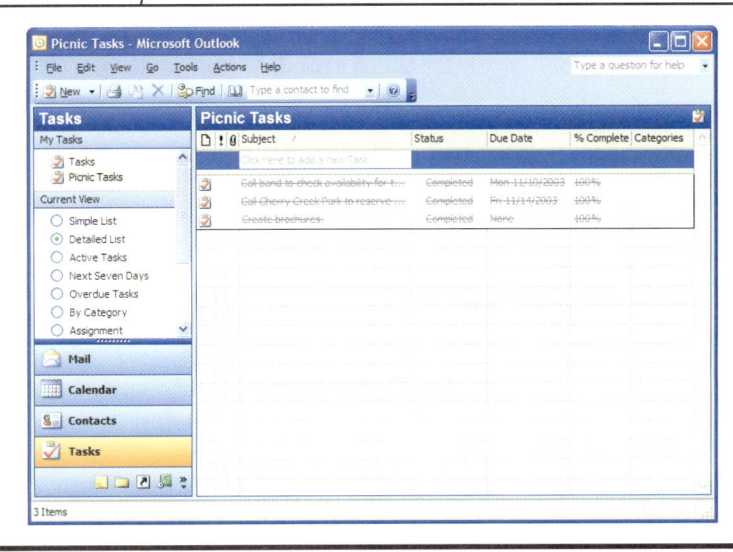

◆ Keep Outlook open for the next exercise.

QUICK REFERENCE ▼

Manually record a task in the Journal

1. Drag a task to the Journal button on the Navigation pane.
2. Click the Save And Close button.

Deleting Tasks

Managing Tasks Assigned to You

THE BOTTOM LINE

When a project is over, you need to delete the associated tasks to reduce clutter.

If you complete a task and mark it as complete, the task still remains as an entry in your task list. Because completed tasks appear with a strikeout line, you can easily identify which tasks have been completed and which tasks are still in progress or have not yet begun. When you know a task has been completed and you don't want the task to clutter your task list, you can delete it. If you delete a task, it is moved to the Deleted Items folder, like other Outlook items. The deleted tasks remain in the Deleted Items folder until you empty the Deleted Items folder or restore the task.

Delete a task

Since you have completed your task, you delete the completed task.

1. If necessary, click the Picnic Tasks folder on the Navigation pane.

The contents of the Picnic Tasks folder are displayed.

2 Click the completed task "Call band to check availability for the picnic" and click the Delete button.

The appointment moves to the Deleted Items folder.

ANOTHER METHOD
Right-click on a task and click Delete.

◆ If you are continuing to the next lesson, keep Outlook open.

◆ If you are Not continuing to the next lesson, close Outlook.

QUICK REFERENCE ▼
Delete a task

1 Click the task.
2 Click the Delete button.

QUICK CHECK
Q: How do you permanently delete a task?
A: Delete the task and empty the Deleted Items folder.

Key Points

✔ *Outlook lets you create and add details to a task.*
✔ *You can sort and organize tasks by using folders and categories.*
✔ *When you assign tasks to others they can accept or decline the tasks. Likewise, you can accept or decline tasks sent to you.*
✔ *Outlook allows you to mark tasks as complete.*
✔ *You can manually record a task in the Journal.*
✔ *When a task is completed and a record of the task is no longer needed, the task can be deleted from the task list.*

Quick Quiz

True/False

T F 1. All tasks must be assigned to a category.
T F 2. Tasks can be stored only with other task items.
T F 3. Overdue tasks are automatically deleted.
T F 4. You must be the owner of a task to assign it to someone else.
T F 5. The Journal automatically tracks all tasks.

Multiple Choice

1. When you receive a task request, you _____.
   a. must accept the task
   b. become the temporary task owner
   c. become the permanent task owner
   d. All of the above

2. When you decline a task, _____.
   a. it is added to your task list
   b. it can be claimed by any Outlook user in your group
   c. it reverts to the previous owner who sent the task request
   d. All of the above

3. The Tasks folder enables you to _____.
   a. track your tasks
   b. receive e-mail
   c. schedule appointments
   d. All of the above

4. A(n) _____ task is red.
   a. in-progress
   b. deleted
   c. completed
   d. overdue

5. A folder containing tasks _____.
   a. must be named Tasks folder
   b. can contain any Outlook item
   c. can hold only task items
   d. can be assigned to another user

Short Answer

1. Identify the columns that appear in the Detailed List view of the task list but do not appear in the Simple List view.
2. How does a completed task appear in a task list?
3. Describe one way to enter a task.
4. If you receive a task request, how do you respond to the request?
5. How can you organize tasks?
6. What happens to deleted tasks?
7. Can you assign a task to someone else? Explain your answer.
8. What is a task?
9. What is the Journal?
10. If you send a task request to someone, how and where does it show up?

On Your Own

Exercise 1

The events coordinator at Adventure Works must begin to plan the company's holiday party. She wants to put all the tasks into Outlook and store them in a folder called Holiday Party. The tasks include the following: find a location, plan the food, buy gifts, book a band or DJ, create invitations, send invitations, and buy decorations. Group all the tasks under the Holiday category. The events coordinator will handle most of the tasks. However, she wants to assign the task of creating invitations to the graphic designer and the task of buying decorations to her assistant (your class partner). Create the tasks and organize them as specified. Use a different name and e-mail address for the graphic designer.

Exercise 2

The following week, the events coordinator needs to update the task list for the holiday party. So far, she has found a location and booked a band. She is halfway through planning the food. She realizes that she needs to buy the gifts quickly. Update the task list.

One Step Further

Exercise 1

The events coordinator wants to track the amount of time she is spending on the holiday party. Record the tasks created for the holiday party in the Journal.

Exercise 2

Use the Journal to access each task. Mark the tasks *Buy decorations* and *Create invitations* as complete.

Exercise 3

The director of marketing asked the events coordinator for a status report. Create a status report for all the tasks related to the holiday party.

LESSON 7

Using Notes

After completing this lesson, you will be able to:

✔ *Create notes in Outlook.*
✔ *Edit notes.*
✔ *Copy and move notes.*
✔ *Forward notes to e-mail recipients.*
✔ *Organize and view notes.*
✔ *Delete notes.*

KEY TERM

- note

Many people use sticky notes to jot down phone numbers, comments, and other reminders to themselves throughout the day. These small notes can be temporarily placed on desks, hung on computer monitors, or attached to other locations where they can't be easily overlooked. Sticky notes are a great invention, but you might already have discovered that they can create clutter, especially when you have several sticky notes attached to your monitor or around your work area.

Microsoft Office Outlook 2003 has electronic notes, which look just like their paper counterparts, except that they appear on the screen. These notes offer you the convenience of sticky notes, but you won't have to worry about further cluttering your desk. Typically, a **note** is a brief text entry that you can save, edit, and move independently of the Outlook window. You can even create notes in different colors. Notes can help you keep track of bits of information, such as an airline reservation number, a reminder to pick up your dry cleaning, or the name of someone you just met.

Use the Notes folder in Outlook to create, store, and organize notes. You can copy notes from the Notes folder to the Microsoft Windows desktop so you can see your notes when Outlook is closed or minimized. You can also convert a note to another Outlook item, such as a task or an appointment.

For example, a co-worker has asked you to review a report she wrote. You quickly use Outlook to create a note reminding yourself to review the report. As your day becomes busier, you realize that you might not have time to review the report by the end of the day. You decide to convert the note to a task so it appears in your task list of things to do tomorrow. When you convert the note to a task, you can also set a high-priority flag to remind yourself to perform this task as soon as possible tomorrow.

In this lesson, you will learn how to create, edit, copy, and move notes. You will also learn how to forward and delete notes, and how to organize notes by using folders, views, and colors.

IMPORTANT

To complete some of the exercises in this lesson, you will need to exchange e-mail messages with a class partner. If you don't have a class partner or you are performing the exercises alone, you can send the message to yourself. Simply enter your own e-mail address instead of a class partner's address.

Creating Notes

Creating, Updating, and Sharing Notes

THE BOTTOM LINE

Notes provide a brief visual reminder or can store small pieces of information.

Notes are easier to create than many other items in Outlook because you don't have to fill in boxes or select options. A note consists of a small window containing a single area for text. Although notes can be any length and size, they are best for short bits of information. For example, because the head chef at Adventure Works has a tendency to forget his e-mail password, he created a note that contains a clue to remind himself of his password.

Notes are intended to be fast and easy to use, so they don't provide most of the capabilities of a word-processing program. You can't make text in a note bold or italic, nor can you apply most other formatting. To display the Notes window, click the Notes button on the Navigation pane.

Figure 7-1

Outlook Notes window

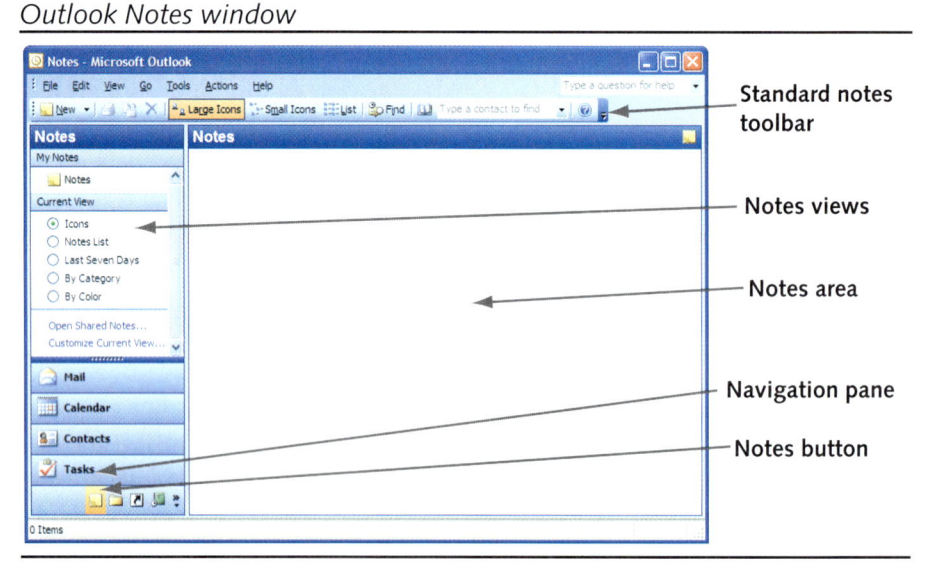

To create a note, on the Standard toolbar, click the New Note button. A blank note is displayed.

Figure 7-2

Note

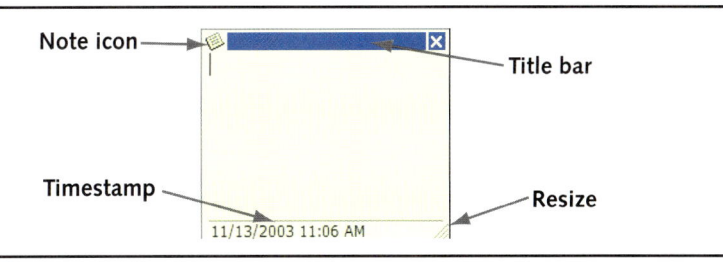

A note icon is located in the top-left corner of a note. When you click the note icon, a menu is displayed. It contains commands for customizing and organizing the note. A Close button is located in the top-right corner of a note. Click the Close button to save and close the note. When you close a note, it is stored in the Notes window.

The date and time that the note was created are displayed at the bottom of the note. If you want to resize a note horizontally, click and drag either the right or left edge of the note. If you want to resize the note vertically, click and drag the bottom edge of the note. If you click and drag the hash marks in the bottom-right corner of the note, you can resize the note horizontally and diagonally at the same time.

After a new note is displayed, type the text you want the note to contain. You can type more text than the note can display as it appears in the Notes pane. However, notes do not have a scroll bar, so you must scroll through the text using the up and down arrow keys to read the text that is not visible or make the note larger. Double-click a note's title bar (the blue bar at the top of the note) to maximize the note. Double-click a note's title bar again to restore it to its previous size.

TIP

You don't need to display the Notes window to create a note. From any Outlook window, you can click the down arrow to the right of the New button and select the Notes option. When you use this method, the note is placed on the Windows desktop. It is treated as the active window until you click a different window or close the note. You can also press Ctrl+Shift+N to create a note.

◆ Be sure to start Outlook before beginning this exercise.

Create notes

You begin this lesson by creating three notes which will be used throughout the exercises in this lesson.

1 On the Navigation pane, click the Notes button.

The contents of the Notes folder are displayed.

2 On the Standard Notes toolbar, click the New Note button.

A new note is displayed. The insertion point is located in the first line of the note.

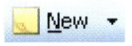

216 **Lesson 7** Using Notes

3 In the note, type Call Andy before 5:00. In the top-right corner of the note, click the Close button.

The note is saved and closed. It is displayed in the Notes pane as an icon.

Figure 7-3

Note icon in the Notes pane

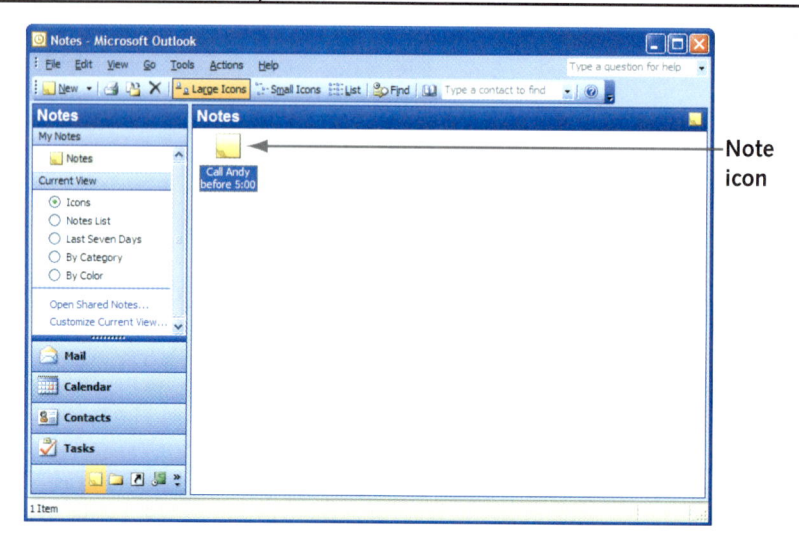

ANOTHER METHOD

You can also press Alt+F4 to close a note.

4 On the Standard toolbar, click the New Note button.

A new note is displayed.

5 In the note, type Make a doctor appointment for Sally. In the top-right corner of the note, click the Close button.

The note is saved and closed. It is displayed in the Notes window as an icon.

6 On the Standard toolbar, click the New Note button.

A new note is displayed.

7 In the note, type Hotel reservation number: K28D62. In the top-right corner of the note, click the Close button.

The note is saved and closed. It is displayed in the Notes window as an icon.

ANOTHER METHOD

You can also double-click the empty, white area of the Notes window to create a new note.

Figure 7-4

Notes displayed in the Notes pane

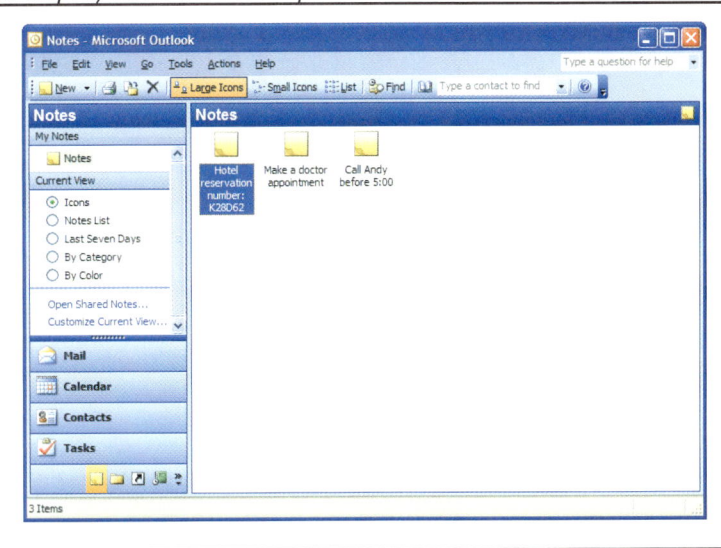

◆ Keep Outlook open for the next exercise.

QUICK REFERENCE ▼
Create a note

1. On the Navigation pane, click the Notes button.
2. On the Standard Notes toolbar, click the New Note button.
3. Type the note.
4. In the top-right corner of the note, click the Close button.

QUICK CHECK

Q: How many words can a note contain?

A: Notes are not limited in length.

Editing Notes

THE BOTTOM LINE
Notes can be edited to change or correct information stored in them.

Creating, Updating, and Sharing Notes

You might want to change the content of a note after you create it. For example, the office manager at Adventure Works typed a note that contained a list of office supplies she needs to order later in the day. One of the employees sent in a late order by e-mail for pencils and a staple remover. The office manager added the two items to the note.

To edit a note, double-click the existing note, add or change information, and click the Close button. The changes are saved and the note closes.

Edit a note

You will now edit one of the notes you created in the previous exercise.

1. **Double-click the note "Call Andy before 5:00" in the Notes window.**

   The note opens.

218   **Lesson 7**   Using Notes

2 In the note, delete 5:00 and type **5:30**. In the top-right corner of the note, click the Close button.

The note is saved and closed. It is displayed as an icon in the Notes window.

Figure 7-5

Edited note

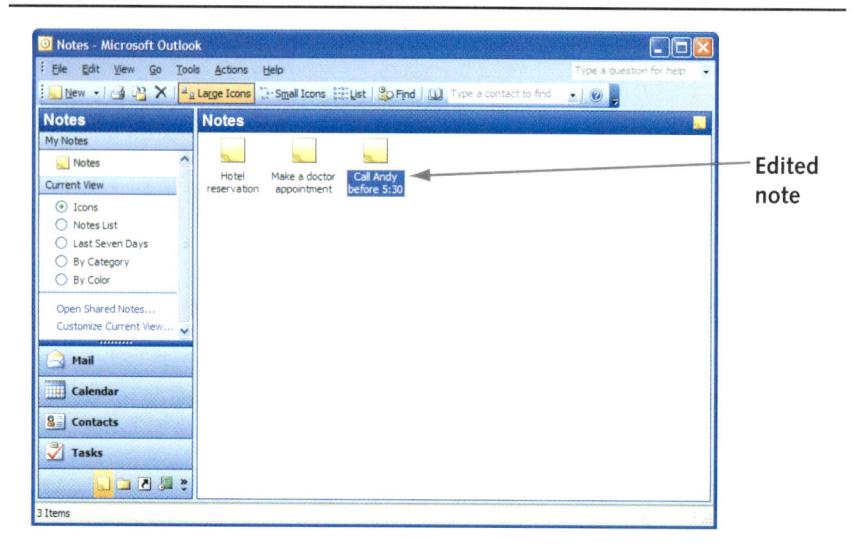

◆ Keep Outlook open for the next exercise.

QUICK CHECK

Q: How do you save a note?

A: **Click the Close button.**

QUICK REFERENCE ▼

Edit a note

1 Double-click the note.

2 Make the changes.

3 Close the note.

Copying Notes

THE BOTTOM LINE

Notes can be copied and moved to save or organize them.

You can copy and move notes the same way you copy and move other Outlook items. For convenience, you can also access a note when Outlook isn't open. You can copy or move a note to the Windows desktop to display it as a reminder even when you're not in Outlook. If you copy or move a note to another Outlook folder, you can convert the note to a different type of Outlook item. For example, if you move a note onto the Calendar shortcut on the Outlook Bar, an appointment window will open so you can convert the note into an appointment by completing the new appointment information.

To copy a note, drag the note onto the appropriate folder shortcut on the Navigation pane or to the Windows desktop. A copy of the note remains in the Notes window.

Lesson 7 Using Notes 219

Copy a note

Using the notes you created, you copy a note onto the Windows desktop. You also create a note and move it to the Tasks folder.

CHECK THIS OUT ▼

Convert Notes to Tasks
You can convert any note into a task. If you do this you can receive a reminder when the task is approaching a deadline.

TROUBLESHOOTING

If a note is already on the Windows desktop when you attempt to drag it to the desktop, a Confirm File Replace dialog box will appear, asking whether you want to replace the file. You might replace a note on the Windows desktop if you edited the note from within the Notes window. To replace the note on the Windows desktop, drag the edited note to the Windows desktop and click Yes in the Confirm File Replace dialog box.

1 If necessary, reduce the size of the Outlook window so you can see the desktop. Select the note "Make a doctor appointment for Sally." Drag the note to the Windows desktop.

The note is copied to the Windows desktop.

Figure 7-6
Note on the Windows desktop

2 In the top-right corner of the Outlook window, click the Maximize button.

The Outlook window is maximized and you can no longer see the note on the desktop.

3 In the top-right corner of the Outlook window, click the Minimize button.

Outlook is minimized to a button on the Windows taskbar and the note is displayed on the Windows desktop.

4 On the Windows taskbar, click the Notes - Microsoft Outlook button.

The Outlook window maximizes.

5 On the Standard toolbar, click the New Note button.

A new note is displayed.

6 In the new note, type **Pick up manager from the airport at 2:30 on Friday.** In the top-right corner of the note, click the Close button.

The note is saved and closed.

7 Select the note "Pick up manager from the airport at 2:30 on Friday." Drag it to the Tasks button on the Navigation pane.

A task window is displayed. Notice that the content of the note is in the Subject box.

220 Lesson 7 Using Notes

> **ANOTHER METHOD**
>
> Drag the note to the Tasks folder in the Folder List.

Figure 7-7

Task created from a note

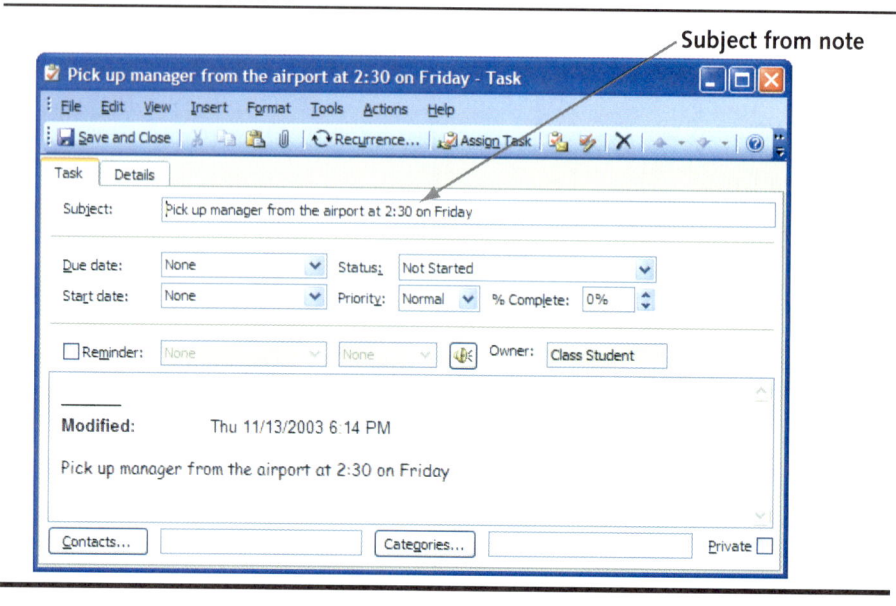

8. **Click the Priority down arrow and select High.**

   The task is assigned a high priority.

9. **On the Standard toolbar in the task window, click the Save And Close button.**

   The task is saved and the window closes.

10. **On the Navigation pane, click the Tasks button, and select the Active Tasks view.**

    The contents of the Tasks folder are displayed. Examine the task "Pick up manager from the airport at 2:30 on Friday." It has been converted into a task with a high-priority flag.

Figure 7-8

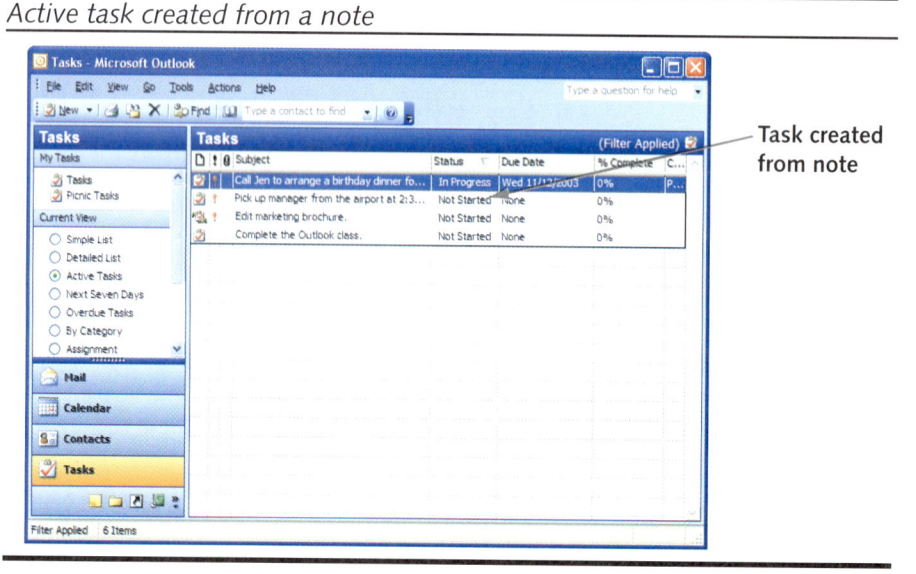

Active task created from a note

Lesson 7 Using Notes 221

◆ Click the Notes button on the Navigation pane to return to the Notes folder.

QUICK CHECK

Q: Why would you copy a note to your desktop?

A: The note is still visible when Outlook is closed.

QUICK REFERENCE ▼

Copy a note

1. Select the note.
2. Drag the note to the desktop or an Outlook folder.

Forwarding Notes

Creating, Updating, and Sharing Notes

THE BOTTOM LINE

You can send a note to a contact to share important information.

Occasionally, you might want to send a note to another person. For example, the office manager at Adventure Works created a note to remind herself to phone the caterer for an upcoming luncheon. However, she was unexpectedly called out of the office. She forwarded the note to Jim, her assistant, so he could complete the task. Instead of copying the text to an e-mail message, she forwarded the note to her assistant as an attachment to an e-mail message.

TIP

You can attach a note to an e-mail message, but you cannot attach a file to a note.

Forward a note

In this exercise, you create a note and forward it to your class partner.

1. **On the Standard Notes toolbar, click the New Note button.**

   A new note is displayed.

2. **Type Lunch with Bill on Friday at 12:30. In the top-right corner of the note, click the Close button.**

   Outlook saves the note and closes it.

3. **In the Notes window, right-click the icon for the note you just created.**

   A shortcut menu is displayed.

4. **On the shortcut menu, click Forward.**

   A message window is displayed. The content of the note is entered in the Subject box as forwarded information. The note is displayed in the bottom of the window as an attachment.

Lesson 7 Using Notes

> **TROUBLESHOOTING**
>
> You might find it difficult to click in front of the note icon. If your click selects the note, just press the left arrow key on your keyboard to move the cursor.

Send

5 In the To box, type the e-mail address of your class partner. Click in the message area before the note icon, and type **Want to join us?** Press Enter, and click the Send button.

The note is sent to your class partner.

Figure 7-9

Forwarded note

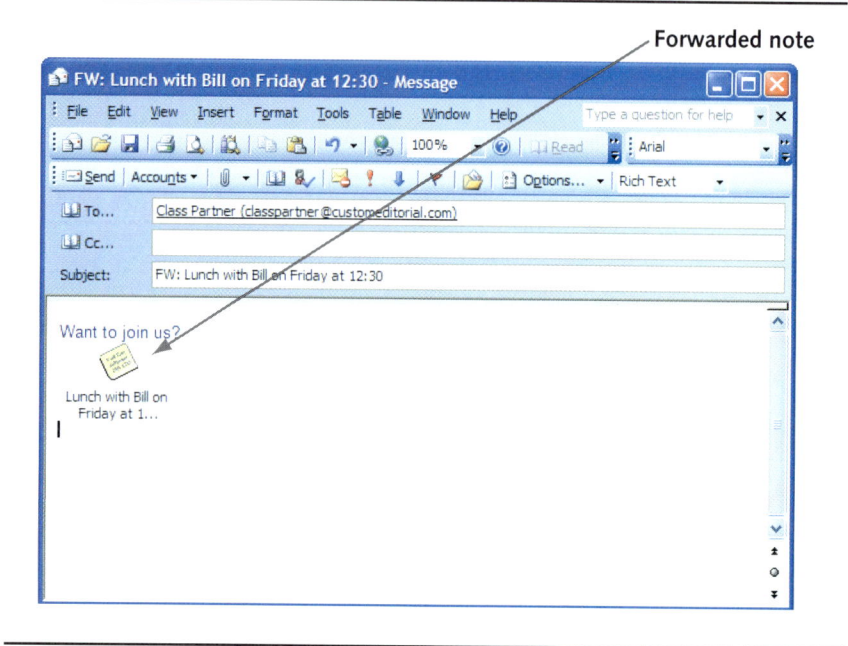

> **TROUBLESHOOTING**
>
> Because this message is not used in another part of the lesson, it is not necessary that the message be sent and received immediately.

◆ If necessary, click the Notes button on the Navigation pane to return to the Notes folder.

QUICK REFERENCE ▼
Forward a note

1 Right-click a note.
2 On the shortcut menu, click Forward.
3 Address and send the e-mail message.

QUICK CHECK

Q: How do you forward a note?

A: Attach it to an e-mail message.

Organizing Notes by View

THE BOTTOM LINE

Outlook lets you use the characteristics of your notes to organize them.

If you have created many notes for a single day or for one particular project, you can organize the notes like you organize other Outlook items. Use views, folders, or colors.

To display notes by view, open the Organize pane and click the Using Views link. Select a view from the Change Your View list. You can also click one of the views on the Navigation panel.

Figure 7-10

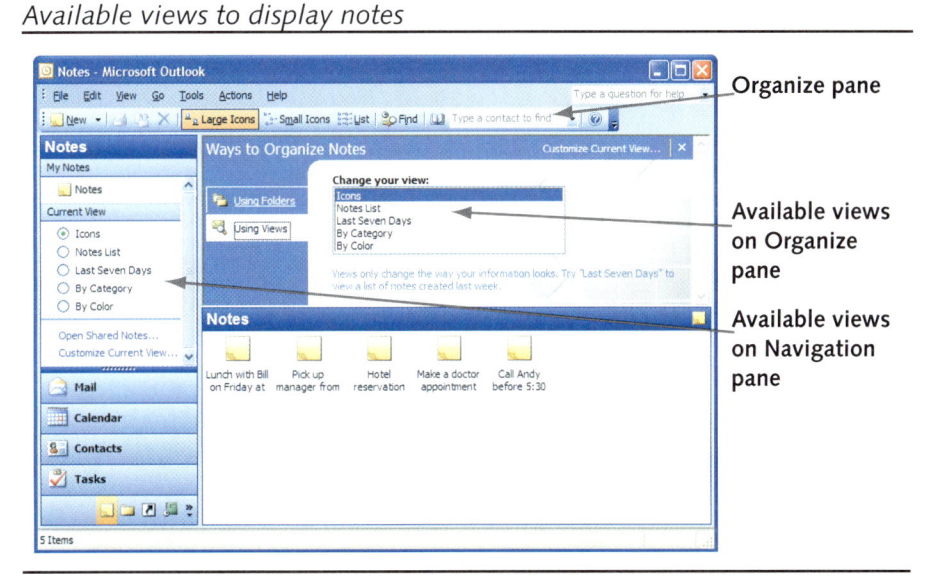

Available views to display notes

The available views you can use are Icons, Notes List, Last Seven Days, By Category, and By Color. The Icons and Notes List do not apply a filter. All notes are displayed. The remaining views apply a filter. Only the notes that meet the requirement are displayed. For example, a note created eight days ago is not displayed on the Last Seven Days view. Filtered and unfiltered views are described in the following table.

View	Description
Icons	Notes are displayed in the Notes folder as icons. Part of the first paragraph of the note is displayed below the icon to identify the note. This is the default view.
Notes List	Notes are displayed in a table divided by the Icon, Subject, Created, and Categories columns.
Last Seven Days	Only notes created in the last seven days are displayed.
By Category	Notes are displayed in a table divided by the Icon, Subject, and Created columns. The notes are grouped by categories, represented by gray boxes with the heading *Categories: (Category) [number] items*. Click the plus sign in a box to view the notes in the group and click the minus sign to hide the notes.

(continued)

(continued)

View	Description
By Color	Notes are displayed in a table divided by the Icon, Subject, Created, and Category columns. The notes are grouped by color, represented by gray boxes with the heading *Color: Color ([number] items)*.

Notes are yellow by default. However, you can change the color of notes. The colors provide a way to organize them. For example, you can display all personal notes in green and all business notes in yellow. To change the color of a note, right-click a note, point to Color on the shortcut menu, and select a color. Notes can be blue, green, pink, yellow, or white.

> **TROUBLESHOOTING**
>
> You can't change the color of a note on the Windows desktop by right-clicking the note. To change the color, open the note, click the note icon in the top-left corner of the note, point to color, and select the desired note color.

Organize notes

Using the notes created previously, you will color two notes and change the view of the Notes window.

1 **In the Notes window, right-click the note "Make a doctor appointment for Sally."**

A shortcut menu is displayed.

2 **Point to Color and click Blue.**

The note changes to blue.

3 **In the Notes window, right-click the note "Hotel reservation number: K28D62."**

A shortcut menu is displayed.

4 **Point to Color and click Green.**

The note changes to green.

5 **Open the Tools menu and select the Organize option.**

The Organize pane is displayed.

6 **In the Organize pane, click the Using Views link.**

The Using Views section of the Organize pane is displayed.

7 **In the Organize pane, click By Color in the Change Your View list. If necessary, click the plus sign (+) in the gray box on the left side of each group.**

Outlook groups the notes by color and displays a description and a gray box for each color group.

Figure 7-11

Views notes by color

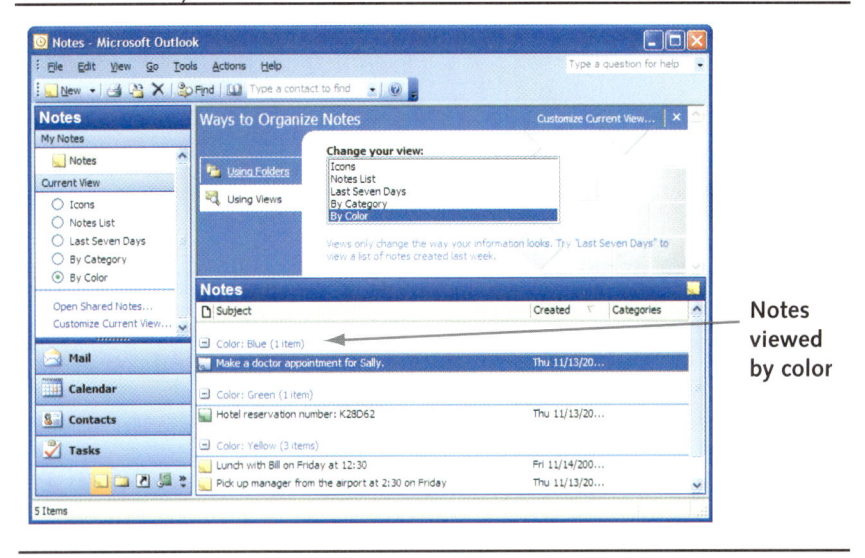

[Screenshot of Notes - Microsoft Outlook showing Ways to Organize Notes pane with Change your view options: Icons, Notes List, Last Seven Days, By Category, By Color. Notes are grouped by color: Blue, Green, Yellow.]

Notes viewed by color

ANOTHER METHOD

Select a view on the Navigation pane.

8 **In the Change Your View list, select Icons.**

Notes are displayed in the Icons view.

◆ Leave the Organize pane open for the next exercise.

QUICK REFERENCE ▼

Organize notes

1 Right-click a note.
2 Change the color or other characteristic.
3 Open the Organize pane and click the Using Views link.
4 In the Change Your View list, select a view.

QUICK CHECK

Q: Why would you change the color of a note?

A: **Use color to organize your notes.**

Organizing Notes by Folder

THE BOTTOM LINE

Just as other components in Outlook are organized in folders, related notes can be kept together in a folder.

Organizing Notes

Related notes can be placed together in a single folder to organize notes. Select a note to be placed in a folder. Display the Organize pane and click the Using Folders option. In the Using Folders section, select a folder in the Move Note Selected Below To field. Click the Move button.

Figure 7-12

Organize pane to assign notes to folders

If the existing folders aren't adequate, create a new one. To add a new folder, click the New Folder button in the top-right corner of the Organize pane, type a name for the folder, and click OK.

Organize notes

You will now create a folder, name it Personal Notes, and move an existing note to the folder.

1 **In the Organize pane, click the Using Folders link.**

The Using Folder section of the Organize pane is displayed.

2 **In the top-right corner of the Organize pane, click the New Folder button.**

The Create New Folder dialog box is displayed. The insertion point is located in the Name box.

3 **In the Name box, type Personal Notes, and verify that Notes is selected as the destination.**

The new folder will be placed in the Notes folder.

Lesson 7 Using Notes 227

Figure 7-13

Creating a new folder for notes

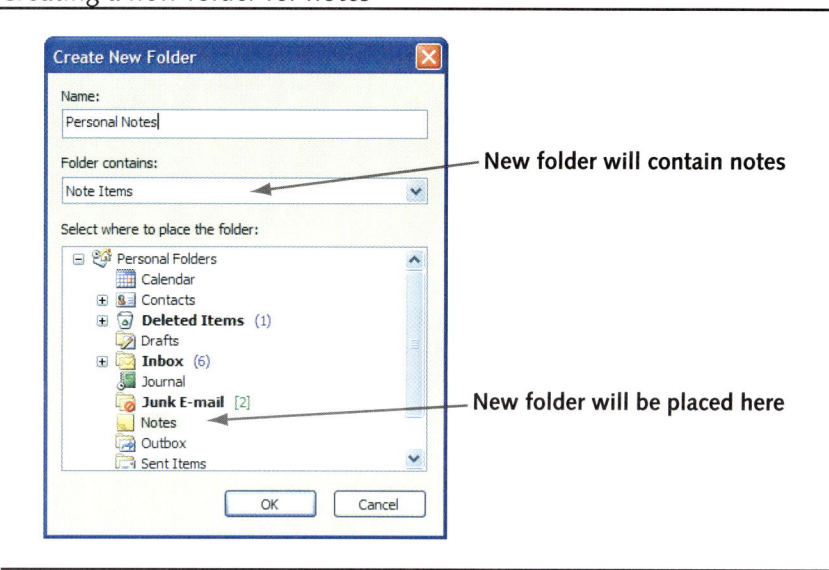

— New folder will contain notes

— New folder will be placed here

4 **Click OK.**

The folder is created.

5 **Click the note "Lunch with Bill on Friday at 12:30."**

The note is selected.

6 **In the Organize pane, click the Move button.**

The note is moved to the Personal Notes folder.

7 **On the Navigation pane, click the Personal Notes folder.**

The Organize pane is closed and the note *Lunch with Bill on Friday at 12:30* is displayed in the Notes window.

Figure 7-14

Note placed in the new folder

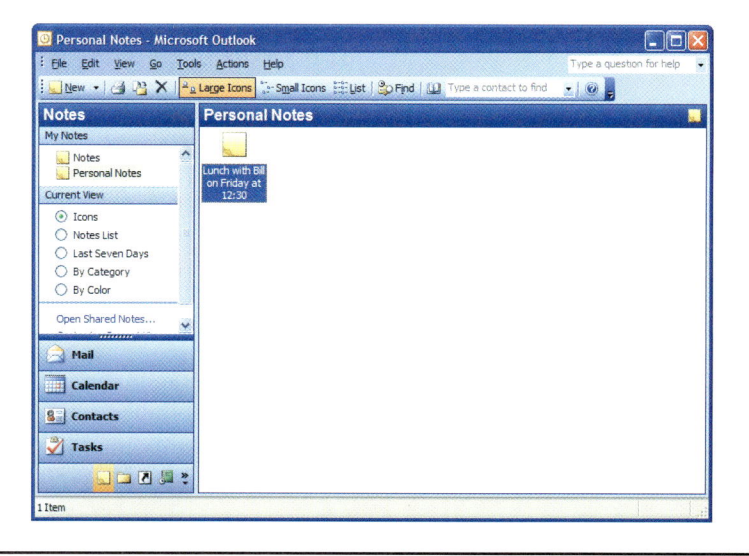

8 On the Navigation pane, click the Notes folder.

The contents of the Notes folder are displayed. The note you moved is no longer displayed.

ANOTHER METHOD

To change a view, you can also open the View menu, point to Arrange By, point to Current View, and select a view.

QUICK REFERENCE ▼
Organize notes by folders

1 Open the Organize pane and click the Using Folders link.
2 In the Organize pane, select or create a folder.
3 In the Notes pane, select a note.
4 In the Organize pane, click the Move button.

QUICK CHECK

Q: What can you do if the standard folders are not appropriate for storing your notes?

A: **Create new folders.**

Deleting Notes

THE BOTTOM LINE

Once they are no longer needed you delete notes to prevent the build-up of clutter on your screen.

When you no longer need a note, you can delete it to remove the item from your Notes window or your Windows desktop. Like other Outlook items, when you delete a note, it is moved to the Deleted Items folder. Deleted notes remain in the Deleted Items folder until you empty it. You can restore a note by opening the Deleted Items folder and dragging the note to the Notes button on the Navigation pane.

Delete a note

Now that you are done with the notes you will delete a note.

1 **In the Notes window, click the note Call Andy before 5:30.**

The note is selected.

2 **On the Standard toolbar, click the Delete button.**

The note moves to the Deleted Items folder.

3 **On the Navigation pane, click the Folder List button, and then click the Deleted Items folder to view the deleted note.**

ANOTHER METHOD

To delete a note, you can also right-click the note and click Delete.

- If you are continuing to the next lesson, keep Outlook open.
- If you are not continuing to the next lesson, close Outlook.

QUICK REFERENCE ▼

Delete a note

1. Select a note.
2. Click the Delete button on the standard toolbar.

QUICK CHECK

Q: Why do you delete notes?
A: Delete notes to reduce clutter.

Key Points

- ✔ Outlook lets you create and edit notes in the Notes folder.
- ✔ Once you have created notes you can copy and move them to your desktop to view reminders when you are not using Outlook.
- ✔ Notes can be converted to another Outlook item, such as a task or message.
- ✔ You can forward a note as an e-mail attachment.
- ✔ Like all Outlook elements, notes can be organized by views, folders, and colors.
- ✔ When notes are no longer needed you can delete them.

Quick Quiz

True/False

T F 1. Notes can hold a maximum of 100 words.
T F 2. You can use the toolbar to format the text in a note.
T F 3. When you close a note, it is saved in the Notes window.
T F 4. Use the scroll bar to view all the text in a long note.
T F 5. You can see notes when Outlook isn't open.

Multiple Choice

1. Drag a note to a different Outlook folder to _____.
   a. save the note
   b. delete the note
   c. convert it to a different type of Outlook item
   d. All of the above

2. Attach a note to a(n) _____ to send it to a friend.
   a. e-mail message
   b. appointment
   c. task
   d. All of the above

3. By default, a note is _____.
   a. blue
   b. yellow
   c. green
   d. pink

4. Some views use a _____ to limit the notes displayed in the view.
   a. maximize button
   b. minimize button
   c. filter
   d. All of the above

5. To restore a note, _____.
   a. edit the note
   b. drag it to the Notes button
   c. change its color
   d. resize the note

Short Answer

1. What is a note?
2. Describe two ways you can organize notes.
3. How do you move a note to another folder?
4. How do you delete a note?
5. How do you copy a note?
6. How do you copy a note to the desktop?
7. How do you create a note?
8. What does a note become when you forward it?

On Your Own

Exercise 1

Create the following notes: Make dentist appointment, Call car repair shop for tune-up appointment, Follow up on picnic activities, and Set up luncheon meeting for the president of Adventure Works. The first two notes are the most important, so copy them to your desktop.

Exercise 2

Move the note "Set up luncheon meeting for the president of Adventure Works" to the Tasks folder. Forward the note "Follow up on picnic activities" to your class partner.

One Step Further

Exercise 1

Move the note "Make dentist appointment" to the Windows desktop. Modify the note by adding the text June 14 at 2:15.

Exercise 2

Change the color of the personal notes to green. Move the green notes to the Personal Notes folder you created earlier in the lesson.

Exercise 3

Create three additional notes. Color-code the notes. Organize the notes by color.

LESSON 8

Customizing Outlook

After completing this lesson, you will be able to:

✔ *Set Outlook startup options.*
✔ *Customize the Navigation pane.*
✔ *Create a shortcut on the Navigation pane.*
✔ *Use and customize Outlook Today.*
✔ *Create a Personal Folders file.*
✔ *Import a Microsoft Access database into Outlook.*
✔ *Export Outlook data to a Microsoft Excel database.*

KEY TERMS

- export
- group
- import
- map
- Outlook Today
- Personal Folders file
- private store

You already know the basics of Microsoft Office Outlook 2003. You can send and receive e-mail messages and create and use items such as contacts, tasks, and appointments. Now you need to organize the information and customize Outlook to fit your needs.

As an illustration, think of your desk at work. Although it is similar to many other desks in your office building (and might even be one of many identical desks in identically sized cubicles), your desk is unique. Your inbox, telephone, and favorite pen are easily accessible. Information about the project that is currently "hot" is carefully placed in a folder and stored in a special location. A picture taken during your last vacation reminds you of the world outside the office. In other words, your office space is set up to suit your preferences.

Microsoft Outlook can also be adjusted to fit your needs. Display the functions you use the most and hide others. Create folders to organize and store project information. Set your preferences to make Outlook work for you and accommodate your work style.

In this lesson, you will learn how to modify the display of the Navigation pane. You will customize the view of your daily tasks and events by using Outlook Today. You will create a backup method for your important messages. Finally, you will learn how to import and export data between Outlook and other Microsoft Office System applications to avoid entering data more than once.

IMPORTANT

Before you can use the practice files in this lesson, you need to install them from the companion CD for this book to their default location. For additional information on how to find and open files used in this book, see the "Using the CD-ROM" section at the beginning of this book.

To complete the exercises in this lesson, you will need to use the files named Guests and AW Address List in the Outlook Practice folder located on your hard disk.

> **IMPORTANT**
>
> To complete some of the exercises in this lesson, you will need to exchange e-mail messages with a class partner. If you don't have a class partner or you are performing the exercises alone, you can send the message to yourself. Simply enter your own e-mail address instead of a class partner's address.

Setting Outlook Startup Options

> **THE BOTTOM LINE**
>
> You can create a desktop shortcut to open Outlook. Then you can adjust the target to determine the folder displayed when Outlook is launched.

When you sit down to work, you want the tools and information you need at your fingertips. Setting a few preferences in Outlook will set you up for success. To start Outlook from your desktop, create a shortcut that launches Outlook when you double-click the icon. Identify the Outlook information you want to see when you launch the application. Adjust the settings to display the Outlook folder you prefer to see when you launch the application.

> **IMPORTANT**
>
> Outlook must be closed to create a shortcut on your desktop. Close Outlook before you start this exercise.

Set startup options

You begin this exercise by creating a shortcut to the Outlook application on your desktop. Then you identify the Outlook function to be displayed when you start the application.

> **TROUBLESHOOTING**
>
> Use the Microsoft Search function to find the Outlook application. Click the Start button in the Microsoft Windows XP taskbar to open the Start menu, and select the Search option. Select the option All Files and Folders. Enter the search text **Outlook.exe** in the first box to find the Outlook application.

Lesson 8 Customizing Outlook 233

1 **Open Windows Explorer and navigate to the Outlook application.**

The name of the Outlook program file contains .exe if your computer displays file name extensions. If icons are displayed, the OUTLOOK.EXE file is identified by the Outlook icon. OUTLOOK.EXE is usually located in C:\Program Files\Microsoft Office\OFFICE11.

Figure 8-1

Outlook application

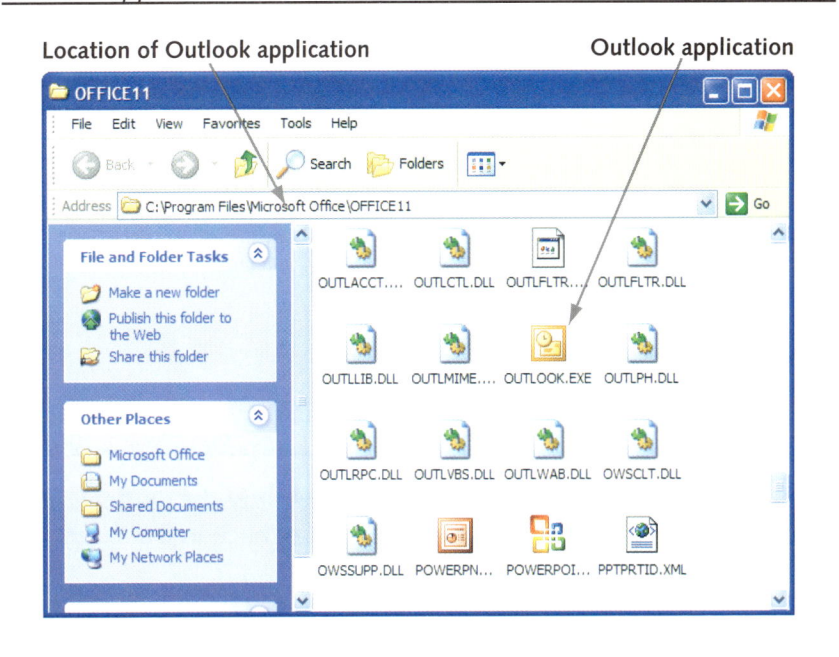

2 **Right-click the OUTLOOK.EXE file. Select the Create Shortcut option from the displayed menu.**

The shortcut is created in the same folder. The file is named Shortcut to OUTLOOK.EXE.

3 **Close or minimize any open windows so you can see the shortcut you just created and a clear area on your desktop. Drag the shortcut to your desktop and close Windows Explorer.**

The shortcut enables you to start Outlook with a simple double-click rather than using the Microsoft XP Start menu.

Figure 8-2

Outlook shortcut on the desktop

4 **Right-click the new shortcut on your desktop, and click Properties. If necessary, click the Shortcut tab.**

This window enables you to identify the events that happen when you start the Outlook application.

234 **Lesson 8** Customizing Outlook

Figure 8-3

Properties of the Outlook shortcut

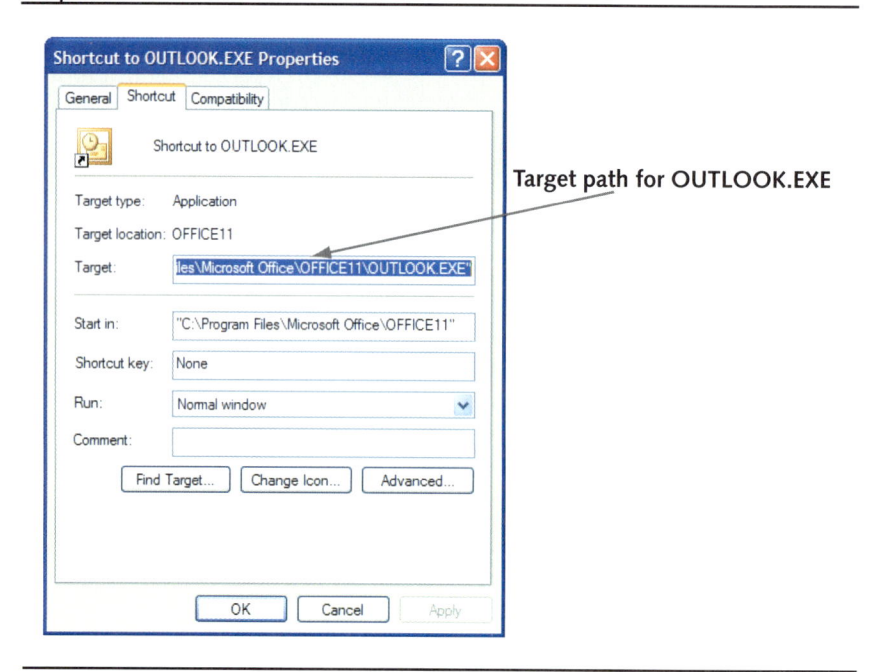

[Screenshot of Shortcut to OUTLOOK.EXE Properties dialog box, with Target path for OUTLOOK.EXE indicated]

5 **To identify the Outlook function you want to display when Outlook opens, click in the Target field, type a space after the target path, and type /select outlook:xxxxx (where xxxxx is the folder name) in the field. Click OK to close the dialog box.**

Foldername identifies the name of the Outlook folder. Don't use spaces in the foldername variable. For example, to start Outlook in the Calendar folder, type /select outlook:calendar in the field. To start Outlook in the Outlook Today folder, type /select outlook:today in the field.

6 **Double click the shortcut to open Outlook.**

Outlook will open to the folder you indicated.

QUICK CHECK

Q: How can you start Outlook from your desktop?

A: **Create a shortcut on the desktop.**

ANOTHER METHOD

This procedure sets the target when this shortcut is used to start Outlook. To set the target to Outlook Today every time Outlook is launched, set the option in Outlook when you customize Outlook Today.

◆ Keep Outlook open for the next exercise.

QUICK REFERENCE ▼

Set startup options

1 Close Outlook.

2 Open Windows Explorer and navigate to the Outlook application.

3 Right-click the OUTLOOK.EXE file. Select the Create Shortcut option from the displayed menu.

4 Drag the shortcut to your desktop and close Windows Explorer.

Customizing the Navigation pane

THE BOTTOM LINE
Adjusting the Navigation pane increases convenience and efficiency for you.

The purpose of the Navigation pane is to make it easier for you to navigate through different areas in Outlook. It has a default setup for the buttons it contains, the size of the pane, and the views it presents in each folder. However, you can change the Navigation pane to make it work for you. In fact, if you prefer to use the Go menu to access the standard Outlook folders and views, you can hide the Navigation pane to provide more room to display folder content.

In the previous lesson, you modified the Navigation pane by adding the Journal button. You can also customize the Navigation pane by changing its width, which changes the size of the viewing area of each folder. To change the width of the Navigation pane, position the mouse pointer over the right edge of the Navigation pane. When the mouse pointer changes to a double-headed arrow, drag the edge right or left to increase or decrease the width of the Navigation pane.

After you have worked with Outlook for a few days, you may find that you use some folders more than others. You might not use the Journal at all, but you are constantly exchanging e-mail messages and making notes to store order information reported by your sales representatives. To increase your effectiveness, you can remove the Journal button from the Navigation pane and move the Notes button up so it is displayed below the Mail button. On your screen, this may mean that the Notes button becomes full-size and a different button is moved to the last row, where it is displayed as an icon.

TIP
To customize the toolbars and menus in Outlook, click Customize on the Tools menu. Three tabs appear in the Customize dialog box. You can display additional toolbars as well as create new ones by using the Toolbars tab. You can add buttons to toolbars and commands to menus by dragging commands from the Commands tab on the dialog box to the appropriate position on the toolbar or menu. You can control the display of the menu commands and the appearance of a toolbar by using the Options tab.

Customize the Navigation pane

With Outlook open you will now change the width of the Navigation pane, and hide and display the pane. You will also hide the Journal button and change the sequence of the buttons in the Navigation pane.

1 **If necessary, click the Mail button on the Navigation pane.**

The contents of the Inbox folder are displayed.

2 **Position the mouse pointer on the right edge of the Navigation pane.**

The mouse pointer appears as a double arrow.

3 **Drag the mouse pointer to the right about one inch.**

The Navigation pane becomes wider, and the panes to the right become smaller.

Figure 8-4

Adjusted pane width

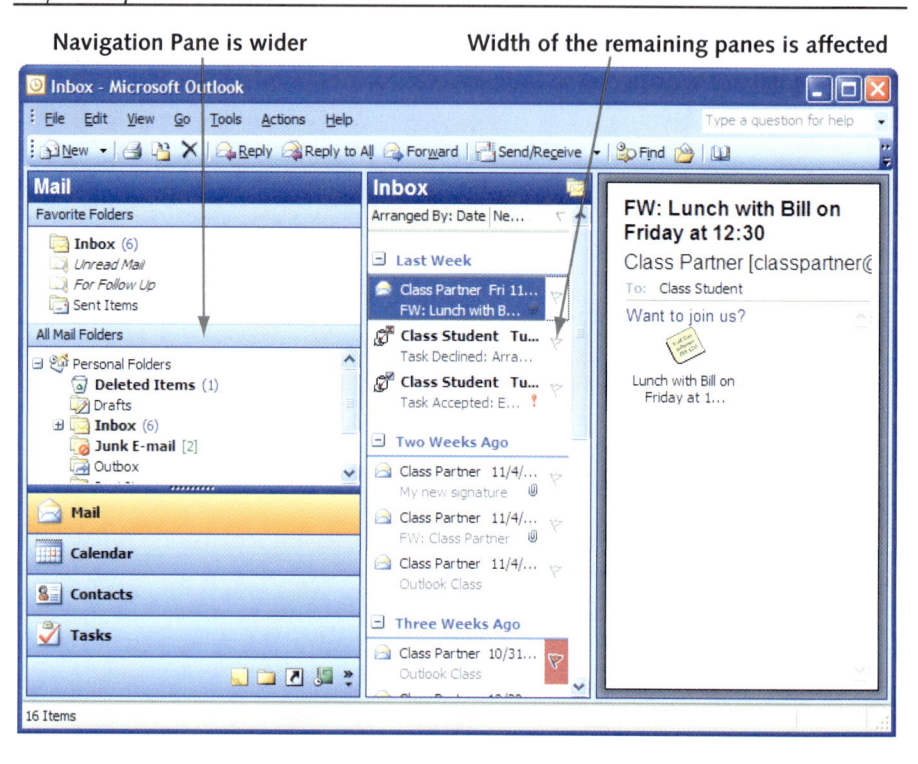

4 **Drag the right border of the Navigation pane to the left about one inch, returning the border to its original location.**

The Navigation pane becomes smaller and the panes to the right become larger.

5 **Open the View menu and select the Navigation pane option.**

The Navigation pane is hidden and the other panes become wider.

Lesson 8 Customizing Outlook 237

Figure 8-5

Navigation pane is not displayed

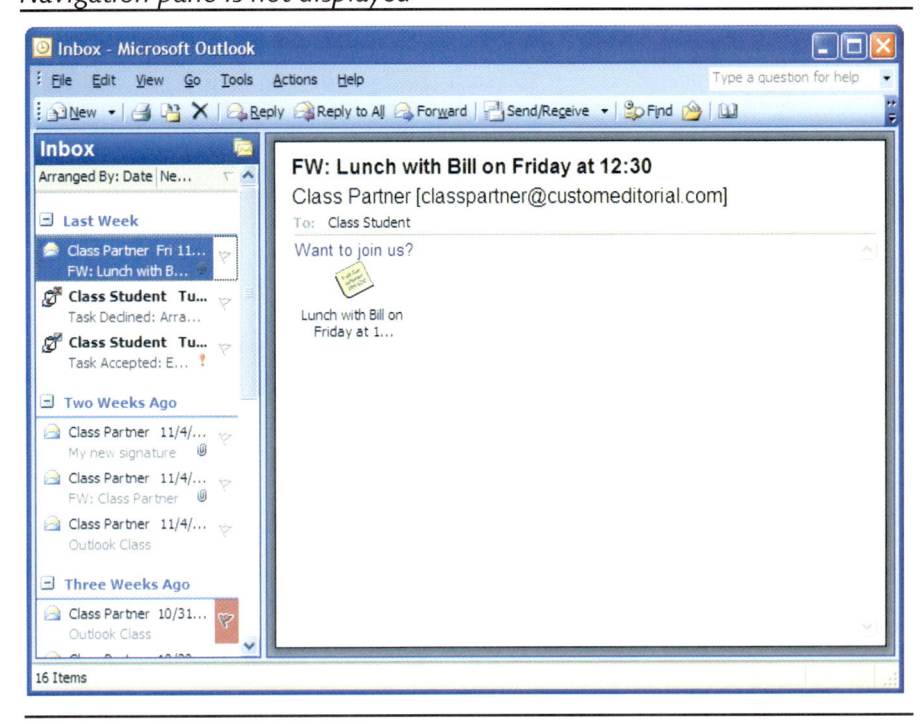

6 Open the View menu and select the Navigation pane option again. Right-click the bottom portion of the Navigation pane and select Navigation pane Options from the displayed menu.

The Navigation pane Options dialog box is displayed.

Figure 8-6

Navigation pane Options dialog box

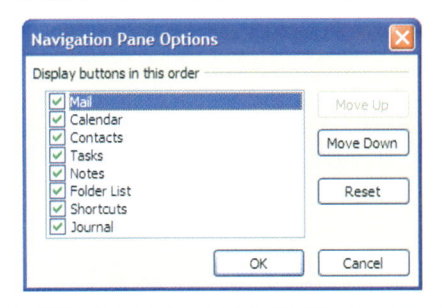

7 Click the box in front of the Journal option.

The Journal option is cleared. When you return to the Outlook window, the Journal button will not be displayed in the Navigation pane.

8 Click the Notes option and click the Move Up button three times. Click the OK button.

The Navigation pane Options dialog box is closed. The Navigation pane has been modified.

Figure 8-7

Modified Navigation pane

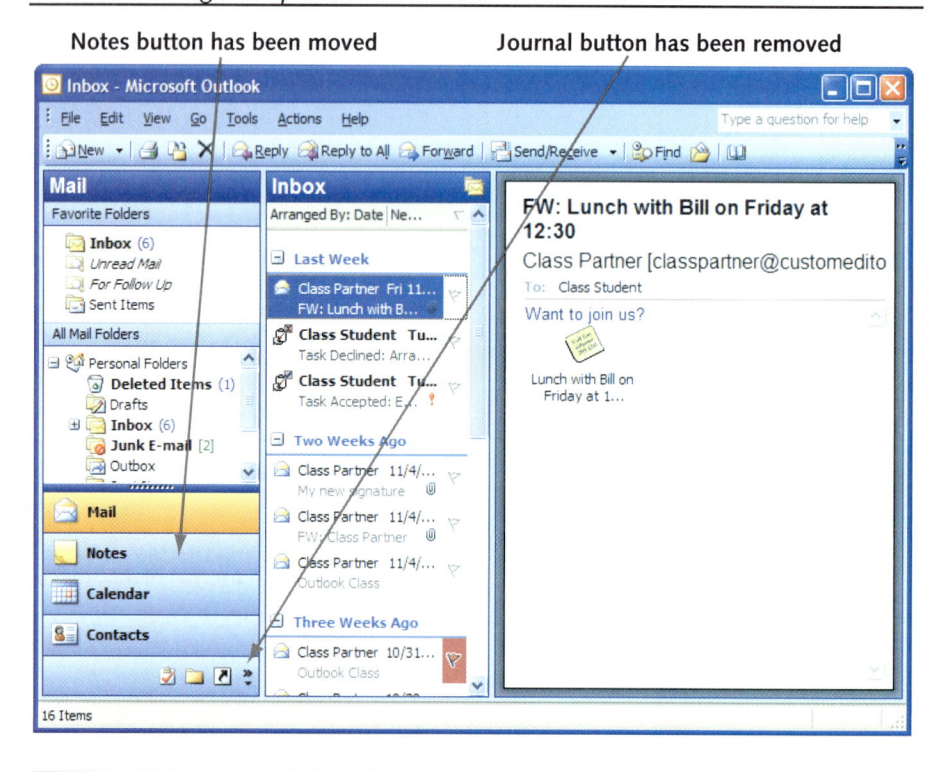

9 Right-click the Navigation pane and select Navigation pane Options from the displayed menu.

The Navigation pane Options dialog box is displayed.

10 Click the Notes option and click the Reset button. Click the OK button.

The Navigation pane Options dialog box is closed. The Navigation pane has been modified. Its configuration now matches its default appearance. The Journal button is not displayed and the Notes button is below the Tasks button.

◆ Keep Outlook open for the next exercise.

QUICK REFERENCE ▼

Change the sequence of buttons in the Navigation pane

1 Right-click the Navigation pane and select Navigation pane Options from the displayed menu.

2 Select an option and click Move Up or Move Down to change the sequence of the buttons.

3 Click the OK button.

QUICK CHECK

Q: Why would you want to hide the Navigation pane?

A: Hiding the Navigation pane provides more viewing area to display the folder content.

Creating a Shortcut on the Navigation Pane

THE BOTTOM LINE

Like other Office System applications, you can create shortcuts to access Outlook folders. These shortcuts can then be placed in groups to organize them.

You can create shortcuts to Outlook folders. This enables you to access frequently used folders with a single click, including folders you created to organize your Outlook items. This is usually faster and easier than using the Folder List because you specify the links in the group. For maximum efficiency, limit the links to ones you use regularly. Don't create a link to every Outlook folder.

To organize your shortcuts, you can create groups. Place shortcuts in a **group**. For example, a manager at Adventure Works is supervising several active projects. She created a group titled Active Projects. This enables her to keep links to the various projects together.

Create an Outlook shortcut

Now you will create the Active Projects group and add shortcuts to the other Outlook folders you have created.

TROUBLESHOOTING

Your shortcuts might be different from the shortcuts displayed in this exercise.

1 **On the Navigation pane, click the Shortcuts button.**

The Shortcuts area is displayed in the upper area of the Navigation pane. The content in the other panes doesn't change. The Inbox is still displayed on the right.

240 Lesson 8 Customizing Outlook

Figure 8-8

Standard shortcuts

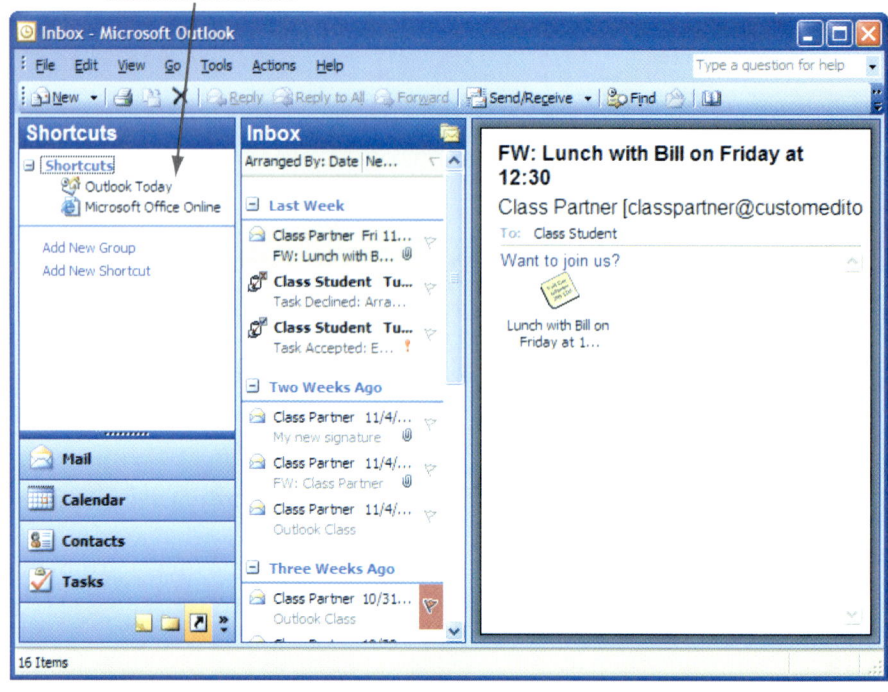

2. **On the Navigation pane, click the Add New Group option.**

   The highlighted text *New Group* is added above the dividing line. The highlight indicates that you can simply type to change the name of the new group.

3. **Type Active Projects and press Enter.**

   The new group is renamed.

> **TIP**
>
> To delete a group, right-click the group and click Remove Group on the shortcut menu that appears.

Figure 8-9

New group added

4. **Right-click the Active Projects folder and select the Add New Shortcut option.**

   The Add To Navigation pane dialog box is displayed.

Lesson 8 Customizing Outlook 241

Figure 8-10

Add To Navigation pane dialog box

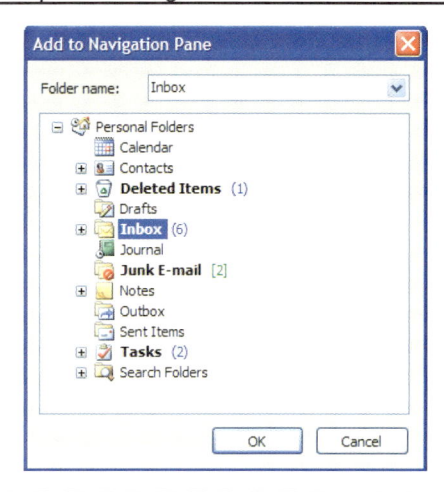

5. **Click the plus sign (+) next to the Inbox folder to display the Parties folder.**

   This folder was created in a previous lesson.

6. **Click the Parties folder and click the OK button.**

   The Parties folder is displayed below the Active Projects folder. It is indented, indicating that it is located in the Active Projects folder.

   Figure 8-11

   New shortcut added

7. **Right-click the Active Projects folder and select the Add New Shortcut option.**

   The Add To Navigation pane dialog box is displayed.

8. **Click the plus sign (+) next to the Tasks folder to display the Picnic Tasks folder.**

   This folder was created in a previous lesson.

242   **Lesson 8** Customizing Outlook

9 Click the Picnic Tasks folder and click the OK button.

The Picnic Tasks folder is displayed below the Parties folder.

Figure 8-12
Shortcuts to active projects

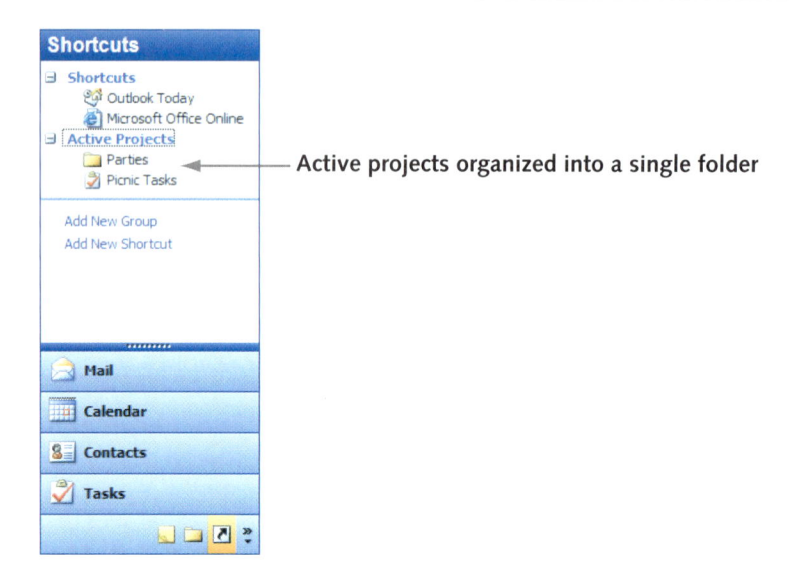

TIP

You can rearrange the shortcuts on the Navigation pane. Simply drag an icon and release the mouse button when a horizontal line appears at the new location.

QUICK CHECK

Q: How can you organize shortcuts on the Navigation pane?

A: **Place the shortcuts into groups.**

◆ Leave this screen open for the next exercise.

QUICK REFERENCE ▼

Add a new group

1 On the Navigation pane, click the Shortcuts button.

2 On the Navigation pane, click the Add New Group option.

3 Type the name of the folder and press Enter.

Add a new shortcut

1 On the Navigation pane, click the Shortcuts button.

2 On the Navigation pane, right-click the destination group for the shortcut and select the Add New Shortcut option.

3 Select the folder and click the OK button.

Using and Customizing Outlook Today

> **THE BOTTOM LINE**
>
> Outlook lets you customize Outlook Today to display the information that is important to you.

The Adventure Works general manager checks her schedule every morning while she drinks her first cup of coffee at the office. Using **Outlook Today**, you can view a summary of tasks and appointments for the day, as well as the number of new e-mail messages in your Inbox. The Drafts, Inbox, and Outbox mail folders appear in Outlook Today by default. You can add other Outlook folders as well. For example, if you created folders for each important project you work on, you can add those folders to Outlook Today so that you can quickly access them.

To set Outlook Today as your start page—the first Outlook window you view each time you start the application—select the Customize Outlook Today option in the right pane and click the check box labeled When starting, go directly to Outlook Today. This has the same result as setting the target for the Outlook shortcut you placed on your desktop. However, this sets the option to go straight to Outlook Today every time you start Outlook. The target in the shortcut works only when you use the shortcut to start the application.

The Outlook Today Calendar automatically displays the events for the current day and the next four days. You can customize the Calendar to display from one to seven days. You can also organize tasks in Outlook Today by selecting options so that you can view all tasks, only the current day's tasks, or tasks with no due date. You can quickly sort tasks by due date, importance, when they were created, or scheduled start date. Choose a style for the Outlook Today page by selecting the number of columns and the color scheme.

Figure 8-13

Outlook Today

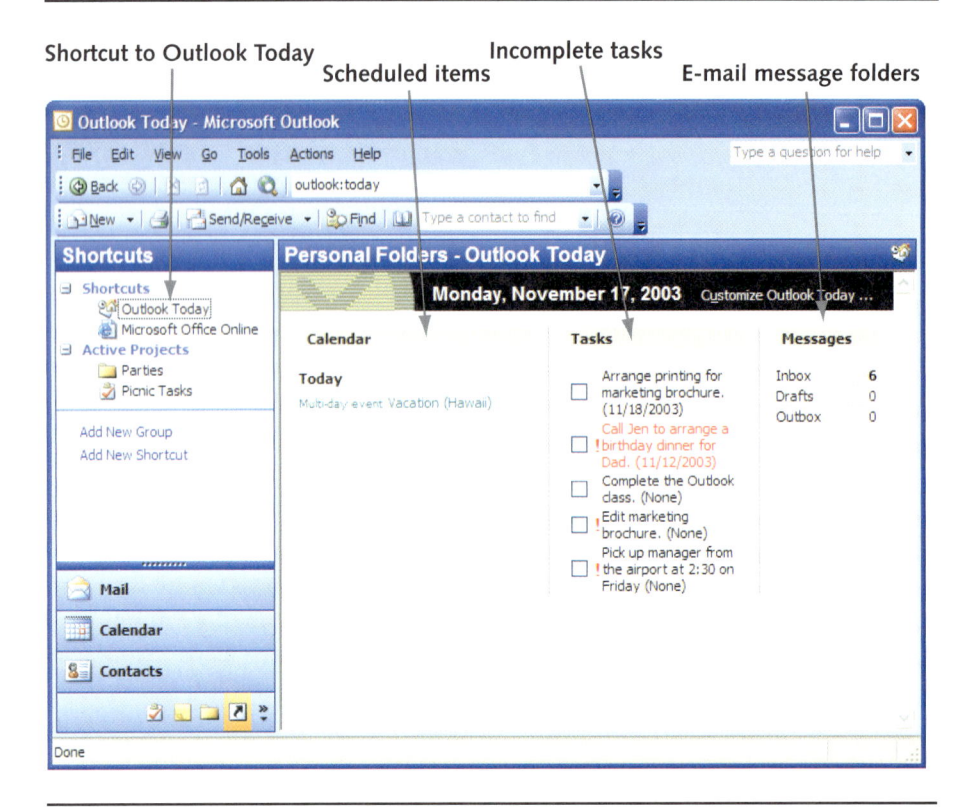

Shortcut to Outlook Today — Scheduled items — Incomplete tasks — E-mail message folders

Customize Outlook Today

You will now work with Outlook Today to customize the look to suit specific needs.

1 **Click the Outlook Today shortcut.**

Outlook Today is displayed.

TROUBLESHOOTING

If you don't have the Outlook Today shortcut, it might be located in your personal folders. Click the Folder List button and click Personal Folders on the folder list.

2 **In the top-right corner of the Outlook Today folder, click the Customize Outlook Today button.**

The Customize Outlook Today pane is displayed.

Lesson 8 Customizing Outlook 245

Figure 8-14

Customization options for Outlook Today

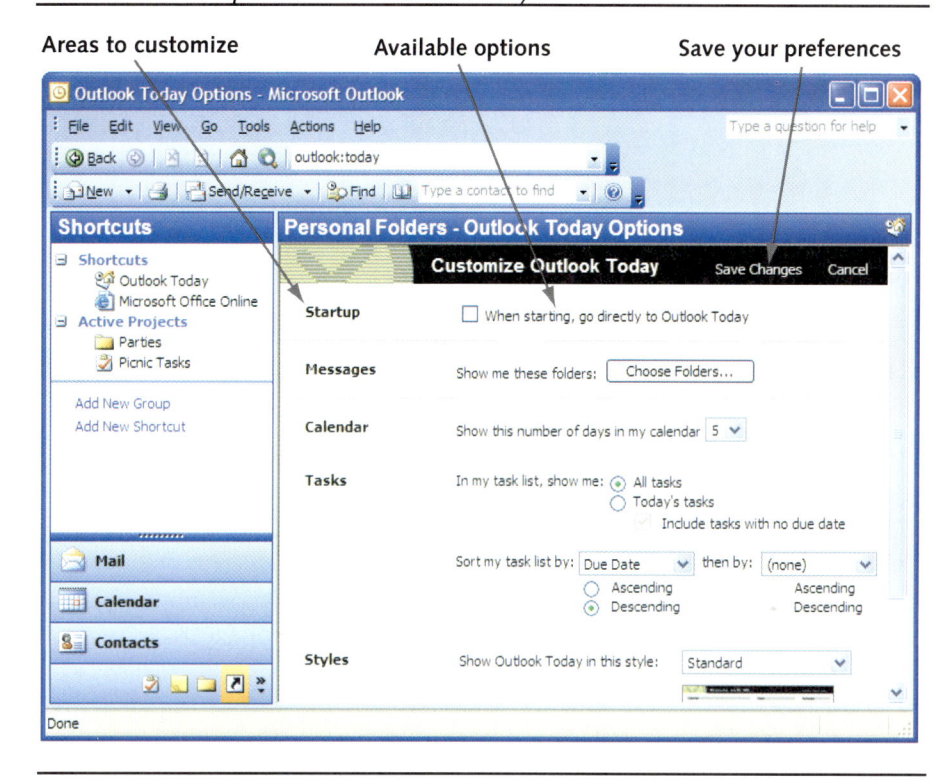

Areas to customize   Available options   Save your preferences

3. **Click the Startup option When Starting, Go Directly To Outlook Today.**

   Every time you start Outlook, Outlook Today will be displayed.

   ### ANOTHER METHOD

   If you double-click a shortcut on your desktop to start Outlook, you can set the starting target to display Outlook Today when the application is launched by using the shortcut.

4. **In the Messages section, click the Choose Folders button.**

   The Select Folder dialog box is displayed.

   Figure 8-15

   Folders that can be displayed in Outlook Today

Lesson 8 Customizing Outlook

5 Select the Notes check box, and click OK.

The number of notes will appear in Outlook Today.

6 In the Calendar section, click the Show This Number Of Days In My Calendar down arrow, and click 7.

Outlook Today will show your appointments for the next seven days.

7 In the Tasks section, click the Sort My Task List By down arrow, and click Importance.

The tasks displayed in Outlook Today will be organized from the most important task to the least important task.

8 In the Styles section, click the Show Outlook Today In This Style down arrow, and click Winter.

A small preview of the Winter style is displayed.

9 In the top-right corner of the Customize Outlook Today pane, click Save Changes.

The customized Outlook Today folder is displayed.

QUICK CHECK

Q: By default, which mail folders are displayed in Outlook Today?

A: The Drafts, Inbox, and Outbox mail folders appear in Outlook Today by default.

Figure 8-16

Customized Outlook Today

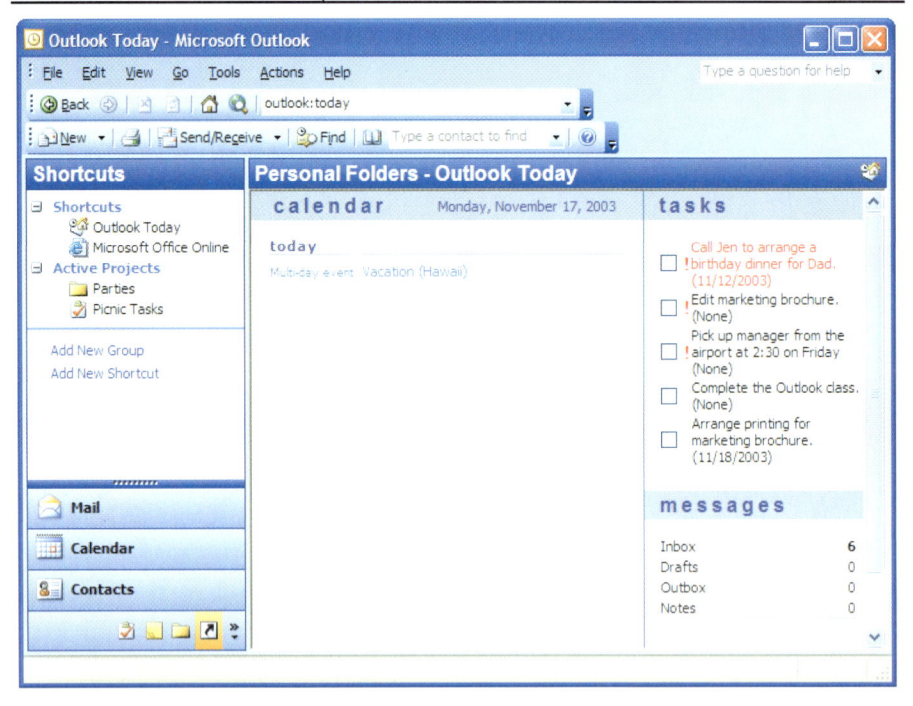

◆ Keep Outlook open for the next exercise.

QUICK REFERENCE ▼

Customize Outlook Today

1 Open Outlook.

2 In the top-right corner of the Outlook Today folder, click the Customize Outlook Today button.

3 Modify any options and click the Save Changes option.

Create Personal Folders

THE BOTTOM LINE

With Outlook, you can create a Personal Folders file to store Outlook items on your computer rather than a server.

All Outlook items are stored in a data file on the Outlook server or on your computer. If the items are stored on the server, they are placed in a file called a **private store**. If the items are stored on your computer, they are stored in a **Personal Folders file** identified by the extension .pst.

Create a Personal Folders file if you want to ensure that items normally stored on the server will be available when you aren't connected to the server. It also enables you to back up or move items for a specific project.

Create a Personal Folders file

You begin this exercise by creating a personal folders file. Then you save items in the folder, and open the folder.

1 Open the File menu, point to New, and click the Outlook Data File option.

The New Outlook Data File dialog box is displayed.

Figure 8-17

New Outlook Data File dialog box

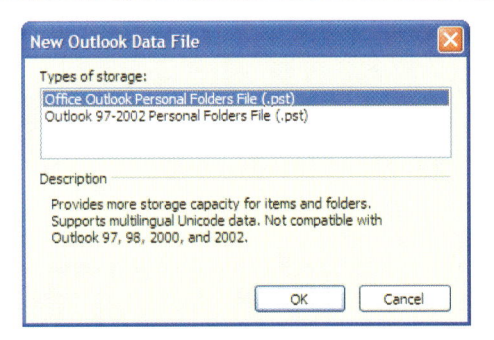

2 Click the OK button.

The Create Or Open Outlook Data File dialog box is displayed.

Figure 8-18

Create Or Open Outlook Data File dialog box

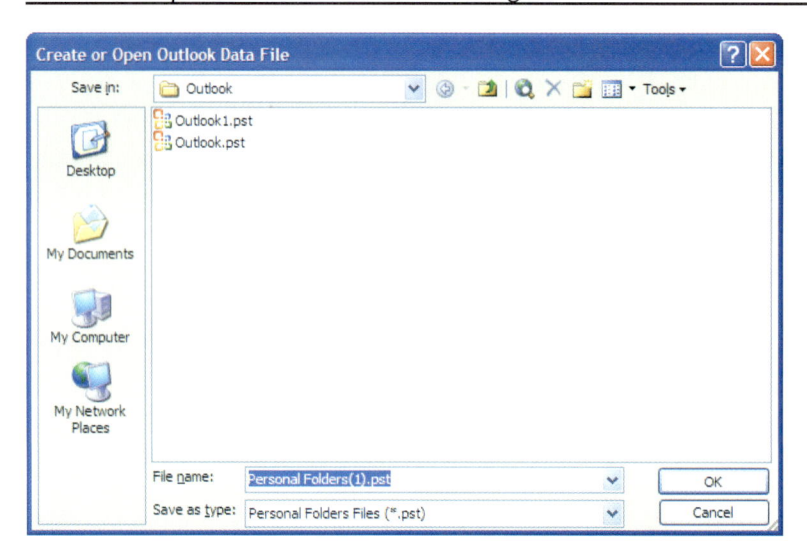

3 In the File Name box, type *classfolder*, and click OK.

The Create Microsoft Personal Folders dialog box is displayed.

4 In the File Name box in this dialog box, type the name *classfolder* again, and click OK.

The folder is created.

5 Click the Folder List button. Click the minus sign (–) to the left of Personal Folders.

The folder is collapsed. Classfolder is displayed at the same level.

6 Click the plus sign (+) to the left of the classfolder folder.

The Deleted Items and Search folders are located in the .pst folder by default.

7 Click the plus sign (+) to the left of Personal Folders and drag the bottom border of the folder list display area down.

This enables you to see most or all of the folders at the same time.

8 Hold the Ctrl key and drag the Inbox folder into the classfolder folder.

The Inbox is copied into the classfolder folder.

Figure 8-19

Inbox copied into .pst folder

◆ Drag the bottom border of the folder list display area to its original location.

◆ Keep Outlook open for the next exercise.

QUICK CHECK

Q: What extension identifies a Personal Folders file?

A: The extension .pst identifies a Personal Folders file.

QUICK REFERENCE ▼

Create a Personal Folders file

1. Open the File menu, point to New, and click the Outlook Data File option.
2. Click OK.
3. Type the name of the folder and click OK.
4. Type the name of the folder again and click OK.
5. Hold the Ctrl key and drag the folders into the .pst folder to be stored.

Importing a Microsoft Access Database into Outlook

THE BOTTOM LINE

Importing contact data enables you to avoid typing the same information again.

You don't want to type the same information twice. If you created a database of names and addresses in a Microsoft Office System application other than Outlook, you can import this information into the Contacts folder in Outlook. When you **import** data, you bring information from another program into the program you're currently using. For example, the marketing director created a database of guests in Microsoft Access. She decided that it would be useful to also have the contacts in Outlook. To avoid retyping each contact's information, she imported the Microsoft Access guest information into Outlook.

TIP

To import data from a text-editing program, the data must be in a tab-separated or comma-separated format before starting the import process.

The Access field names (such as First Name, Street, or City) are not required to match the field names in the Contacts folder (where you add the contact information). The Import and Export Wizard has a feature that lets you **map** your Access field names (which are called values) to similar Outlook field names. Mapping pairs an application's field names with similar field names in Outlook. For example, you would pair the field name Zip/Postal from another application to the field Business Postal Code in Outlook. Mapping is not a requirement. However, if you choose not to map values to fields, some of the information that you typed in Access might not appear in Outlook.

IMPORTANT

The Import/Export engine feature must be installed for this exercise to work. If an alert box appears during the exercise asking whether you want to install the feature, insert the Office or Outlook 2003 CD-ROM, and click Yes.

Import an Access database

You will now import an Access database of addresses into the Contacts folder.

1 **Click the Contacts button.**

The Contacts folder is displayed.

2 **On the File menu, click the Import And Export option.**

The Import And Export Wizard is initiated. The option Import From Another Program or file is already selected.

Figure 8-20

Import And Export Wizard dialog box

Lesson 8 Customizing Outlook 251

3 Click Next.

The next wizard dialog box is displayed. It asks you to select a file type to import from.

Figure 8-21
Import A File dialog box

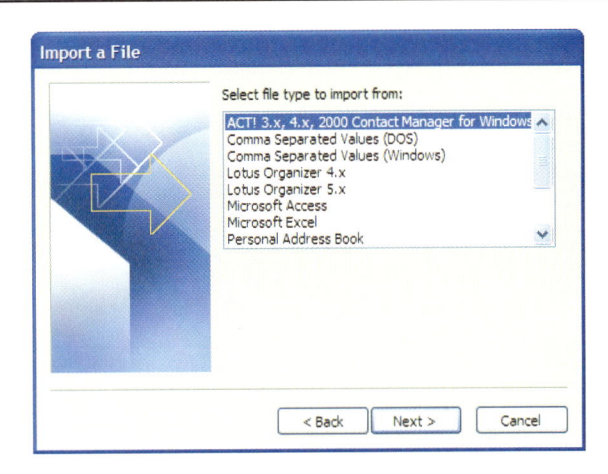

4 Scroll down if necessary, click Microsoft Access, and then click Next.

The next wizard dialog box is displayed. It asks you to locate the file to import.

Figure 8-22
Second Import A File dialog box

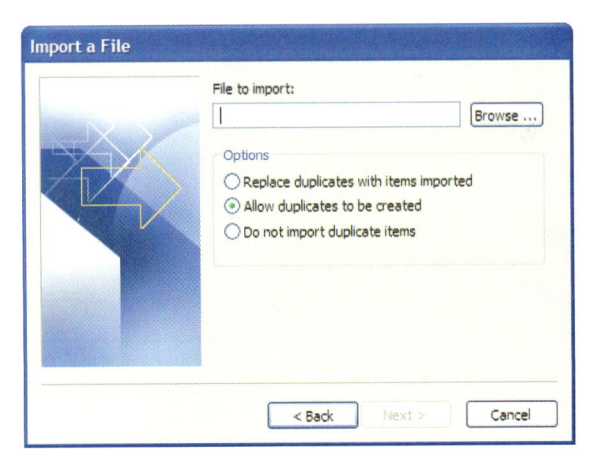

5 Browse to navigate to the Outlook Practice folder on your hard disk, and double-click the Guests file. Click Next.

The next wizard dialog box is displayed. It asks you to select the Outlook folder in which you want the imported information to be placed.

Figure 8-23

Third Import A File dialog box

6 **If necessary, scroll to display the Contacts folder, click the Contacts folder, and then click Next.**

The final wizard dialog box is displayed.

Figure 8-24

Final Import A File dialog box

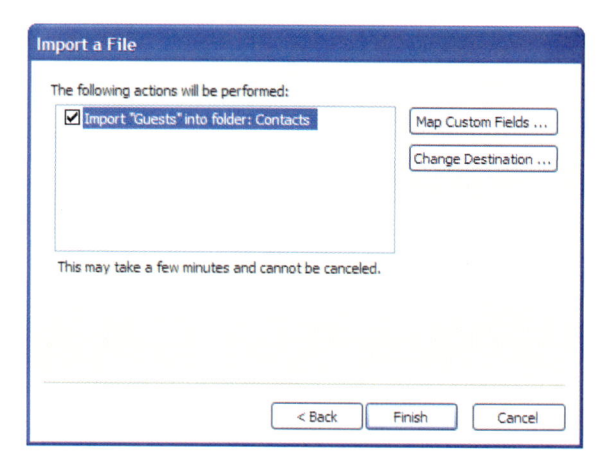

7 **Click the Map Custom Fields button.**

The Map Custom Fields dialog box is displayed.

Figure 8-25

Map Custom Fields dialog box

> **TROUBLESHOOTING**
>
> Notice that the values First Name and Last Name appear under the Mapped From column in the To section. Because the value in the From section and field in the To section are already the same, you do not have to drag these values onto the name fields.

8 In the To section, click the plus sign (+) to the left of the Name field.

The Name field is expanded, showing the elements of the field.

Figure 8-26

Expanded field in the Map Custom Fields dialog box

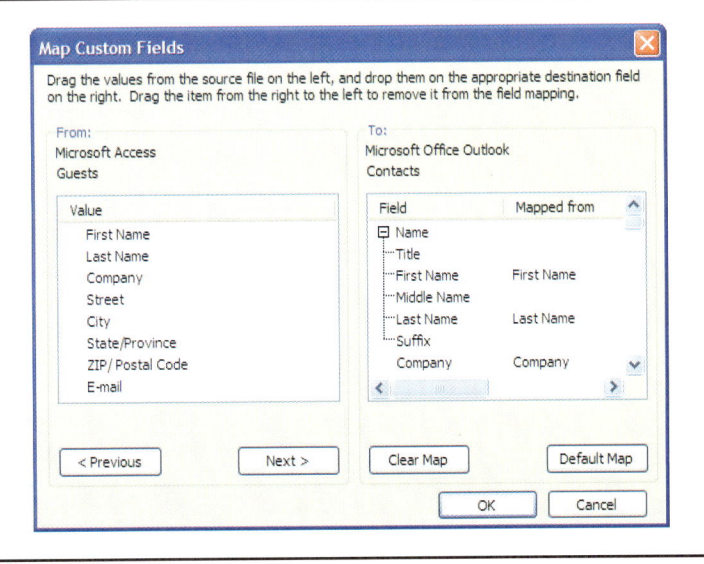

9 In the To section, scroll down to the Business Address field (so that it appears at the top of the list). In the To section, click the plus sign (+) to the left of the Business Address field.

The Business Address field expands, showing the elements of the field.

> **TROUBLESHOOTING**
>
> Outlook tries to "remember" values that have already been mapped to fields. It is possible that some values and fields already match because someone worked through this exercise before you mapped the fields.

10 In the From section, drag the Street value onto the first Business Street field in the To section.

The Street value is displayed next to the Business Street field, in the Mapped From column.

Figure 8-27

Street address mapped in the Map Custom Fields dialog box

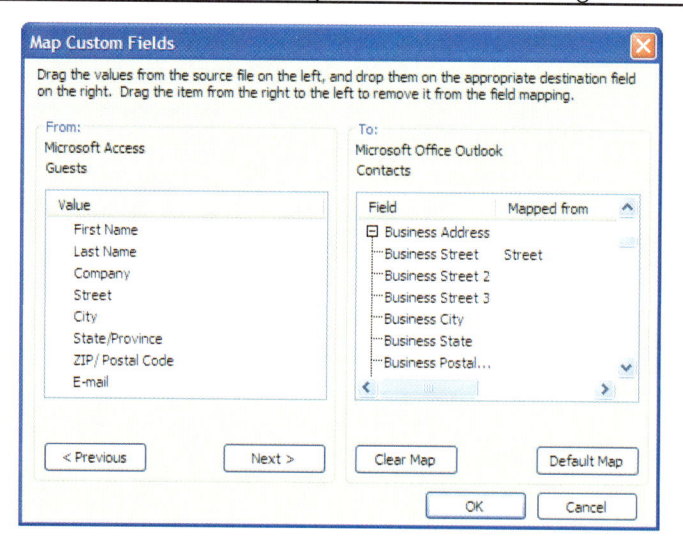

11 In the From section, drag the City value onto the Business City field in the To section.

The City value is displayed next to the Business City field, in the Mapped From column.

12 In the From section, drag the State/Province value onto the Business State field in the To section.

The State/Province value appears next to the Business State field, in the Mapped From column.

13 In the From section, drag the ZIP/Postal Code value onto the Business Postal Code field in the To section.

The ZIP/Postal Code value appears next to the Business Postal field, in the Mapped From column.

Lesson 8 Customizing Outlook 255

Figure 8-28

Complete address mapped in the Map Custom Fields dialog box

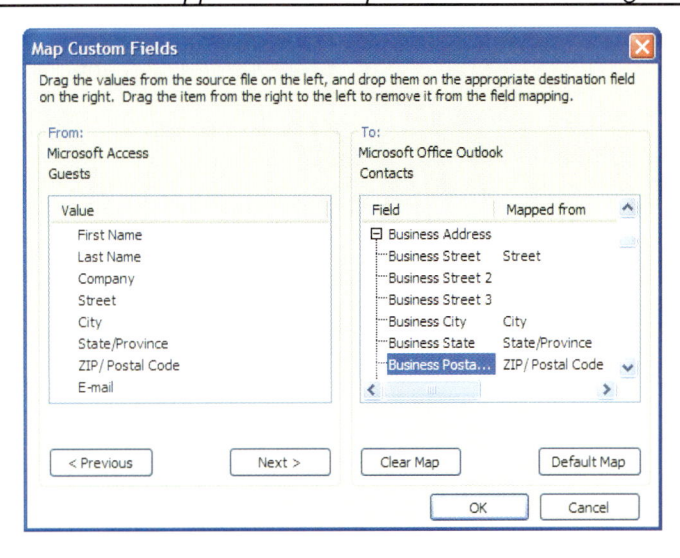

14 In the To section, scroll down until you see the E-Mail field.

The E-Mail field and the Mapped From value are the same, so you don't need to drag the value onto the field.

15 Click OK and click Finish.

A progress bar is displayed as the Access files are imported into the Contacts folder.

Figure 8-29

Outlook Contacts contains the imported data

◆ Keep Outlook open for the next exercise.

QUICK CHECK

Q: What do you do if the field names in the data source don't match the field names in Outlook?

A: Map the fields when you import the data.

QUICK REFERENCE ▼
Import an Access database

1. On the File menu, click the Import And Export option.
2. Select the file type to import from.
3. Select the file to import.
4. Select the destination folder.
5. Map any fields if necessary.
6. Click OK and click Finish.

Exporting Outlook Data to a Microsoft Excel Database

THE BOTTOM LINE

Outlook data can be exported to a variety of applications to share, store, or modify in another application.

In addition to importing information into Outlook, you can also **export** data, moving Outlook information out to other Office applications such as Microsoft Access or Microsoft Excel. Suppose you have been compiling a database of addresses in Excel. If your Excel database does not already contain addresses that you just added to Outlook, you could export the Outlook addresses to Excel. Before you export data, you must convert the Outlook data to a file that the other program can use. For example, if you want to export the contents of your Contacts folder to Excel, you must convert the Outlook information to an Excel file (.xls file). After you perform the export, you can simply navigate to the folder where you stored the .xls file, and then open the file. Excel starts and the Outlook information you exported is available in an Excel database.

IMPORTANT

You must have the Import/Export feature installed for this exercise to work. If an alert box appears during this exercise asking whether you want to install the feature, insert the Office or Outlook 2003 CD-ROM, and click Yes.

Export Outlook data to Excel

Now you export the contents of the Contacts folder to an Excel file.

Lesson 8 Customizing Outlook 257

> **IMPORTANT**
>
> You must have Microsoft Excel installed on your computer to perform all of this exercise.

1 **On the File menu, click the option Import And Export.**

The Import And Export Wizard is displayed.

2 **Click the Export To A File option and click Next.**

The next wizard dialog box is displayed. It asks you to choose a file type for the export.

Figure 8-30

Export To A File dialog box

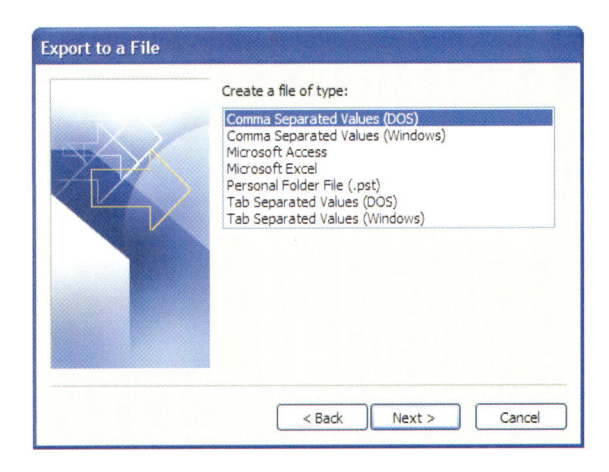

3 **Click Microsoft Excel and click Next.**

The next wizard dialog box is displayed. It asks you to choose a source folder for the data to be exported. The Contacts folder is already selected.

4 **Click Next.**

The next wizard dialog box is displayed. It asks you to browse to a location in which to save the exported file.

5 **Click the Browse button.**

The Browse dialog box is displayed.

6 **If necessary, click the Save In down arrow and navigate to the Outlook Practice folder. Click in the File Name box, delete any existing text, type [your name]'s Addresses, and click OK.**

This determines where the data will be loaded.

7 **Click Next.**

The final wizard dialog box is displayed.

8 **Click Finish.**

A progress bar is displayed as the Contact information is exported to an Excel file.

258   Lesson 8   Customizing Outlook

9 Start Windows Explorer, and navigate to the Outlook Practice folder on your hard disk.

> **TIP**
>
> Several columns, such as the highlighted Middle Name field in this example, might not contain any data. Right-click the letter above the column name and click Delete on the displayed shortcut menu. Other fields, such as the Company field, need to be lengthened to display all the text.

10 Double-click the file [your name]'s Addresses.

Excel starts and the file opens.

Figure 8-31

Exported data opened in Excel

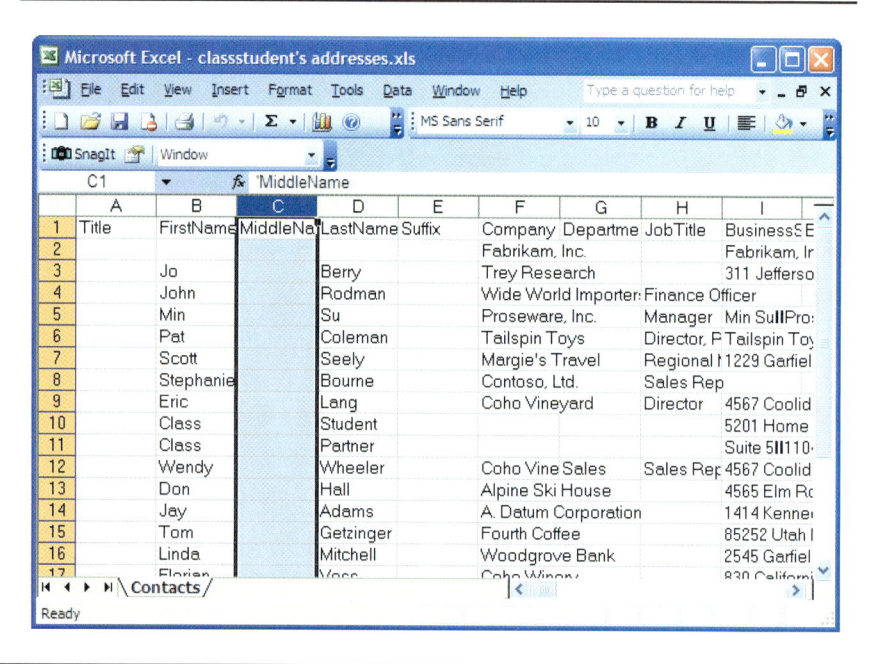

◆ Close Excel.

◆ If you are continuing to the next lesson, keep Outlook open.

◆ If you are not continuing to the next lesson, close Outlook.

QUICK REFERENCE ▼

Export Outlook data

1 On the File menu, click the Import And Export option.

2 Click the Export To A File option and click Next.

3 Select the destination application and click Next.

4 Select the location where the file will be saved. Click OK.

5 Click Next and click Finish.

QUICK CHECK

Q: What is necessary to export data?

A: You must convert the Outlook data to a file that the other program can use.

Key Points

✓ With Outlook, you can create a shortcut to start the application from your desktop. In the shortcut, you can specify the Outlook folder you want to see when Outlook starts.

✓ The Navigation pane can be customized by changing its size, hiding and displaying buttons, and changing the sequence of the buttons.

✓ Shortcuts to Outlook folders can be organized by placing them in groups.

✓ You can use Outlook Today to summarize your schedule, list your tasks, and count your unread messages.

✓ A Personal Folders file stores Outlook items on your hard drive.

✓ You can import data into Outlook from other applications, such as Microsoft Access. This enables you to add information to your Contacts folder without typing it.

✓ Likewise, you can export data from Outlook to other applications, including Microsoft Excel. This enables you to share Outlook information with others or use it in a different way.

True/False

T   F   1. Change the desktop shortcut for the Outlook application to set the colors used by Outlook.

T   F   2. Outlook must be closed to create a shortcut on your desktop.

T   F   3. You can change the sequence of the buttons in the Navigation pane.

T   F   4. You can use the Navigation pane to place a shortcut to a file located on your computer.

T   F   5. The Outlook Today Calendar automatically displays the events for the current day and the next four days.

Multiple Choice

1. The file that runs the Outlook application is _____.
   a. Outlook.pst
   b. Outlook.exe
   c. Outlook.bmp
   d. all of the above

2. The Navigation pane can be _____.
   a. hidden
   b. widened
   c. modified to display the buttons in a different sequence
   d. all of the above

3. To organize _____, place them in a group.
   a. messages
   b. shortcuts
   c. preferences
   d. modifications

4. By default, Outlook Today displays _____.
   a. information in a single column
   b. the target of the Outlook shortcut
   c. the events for today
   d. the appointments for the entire week
5. A _____ is located on the Outlook server.
   a. private store
   b. Personal Folders file
   c. shortcut
   d. all of the above

Short Answer

1. How do you create a shortcut to Outlook on your desktop?
2. How do you specify the Outlook folder to display when you launch Outlook from the desktop?
3. How can you customize the Navigation toolbars?
4. How do you customize Outlook Today?
5. What is mapping?
6. How do you hide the Navigation pane?
7. How do you create a new group?
8. How do you set Outlook Today as the default start page?

On Your Own

Exercise 1

Create a folder called **Expenses** in your Inbox. Add it to the Active Projects group created in this lesson.

Exercise 2

Modify Outlook Today as follows: display the Inbox, Drafts, and Outbox in the Outlook Today pane, display two days of events for the Calendar, and display all tasks by due date.

One Step Further

Exercise 1

Import the Access database called AW Address List into the Contacts folder.

Exercise 2

After completing the previous exercise, export your Contacts in Excel format.

Exercise 3

Use Outlook Help to identify the formats you can use to import and export data.

LESSON 9

Using Advanced E-Mail Features

After completing this lesson, you will be able to:
- ✔ Create and use message templates.
- ✔ Create a distribution list.
- ✔ Protect your privacy.
- ✔ Use the Rules Wizard.
- ✔ Track when messages are delivered and read.
- ✔ Set up a news account.
- ✔ View newsgroups and newsgroup messages.
- ✔ Subscribe to a newsgroup.

KEY TERMS

- actions
- conditions
- delivery receipt
- desktop alert
- distribution list
- exceptions
- newsgroup
- newsreader
- news server
- posts
- read receipt
- subscribe
- template
- thread
- Web beacon

The office manager at Adventure Works has noticed that the e-mail messages she receives are more specialized than the messages she sends. For example, around holidays, she receives festive messages that have backgrounds and borders. One time she received an important message that displayed an alert box asking whether Microsoft Outlook could notify the sender that she had read the message. Perhaps you have also received such specialized e-mail messages and would like to know how you, too, can create them. Advanced features in Microsoft Outlook enable you to track the messages you send and receive, organize your Inbox by using the Rules Wizard, and participate in newsgroups.

In this lesson, you will learn how to create and use message templates and how to use the Rules Wizard to set rules specifying how messages should be handled when they arrive in your Inbox. You will set privacy options, track when messages are delivered and read, use a newsreader, and subscribe to a newsgroup.

IMPORTANT

To complete some of the exercises in this lesson, you will need to exchange e-mail messages with a class partner. If you don't have a class partner or you are performing the exercises alone, you can send the message to yourself. Simply enter your own e-mail address instead of a class partner's address.

Creating and Using Message Templates

> **THE BOTTOM LINE**
>
> Templates reduce errors and provide consistency in content and format.

If you have a certain message that you send over and over again, you can save the message as a template so that it can be easily reused. In Outlook, a **template** is an e-mail message that is used as a pattern to format similar e-mail messages.

The customer service manager at Adventure Works requires a daily e-mail message from all the customer service representatives. The message contains guest complaints, suggestions, compliments, and how problems were solved. To save time, one of the customer service representatives created a template of the daily e-mail message. He simply typed Customer Complaints, Customer Suggestions, Customer Compliments, and Solutions, and left space to fill in the actual daily customer comments.

You create templates within a standard message window by saving the message as a template. When you save the message as a template, Outlook saves it in the Templates folder in Windows Explorer by default. Saving templates in the Templates folder is helpful because all templates are stored in one location where they can be found quickly.

Creating a Template

To create a template for e-mail messages, you must modify the Outlook options. You can't save a message as an Outlook template (*.oft) if Microsoft Word is the default editor for e-mail messages. Therefore, turn off Microsoft Word as the default editor, create the template, and turn on Microsoft Word as the default editor again. This is a simple process.

Turn off Microsoft Word as the default editor

1. On the Tools menu, select Options.

2. In the Options dialog box, click the Mail Format tab.

3. In the Message Format area, click the check box Use Microsoft Word To Edit E-Mail Messages so the option is not selected.

4. Click the Apply button and click the OK button to close the dialog box.

With Microsoft Word disabled as the editor, you can use Outlook to create a template. After creating a template, restore Microsoft Word as your default editor.

Restore Microsoft Word as the default editor

1. On the Tools menu, select Options.

2. In the Options dialog box, click the Mail Format tab.

3. In the Message Format area, click the check box Use Microsoft Word To Edit E-Mail Messages. That option is now selected.

4. Click the Apply button and click the OK button to close the dialog box.

◆ Be sure to start Outlook before begging this exercise.

Create a template

You begin this lesson by creating a message template.

1 On the Tools menu, select Options.

The Options dialog box is displayed.

2 In the Options dialog box, click the Mail Format tab.

These options control the format of the messages you create.

3 In the Message Format area, clear the template by clicking the check box Use Microsoft Office Word 2003 To Edit E-Mail Messages.

Some formatting options available in Microsoft Word are no longer available in the e-mail messages you create.

4 In the Signature For New Messages box, select <None>.

If someone else uses the template, you don't want your signature to be part of the message.

Figure 9-1

Disable Microsoft Word as the default editor

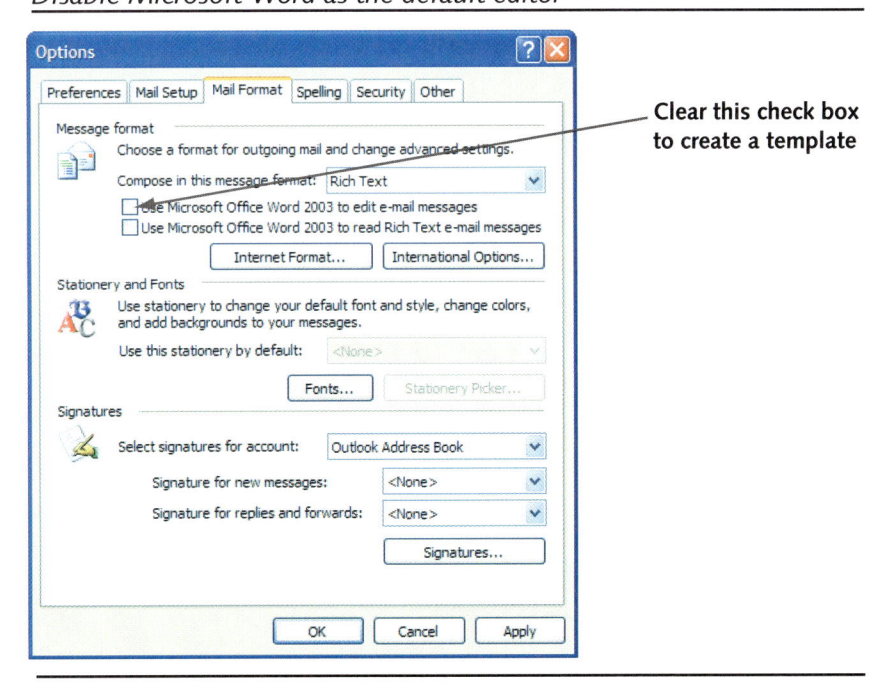

264 **Lesson 9** Using Advanced E-Mail Features

5 Click the Apply button and click the OK button to close the dialog box.

Microsoft Word is no longer your default editor. You are ready to create the template.

6 On the Standard toolbar, click the New Mail Message button.

A message window is displayed.

7 Click in the Subject box, type Update, and press Enter.

The insertion point moves to the message area.

8 Type Customer Complaints: and press Enter four times. Type Customer Suggestions: and press Enter four times. Type Customer Compliments: and press Enter four times. Type Solutions: and press Enter four times.

The message is created and is ready to be saved as a template.

Figure 9-2
The subject and the content will be part of the template

Subject becomes suggested title of the template

Content becomes part of the template

9 On the File menu in the Message window, click Save As.

The Save As dialog box is displayed.

> **TIP**
>
> When you designate a file as an Outlook Template, Outlook automatically saves it to the Templates folder.

10 Click the Save As Type down arrow, click Outlook Template (*.oft), and click the Save button.

The subject of the message is used as the name of the template.

11 Click the Close button in the top-right corner of the Message window. If an alert box is displayed asking you to save a draft of the message, click No.

The message is now a template, and you are ready to restore Microsoft Word as the default editor.

12 On the Tools menu, select Options.

The Options dialog box is displayed.

13 In the Options dialog box, click the Mail Format tab.

These options control the format of the messages you create.

14 In the Message Format area, click the check box Use Microsoft Word To Edit E-Mail Messages. Select your signature in the Signature For New Messages box.

The formatting options available in Microsoft Word are now available in the e-mail messages you create. Your signature will be placed in new messages.

15 Click the Apply button and click the OK button to close the dialog box.

Microsoft Word is restored as your default editor. You are ready to compose new messages and use the template you created.

◆ Keep Outlook open for the next exercise.

QUICK CHECK

Q: Why do you turn off Microsoft Word as the default editor?

A: This enables you to save a template.

QUICK REFERENCE ▼

Create a template

1 Turn off Microsoft Word as the default editor.
2 Create the message.
3 Save it as a template.
4 Restore Microsoft Word as the default editor.

Using a Template

Some messages you send regularly are very similar. Status reports, a response to customer comments, and meeting announcements are just a few examples. Using a template to fill in the standard text saves time and reduces errors. The text in the template provides a framework for the information you need to send.

Use a template

Now you will use the template you created in the previous exercise.

1 On the File menu, point to New and click Choose Form.

The Choose Form dialog box is displayed.

Figure 9-3

Choose Form dialog box

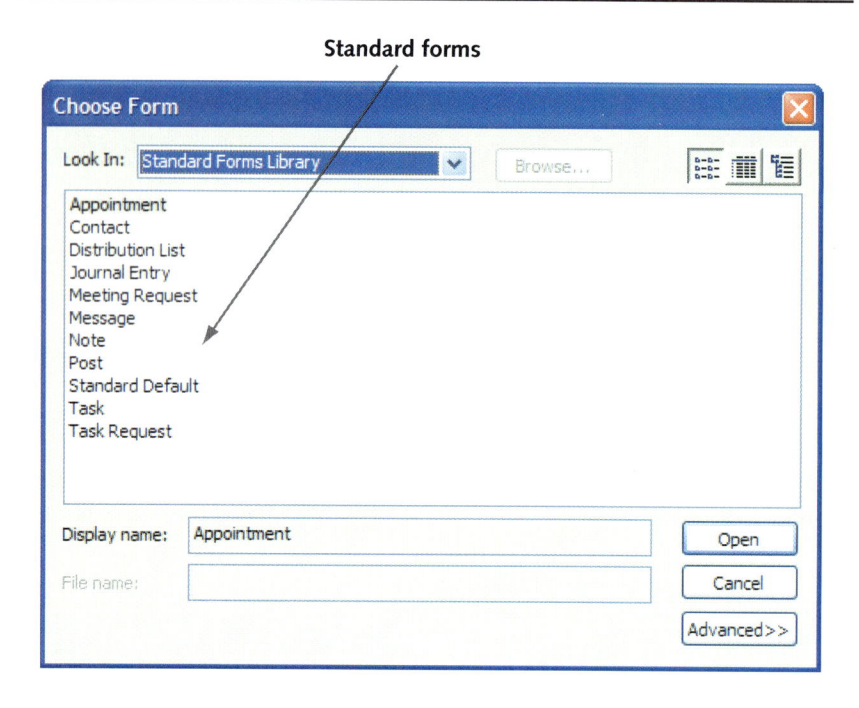

Standard forms

[Choose Form dialog box screenshot showing Standard Forms Library with list: Appointment, Contact, Distribution List, Journal Entry, Meeting Request, Message, Note, Post, Standard Default, Task, Task Request]

2 Click the Look In down arrow, and click **User Templates In File System**.

The name of the template that you created is displayed.

3 Click the **Update** template and click **Open**.

A message box containing the template is displayed.

4 In the **To** box, type your class partner's e-mail address.

The complete message will be sent to your class partner.

> **TIP**
>
> To distinguish between the headings and responses, use the Formatting toolbar to change the appearance of the headings. In this example, the headings are bold.

5 In the message area, click the blank line after the text "Customer Complaints," and type None.

6 Click the blank line after the text "Customer Suggestions," and type Customer wants magazines by the hot tub.

7 Click the blank line after the text "Customer Compliments," and type Adventure Works is in a beautiful location!

8 Click the blank line after the text "Solutions," and type Put magazines by the hot tub.

Figure 9-4

Message created from a template

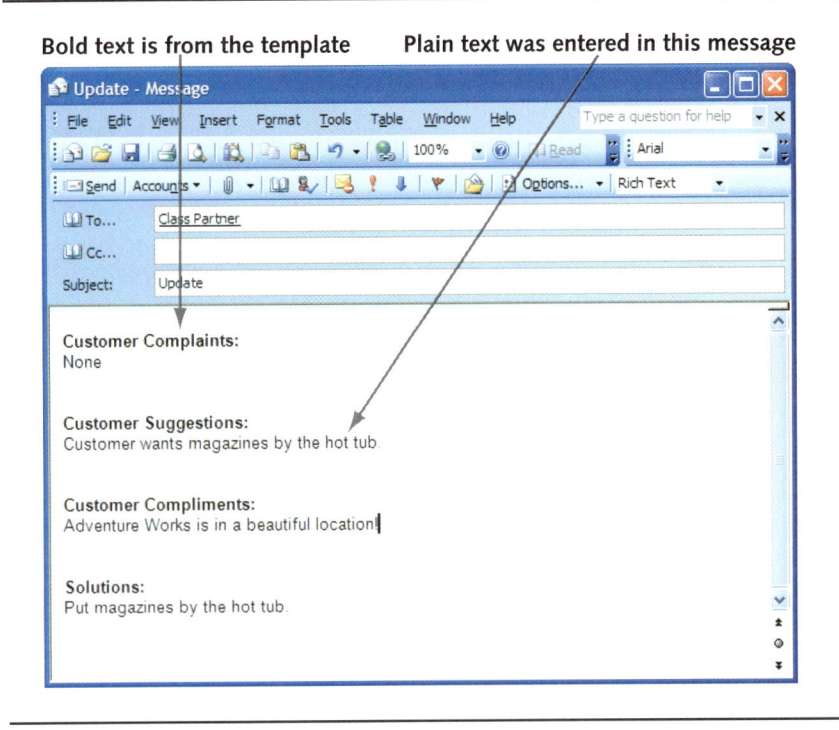

Bold text is from the template   Plain text was entered in this message

[Screenshot of Update - Message window showing:
- To: Class Partner
- Subject: Update
- Customer Complaints: None
- Customer Suggestions: Customer wants magazines by the hot tub.
- Customer Compliments: Adventure Works is in a beautiful location
- Solutions: Put magazines by the hot tub.]

9 On the Standard toolbar in the message window, click the Send button.

The message is sent to your class partner.

10 On the Standard toolbar, click the Send/Receive button, and click the Update message received from your class partner in the message list.

The body of the message is displayed in the Reading pane.

◆ Keep Outlook open for the next exercise.

QUICK CHECK

Q: What benefit do you get from a template?

A: Using a template to fill in the standard text saves time and reduces errors.

QUICK REFERENCE ▼

Use a template

1 On the File menu, point to New and click Choose Form.
2 Click the Look In down arrow, and click User Templates In File System.
3 Click the template and click Open.

Creating a Distribution List

THE BOTTOM LINE

You can send the same e-mail message to several individuals at the same time with a single click by using a distribution list.

Using Address Books

268   Lesson 9   Using Advanced E-Mail Features

Sending everyone in your organization a message every week can be a big job. In previous lessons you typed individual e-mail addresses or selected a name from the address book by clicking the To button. This can be time-consuming. Even if you belong to a small group, addressing a message to every member time after time can be tedious.

A distribution list can make a long task into a job that takes only a few clicks. A **distribution list** is a single address book entry that contains several individual addresses. For example, if you want to send a message to everyone in your family, you can create a single entry for Smith. Within the Smith entry, you include your father, John, your mother, Jane, your brother, John Jr., your sister, Janie, and your cousin, Johnny. To send an e-mail to all your family members, you address the message to Smith. Because Smith is a distribution list, the message is sent to all five members of your family.

Microsoft Office Outlook 2003 provides the ability to edit a distribution list for a single message. This enables you to send a message to exclude one or two members of the group. To send a message about a surprise birthday party to everyone but your father, click the plus sign next to the distribution list in the To field to see the individual members of the list. Delete your father's name from the message and click the Send button.

Create a distribution list

Now you will create a distribution list of several business people who are registered for a series of sales presentations to be held at your facility. Then you will view this list in your Address Book.

1 Open the Tools menu and click the Address Book option.

The Address book is displayed.

2 If necessary, select Contacts in the drop-down list on the right.

Contacts are displayed in the lower area.

Figure 9-5

List of contacts in the Address Book

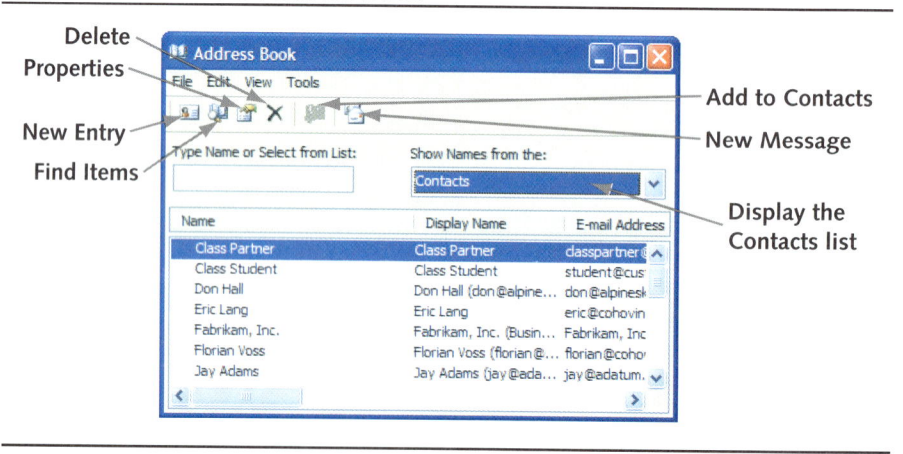

3 Click the New Entry button, click New Distribution List, and click OK.

The Select Members dialog box is displayed. You are ready to name the distribution list and select the contacts to be added to the distribution list.

Lesson 9 Using Advanced E-Mail Features 269

Figure 9-6

New Distribution List dialog box

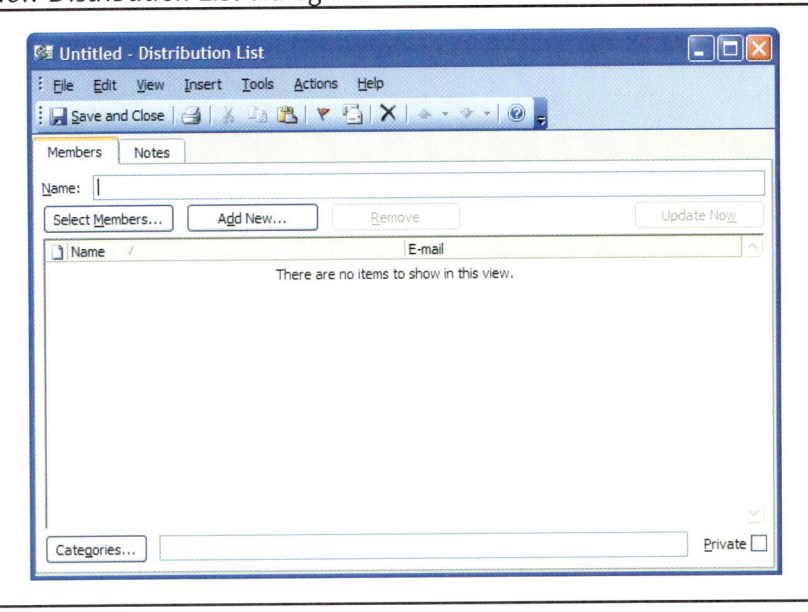

[Screenshot: Untitled - Distribution List dialog box with Members and Notes tabs, Name field, Select Members, Add New, Remove, and Update Now buttons, and Name/E-mail columns showing "There are no items to show in this view."]

4 In the Name box, type Sales Presentation Fall Series, and click the Select Members button.

The Select Members dialog box is displayed.

Figure 9-7

Select Members dialog box

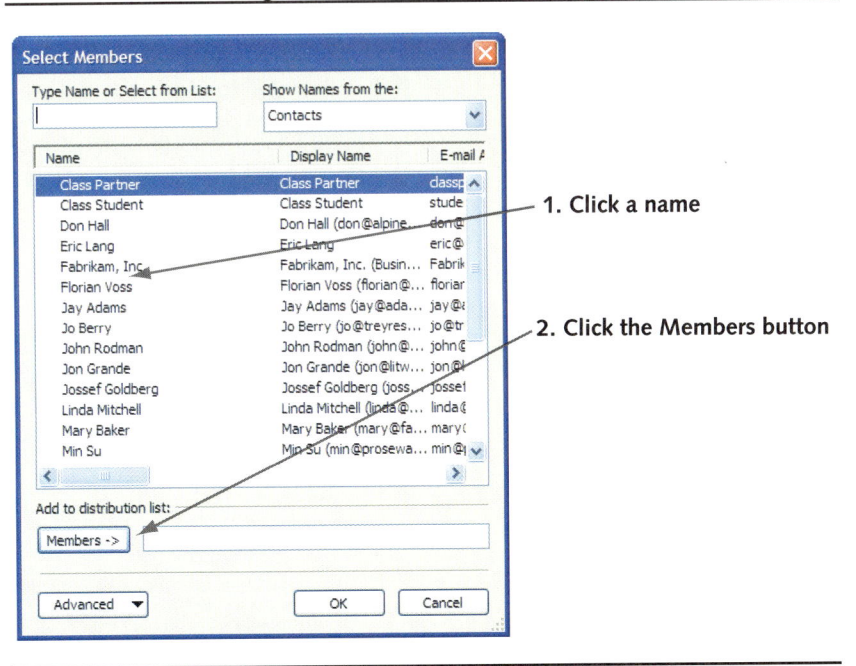

[Screenshot: Select Members dialog box showing list of names including Class Partner, Class Student, Don Hall, Eric Lang, Fabrikam Inc., Florian Voss, Jay Adams, Jo Berry, John Rodman, Jon Grande, Jossef Goldberg, Linda Mitchell, Mary Baker, Min Su, with callouts "1. Click a name" and "2. Click the Members button"]

5 Select John Rodman and click the Members button.

John Rodman is added to the distribution list.

6 Select Mary Baker and click the Members button.

Mary Baker is added to the distribution list.

270 **Lesson 9** Using Advanced E-Mail Features

7 **Select Stephanie Bourne and click the Members button.**

Stephanie Bourne is added to the distribution list.

8 **Select Wendy Wheeler and click the Members button.**

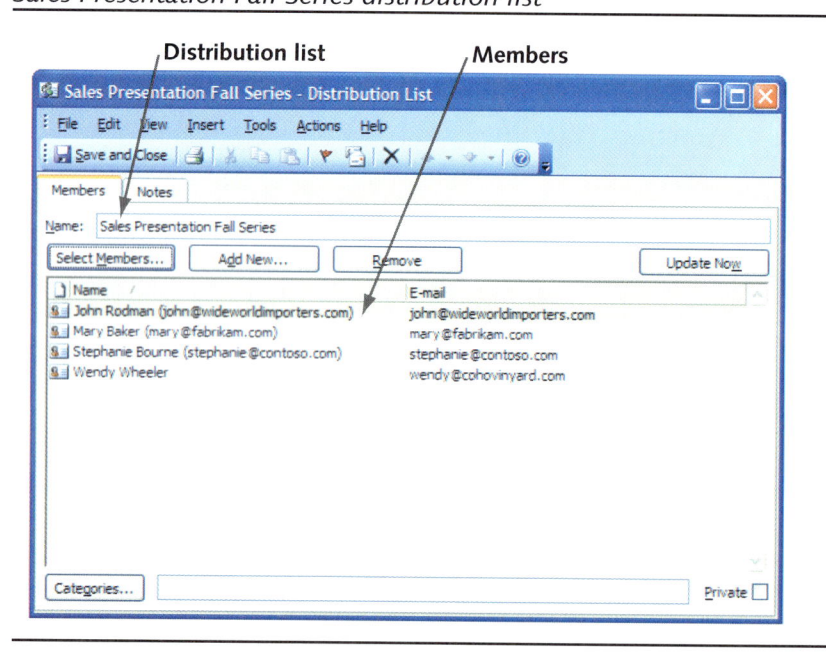

Wendy Wheeler is added to the distribution list.

Figure 9-8

Members of the Sales Presentation Fall Series distribution list

9 **Click OK to close the Select Members dialog box.**

The Distribution List dialog box is displayed. The individuals you selected are listed as members.

Figure 9-9

Sales Presentation Fall Series distribution list

Lesson 9 Using Advanced E-Mail Features 271

Save and Close

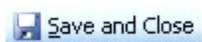

10 Click the Save And Close button. If necessary, scroll down to see the Sales Presentation Fall Series distribution list in the Address Book.

The distribution list is saved and the Address Book window is displayed. The icon indicates that the entry is a distribution list.

Figure 9-10

Address Book containing the Sales Presentation Fall Series distribution list

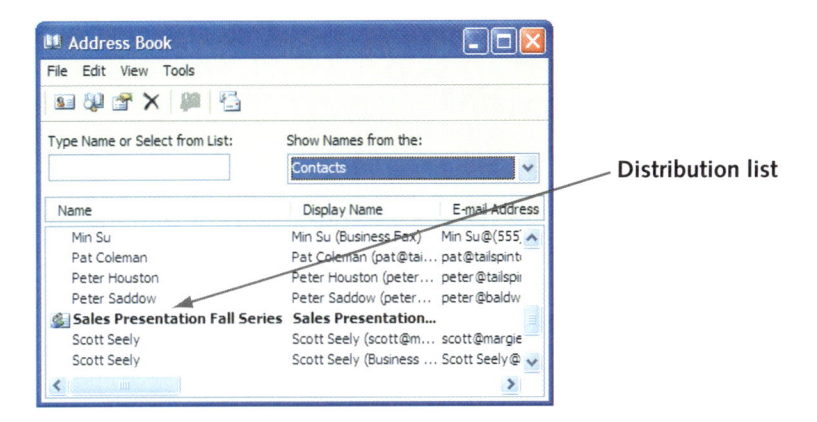

◆ Close the Address Book.

◆ Keep Outlook open for the next exercise.

QUICK CHECK

Q: Why would you use a distribution list?

A: You can use a single Address Book entry to send e-mail to several addresses.

QUICK REFERENCE ▼

Create a distribution list

1 Open the Address Book.
2 Click the New Entry button, click New Distribution List, and click OK.
3 Name the entry and click the Select Members button.
4 Select an existing entry and click the Members button.
5 Click OK and click the Save And Close button.

Protecting Your Privacy

THE BOTTOM LINE

You can protect yourself by blocking offensive images from your Inbox. You can also provide a different type of protection by limiting the distribution of e-mail messages you send.

E-mail threatens your privacy when it comes in and when it goes out. You need to protect yourself from invasions of your privacy in both directions. You have probably thought of blocking offensive e-mail from arriving in your mailbox, but have you thought of the privacy that you sacrifice every time you send an e-mail message? For example, Shelley sent her co-worker a message that contained a story about her supervisor. It was funny, but it made her supervisor look a little foolish. Her friend thought the story was funny enough to share. She forwarded Shelley's message to another friend in the company, who forwarded it to four additional co-workers. Each of them forwarded the message to several friends and acquaintances in the company. By that afternoon, the story was passed around the water cooler.

Outlook provides protection in both directions. It protects you from seeing messages you don't want to view and limits the distribution of messages you send.

Controlling Incoming Messages

Outlook's improved privacy features enable you to block or allow external Web content such as pictures or sounds in e-mail messages. You can also prevent a Web beacon from validating your e-mail address to junk mail senders.

You might want to block images included in many junk mail messages. The images might be offensive, or you might not want to waste time downloading images of items that have no interest to you.

A **Web beacon** is a program that informs the sender that you have read or previewed a message. The Web beacon tells the sender that your e-mail address is valid. Validated addresses might be sold or distributed to other junk mail senders, increasing the amount of junk mail you receive.

Control the content of incoming messages

To protect your privacy, in this exercise you limit the content of the messages you receive.

1 Open the Tools menu and click Options.

The Options dialog box is displayed.

2 Click the Security tab and click the button Change Automatic Download Settings.

The Automatic Picture Download Settings dialog box is displayed.

Figure 9-11

Automatic Picture Download Settings dialog box

3 Select the options you want and click OK twice to return to the main Outlook window.

Your changes are saved.

Keep Outlook open for the next exercise.

Controlling Outgoing Messages

Microsoft Office Outlook 2003 has a new feature that enables you to restrict the recipient of your message. You can prevent the recipient from forwarding, copying, or printing your message. To use this feature, create a new message and click the Permission button on the individual message. Several criteria must be met before you can control the distribution of messages you send.

- The message must be sent from an Exchange Server account.
- The Exchange Server account must have a digital ID.
- The recipient must have Outlook 2003 or the Rights Management Add-on for Internet Explorer. (The add-on is a free download from the Microsoft Web site.)

Using the Rules Wizard

> **THE BOTTOM LINE**
>
> Outlook provides a wizard to create rules that organize your e-mail messages as they arrive.

In Lesson 3, you used the Organize pane to create a rule that applied color to messages from specific senders. The Rules Wizard provides another method of creating rules to organize messages. Rules consist of three elements—conditions, actions, and exceptions—that, when combined, process and organize messages in a certain way. **Conditions** are requirements that a message must meet before an action is performed (e.g., messages that you receive must have the word meeting in the subject and have an attachment). **Actions** specify what Outlook does with a message that meets the conditions, such as delete it, forward it, or move it to a folder upon receipt. **Exceptions** are provisions for a message that, if met, exclude a message from being acted upon (e.g., messages that are received between January 1 and January 7 will not be automatically deleted). When you create a rule, you must describe a condition and an action; describing an exception is not required.

The human resource manager at Adventure Works placed an ad in the newspaper for a cook. The ad instructed applicants to e-mail their resumes to her. To quickly separate her general e-mail from the many applicants' e-mail messages, the human resource manager created a rule that automatically sends any messages containing the word *cook* in the message body (condition) to a folder called Cook Position (action), unless the message was marked with high importance (exception).

After a rule is created, you can turn the Rules Wizard on and off (enable or disable the feature) as desired. You can also modify the rules to include different conditions or actions, based on what you need at that time. For example, if you created a rule that has an exception that you no longer want, you can remove the exception.

QUICK CHECK

Q: What does a Web beacon do?

A: **The Web beacon tells the sender that your e-mail address is valid.**

Managing Messages through Rules

At any time, you can run a rule on messages already in the Inbox. Open the Tools menu and select the Rules and Alerts option. Select the check box for the rule and click the Run Now button. In the Run Rules Now dialog box, select the rule and click the Run Rules Now button.

Create a rule

To Illustrate the usefullness of the Rules Wizard, in this exercise, you create a rule that places messages that have the word *cook* in the subject into a folder you create called Cook Position.

1 **On the Tools menu, click Rules and Alerts.**

The Rules And Alerts dialog box is displayed. Any existing rules are listed.

Figure 9-12

Rules And Alerts dialog box

Click the New Rule button to start the Rules Wizard

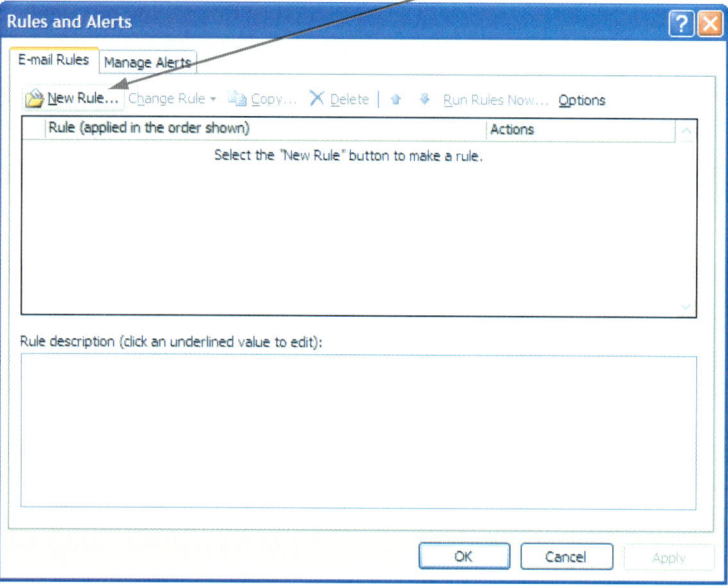

> **TIP**
>
> If the Office Assistant asks whether you want help, reject the help to hide the Assistant.

2 **Click the New Rule button.**

The first Rules Wizard dialog box is displayed. The option Start Creating A Rule From A Template is already selected.

Figure 9-13

First Rules Wizard dialog box

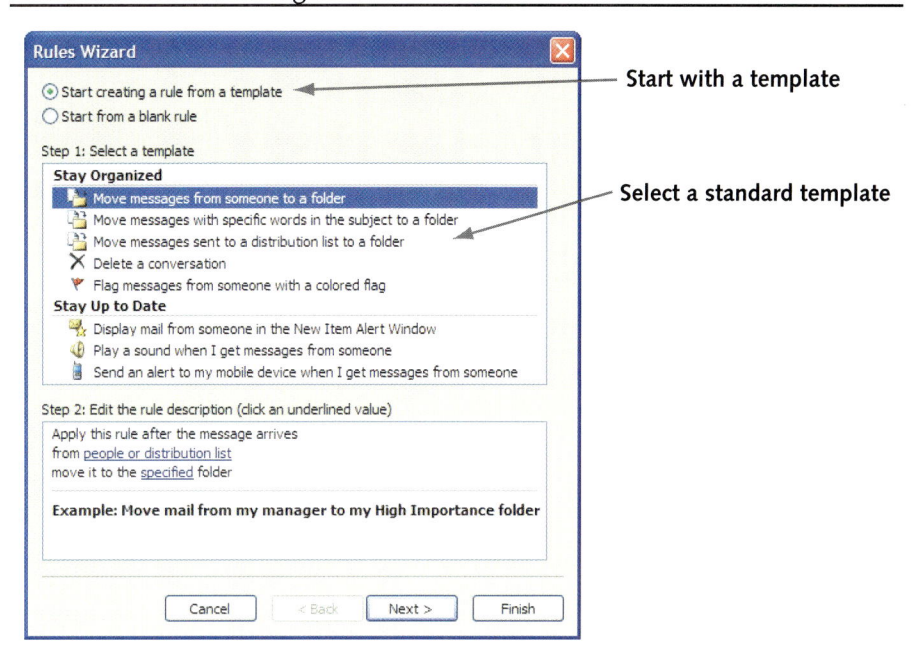

- Start with a template
- Select a standard template

3. **Select the option Move Messages With Specific Words In The Subject To A Folder. Click the Next button.**

   The next wizard dialog box is displayed, asking you to identify the conditions you want to set.

4. **In the Which Condition(s) Do You Want To Check? list, select two options: With Specific Words In The Subject and With Specific Words In The Body.**

Figure 9-14

Conditions selected

5 In the lower area of the dialog box, click the underlined words in the first phrase "with specific words in the subject."

The Search Text dialog box is displayed.

6 Type cook. Click the Add button and click OK.

The condition is added.

7 In the lower area of the dialog box, click the underlined words in the second phrase "with specific words in the body."

The Search Text dialog box is displayed.

8 Type cook. Click the Add button and click OK.

The condition is added. You are ready to specify where the messages will be placed.

Figure 9-15

Conditions have been specified

9 In the Rule Description list, click the underlined word in the third phrase "move it to the specified folder."

The next wizard dialog box displays your Outlook folders.

Lesson 9 Using Advanced E-Mail Features 277

Figure 9-16

Available Outlook folders

10 **Click the Inbox folder and click the New button.**

The Create New Folder dialog box is displayed. The insertion point is in the Name box.

11 **Type Cook Position.**

The folder will be created in the Inbox.

Figure 9-17

Creating a new Outlook folder to store messages about the cook position

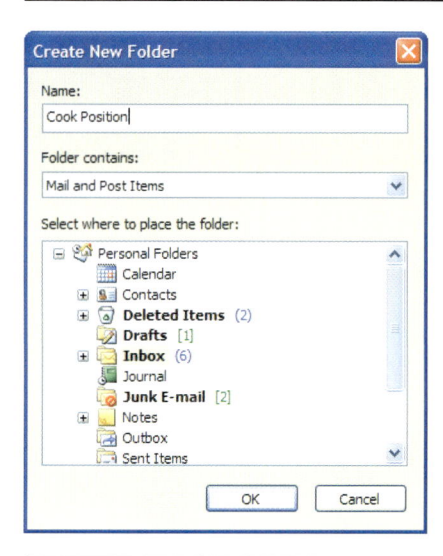

12 **Click OK.**

The new folder is displayed.

278   Lesson 9   Using Advanced E-Mail Features

Figure 9-18

Cook position folder

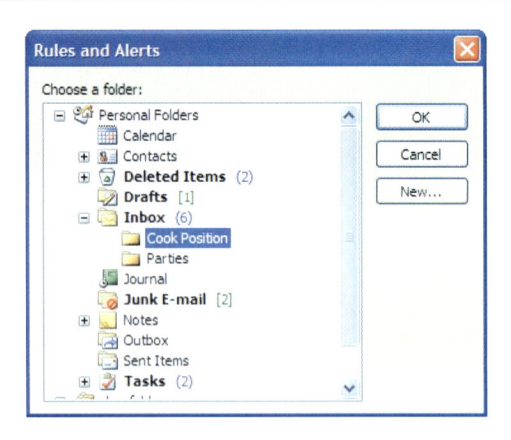

13 Click OK.

The Rules Wizard dialog box is displayed. The rule is complete.

Figure 9-19

The required parts of the rule are complete

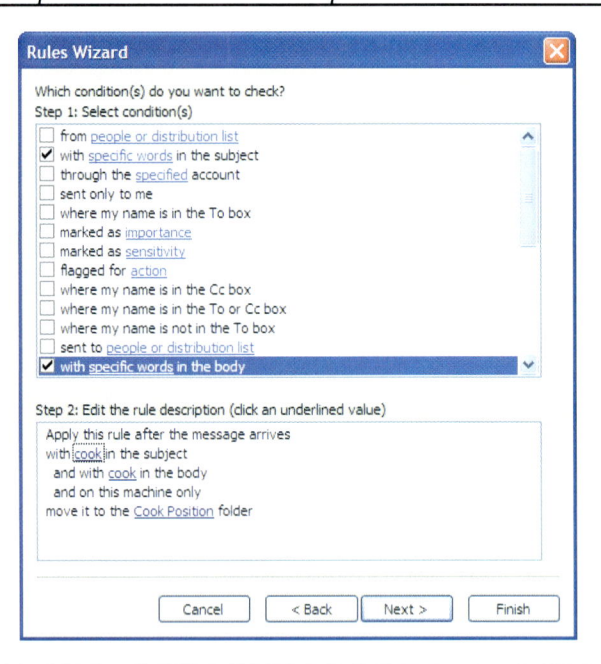

14 In the wizard dialog box, click Next.

Because you specified a folder on your computer where the messages will be placed, the phrase *and on this machine only* has been added to the rule. The next dialog box enables you to specify any exceptions to the rule.

Figure 9-20

Exceptions are not required

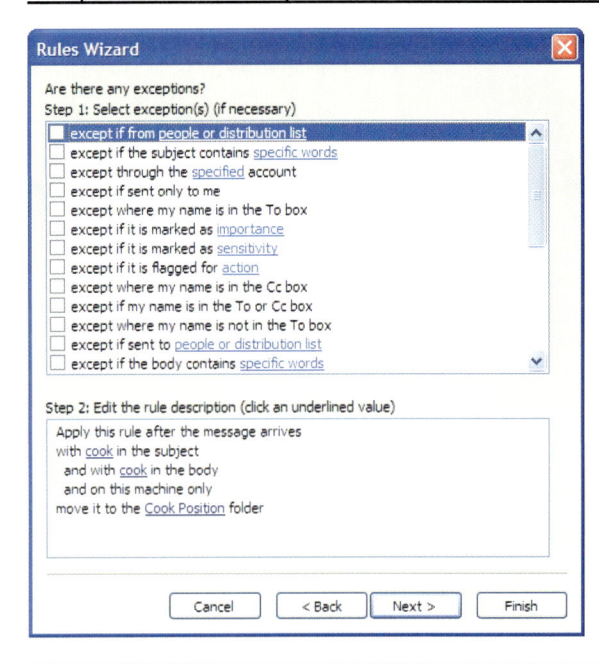

15 **Click Next to choose not to select an exception.**

The next wizard dialog box is displayed. It asks you to name the rule. The word *cook* is already inserted in the box Step 1: Specify A Name For This Rule.

Figure 9-21

Name the rule

280 Lesson 9 Using Advanced E-Mail Features

> **TROUBLESHOOTING**
>
> After you create a rule, you should test it several times to verify that it is performing the actions you expect.

16 **Click Finish.**

The Rules And Alerts dialog box is displayed. The rule you just created is displayed.

Figure 9-22

Rule is complete

QUICK CHECK

Q: What does a rule do?

A: A rule processes and organizes messages in a certain way.

- Close the Rules And Alerts dialog box.
- Keep Outlook open for the next exercise.

QUICK REFERENCE ▼

Create a rule

1 On the Tools menu, click Rules and Alerts.
2 Click the New Rule button.
3 Complete the Rules Wizard and click Finish.

Tracking When Messages Are Delivered and Read

THE BOTTOM LINE

Some messages are more important than others. You can request a delivery receipt or a read receipt to verify that a recipient received the important message you sent.

Have you ever wondered if someone has read an important message that you sent? With Outlook, you can track the day and time a message was received and read by a recipient. Before you send a message, you can set up Outlook to request a delivery receipt or a read receipt. A **delivery receipt** is sent to the sender when the message arrives in the recipient's mailbox. It does not guarantee that the message was read. A **read receipt** is sent to the sender when the message is opened. Read receipts are sent to the sender in the form of an e-mail message.

To use the delivery receipt option, you must be using Microsoft Exchange Server as your mail service. Read receipts work with the Microsoft Exchange Server or Internet mail service.

The recipient can choose to accept or decline the request to send a read receipt. If the recipient accepts, a read receipt is automatically sent to you.

Read receipts verify that the message was received. However, they do not necessarily verify that the message was read. A recipient could delete your message without reading it and send a read receipt to you. Even though the recipient didn't read the message, the read receipt still displays a date and time at which the message was read.

It is a good idea to read messages that request read receipts because the information in the message is probably important—so important that the sender needs to make sure that you read it and possibly acted upon it after reading it. A dispute might arise if you send a read receipt without reading the message. The sender has the advantage in the dispute because he or she has proof that the read receipt was sent, thus placing the blame solely on you. For example, if the message asks you to pick up your boss at the airport, you have only yourself to blame if you really didn't read the message.

While you work in other applications, you can receive an Outlook desktop alert. A **desktop alert** is displayed briefly when an e-mail message, meeting request, or task request arrives. The small box contains information about the Outlook item that arrived.

TIP

Desktop alerts are available for Microsoft Exchange Server and POP3 e-mail accounts.

You can change the characteristics of a desktop alert, including the length of time the alert is displayed and the transparency of the box. To change the settings, open the Tools menu, click Options, click the E-mail Options button, click the Advanced E-mail Options button, and click the Desktop Alert Settings button.

Request a read receipt

In this exercise, you will first create a message that requests a read receipt. Then you will receive this type of message from your class partner.

1 On the Standard toolbar, click the New Mail Message button.

A message window is displayed. The insertion point is already in the To box.

2 In the To box, type your class partner's e-mail address, and press Tab twice.

This places the cursor in the Subject box.

3 In the Subject box, type **Urgent!** Click in the message area and type **Please pick up the boss at the airport at 12:15 P.M. Airways, gate 24.**

The message is complete.

4 On the Standard toolbar in the message window, click the Options button.

The Message Options dialog box is displayed.

Figure 9-23
Tracking options in the Message Options dialog box

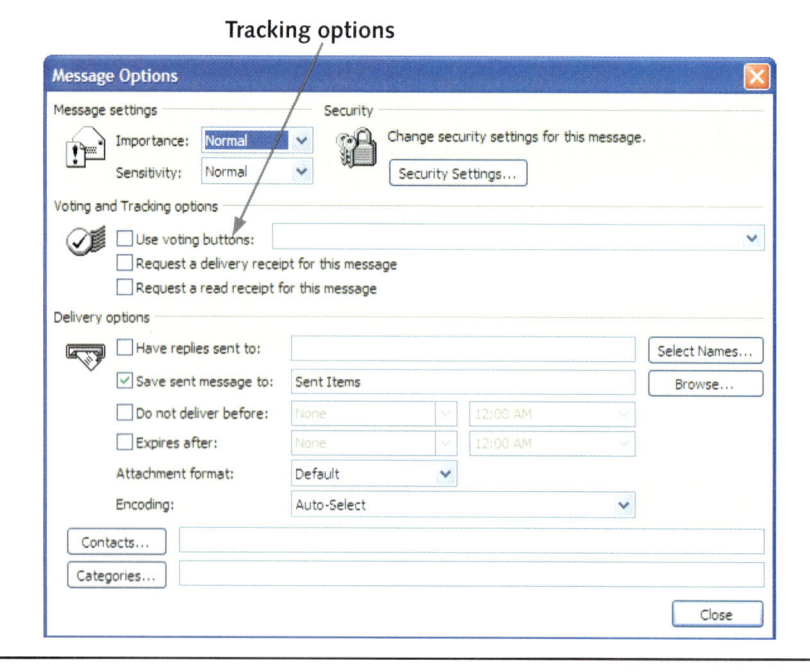

5 In the Voting And Tracking options section, select the Request A Read Receipt For This Message check box, and click Close.

You return to the message window.

Lesson 9 Using Advanced E-Mail Features 283

6 On the Standard toolbar in the message window, click the Send button.

The message is sent.

7 On the Standard toolbar, click the Send/Receive button.

The Urgent message from your class partner arrives in your Inbox.

8 Double-click the message.

An alert box is displayed. It requests that you send a read receipt. The box identifies the sender and the subject of the message.

Figure 9-24

Read receipt request

9 Click Yes. Close the message.

The read receipt has been sent.

10 On the Standard toolbar, click the Send/Receive button.

The Read: Urgent! message arrives in your Inbox. Notice that a read receipt icon appears in the Icon column.

11 Click the Read: Urgent! message header.

The receipt appears in the Reading pane.

Figure 9-25

Read receipt

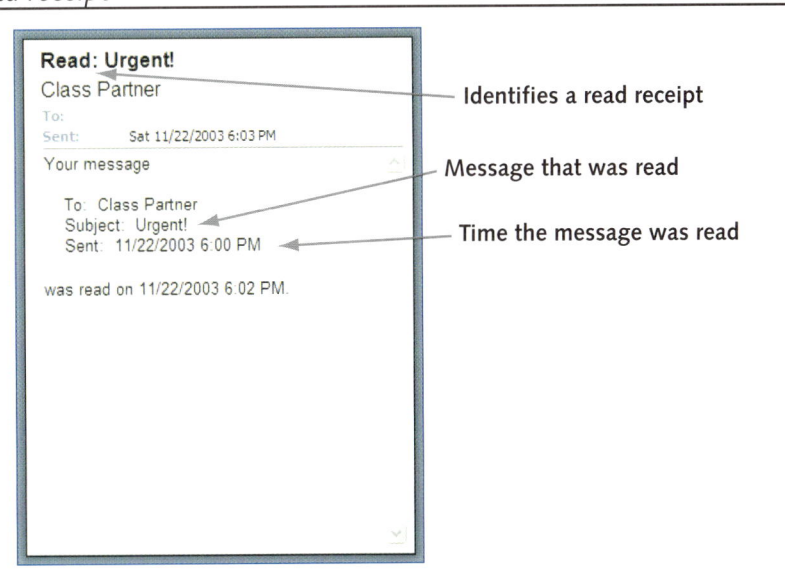

QUICK CHECK

Q: What is a requirement for using delivery receipts?

A: **You must be using Microsoft Exchange Server as your mail service.**

◆ Keep Outlook open for the next exercise.

> **QUICK REFERENCE ▼**
>
> **Request a read receipt**
>
> 1. Create a new message.
> 2. Click the Options button.
> 3. In the Voting And Tracking options section, select the Request A Read Receipt For This Message check box, and click Close.
> 4. Send the message.

Preparing to Access a Newsgroup

> **THE BOTTOM LINE**
>
> Newsgroups are a valuable source of information and enable you to communicate with other people who have similar interests or occupations.

You can send a different kind of e-mail message to a newsgroup. A **newsgroup** is a collection of messages that are constantly being sent and responded to by people within the group. Each newsgroup discusses a specific topic, such as gardening, rock bands, or television programs. The gardener at Adventure Works likes to visit newsgroups that talk about gardening to troubleshoot insect problems and get tips on growing flowers.

The messages (also called **posts**) appear on a news server. A **news server** is a computer that is maintained by a company, group, or individual, and is configured to accept posts from newsgroups. (Your Internet service provider most likely has a news server you can access.) To read these posts, you must use a newsreader. A **newsreader** is an application that you use to send and receive newsgroup posts. Outlook uses the Microsoft Outlook Express newsreader.

Adding News to the Go Menu

Before you can access newsgroups, you must add News to the list of destinations in the Go menu. To add the News option, you'll drag the command to the Go menu from the dialog box used to customize toolbars and menus.

> **Add News to the Go menu**
>
> To begin working with newsgroups, you will add News to the Go menu.
>
> 1. Click the Toolbar Options button on the right end of the current toolbar. Point at the option Add Or Remove Buttons, and click the Customize option. If necessary, click the Commands tab.
>
>   The Customize dialog box is displayed.

Figure 9-26

Customize dialog box

2. **Click Go in the Categories list on the left.**

   The commands displayed on the right change to list commands available for the Go category.

3. **Scroll down the list of commands if necessary. Click the News command.**

   The News command in the Go category is selected.

Figure 9-27

News command selected in the Customize dialog box

4. **Drag the News command to the Go menu in the menu bar.**

   The Go menu opens and a dark line is displayed in the current list of commands on the Go menu.

5. **Drop the News command when the dark line is located where you want the News command to be displayed.**

   The News command has been added to the Go menu.

◆ Close the Customize dialog box.

◆ Keep Outlook open for the next exercise.

Setting Up a News Account

Before you can view newsgroups in a newsreader, you must set up a news account. Setting up a news account is similar to setting up an e-mail account.

Ask your instructor or Internet service provider for the name of your news server.

You need the following information to set up a news account.

- Your e-mail address
- Your news server name (NNTP server name)
- Your user name
- Your password

After your news account is set up, Outlook Express downloads the newsgroups from the news server. Because there are thousands of newsgroups, the downloading process might take a few minutes. However, you only have to download once.

Set up a news account

Continuing your work with newsgroups, you now set up a news account.

IMPORTANT

You will need to know the name of your news server to complete this exercise.

1 On the Go menu, click News.

The Outlook Newsreader, a component of Outlook Express, is displayed.

TIP

An alert box might be displayed asking whether you want to make this application your default newsreader. Click Yes or No to close the alert box.

CHECK THIS OUT ▼

Safety on the Internet
Newsgroups are an excellent way to communicate with others who share your interests. However, be careful to protect your personal information. Use a screen name rather than your legal name. Set up a separate e-mail account that uses only your screen name. Do not provide any additional contact information in your posts. If you use a signature, make sure that it does not automatically place your information in any message you post. Remember that other subscribers to the newsgroup could be anyone in the world with an Internet connection.

Lesson 9 Using Advanced E-Mail Features 287

Figure 9-28

Microsoft Outlook Newsreader

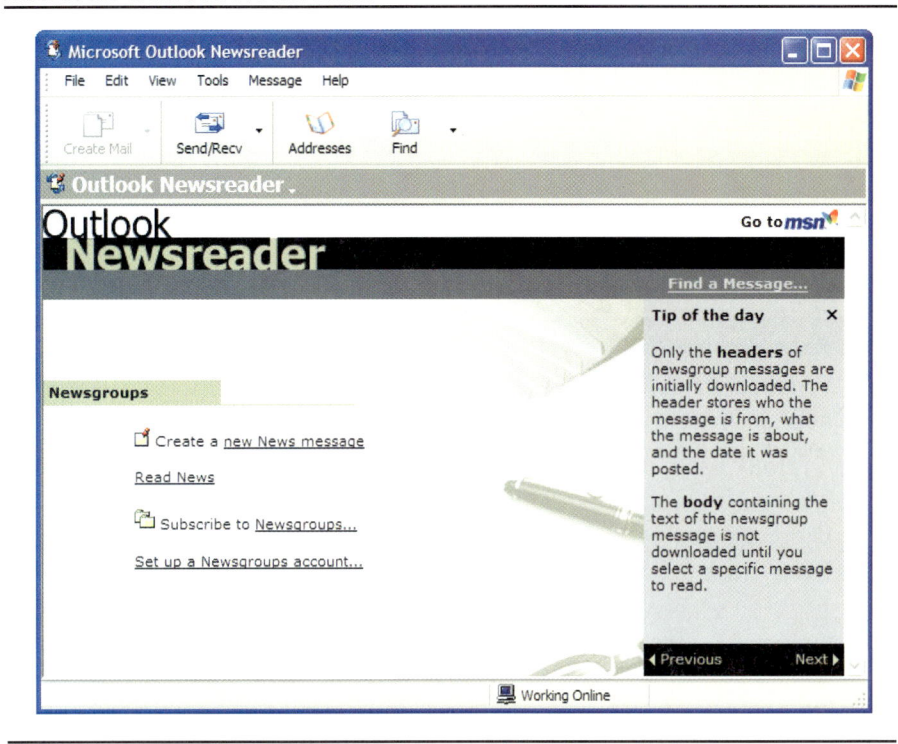

2 Click the Set Up A Newsgroups Account link. (This step may not be necessary for you. If you do perform this step, it only has to be done the first time this procedure is performed.)

The Internet Connection Wizard dialog box is displayed.

TROUBLESHOOTING

If you did not perform Step 2, this figure will not be displayed.

Figure 9-29

Internet Connection Wizard dialog box

3 In the Display Name box, type your name (if necessary), and click Next.

The next wizard dialog box is displayed.

4 In the E-Mail Address box, type your e-mail address (if necessary), and click Next.

The next wizard dialog box is displayed.

5 Type the news server name, click Next, and click Finish.

The Internet Connection Wizard closes and an alert box is displayed. It asks whether you want to download a list of available newsgroups.

6 Click Yes.

The list of newsgroups is downloaded, and the Newsgroup Subscriptions dialog box is displayed.

◆ Keep this window open for the next exercise.

QUICK CHECK

Q: What application accesses newsgroups?

A: Outlook uses the Microsoft Outlook Express newsreader.

QUICK REFERENCE ▼

Set up a news account

1 Add the News command to the Go menu.
2 On the Go menu, click the News command.
3 Click the Set Up A Newsgroups Account link.
4 Complete the Wizard.

Viewing Newsgroups and Newsgroup Messages

THE BOTTOM LINE

There are thousands of newsgroups from which to choose. One or more newsgroups may appeal to you and you can establish subscriptions with multiple newsgroups.

After you create a news account and download the newsgroups, you can view newsgroups. You use the Newsgroups Subscriptions dialog box to choose a newsgroup to view.

Viewing posts in a newsgroup is similar to viewing e-mail messages. Outlook Express displays the post headers in the message list and posts content in the Preview pane. Like e-mail messages in Outlook, unread posts appear in bold. The plus and minus signs to the left of the posts indicate the originating message of a message thread. A **thread** includes a message and all of the replies to that message. When you click a plus sign to the left of a post, the responses to that post appear indented under the original post. When you click a minus sign, the responses are hidden.

Sending posts to newsgroups is similar to sending e-mail messages. To send a message to the newsgroup, click the New Post button on the toolbar,

Lesson 9 Using Advanced E-Mail Features 289

type a subject and a message, and click the Send button. To reply to a post, click the post that you want to reply to and click the Reply Group button (so that the post can be seen by the newsgroup), or click the Reply button (so the post can be seen by only the person who posted it).

View newsgroup posts

Now that you have a news account setup and a newsgroup link, you will view a gardening newsgroup and read various posts.

1 In the Newsgroup Subscriptions dialog box, type *gardens* in the Display Newsgroups Which Contain box.

After a few seconds, the names of newsgroups that discuss gardens are displayed.

TROUBLESHOOTING

Your Internet service provider's news server might not offer certain newsgroups. If the aus.gardens newsgroup does not appear, choose another.

2 Click aus.gardens, and click the Go To button.

The Newsgroup Subscription dialog box closes, and the folder banner displays the newsgroup name. After a few seconds, the newsgroup posts appear in the message list.

Figure 9-30

aus.gardens newsgroup

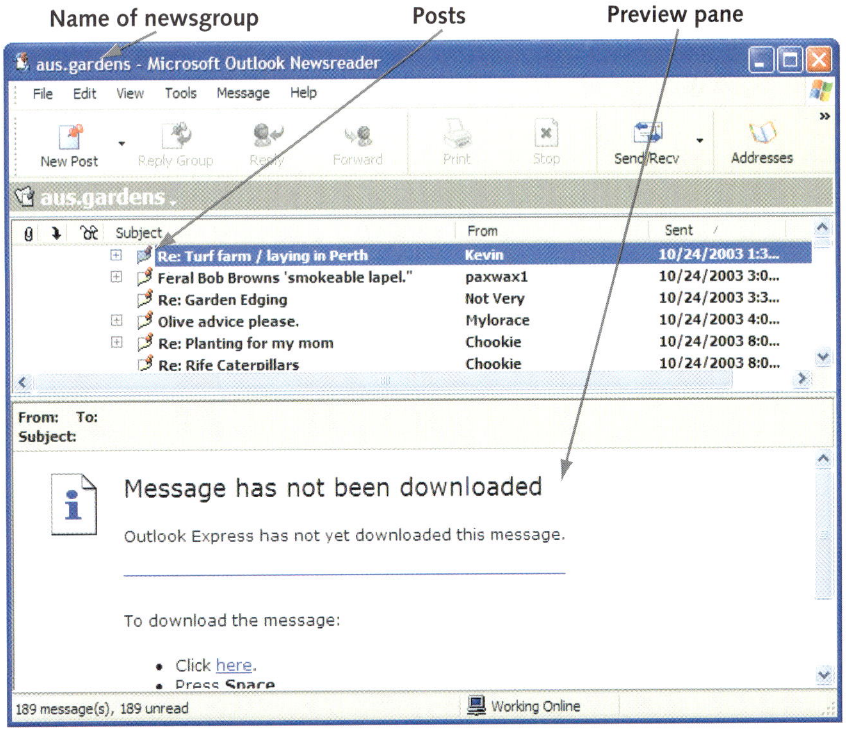

3 Click a post header.

The message body is displayed in the Preview pane.

290 | **Lesson 9** Using Advanced E-Mail Features

> **ANOTHER METHOD**
>
> You can double-click a post to display it in its own message window.

QUICK CHECK

Q: What is a thread?

A: A thread includes a message and all of the replies to that message.

4 Click the plus sign to the left of a post.

The thread expands and shows all posts sent in response to the original post.

5 Click a post that has a minus sign to the left of it.

The thread collapses and responses are hidden.

QUICK REFERENCE ▼

View newsgroup posts

1 Select a newsgroup and click the Go To button.

2 Click a post header.

3 Click the plus sign to the left of a post.

Subscribing to a Newsgroup

> **THE BOTTOM LINE**
>
> You should keep your newsgroup subscriptions up to date. To do so, subscribe to newsgroups that interest you and unsubscribe from newsgroups you no longer post to or view.

If you decide that you really like a particular newsgroup, you can subscribe to it. In Outlook Express, to **subscribe** means to add a newsgroup's name to Outlook Express's Folders list. Subscribing makes it easier for you to access a newsgroup. You can subscribe to as many newsgroups as you like. If you find that you rarely visit a newsgroup that you've subscribed to, you can easily unsubscribe from the newsgroup, thus removing it from the Folders list.

Subscribe to a newsgroup

In order to learn how to manage newsgroup subscriptions you will subscribe to the aus.gardens newsgroup, and then unsubscribe from it.

1 If necessary, click the Folder Banner to display the list of folders. Right-click the aus.gardens newsgroup name (or the newsgroup that you chose), and click Subscribe on the shortcut menu that appears.

You are now subscribed to the newsgroup.

2 In the Folders list, right-click the aus.gardens newsgroup (or the newsgroup that you chose), and click Unsubscribe on the shortcut menu that appears.

An alert box appears, asking whether you are sure that you want to unsubscribe from the newsgroup.

TROUBLESHOOTING

If an alert box appears telling you that you are not subscribed to any newsgroups and asking whether you would like to see a list of available newsgroups, click No.

3 **Click OK.**

The newsgroup is no longer listed in the Folders list and it is removed from the newsgroup window.

ANOTHER METHOD

You can also subscribe to a newsgroup by clicking the Newsgroups button on the toolbar to display the Newsgroup Subscription dialog box. Select the newsgroup's name in the list, and click the Subscribe button.

QUICK CHECK

Q: Why would you subscribe to a newsgroup?

A: Subscribing makes it easier for you to access a newsgroup.

◆ If you are continuing to the next lesson, keep Outlook open.

◆ If you are not continuing to the next lesson, close Outlook.

QUICK REFERENCE ▼

Subscribe to a newsgroup

1 Right-click the newsgroup name.
2 Click Subscribe on the shortcut menu.

Key Points

✔ *Outlook allows you to create specialized e-mail messages by creating and using message templates.*
✔ *You can create a distribution list to make it easier to send e-mail to a group of several recipients.*
✔ *Your privacy can be protected by blocking offensive or useless images and limiting the distribution of messages you send.*
✔ *The Rules Wizard lets you establish rules for handling e-mail messages as they arrive.*
✔ *You can track when messages are delivered and read to verify that your message was received.*
✔ *With Outlook you can use a newsreader and subscribe to a newsgroup, which can be a valuable source of information.*

Quick Quiz

True/False

T F 1. Templates are saved with the extension .dot.
T F 2. A template is a type of form.
T F 3. Individual members can be removed from a distribution list for a specific message.
T F 4. An exception is not required when you create a rule.
T F 5. Read receipts work with the Microsoft Exchange Server or Internet mail service.

Multiple Choice

1. A desktop alert tells you when you receive a(n) _____.
   a. e-mail message
   b. meeting request
   c. task request
   d. All of the above

2. To view newsgroups, Outlook uses _____.
   a. Outlook newsreader
   b. Outlook Express newsreader
   c. Outlook Mail folder
   d. a previous version of Outlook

3. The News command must be added to the _____ menu.
   a. Go
   b. News
   c. View
   d. Newsreader

4. Templates are stored in the _____ folder.
   a. Templates
   b. Forms
   c. Mail
   d. Contacts

5. You can prevent a recipient from _____ a message you sent.
   a. printing
   b. forwarding
   c. copying
   d. All of the above

Short Answer

1. How do you mark a message for a read receipt?
2. How do you access the Outlook Express newsreader?
3. Identify the three parts of a rule.
4. When can you run a rule?
5. What is the purpose of a read receipt?
6. How do you save a message as a template?
7. Where are Outlook templates saved?

On Your Own

Exercise 1

Create a birthday e-mail message for a friend. Make the font size of the text 18, and change the font color to a color that appeals to you. Save the message as a template, and use the template to create a birthday e-mail message for your class partner. Request a read receipt and then send the message.

Exercise 2

Create a rule that takes messages that arrive in your Inbox marked with high importance and moves them to a new folder named To Do Today. Send a message identified as important to your class partner.

One Step Further

Exercise 1

View the list of newsgroups you can access. Subscribe to a newsgroup that interests you.

Exercise 2

Your employer is considering the advantages and disadvantages of enabling its employees to access newsgroups. Write a paragraph that supports those in favor of accessing newsgroups or those opposed to newsgroup access.

Exercise 3

Create a folder to hold read receipts or delivery receipts. Write a rule that moves any read receipts or delivery receipts you receive to the new folder.

LESSON 10
Using Advanced Calendar Features

After completing this lesson, you will be able to:
✓ *Customize Calendar options.*
✓ *Change time zone settings.*
✓ *Set private appointments.*
✓ *Update meetings.*
✓ *Schedule online meetings using NetMeeting.*
✓ *Share Calendar information over the Internet.*
✓ *Create side-by-side calendars.*

KEY TERMS
- chat
- iCalendar
- NetMeeting
- private
- Whiteboard

When you first began using the Microsoft Outlook Calendar, you probably just typed in a few appointments and scheduled a few meetings. As you continue to use the Calendar, you might want to use more of its features or customize it to fit the way you work. For example, you might prefer to display the time slots in the Appointment Area in a different color. You might want to change the Appointment Area so that the start and end times match the times when you arrive and leave work. As you view different menus, you might wonder about some of the more advanced features that are represented on the menus, such as online meetings.

In this lesson, you will learn how to customize Calendar options and change time zone information. You will set private appointments, update meetings, and schedule online meetings with Microsoft NetMeeting. Finally, you will share Calendar information with others over the Internet or over an intranet.

IMPORTANT
To complete some of the exercises in this lesson, you will need to exchange e-mail messages with a class partner. If you don't have a class partner or you are performing the exercises alone, you can send the message to yourself. Simply enter your own e-mail address instead of a class partner's address.

Customizing Calendar Options

THE BOTTOM LINE

In Outlook, you can change the characteristics of your calendar to match the way you work.

In earlier lessons, you used the Calendar to perform simple tasks such as scheduling meetings, reminding you of appointments, and creating tasks. In fact, you were so busy *using* the Outlook Calendar that you might not have noticed how the new streamlined format of the Calendar window made it easy to perform these actions. Every action can be completed with fewer clicks and less work than you anticipated. The Date Navigator and the Calendar display area that can display the date, day, and time provide single-click access to the schedule for a specific day. In Microsoft Office Outlook 2003, you can also view more than one calendar at a time in the Calendar display area. You will look at this feature later in the lesson.

Figure 10-1

Streamlined Calendar folder

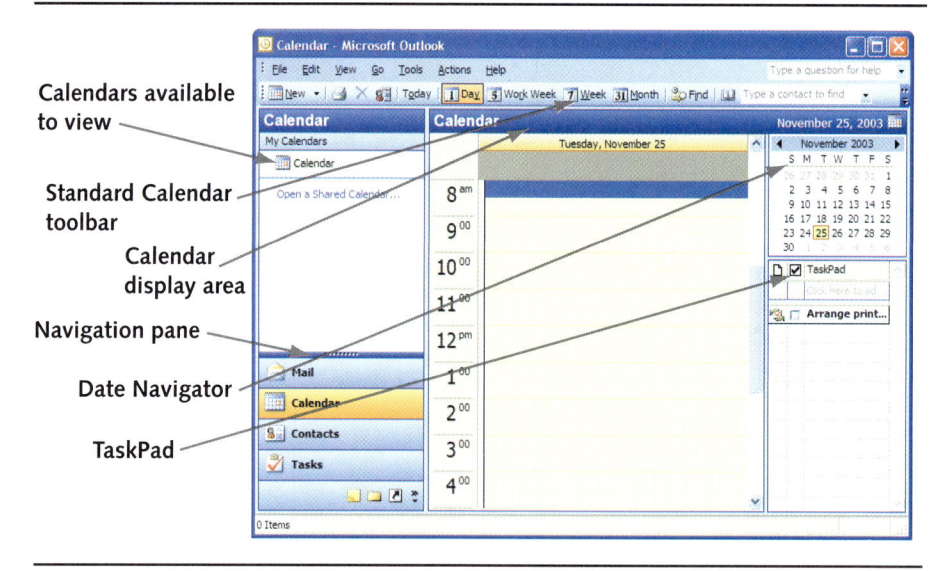

If all the information you need on your calendar isn't visible, change your calendar options to display the information. Change the default settings to customize the Calendar to fit your needs. By default, the Outlook Calendar displays a Monday through Friday, 8:00 AM to 5:00 PM, work week. However, this work week might not fit your work schedule. For example, your work week might start on a Tuesday and end on a Saturday. Also, the Calendar doesn't automatically show holidays from different countries, different time zones, or the numbers of the weeks (1 through 52). However, you can change any of these options to reflect your work environment. The following table details some of the Calendar options you can change by using the Calendar Options dialog box.

Calendar Option	Description
Sun, Mon, Tue, Wed, Thu, Fri, Sat	Display the selected days as working days in Work Week view. This is useful if your work week isn't Monday through Friday. If your work schedule changes, you can select different check boxes.
First day of week	Arrange the Calendar so the specified day is the first day of the work week.
First week of year	Specify whether you want the first week of the year to start on January 1, the first four-day week, or the first full week.
Start time	Specify the time you begin your work day.
End time	Specify the time you end your work day.
Show week numbers in the Date Navigator	Display the numbers of the weeks of the year from 1 to 52 to the left of each week in the Date Navigator.
Allow attendees to propose new times for meetings you organize	Individuals invited to a meeting you set up can suggest a different time for the meeting.
Use this response when you propose meeting times	This sets the default response for suggesting a new time when invited to a meeting. Responses are Tentative, Accept, and Decline.
Background color	Change the background color for the time slots in the Appointment Area.
Planner Options	Select this option to modify the Planner functions when you schedule meetings.
Add Holidays	Display holidays from a country you specify. If you have customers or associates who work in a different country, display holidays for that country so you know when they will be out of the office.
When sending meeting requests over the Internet, use iCalendar format	Internet Calendaring (iCal) is a file type that enables you to send meeting requests, save an appointment, and import or export information in your calendar.
Free/Busy Options	This lets other people know when you are available for meetings. You can set the amount of information you want to share.
Resource Scheduling	You can reserve resources such as meeting rooms and presentation equipment.
Time Zone	Display a time zone from a country you specify. If you have customers or associates who work in a different time zone, set the Appointment Area so it displays the times for your time zone with the corresponding times for a second time zone.

298 Lesson 10 Using Advanced Calendar Features

◆ **Be sure to start Outlook before beginning this exercise.**

Customize Calendar options

You begin this exercise by creating a work week that starts on Wednesday and ends on Sunday. Then you set the daily start time to 2:00 PM and set the end time to 10:00 PM and change the color of the Appointment Area. Finally, you set up Outlook to show holidays from the United Kingdom.

1 **In the Navigation pane, click the Calendar button to display the Calendar.**

The most recent type of time period (day, work week, week, or month) viewed by you or another user is displayed.

2 **If necessary, click the Work Week button on the Standard toolbar.**

The Calendar is displayed in Work Week view. Notice that the default work week is Monday through Friday, 8:00 AM to 5:00 PM.

3 **On the Tools menu, click Options.**

The Options dialog box is displayed.

Figure 10-2

Options dialog box

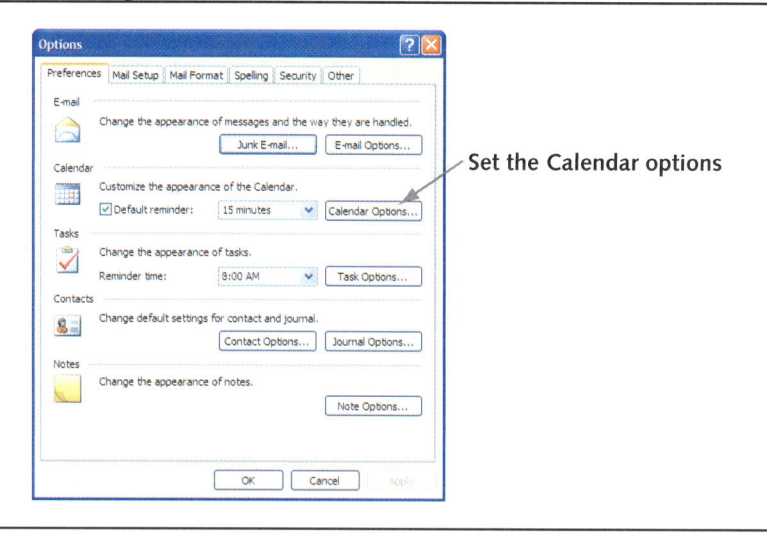

4 **Click the Calendar Options button.**

The Calendar Options dialog box is displayed.

Lesson 10 Using Advanced Calendar Features 299

Figure 10-3

Calendar Options dialog box

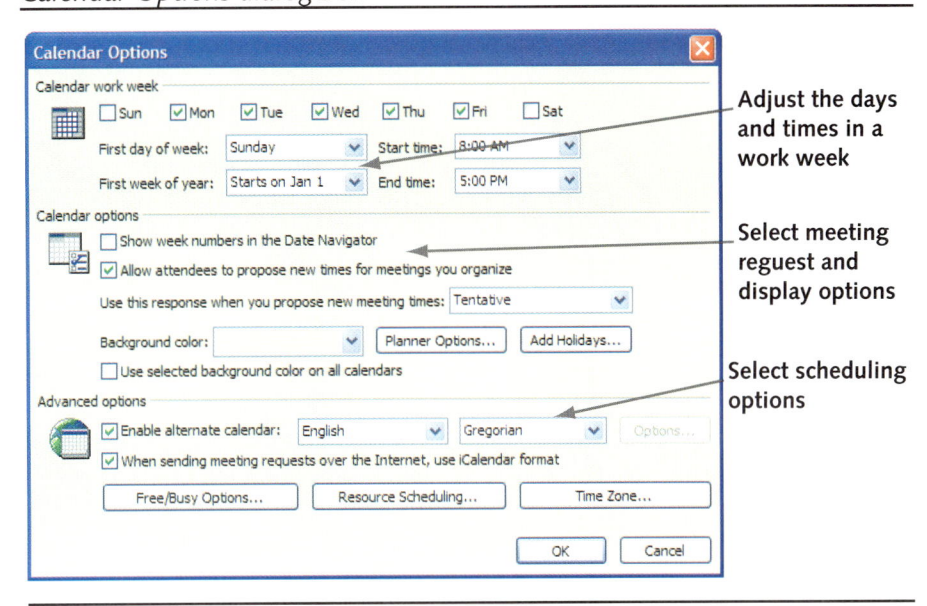

- Adjust the days and times in a work week
- Select meeting request and display options
- Select scheduling options

5 Select the Sun check box, clear the Mon and Tue check boxes, and then select the Sat check box.

The new workdays are selected.

6 Click the First Day Of Week down arrow, and click Wednesday.

Wednesday is now specified as the first day of the work week.

7 Click the Start Time down arrow, scroll down, and then click 2:00 PM. Click the End Time down arrow, scroll down, and then click 10:00 PM.

The start and end time of each work day is specified.

8 Click the Background Color down arrow, and click a blue section.

The background of the Calendar is blue.

9 Click the Add Holidays button.

The Add Holidays To Calendar dialog box is displayed.

TIP

You can select holidays for as many countries as you want. A dialog box will be displayed if the holidays have already been added. Click OK in the box to continue.

Figure 10-4

Add Holidays To Calendar dialog box

10 Select the United Kingdom check box, clear the United States check box, and then click OK.

A progress bar might be displayed while the holidays from the United Kingdom are added to the Calendar.

11 Click OK in the alert window displayed after the holidays have been added.

The new holidays will be displayed in your calendar.

12 In the Calendar Options dialog box, click OK. In the Options dialog box, click OK.

The new options that you specified are activated. Notice that the time slots in the Appointment Area are now blue and that the days Wednesday through Sunday appear as the days in the work week.

> **TIP**
>
> If you decide that you can no longer want to see holidays for a specific country, you can quickly delete the holidays from the Calendar. On the View menu, point to Arrange By, point to Current View, and click Events. Click the Location column heading to sort by country, select all holidays for the country that you want to remove, and then press Delete.

Figure 10-5

Customized calendar

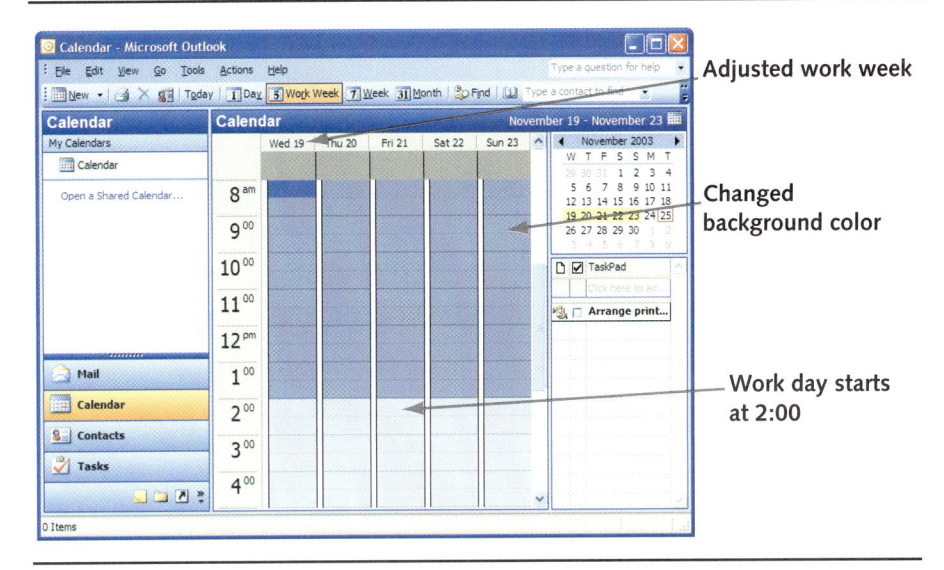

- Adjusted work week
- Changed background color
- Work day starts at 2:00

13 On the Standard toolbar, click the Day button, and then click the Today button.

The current day is displayed.

◆ Keep Outlook open for the next exercise.

QUICK REFERENCE ▼
Customize Calendar options

1 On the Tools menu, click Options.
2 Click the Calendar Options button.
3 Make any necessary changes.
4 Click the OK button several times to return to the main window.

QUICK CHECK

Q: What is the default work week?

A: By default, the Outlook Calendar displays a Monday through Friday, 8:00 AM to 5:00 PM, work week.

Changing Time Zone Settings

THE BOTTOM LINE

If you work with others who live in an area different from you, you may need to change or add a time zone. Fortunately, Outlook makes viewing and changing time zones easy.

You can change the time zone used by Outlook if you move to a different location or if the current time zone is incorrect. When you change the time zone in Outlook, you are changing it for all other programs as well—just as if you had changed the time zone by using the Date/Time Properties dialog box in Microsoft Windows. You can also add a second time zone to the Calendar, which is useful if you frequently work with people in a different time zone or country, or if you are planning a business trip and want to view the time difference.

302 Lesson 10 Using Advanced Calendar Features

For example, reservation agents at Adventure Works frequently phone guests to confirm upcoming reservations. Adventure Works is located in the United States, but it has many visitors from France. The reservation agents have set up France as an additional time zone to ensure they call guests at reasonable hours.

Add a time zone

You will now add the time zone for Paris to your Calendar as a second time zone.

1 On the Tools menu, click Options.

The Options dialog box is displayed.

2 Click the Calendar Options button.

The Calendar Options dialog box is displayed.

TROUBLESHOOTING

Depending on your location, the settings in your Time Zone dialog box might be different than those in the illustration shown here.

3 Click the Time Zone button.

The Time Zone dialog box is displayed.

Figure 10-6
Time Zone dialog box

TIP

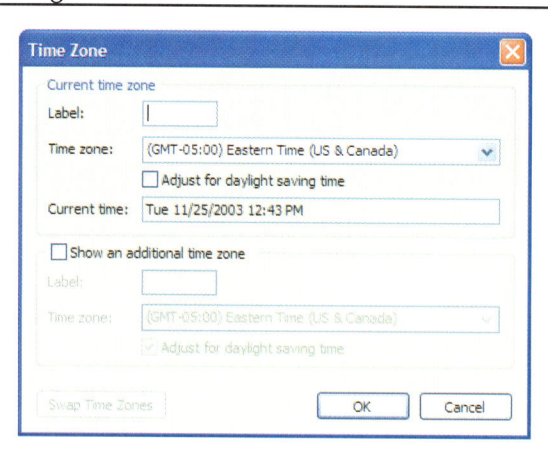

If you decide you no longer want to show an additional time zone, simply clear the Show An Additional Time Zone check box.

4 Select the Show An Additional Time Zone check box.

This activates the fields for the additional time zone.

Lesson 10 Using Advanced Calendar Features 303

5 In the Show An Additional Time Zone section, click in the Label box, and type France.

The label you enter should easily identify the location or individual in the time zone you display.

6 Click the Time Zone down arrow, scroll down, click the line (GMT + 01:00) Brussels, Copenhagen, Madrid, Paris, and then click OK.

The time zone is selected.

7 In the Calendar Options dialog box, click OK. In the Options dialog box, click OK.

The time zone information for France now appears in the Calendar.

Figure 10-7

Additional time zone displayed

QUICK CHECK

Q: How do you delete a time zone after it is added to your calendar?

A: If you decide you no longer want to show an additional time zone, simply clear the Show An Additional Time Zone check box in the Time Zone dialog box.

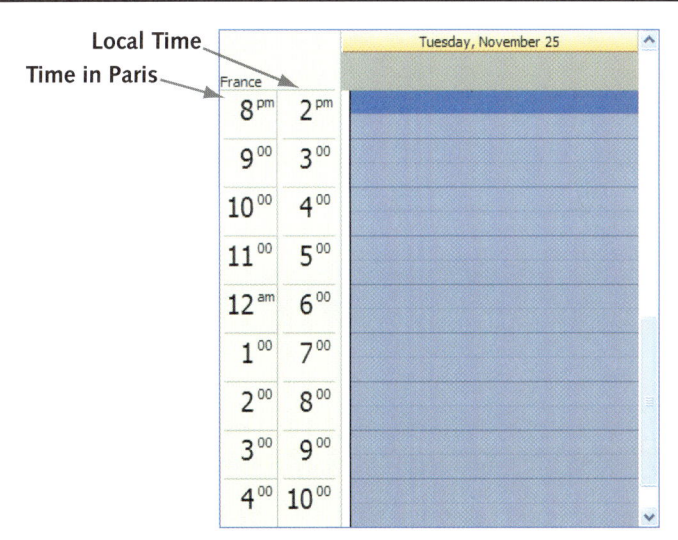

◆ Keep Outlook open for the next exercise.

QUICK REFERENCE ▼

Add a time zone

1 On the Tools menu, click Options.
2 Click the Calendar Options button and click the Time Zone button.
3 Select the Show An Additional Time Zone check box.
4 Select and label the time zone.
5 Click OK three times to return to the main window.

Setting Private Appointments

> **THE BOTTOM LINE**
>
> There are times when you may need to keep appointments private. You can protect the details of a personal appointment in Outlook by making the appointment private.

Scheduling Appointments and Events

> **TIP**
>
> See Lesson 5 for basic information about setting appointments.

Every day, you perform a variety of actions and make a number of appointments. Some of these actions are company business; others are performed for you. For example, you may attend a planning meeting in the morning and use some personal time in the afternoon to visit a doctor or pick up your daughter from school. Although you don't want to share your doctor appointment with your co-workers, you want to save the information in Outlook so you don't forget the appointment. When you enter the appointment in Outlook, identify the appointment as **private**. Other users can't see your private items, even if they access your Outlook folders.

Set a private appointment

In this exercise, you set a private appointment to pick up your son after a cross-country track meet next week.

1 **In the Date Navigator, click next Thursday's date.**

The Appointment Area displays next Thursday's date.

2 **On the Standard toolbar, click the New Appointment button.**

An appointment window is displayed. The insertion point is already in the Subject box.

3 **In the Subject box, type Pick up Michael and press the Tab key.**

The insertion point moves to the Location box.

4 **In the Location box, type Track meet at school.**

Enter any information that identifies the location.

5 **In the Start Time drop-down list, select 5:30 PM.**

This identifies the time that the appointment starts.

6 **In the lower-right corner of the window, click the Private box.**

The details of a private appointment are not visible to others.

Figure 10-8

Private appointment

[Screenshot of appointment window with "Private appointment" label pointing to the Private checkbox in the lower-right corner]

7 **Click the Save And Close button.**

The appointment is saved to your calendar.

◆ Click the Today button to display today's schedule.

◆ Keep Outlook open for the next exercise.

QUICK REFERENCE ▼

Set a private appointment

1 Create an appointment.

2 In the lower-right corner of the window, click the Private box.

3 Click the Save And Close button.

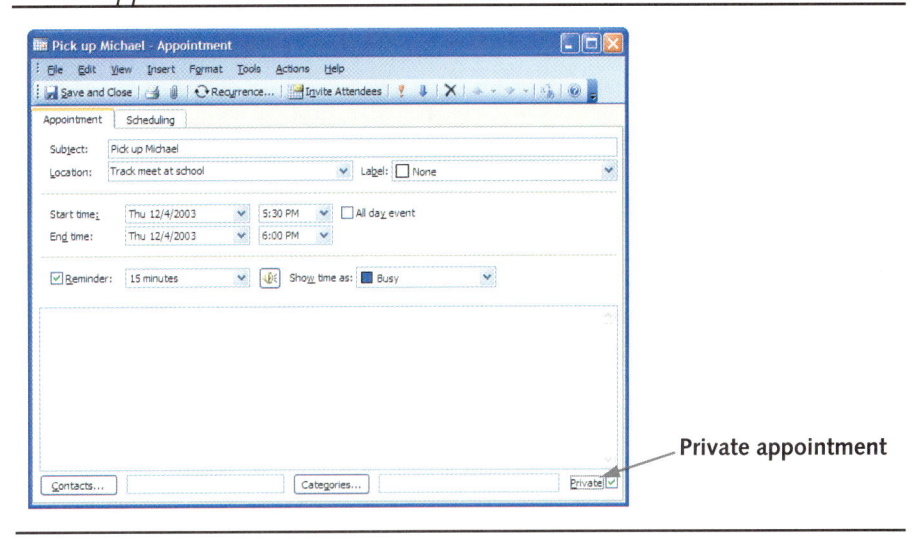

QUICK CHECK

Q: How confidential is a private appointment?

A: The details of a private appointment are not visible to others.

Updating Meetings

Updating and Organizing Appointments

THE BOTTOM LINE

Once a meeting is set up, whether through Outlook or not, the details and information about that meeting may change. After a meeting is created in Outlook, it can be modified and updated.

TIP

See Lesson 5 for basic information about planning a meeting, creating a meeting, inviting attendees to a meeting, responding to a meeting request, and proposing a new time for the meeting.

You have probably attended plenty of meetings that were nothing more than a waste of time for every attendee. Using Outlook doesn't guarantee that the meetings you create will be filled with valuable information. However, Outlook does provide tools to help you create meetings that result in success in the business world. After creating a meeting, you may need to update information about the meeting. The following table describes how meetings can be modified after they are created.

Action	Example
Change a meeting to a recurring series	A meeting held to kick off a project can be changed to become a weekly status meeting.
Change the time the meeting starts	Several attendees are unavailable for the company morale meeting on Friday morning. Change the meeting to Friday afternoon so everyone can participate.
Add or delete attendees and resources	A trainer requires a specific room or piece of equipment for his presentation. Ensure that the needed resources are present.
Change the status of an attendee	A required attendee is unavailable, but the meeting must be held at the specified time. Change the attendee's status from required to optional.
Change the meeting to a NetMeeting	A participant was planning to fly into your city for a meeting, but cannot leave his office due to other commitments. Change the meeting to a NetMeeting so he can still participate.

The public relations manager at Adventure Works set up a kick-off meeting for the summer season. Although the meeting was planned several weeks in advance, she has to make several changes. First, the vendor giving a presentation about new equipment requested a large television screen and a DVD player to view a movie about the product. Next, the vice president told her that he would be out of town for the meeting and the groundskeeper sent an e-mail message about the building where the meeting was scheduled. She used Outlook to make each change.

Canceling a Meeting

Sometimes, a meeting just doesn't work out. Participants can't attend. Equipment isn't available. The scheduled speaker won't give a presentation if the wind is blowing from the North. You can't do anything but cancel the meeting. To cancel a meeting:

1. Double-click the meeting on your daily planner.

2. In the Actions menu, select Cancel Meeting.

3. In the alert window, choose to send a cancellation notice or not send a notice when you delete the meeting, and click the OK button.

Lesson 10 Using Advanced Calendar Features 307

Update a meeting

To demonstrate how a meeting would be updated, you create a meeting that requires your class partner and another student, you change the meeting to a recurring meeting, and then you change the status of an attendee.

1 On the Navigation pane, click the last Wednesday of next month.

The last Wednesday of next month is displayed in the Appointment Area.

2 Click the 9:00 AM time slot.

Because you modified the start of the workday in a previous exercise, the 9:00 AM time slot is darker than the workday time periods.

3 On the Standard toolbar, click the down arrow to the right of the New Appointment button, and select the Meeting Request option.

The meeting window is displayed.

Figure 10-9

New meeting request

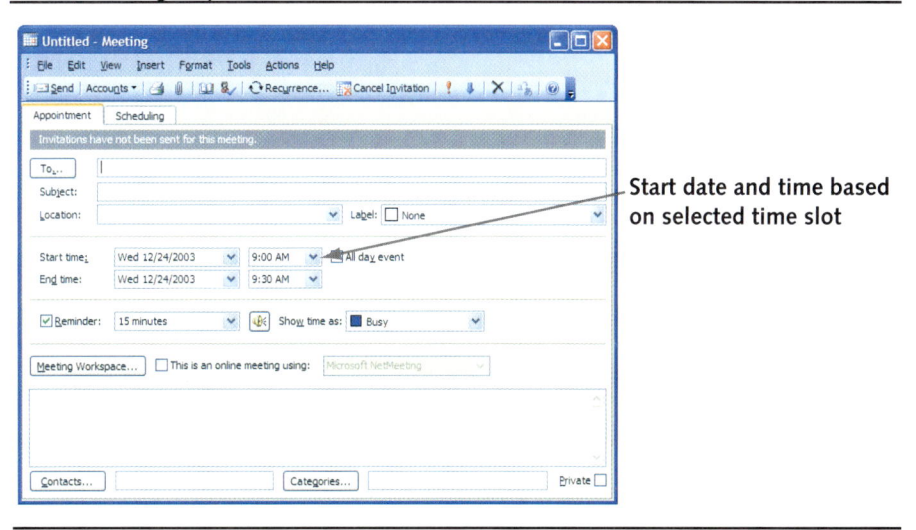

Start date and time based on selected time slot

4 Click the To button.

The Select Attendees And Resources dialog box is displayed.

5 Select your class partner, and click the Required button. Select another student, click the Required button, and click the OK button.

The Untitled Meeting window is displayed again.

6 Click in the Subject field and type New Season Kick-Off Meeting. Click in the Location field and type Conference Room A.

The subject is the subject of the meeting request and the topic to be discussed in the meeting.

7 Select the End Time of 11:00 AM.

The meeting information is complete.

Figure 10-10

Meeting request

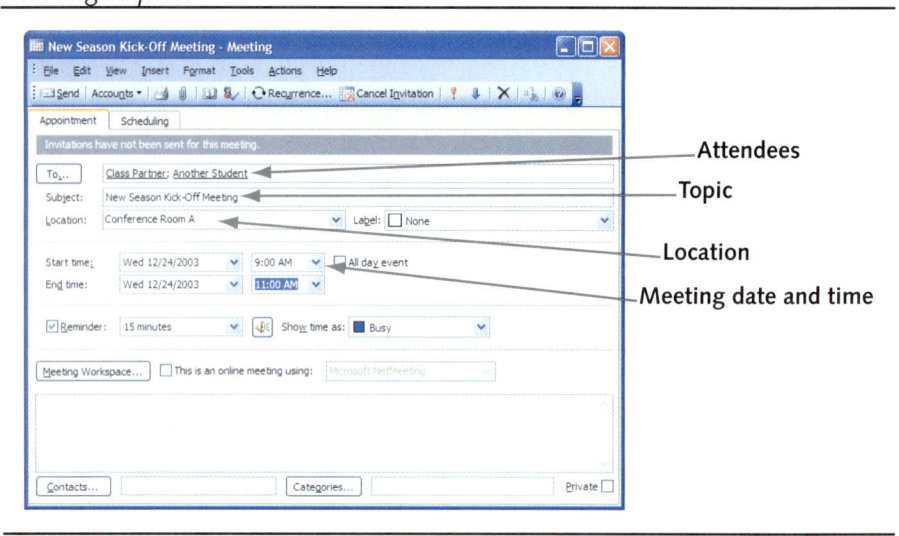

- Attendees
- Topic
- Location
- Meeting date and time

8 **Click the Send button.**

The meeting is scheduled in your planner.

Figure 10-11

Meeting is scheduled

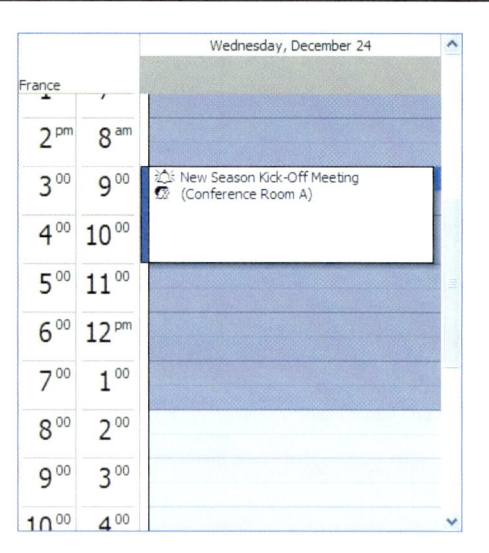

9 **Double-click the meeting on your daily planner.**

The window containing detailed information about the meeting is displayed.

10 **Click the Recurrence button.**

The Appointment Recurrence dialog box is displayed. The suggested recurrence pattern is generated by the day and time of the original meeting.

Lesson 10 Using Advanced Calendar Features 309

Figure 10-12

Appointment Recurrence dialog box

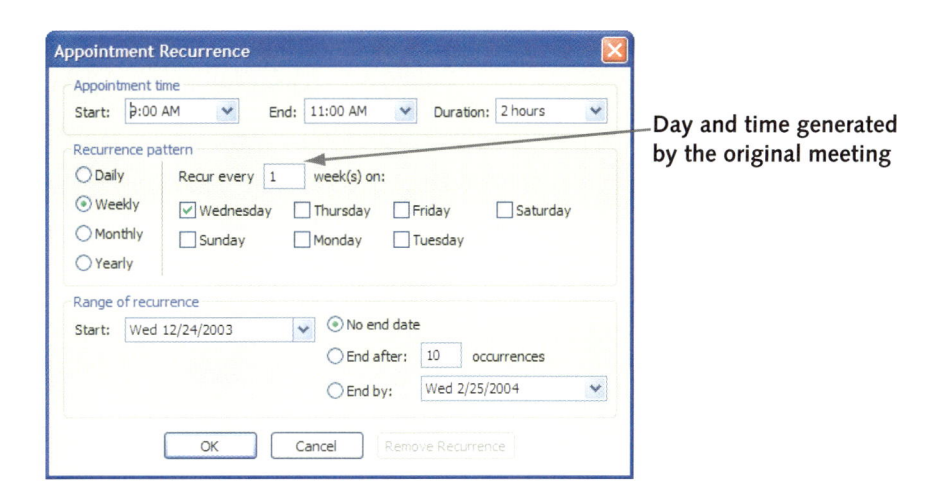

Day and time generated by the original meeting

11 In the Recurrence Pattern area, click Monthly and the third Monday of every month. Click the OK button.

The meeting is scheduled for the third Monday of every month.

Figure 10-13

Modified recurrence pattern

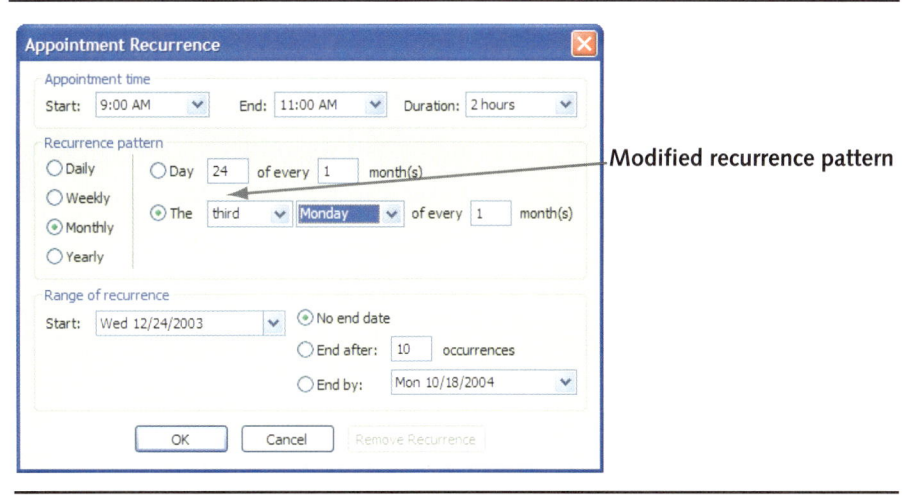

Modified recurrence pattern

12 Click the Tracking tab.

Information about the attendees is displayed. Currently, both invitees are required.

Figure 10-14

Tracking information

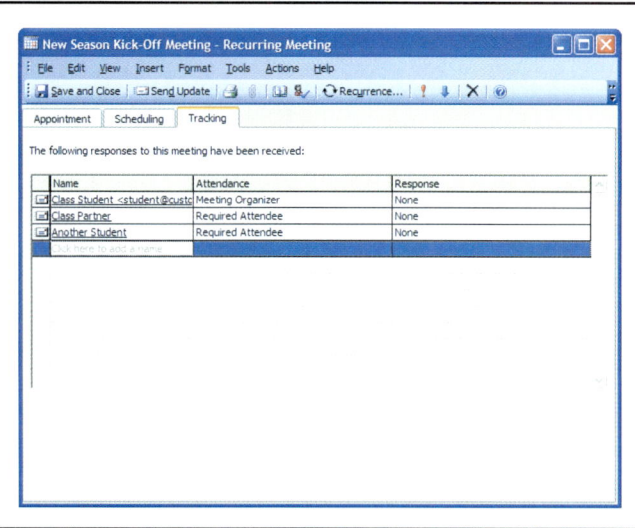

13 Click the field labeled Required Attendee in the Attendance column for your class partner.

A drop-down list is displayed.

14 Select Optional Attendee.

Your class partner's attendance is no longer required.

Figure 10-15

Modifying attendance requirements

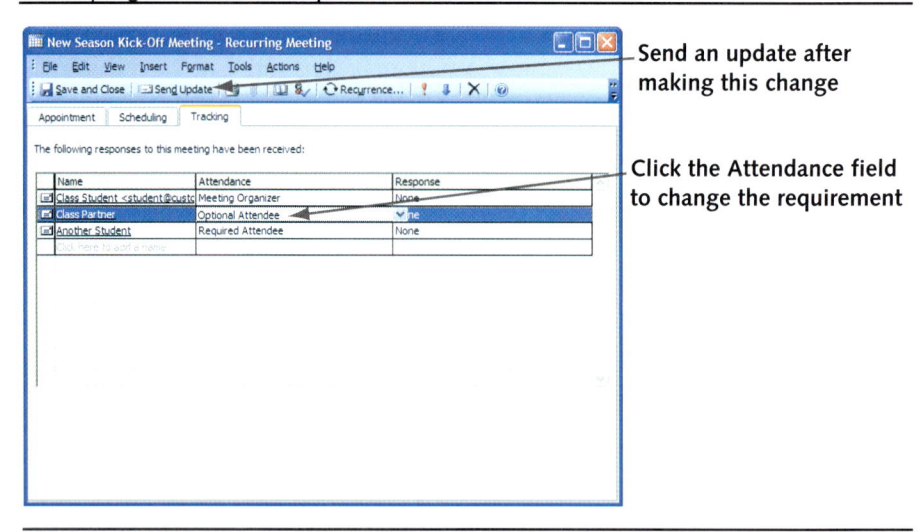

— Send an update after making this change

— Click the Attendance field to change the requirement

15 Click the Send Update button.

A message is sent to each attendee.

◆ Click the Today button to display today's schedule.

◆ Keep Outlook open for the next exercise.

Lesson 10 Using Advanced Calendar Features 311

QUICK CHECK

Q: Can you change a standard meeting to an online meeting?

A: You can change the meeting and update the attendees.

QUICK REFERENCE ▼

Update a meeting

1. Double-click the meeting on your daily planner.
2. Make any needed changes.
3. Click the Send Update button.

Scheduling Online Meetings Using NetMeeting

THE BOTTOM LINE

Working with NetMeeting, you can schedule an online meeting if you can't conduct a meeting in person.

In addition to using Calendar to schedule meetings with participants who can attend a meeting in person, you can also schedule an online meeting for participants who cannot attend the meeting in person. For example, Adventure Works is planning to host a seminar for the hotel industry on how to attract international guests. The guest relations manager at Adventure Works has a business associate in Ireland who would like to attend this seminar, but he won't be able to make the trip from Ireland to California. As an alternative, she invited her associate to attend the conference via an online meeting.

TIP

Online meetings can also be conducted by using a Windows Media Services broadcast or a Microsoft Exchange conference.

To conduct such a meeting, you can use Microsoft NetMeeting. **NetMeeting** is an add-on program that comes with Microsoft Internet Explorer. Using NetMeeting, you can conduct meetings over the Internet or over an intranet. NetMeeting supports two-way communication among meeting participants by using sound and video. To communicate in this way, you must have a sound card, speakers, a microphone, and a video camera installed on your computer. If you do not have these items, you can still exchange information by typing messages in a **chat** window (a window used to exchange typed messages instantaneously), drawing on an electronic **Whiteboard** (a blank screen that simulates marker boards used in classrooms or conference rooms), or sharing files and applications.

You can schedule an online meeting within Outlook. The steps for scheduling an online meeting are similar to the steps for scheduling a normal meeting using the Calendar. Simply follow the same steps and then specify that the meeting will be held online using NetMeeting. You can set up a reminder in Outlook to remind each attendee before the meeting is about to occur. When it is time for the meeting, the organizer who created the meeting opens the meeting request and clicks Start Meeting on the Actions menu. Other participants join the meeting by opening the meeting in the Calendar and clicking Join Meeting on the Actions menu.

Figure 10-16
Microsoft NetMeeting

312 Lesson 10 Using Advanced Calendar Features

> **IMPORTANT**
>
> You must be set up for NetMeeting before you begin using the application. To set up NetMeeting, start Internet Explorer. On the File menu, point to New, and click Internet Call. Follow the steps in the wizard.

Starting a NetMeeting

To actually participate in a NetMeeting, you must first start NetMeeting and then set up NetMeeting by entering your personal information in the NetMeeting dialog box. Start NetMeeting by right-clicking an online meeting, which is not currently selected, in the Calendar and then clicking Start NetMeeting. (If you don't have an existing meeting in the Calendar, you can access NetMeeting by starting Internet Explorer. Then on the File menu, point to New, and click Internet Call.)

To start a meeting:

1. Double-click the meeting in the Calendar.

2. Click the Start Meeting button near the top of the pane.

To find out more information about how to set up and use NetMeeting, use the online Help in Outlook and search for NetMeeting.

> **Schedule an online meeting**
>
> To simulate an online meeting, in this exercise, you schedule an online meeting with your class partner using NetMeeting.
>
> **1** In the Calendar, display next Thursday and click the 11:00 AM time slot.
>
> Remember that the calendar runs from Wednesday to Sunday. Click the 11:00 AM time slot for your time zone—not France's.
>
> **2** On the Standard toolbar, click the down arrow to the right of the New Appointment button and click the Meeting Request option.
>
> The meeting window is displayed.

> **ANOTHER METHOD**
>
> You can also display the meeting window by right-clicking the time at which the meeting is to begin (in the Appointment Area) and clicking New Meeting Request on the shortcut menu.

> **3** Click the To button.
>
> The Select Attendees And Resources dialog box is displayed.
>
> **4** Scroll to see your class partner's name if necessary, and click your class partner's name. Click the Required button, and click OK.
>
> The meeting request is addressed to your class partner.
>
> **5** Click in the Subject box, and type **Environmental NetMeeting**.
>
> This is the subject of the message and the topic of the online meeting.

Lesson 10 Using Advanced Calendar Features 313

6 **Select the This Is An Online Meeting Using check box.**

The meeting window expands, showing more options. Notice that Microsoft NetMeeting already appears in the This Is An Online Meeting Using box.

Figure 10-17
Additional fields are displayed when you request an online meeting

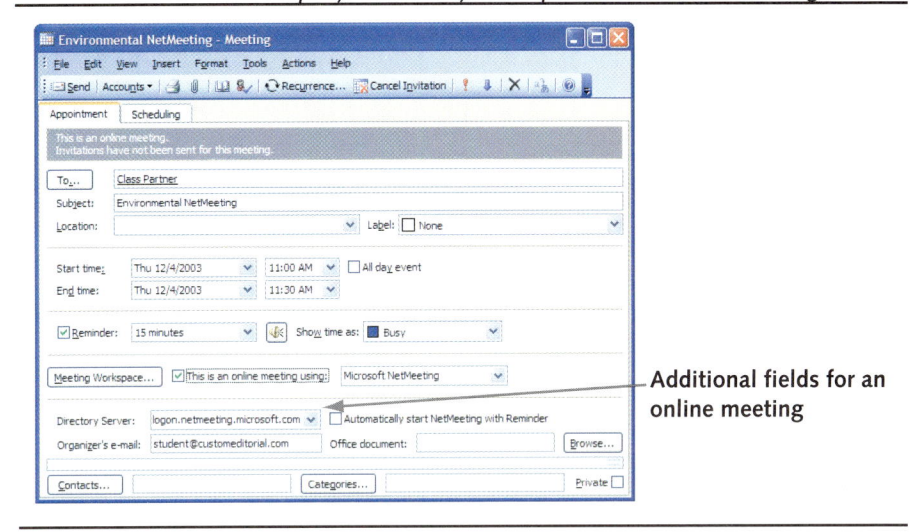

—Additional fields for an online meeting

7 **If necessary, enter or select the server hosting the NetMeeting in the Directory Server box.**

Ask your system administrator for assistance if necessary.

8 **If necessary, enter your e-mail address in the Organizer's e-mail box.**

If you choose to send a reminder by using the Reminder check box and the Automatically Start NetMeeting With Reminder check box, Outlook will remind you and the attendees that you have fifteen minutes (or any other time you specify) before the NetMeeting automatically starts.

9 **Click the second End Time down arrow, and click 1:00 PM (2 Hours).**

This identifies the time the online meeting will end.

Figure 10-18
Meeting request for an online meeting

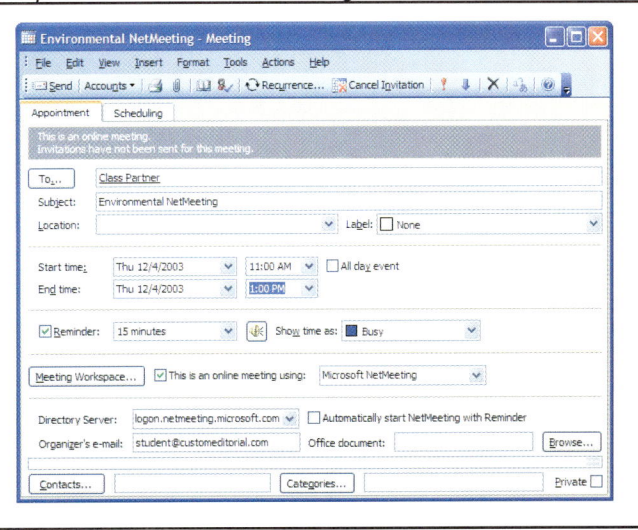

QUICK CHECK

Q: What is NetMeeting?

A: It is an add-on program that comes with Microsoft Internet Explorer.

10 On the Standard toolbar in the meeting window, click the Send button.

The NetMeeting request is sent to your class partner. The meeting is displayed in your Calendar.

◆ Keep Outlook open for the next exercise.

QUICK REFERENCE ▼

Schedule an online meeting

1 Schedule the meeting.

2 Select the This Is An Online Meeting Using check box.

3 Enter the meeting information.

4 On the Standard toolbar in the meeting window, click the Send button.

Sharing Calendar Information over the Internet

THE BOTTOM LINE

With Outlook you can send a meeting request to an attendee who is outside your network by using the Internet.

Outlook has a component called **iCalendar** (Internet Calendaring), which allows you to send meeting requests and receive responses from invitees outside your company's network. For example, the events coordinator at Adventure Works sent a meeting request to her son's English teacher to schedule a time to discuss her son's performance.

IMPORTANT

iCalendar won't work properly if you send a meeting request to a recipient who uses a mail program that does not have iCalendar.

When you send a meeting request over the Internet, Outlook sends an iCalendar attachment that contains the meeting information. When an invitee receives a meeting request, he or she can open or save the attachment to his or her hard disk and then either accept or decline the invitation. If the invitee accepts, he or she can then add the meeting to his or her own Calendar.

Lesson 10 Using Advanced Calendar Features 315

Share calendar information

In this exercise, you will first create a meeting request and then send an iCalendar attachment to your class partner. Then you will accept a meeting request from your class partner.

1 Display next Wednesday in Day view. In the Calendar, click the 7:00 PM time slot.

The date and time will be used to create the meeting request.

2 On the Standard toolbar, click the down arrow to the right of the New Appointment button, and click Meeting Request.

A meeting window is displayed.

3 Click the To button.

The Select Attendees And Resources dialog box is displayed.

4 If necessary, scroll down until you see your class partner's name, and then click your class partner's name. Click the Required button, and click OK.

The meeting request will be addressed to your class partner.

5 Click in the Subject box, and type Rock Climbing Club Meeting. Click in the Location box, and type Adventure Works. Click the second End Time down arrow, and click 8:00 PM (1 Hour).

This provides the basic meeting information.

6 In the meeting window, on the Actions menu, click Forward As iCalendar.

A message window is displayed. Enter your class partner's e-mail address if necessary. The iCalendar appears as an attachment.

Figure 10-19

Forwarding an iCalendar

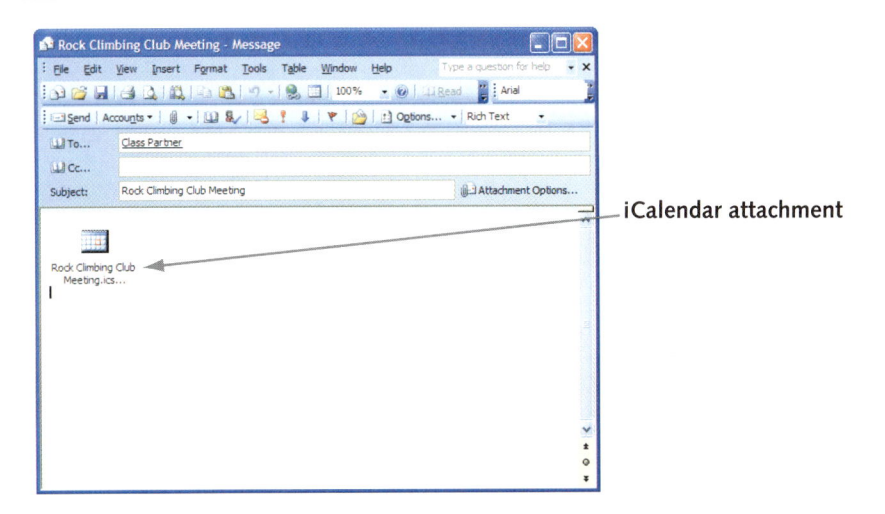

7 Click the Send button.

The meeting request will be sent to your class partner.

8 **In the top-right corner of the meeting window, click the Close button.**

An alert box is displayed, asking whether you want to save changes.

> **TROUBLESHOOTING**
>
> Normally you would click Yes in the alert box so that the meeting would appear in your Calendar, but because your class partner is going to send this same meeting request to you, you need your Calendar to be open on this day for this exercise to work properly. Otherwise, when you open the iCalendar attachment from your partner, a meeting window will appear, alerting you that you already have a meeting on that day (the meeting you tried to schedule).

9 **Click No in the alert window.**

This prevents conflict between the meeting you organized and the meeting your class partner organized.

10 **Display the Inbox, and on the Standard toolbar, click the Send/Receive button.**

A meeting request from your class partner arrives in the Inbox.

11 **Double-click the attachment in the Rock Climbing Meeting message. If an alert box is displayed, choose to open the attachment.**

A window is displayed. You can click the Tentative button if you think that you might be able to attend the meeting, or click the Decline button if you can't attend the meeting. If you want to quickly look at your Calendar to see whether you are available, you can click the Calendar button.

12 **On the Standard toolbar, click the Accept button.**

An alert box informs you that the meeting will be added to your Calendar and asks whether you want to include comments with your response.

13 **Click OK, and click the Send/Receive button.**

An e-mail message arrives in your Inbox stating that your class partner has accepted.

> **TIP**
>
> After the response is sent, the meeting organizer can see who has responded to the meeting by double-clicking the meeting in the Calendar and clicking the Tracking tab.

14 **Display the Calendar. In the Calendar, display the date of the meeting.**

The meeting appears in your Calendar.

Lesson 10 Using Advanced Calendar Features 317

Figure 10-20

The meeting is scheduled

- Keep Outlook open for the next exercise.

QUICK CHECK

Q: How is iCalendar information sent?

A: **It is sent as an attachment.**

QUICK REFERENCE ▼

Share calendar information

1. Create the meeting request.
2. In the meeting window, on the Actions menu, click Forward As iCalendar.
3. Click the Send button.

Side-by-Side Calendars

Using Multiple Calendars

THE BOTTOM LINE

Outlook allows you to keep and view multiple calendars at the same time.

You're a busy person. You work, take night classes, and drive your children to a variety of weekend and evening activities. You have a calendar for your schedule at work, a calendar of your son's club activities, a calendar of your daughter's sports activities, and a calendar of your husband's travel schedule. Keeping track of several calendars is taking too much time and energy.

Outlook 2003 enables you to view several calendars at the same time. Even better than viewing the calendars, you can copy and move items from one calendar to another. When you view calendars at the same time, they all display the same dates and scroll together.

318 **Lesson 10** Using Advanced Calendar Features

View multiple calendars

First you will create a second calendar for your personal appointments and view it next to your standard calendar. Then you will copy an appointment from one calendar to the other.

TROUBLESHOOTING

If you do not have the appointments used in this exercise, create two new appointments in your standard calendar.

1 **Display the calendar for next Thursday. If necessary, scroll to display the appointments for this date.**

Two appointments are scheduled. You have an online meeting at 11 AM and you have a private appointment to pick up your son at 5:30 PM. You will move the personal appointment to the calendar you create.

2 **Click the down arrow next to the New button and click the Folder option.**

The Create New Folder dialog box is displayed.

3 **Name the new folder Second Calendar, click the Personal Folders directory to identify where the folder is created, and click the OK button.**

The new calendar is displayed in the list.

Figure 10-21

Second Calendar is created

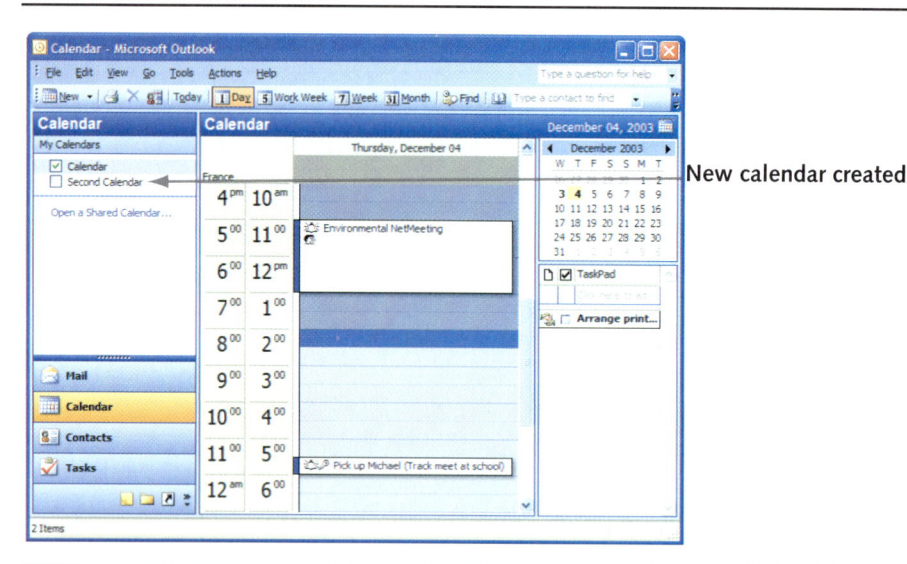

4 **Click the check box in front of the Second Calendar.**

The new calendar is displayed next to the original calendar. The name of each calendar is at the top of the column holding the calendar. The columns are also color-coded to match the color used to highlight the color of the calendar identified in the Navigation pane.

CHECK THIS OUT ▼

Using Multiple Calendars

The ability to keep multiple calendars has many uses. For example, you could use this feature to track schedules for your department. You could display the calendar for several sales representatives to see where they spend their time or you could pinpoint customers who receive too much or too little attention from your staff.

Figure 10-22

Second Calendar is displayed

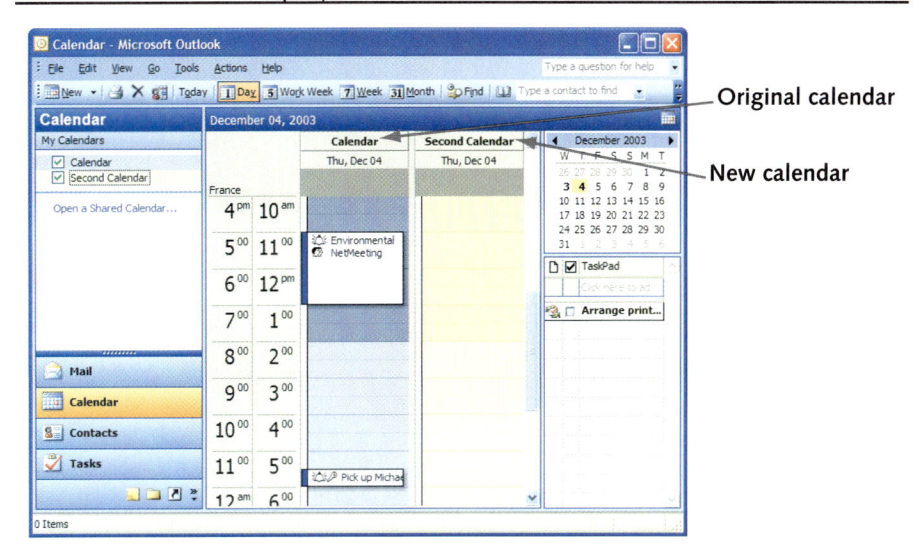

— Original calendar
— New calendar

5 Drag the personal appointment, "Pick up Michael," to the Second Calendar.

The appointment is moved to the new calendar.

Figure 10-23

The appointment is moved to the Second Calendar

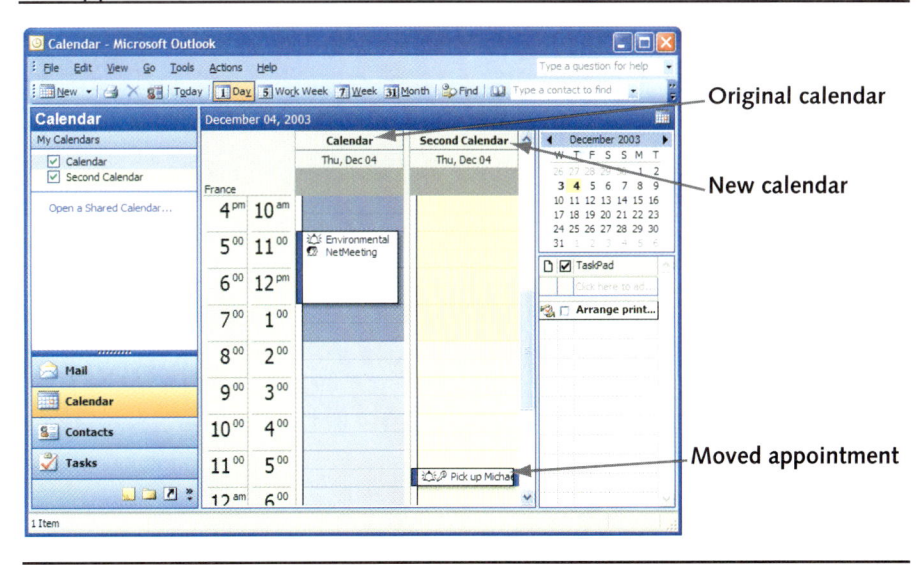

— Original calendar
— New calendar
— Moved appointment

6 Right-click on the moved appointment and drag it to the original calendar. Select the Copy option from the drop down menu displayed when you drop the appointment in the original calendar.

The appointment is copied to the original calendar. It is displayed on both calendars.

Figure 10-24

The appointment is copied to the original calendar

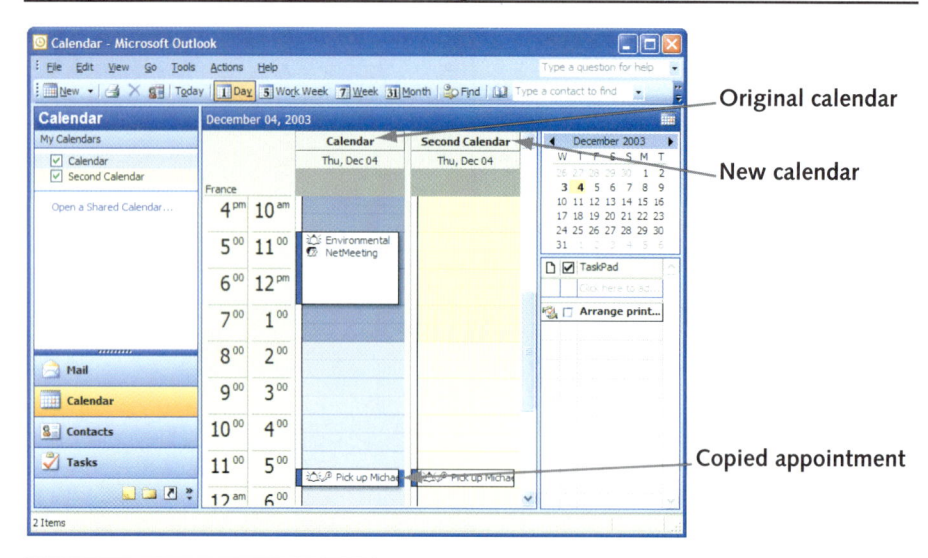

- Original calendar
- New calendar
- Copied appointment

QUICK CHECK

Q: How do you move an appointment to a different calendar?

A: **Display both calendars and drag the appointment to the other calendar.**

- Clear the check box before the Second Calendar in the list of calendars.
- Reset any customization options that you do not want to keep, including the additional time zone, changes to the work week, and changes to the start and end time of the workday.
- If you are continuing to the next lesson, keep Outlook open.
- If you are not continuing to the next lesson, close Outlook.

QUICK REFERENCE ▼

View multiple calendars

1. Display the Calendar.
2. In the Navigation pane, click the check box in front of each calendar.

Key Points

✓ *Outlook lets you customize different Calendar options to help you work more effectively.*
✓ *You can change a time zone or add a second time zone to accommodate customers or co-workers in a different location.*
✓ *With Outlook, you can set private appointments that can't be viewed by others.*
✓ *Meeting details can be changed and attendees can be updated.*
✓ *Through NetMeeting you can schedule and start online meetings.*
✓ *iCalendar lets you share your schedule over the Internet.*
✓ *Two or more calendars can be viewed next to each other. Calendar items can be copied and moved from one calendar to another.*

Quick Quiz

True/False

T F 1. A work week can only start on Monday or Wednesday.

T F 2. Attendees can suggest a new time for a meeting.

T F 3. Your calendar can include holidays celebrated in a different country.

T F 4. Invite a meeting room to attend a meeting to reserve the room.

T F 5. The details of a private meeting can be viewed by an attendee on your calendar.

Multiple Choice

1. Drag an appointment from one calendar to another to _____ it.
   a. move
   b. copy
   c. delete
   d. accept

2. The details of a(n) _____ meeting can't be seen by others.
   a. confidential
   b. updated
   c. private
   d. copied

3. An attendee who must be at a meeting is _____.
   a. a resource
   b. required
   c. recurrent
   d. optional

4. Communicate during an online meeting by _____.
   a. e-mail
   b. talking
   c. sending an update
   d. All of the above

5. Internet Calendaring enables you to _____.
   a. use NetMeeting
   b. attend online meetings
   c. send a meeting request
   d. All of the above

Short Answer

1. Describe a customization method you find helpful.
2. Why are NetMeetings used?
3. Why would you make a private appointment?
4. Identify the meeting updates you can perform.
5. How do you add a time zone to the Calendar?
6. For what reason do you use iCalendar?
7. Why do you share Calendar information?

On Your Own

Exercise 1

Modify the following Calendar options: change the work week to go from Tuesday through Friday, 9:00 AM to 7:00 PM; designate Tuesday as the first day of the work week; change the background color to yellow; and display a second time zone labeled Tokyo. (Select the appropriate time zone.)

Exercise 2

Invite your class partner to an online meeting to discuss some of the features of NetMeeting; the meeting will be held the second Tuesday of next month from 1:00 PM to 2:00 PM. Using iCalendar, invite your instructor (or a second friend) to a canned food drive meeting, which will be held in the parking lot the first Thursday of next month from noon to 2:00 PM.

One Step Further

Exercise 1

Visit Microsoft at *www.microsoft.com*. Investigate the Microsoft Office Internet Free/Busy Service.

Exercise 2

You can also conduct online meetings using Windows Media Services or Microsoft Exchange Conferencing. Visit Microsoft at *www.microsoft.com* to investigate these options.

Exercise 3

Compare the chat features of two online tools. Why is one of the tools a better choice?

LESSON 11

Managing Information

After completing this lesson, you will be able to:
✔ Work offline.
✔ Modify Mail Service.
✔ Create and use Outlook forms.
✔ Create Search Folders.
✔ Grant permissions to your folders.
✔ Use Outlook with Windows SharePoint Services.

KEY TERMS

- alert
- Cached Exchange Mode
- control
- Design view
- field
- form
- permission
- public folder
- publish
- roles
- Search Folder
- shared attachment
- virtual folder

After you have used Microsoft Outlook for any length of time, you will quickly realize just how much information it contains. Appointments, addresses, and task lists barely scratch the surface of the information that Outlook can track. Managing the information correctly keeps you at the top of your game and ensures that you arrive at the right place at the right time to meet and greet the right people.

The new Cached Exchange Mode enables you to maximize your productivity when you are away from the office. You can receive important messages that require a response or fast action.

Advanced mail features enable you to set options for mail handling. This includes saving a draft of a message as you write it, setting alerts that occur when mail arrives, and providing assistance while you compose new messages.

In this lesson, you will learn how to enable the Cached Exchange Mode, modify your Mail Service, create forms, and grant permission to access your folders.

IMPORTANT

Before you can use the practice files in this lesson, you need to install them from the companion CD for this book to their default location. For additional information on how to find and open files used in this book, see the "Using the CD-ROM" section at the beginning of this book.

The practice file Guests.mdb is required to complete the exercises in this lesson.

> **IMPORTANT**
>
> To complete some of the exercises in this lesson, you will need to exchange e-mail messages with a class partner. If you don't have a class partner or you are performing the exercises alone, you can send the message to yourself. Simply enter your own e-mail address instead of a class partner's address.

Working Offline

> **THE BOTTOM LINE**
>
> When you are working off site, you can establish a remote connection to your server. When connected, you use Cached Exchange Mode to update your folders.

Offices and organizations don't always fit inside a single building. Workers and members travel to meetings in other cities, work from home, or check their e-mail while eating lunch in the park down the street. Outlook has several features that help you work, even when you aren't physically located in the office.

Establishing a Remote Connection

Mobility is important. You may need to access your e-mail while you are on a business trip, vacationing with your family, or working from home. Whether you are connecting to your school, your office, or an organization, you have a variety of options to make a remote connection to access your e-mail. Outlook enables you to connect via dial-up, broadband, virtual private networks (VPN), and exchange server access through the Internet (RPC over HTTP).

> **IMPORTANT**
>
> Consult your systems administrator or Internet service provider (ISP) for additional setup information.

- *Dial-up connection*—In the past, this was the most common type of remote connection. Using a regular phone line, your computer modem dials a phone number and connects to your Outlook server over the Internet. The speed at which data are transferred is limited by the hardware and the phone line. It is slow and tedious to download large attachments or a large number of messages.
- *Broadband*—This is a much faster connection than the dial-up option. Your computer uses a cable or satellite connection to access the Internet.
- *Virtual private network*—This option provides a secure connection to the network that includes your Outlook server. You can access the entire network and connect directly to the Outlook server. The connection is made through the Internet, so your system administrator may require special hardware to ensure security.

- *Exchange server access through the Internet (RPC over HTTP)*—This new option requires Microsoft Exchange Server 2003. It enables you to connect to your Outlook server over the Internet without using a special connection or special hardware.

Activating Cached Exchange Mode

> **IMPORTANT**
>
> Cached Exchange Mode requires Microsoft Exchange Server.

Microsoft Office Outlook 2003 includes the new **Cached Exchange Mode**, a feature that simplifies the switch between working online and working offline. It creates a copy of your mailbox on your computer. If you are connected to your Exchange Server, the Cached Exchange Mode ensures that all of your mailbox folders are up to date. When you are not connected, you can continue to work with the messages stored on your computer. If you compose new messages while you are disconnected, the new messages are sent to your Outbox. When you connect to your server again, the content of all your mail folders is updated. This means the messages in your Outbox are sent and new messages received are copied to your Outlook mailbox on your local hard drive.

> **IMPORTANT**
>
> The Cached Exchange Mode is not compatible with Remote Mail, a separate, older function that works only with your Inbox and requires you to configure and synchronize special folders that are available when you are offline.

Several connection settings are available when you use the Cached Exchange Mode. The setting you select should be determined by the type of connection you usually use and the amount of time you have available.

- *Download Full Items*—This option downloads all your messages and attachments. Use this option when you keep Outlook running and you are connected to a network most of the time. Messages and attachments are downloaded to your computer as they arrive. If you frequently work offline, this option takes the most time to update your local mailbox.
- *Download Headers And Then Full Items*—This option downloads all the message headers first, and then downloads the message content and attachments. This option lets you "see what's coming" by providing the message headers first.
- *Download Headers*—This option downloads only the message headers unless you choose to preview or open a specific message. After you click a message header, the body of the message and any attachments are downloaded. Use this option if you have a slow connection and want to view only a few of the messages you receive. This is convenient if you just have a few minutes to connect to your server and you need to select the messages you will deal with when you are offline. It's also a way of screening your messages when you are in a hurry, leaving less important messages on the server until you have more time to download them.

QUICK CHECK

Q: Which connection option requires Microsoft Exchange Server 2003?

A: **Exchange Server Access through the Internet (RPC over HTTP) requires it.**

- *On Slow Connections Only Download Headers*—This option downloads only message headers if you are using a slow connection. Outlook monitors the speed of your connection. If the connection is slow, Outlook automatically stops downloading full messages and attachments. This prevents a long wait while large messages and attachments are downloaded byte by byte.

◆ Be sure to start Outlook before you begin this exercise.

Activate Cached Exchange Mode

In this exercise, you activate Cached Exchange Mode and select a connection option.

IMPORTANT

You must have an active connection to your network before beginning this exercise.

1 Open the Tools menu and click the E-mail Accounts option.

The first screen in the E-mail Accounts Wizard is displayed.

Figure 11-1

First E-mail Accounts pane

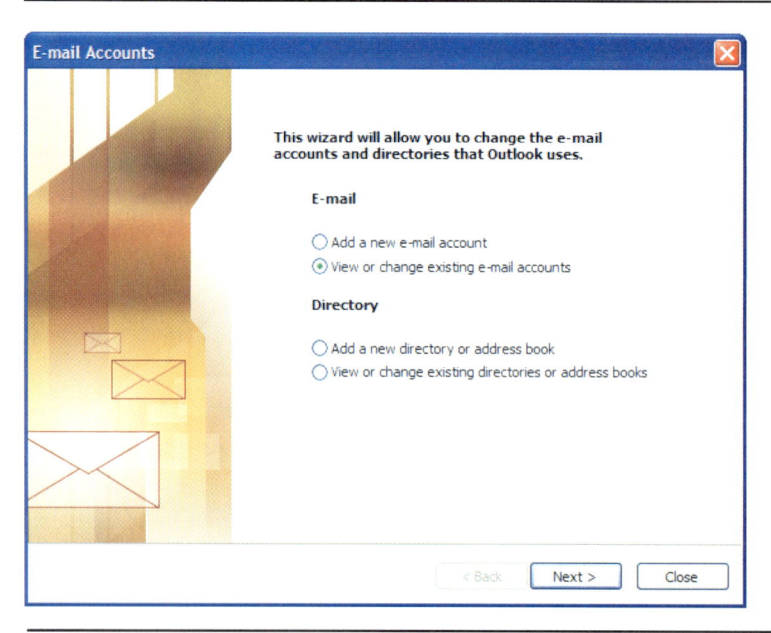

2 If necessary, select the option View Or Change Existing E-mail Accounts. Click the Next button.

This displays accounts that have already been created.

3 Click Microsoft Exchange Server and click the Change button.

The settings for the account are displayed.

4 Select the option Use Cached Exchange Mode.

An alert box might be displayed. It informs you that you must restart Outlook for your change to take effect. Click OK to continue.

5 Click Next in the Wizard screen and click Finish.

This completes the Wizard.

6 Exit Outlook and restart the application.

The change will take effect.

7 In the bottom-right corner of the application, click the word "Connected."

A shortcut menu displaying your connection options is displayed.

8 Select one of the connection options.

Outlook uses the option you select when connected to the server.

◆ Keep Outlook open for the next exercise.

QUICK REFERENCE ▼
Activate Cached Exchange Mode

1 Connect to your network.
2 Open the Tools menu and click the E-mail Accounts option.
3 Use the wizard to change existing e-mail accounts.
4 Select the Microsoft Exchange Server account and click the Change button.
5 Select the option Use Cached Exchange Mode and finish the wizard.
6 Exit Outlook and restart the application.

Modifying Mail Service

THE BOTTOM LINE
You can further customize Outlook by selecting options that alert you when a message arrives.

Timely communication is more important to some businesses than others. For example, Adventure Works often receives e-mail from guests before their arrival. They ask for information about the facilities, confirm reservations, and schedule tours. By company policy, each guest must receive a response within an hour if the e-mail is received between 9 AM and 4 PM. To ensure this, e-mail from guests is directed to the reception desk. Several staff members are responsible for replying when mail arrives. Advanced e-mail options enable the staff to respond quickly and keep a record of the information sent.

To set advanced e-mail options, start in the Inbox. Open the Tools menu, and click Options to display the Options dialog box. Click the E-mail Options button to display the E-mail Options dialog box. Click the Advanced E-mail Options button to display the following Advanced E-mail Options dialog box. Set the options you need and click the OK button in each dialog box to apply the changes.

CHECK THIS OUT ▼

Working Offline
You can choose to work offline, even if you are connected to the server. This prevents updates and allows you to work without interruption.

QUICK CHECK

Q: Which connection option should you use if you have a slow connection?

A: Use the Download Headers option.

Figure 11-2

Advanced E-mail Options dialog box

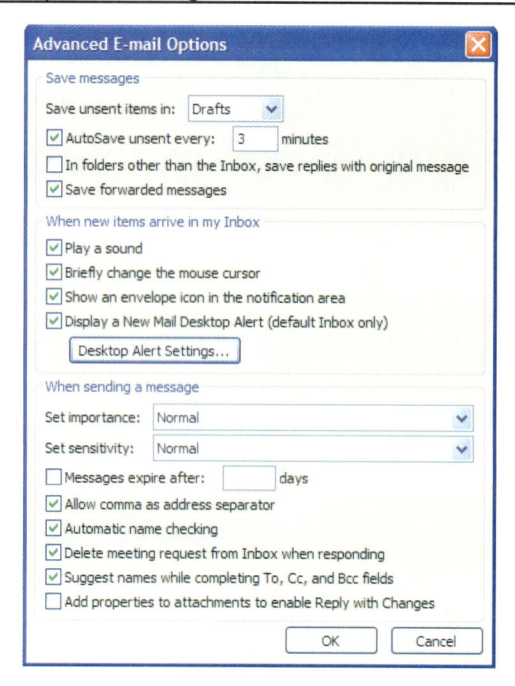

The settings for the reception desk ensure that an e-mail is noticed when it arrives. A sound is played, the mouse cursor changes, and an envelope is displayed. The staff is alerted visually if they don't hear the sound. The e-mail icon remains in the system tray until the message is read.

QUICK CHECK

Q: How can you be notified when mail arrives?

A: Outlook provides visual notification and plays a sound.

QUICK REFERENCE ▼
Modify mail service

1. In the Inbox, open the Tools menu, and click Options.
2. Click the E-mail Options button.
3. Click the Advanced E-mail Options button.
4. Set the options you need and click OK in each dialog box to apply the changes.

Creating and Using Outlook Forms

THE BOTTOM LINE

Outlook provides many standard forms which may be very useful. If one of these forms is close to what you need, but not exact, you can start with a standard Outlook form and customize it for your use.

Many of the detailed windows that you see in Microsoft Outlook are actually forms. A **form** is a collection of fields and field labels for a particular record, formatted and organized for a particular use. A **field** is a single item of data, such as a person's name, e-mail address, or phone number. For example, the Task, Calendar, and Contacts windows are all forms; when you use any of these windows, you are essentially entering fields and records into a database that is controlled and managed by Outlook.

The ready-made forms that you use to create, view, and edit Outlook records provide plenty of flexibility, but like many components in Outlook, you can extend the capabilities of these forms. Specifically, you can modify an existing form to create a format that better matches the way you work.

You can alter an existing Outlook form in several ways: you can delete unwanted fields, add new fields, rename existing field labels, and move and resize fields. For example, in the Contact window, you might change the Company field label to Organization to accommodate government agencies and nonprofit organizations. Or you might want to lengthen the size of the E-mail and Web Page Address fields so that you can see complete addresses in the boxes. The following screen shows the form used to enter fields for a contact record. Notice that the form looks similar to the Contact window—in fact, it *is* the Contact window, but it appears in a **Design view** that allows you to modify the appearance of the window.

Figure 11-3

Contact window in Design view

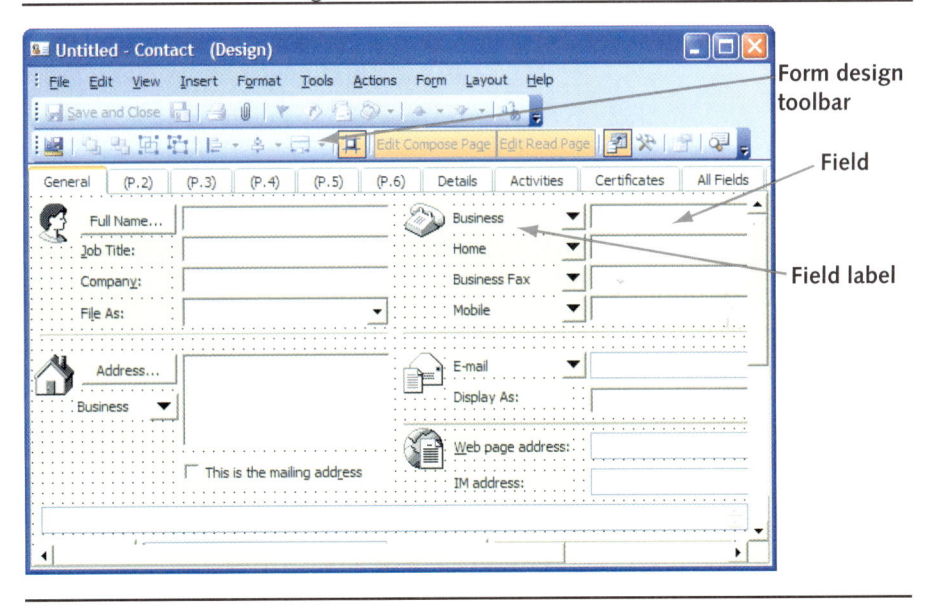

To resize a field, field label, or other object, click one of the resize handles and drag in the desired direction. To move a field, field label, or other object, click and drag until the object is positioned where you want. To delete a field, field label, or other object, click the object's border and press Delete. If you move, size, or delete an object and then change your mind, click Undo on the Edit menu to cancel the changes. To change the text for a field label, click the label, select the text, and then type the new text.

After you have finished customizing a form, you **publish** it—that is, you save the new form to a folder location that Outlook can find. The ready-made forms in Outlook are stored in the Standard Forms Library by default; you can store forms that you create in the Personal Forms Library or in a specific Outlook folder that you select.

You can also add new fields and controls to a form. A **control** is a field or window that provides a way for users to enter data into the form. You can add controls that create text boxes (for entering fields) and field labels, lists, check boxes, option buttons, and more. For example, instead of using the lengthy list of Outlook categories, you might create a list of frequently used categories on your custom contact form. To use controls, you open the form, and click Control Toolbox on the Form menu to display the Toolbox.

Figure 11-4

Control Toolbox

To add a control, drag the desired control button from the Control Toolbox onto the form at the desired location. Editing a control, such as changing the label for a control, is simple. Right-click the control on the form and click Properties. The dialog box that appears varies, depending on the type of control you are using.

You can also quickly add any of Outlook's ready-made fields to a form. To use ready-made fields, open the form and click Field Chooser on the Form menu if the Field Chooser isn't already displayed.

Figure 11-5

Field Chooser

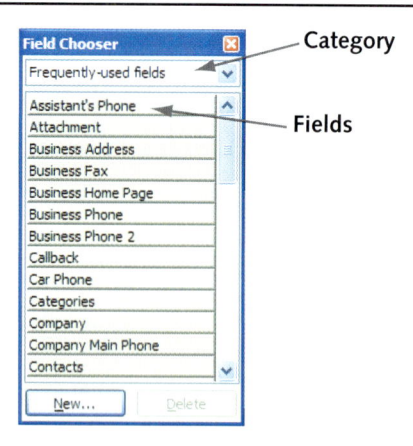

Click the down arrow to the right of the box at the top of the Field Chooser, and select the desired field category. Then scroll down (if necessary) until you see the field that you want to add, and drag the field to the desired location on the form. Outlook adds a field label and a text box (for field entry) when you drag the field onto the form. The following general steps explain how to create a form.

1. In any Outlook window, click the Tools menu, point to Forms, and then click Design A Form. The Design Form dialog box is displayed. The forms in the Standard Forms Library appear in the list.

Figure 11-6

Design Form dialog box

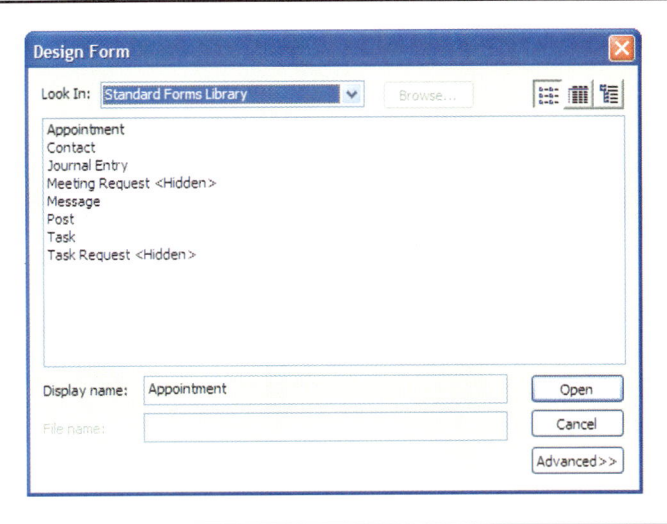

2. In the list, click the form on which you want to base your customized form, and click Open. The Design window for the selected form is displayed.

3. Make changes to the layout of the form by moving, resizing, adding, or deleting field labels, fields (the boxes in which you enter data), and other objects (such as pictures or other icons). Adjust the form until it contains everything you need.

4. When you are finished customizing the form, click the Publish Form button on the toolbar to display the Publish Form As dialog box. A published form can be used for data entry.

ANOTHER METHOD

Open the Tools menu, point to Forms, and select the Publish Form option.

Figure 11-7

Publish Form As dialog box

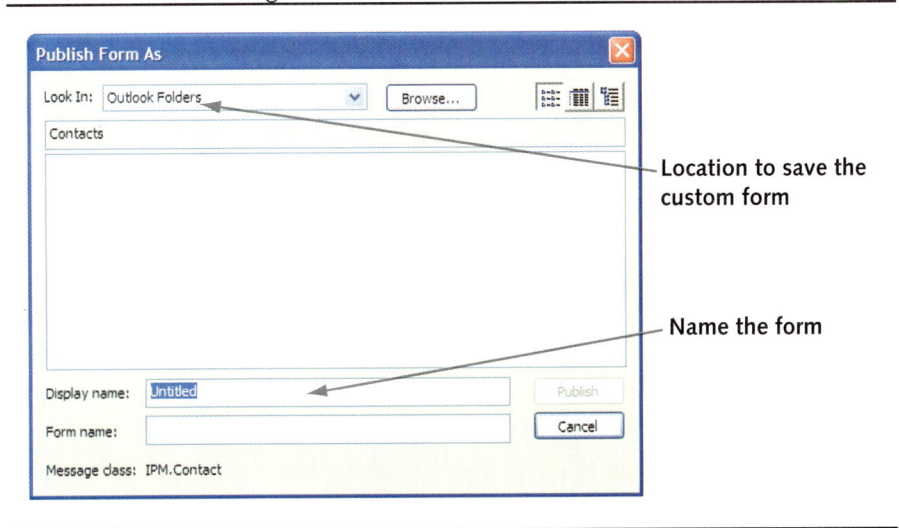

5. Click the Look In down arrow, and click the folder where you want the form to be located. Click in the Display Name box, delete the existing text, and then type a display name.

> **TROUBLESHOOTING**
>
> If you click the Save button instead of the Publish button, Outlook attempts to save the form as a record (such as a contact record or a task item). It will probably tell you that a required field is missing. Use the Save button to save a record after you have entered data; use the Publish button to save a customized form to a designated folder.

6. Click the Publish button. The form is published, making it available for use.

7. Close the Design window without saving changes. The form has been published. It is not necessary to save the form.

After you publish a custom form, you can use it the same way you use any other Outlook form. For example, if you modify the Contact form and publish it, you can open this form and enter information when you create a new contact record.

1. On the Tools menu, point to Forms, and click Choose Form. The Choose Form dialog box is displayed.

2. Click the Look In down arrow, and navigate to the location where you published the custom form. Any customized forms published to the selected location are displayed.

3. Click the name of the form, and click Open. The form is ready to use.

QUICK CHECK

Q: What happens if you try to save a form?

A: **Outlook tries to save the form as a data record.**

QUICK REFERENCE ▼

Create an Outlook form

1. Click the Tools menu, point to Forms, and then click Design A Form.
2. Open a standard form to serve as the base for a new form.
3. Make any necessary changes.
4. Publish the form.

Searching for Information

THE BOTTOM LINE

When you want to find messages that meet specific criteria, you can create Search Folders. These Search Folders are always up to date.

Using Search Folders

You receive information in your e-mail every day. Some of it is important. Some of it is trivial. Outlook can store a lot of data, but all of it is useless if you cannot find the information you need when you want it. Outlook 2003 includes the standard Find feature, an advanced Find, and the new Search folders

The basic Find tool is simple to use. Open the Tools menu, point at Find, and click the Find option to display a small pane in the Outlook window. Use this pane to specify basic search criteria. Tell Outlook what to look for and where to look.

Figure 11-8

Find pane

The advanced Find tool has more options, but it provides the same function. Open the Tools menu, point at Find, and click the Advanced Find option. The Advanced Find dialog box is displayed. Like the basic Find function, you tell Outlook what to look for and where to look. However, you can narrow the search criteria by specifying more details about the message you want to find.

Figure 11-9

Advanced Find dialog box

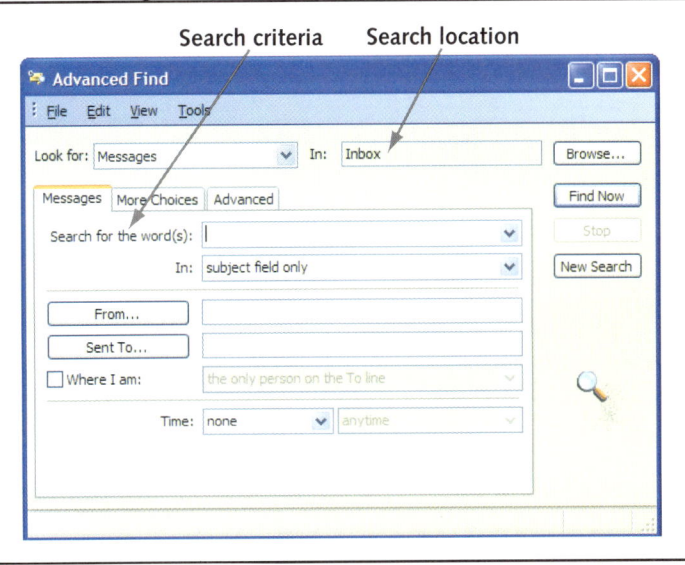

A **Search Folder** is a virtual folder that shows you the messages that fit the search criteria. A **virtual folder** doesn't actually hold anything. The items in a virtual folder are stored in another folder. In fact, a message could appear in more than one Search Folder, even though it is only located in the Inbox. For example, you might create a Search Folder to show you all the messages about a specific project. A second Search Folder might show you all the messages you received from Chris Ashton, one of the project managers. A message from Chris Ashton is displayed in both Search Folders, but it is located in your Inbox.

Information in your Search Folders is automatically kept up to date. As you receive messages that fit the search criteria, they will be displayed in the appropriate Search Folder.

IMPORTANT

You can delete an entire Search Folder without deleting any of the messages. However, if you open a Search Folder and delete individual messages from the folder, the messages are deleted from the real location where they are stored.

You can create custom Search Folders, but for your convenience, Outlook 2003 includes three default Search Folders. They are the For Follow Up folder, Large Messages folder, and the Unread Mail folder.

- *For Follow Up*—This virtual Search Folder displays messages that have been flagged for follow-up actions.
- *Large Messages*—This virtual Search Folder displays messages that are larger than 100 KB.
- *Unread Mail*—This virtual Search Folder displays messages that are marked as unread.

Figure 11-10

Default Search Folders

Create a new Search Folder

To find messages that meet specific criteria you will create a new Search Folder.

1 **In the All Mail Folders list, right-click the Search Folders item. Select New Search Folder on the shortcut menu.**

The New Search Folder dialog box is displayed.

Figure 11-11

New Search Folder dialog box

Lesson 11 Managing Information 335

2 Click the option Mail From Specific People.

The appearance of the dialog box changes. It displays an area that enables you to choose specific individuals.

Figure 11-12

Select individuals who sent messages

— New area to select individual senders

3 Click the Choose button.

The Select Names dialog box is displayed.

4 If necessary, select Contacts in the Show Names From The field. Select your class partner, click the From button, and click the OK button.

The New Search Folder dialog box is displayed. Your class partner's name is specified.

Figure 11-13

Search criterion is identified

— Your class partner is specified

5 Click OK.

The Search Folder is created. It is automatically selected in the list, so all messages from your class partner are listed in the middle pane.

Figure 11-14

New Search Folder is created

Keep Outlook open for the next exercise.

QUICK CHECK

Q: Why is a Search Folder a virtual folder?

A: It doesn't hold any items.

QUICK REFERENCE ▼

Create a new Search Folder

1. In the All Mail Folders list, right-click the Search Folders item. Select New Search Folder on the shortcut menu.
2. Set your search criteria.
3. Click OK.

Granting Permissions to Your Folders

THE BOTTOM LINE

After you have created folders you can place them in the Public Folders directory and specify the users who can access your folder's content.

By default, the folders you create are private. Only you can access them. If you work on a network that includes Microsoft Exchange Server, you can share Outlook items with others by putting the items in a public folder. A **public folder** can contain messages or information that can be shared with designated users. This makes it easier to work together and share information. For example, the human resources manager at Adventure Works likes to have access to the Calendars for all departmental managers so that she can see when a particular manager will be available to interview applicants.

IMPORTANT

This feature requires the use of Microsoft Exchange Server.

When you share an Outlook folder, anyone on the network with the appropriate permission can make changes to the folder, and all other users will see those changes. For example, if you share a task list with others, someone can mark a task as complete so that everyone involved can see that the task no longer needs to be performed.

Before someone on the network can access a public folder that you create, you must grant him or her permission to use the folder. When you grant **permission** to a person on the network, you specify what exactly this person can do to the information in the folder. For example, the events coordinator at Adventure Works lets her assistant view her Calendar (however, the assistant cannot create, edit, or delete Calendar items) and lets her manager view and create Calendar items (however, the manager cannot delete or edit existing items). These levels of involvement are called **roles**. Outlook has several different roles that you can assign to a user.

Role Type	Available Options
Owner	Has all permissions
Publishing Editor	Can create, read, edit, and delete items in the folder and create subfolders
Editor	Can create, read, edit, and delete items in the folder
Publishing Author	Can create and read items in the folder, create subfolders, and edit and delete items that he or she created
Author	Can create and read items in his or her folder, and edit and delete items that he or she created
Reviewer	Can only read items
Contributor	Can only create items; contents of the folder do not appear
None	None

IMPORTANT

To complete this exercise, you must be connected to a network that includes a Microsoft Exchange Server.

Grant permission to your folder

First you will create a tasks folder and share it with others. Then you grant your class partner permission to access your Company Party Tasks folder.

1 Click the Tasks button in the Navigation pane. On the File menu, point to New, and click Folder.

The Create New Folder dialog box is displayed.

Figure 11-15

Create New Folder dialog box

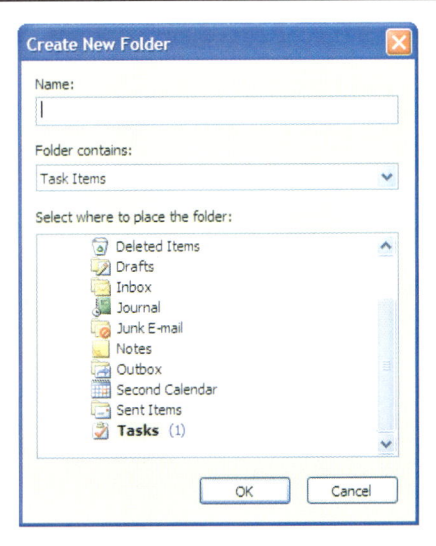

2 In the Name box, type [Your first and last name]'s Company Party Tasks. Click the Folder Contains down arrow, and click Task Items if necessary. In the Select Where To Place The Folder list, scroll down if necessary, click the plus sign to the left of Public Folders, navigate to a location specified by your system administrator, and click OK.

The new folder is created.

3 If necessary, click your Company Party Tasks folder.

The Company Party Tasks folder is opened.

4 Click in the box that contains the text "Click here to add a new Task."
Type Order invitations, and press Enter.
Type Book a band, and press Enter.
Type Call caterer, and press Enter.

The tasks are created.

5 In the Folder List, right-click your Company Party Tasks folder.

A shortcut menu is displayed.

6 On the shortcut menu, click Sharing.

The Properties dialog box is displayed. The Permissions tab is already selected.

TROUBLESHOOTING

If the Permissions tab is not available on the Properties dialog box, either you are not the owner of the folder or you are not connected to the network.

7 Click the Add button.

The Add Users dialog box is displayed.

8 Scroll down if necessary, and click your class partner's name. Click the Add button, and click OK.

Your class partner is added to the list.

9 In the Name list, click your class partner's name. In the Permissions section, click the Permission Level down arrow. Scroll up or down and click Editor.

Your class partner will be able to create, edit, and delete items in the folder and create subfolders.

10 Click OK.

The permissions are set.

◆ Close the Public folder and return to the Inbox.

◆ Keep Outlook open for the next exercise.

Lesson 11 Managing Information 339

QUICK CHECK

Q: Which role can only read items?

A: The reviewer can only read items.

QUICK REFERENCE ▼
Grant permission to your folder

1. Create a folder in the Public Folders directory.
2. Right-click the folder and select Sharing from the shortcut menu.
3. Click the Add button.
4. Select the user, click the Add button, and click OK.
5. Click the permission level and click OK.

Using Outlook with Windows SharePoint Services

THE BOTTOM LINE
Outlook displays an alert when content on the SharePoint site changes, identifies individuals who can access the site, and enables you to post shared documents.

SharePoint sites provide a central location for documents and information. Windows SharePoint Services supplies Web sites with document storage and retrieval functions that require users to check in and check out documents. It maintains version history for the documents it holds and provides a number of standard and customizable ways to view the site.

Outlook, like other Microsoft Office applications, works with SharePoint Services to enhance your work environment and abilities. Outlook displays an alert when content on the SharePoint site changes, provides a list of individuals who can share your items, and enables you to post shared attachments.

IMPORTANT
Consult your systems administrator for assistance with Windows SharePoint Services.

Displaying Alerts from a SharePoint Site

SharePoint sites are designed to help your organization work together more productively than you can work alone on separate computers. Co-workers post a variety of documents, lists, and other information. The individuals who post the items are frequently responsible for keeping the items current by updating the content. Rather than asking these content suppliers to tell everyone when an item is updated, you can choose to receive an **alert,** an automatic notice when items you specify are updated. Alerts are sent to you as e-mail messages that notify you that selected content on a SharePoint site has changed.

CHECK THIS OUT ▼

Rules for Alerts

You can create a rule that automatically delivers alerts to a specific directory. This reduces clutter in your Inbox and organizes your alerts.

Manage alerts

In this exercise, you create alerts for a SharePoint site you have visited.

IMPORTANT

You must have access to a SharePoint site to complete this exercise.

1 **If necessary, click the Mail button in the Navigation pane. Open the Tools menu and select the option Rules And Alerts.**

The Rules And Alerts dialog box is displayed.

TROUBLESHOOTING

If you did not delete rules created in previous lessons, they are listed in the dialog box.

Figure 11-16
Rules And Alerts dialog box

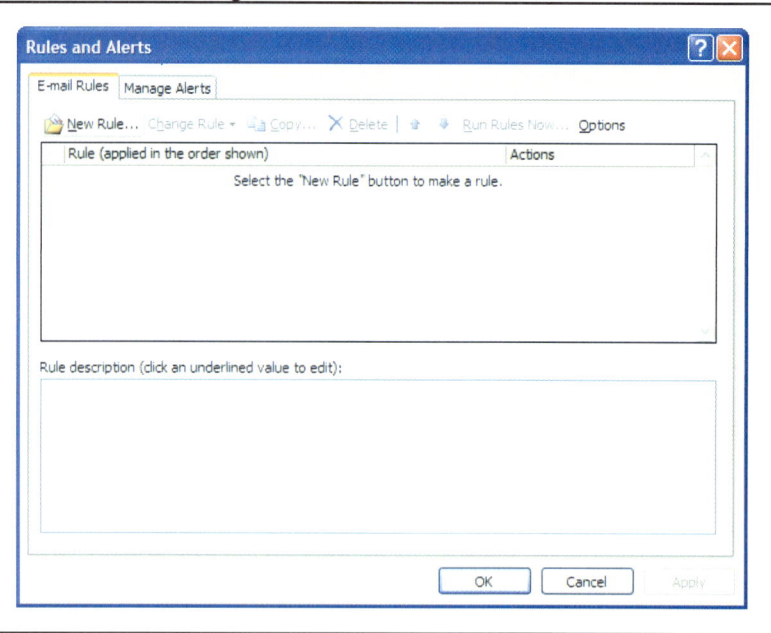

2 **Click the Manage Alerts tab.**

Any existing alert management specifications are displayed. Each alert specification identifies the SharePoint site generating the alert, a description of the reason the alert was generated, and the method used to deliver the alert (usually an e-mail message).

Figure 11-17

Manage Alerts tab

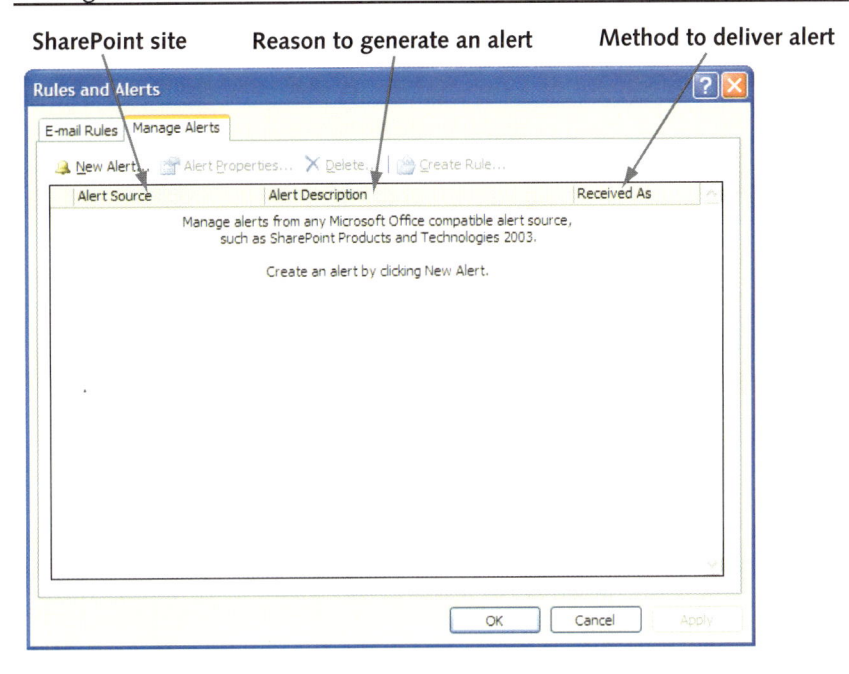

SharePoint site — Reason to generate an alert — Method to deliver alert

3 **Click the New Alert button.**

The New Alert dialog box is displayed.

Figure 11-18

New Alert dialog box

4 **Click the plus sign next to the Sources I Have Visited option.**

The SharePoint sites you have visited are listed.

5 **Select the site and click Open. Navigate to the page containing the content.**

The content you want to track is identified.

6 **Under Actions, select the option Alert Me. Identify the type of changes that should generate an alert, the frequency of the alert, and the method to deliver the alert message. Apply the changes.**

You will immediately receive an e-mail message informing you that the alert has been created.

342   Lesson 11   Managing Information

> **QUICK CHECK**
>
> **Q:** What is the purpose of an alert?
>
> **A:** It tells you that an item has been changed.

◆ Keep Outlook open for the next exercise.

QUICK REFERENCE ▼
Manage alerts

1. Click the Mail button in the Navigation pane. Open the Tools menu and select the option Rules And Alerts.
2. Click the Manage Alerts tab.
3. Click the New Alert button.
4. Select the site, click Open, and navigate to the page containing the content.
5. Select the option Alert Me and define the criteria for an alert. Apply the changes.

Identifying Available Contacts

Windows SharePoint Services maintains a list of individuals who can access the SharePoint Services site. This information must be created on the SharePoint Services site, but it can easily be added to your contact information in Outlook. Use your Web browser to access the contact list. Click the option Link To Outlook. Click Yes to add the Windows SharePoint Services contacts to Outlook.

> **QUICK CHECK**
>
> **Q:** Where is the contact list for a SharePoint site created?
>
> **A:** It is created on the SharePoint site.

QUICK REFERENCE ▼
Identify contacts on a SharePoint Services site

1. Navigate to the contact list on the site.
2. Click the option Link To Outlook and click Yes.

Attaching Files to Messages

Using Shared Attachments

Send a document as a **shared attachment** to create a Document Workspace, a SharePoint Services site centered on the document where recipients can open and edit the attached document. This enables several people to collaborate on a single document or a group of documents.

Send a shared attachment

Now you will send a shared attachment to your class partner.

> **IMPORTANT**
>
> You must have access to a SharePoint site to complete this exercise.

1. If necessary, click the Mail button in the Navigation pane. Click the New Message button.

   A new message window is displayed.

2. Address the message to your class partner. In the Subject box, type Guests.

The message recipients in the To and CC fields are automatically given access to the Document Workspace site.

3 **Open the Insert menu, select File, and navigate to the Outlook Practice directory. Select the document Guests.mdb and click the Insert button.**

The file is attached to the message.

4 **Click the Attachment Options button.**

The Attachment Options task pane is displayed.

> **TROUBLESHOOTING**
>
> Your message also contains your signature, and your attachment might be displayed in a different location. This is determined by your current settings.

Figure 11-19

New Message window with the Attachment Options task pane

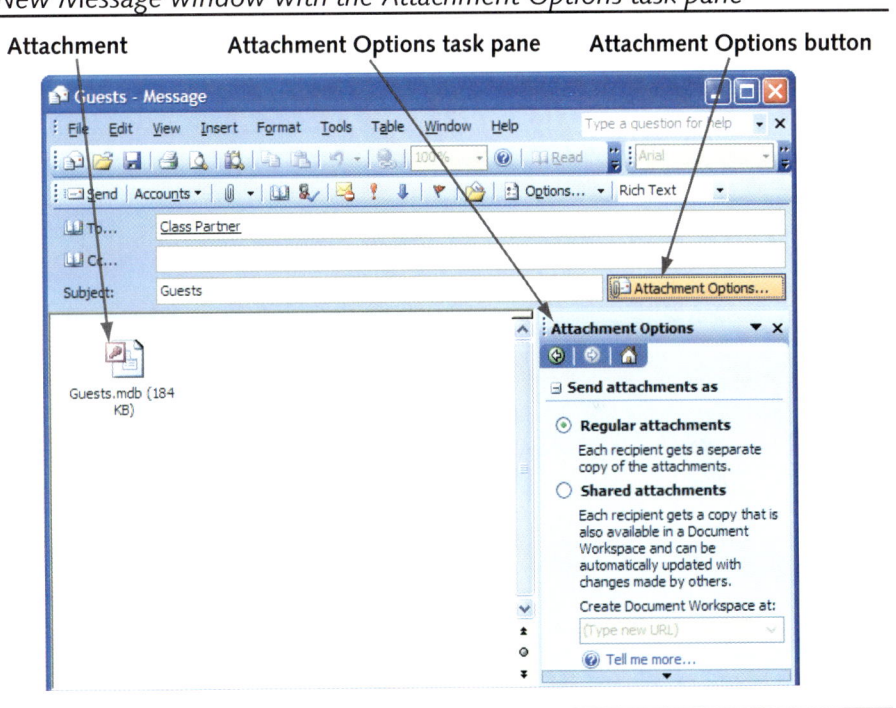

5 **In the Attachment Options task pane, click the Shared Attachments option. Type the URL of the SharePoint site, and click the Send button.**

The message is sent. The Document Workspace site is created and access is granted to the message recipients identified in the To field.

◆ If you are continuing to the next lesson, keep Outlook open.

◆ If you are not continuing to the next lesson, close Outlook.

Lesson 11 Managing Information

QUICK CHECK

Q: What does a shared attachment create?

A: **It creates a Document Workspace site.**

QUICK REFERENCE ▼
Send a shared attachment

1. Create a new message.
2. Address the message and add the subject.
3. Insert a file.
4. Click the Attachment Options button.
5. In the Attachment Options task pane, click the Shared Attachments option. Type the URL of the SharePoint site, and click the Send button.

Key Points

- ✔ *You can use Cached Exchange Mode to update Outlook after working offline.*
- ✔ *Mail options can be modified to provide alerts when you receive a message.*
- ✔ *You can create customized Outlook forms based on standard forms.*
- ✔ *To find messages that meet specific requirements, you can create a Search Folder.*
- ✔ *You can choose to grant permission for other users to view and use items in your folders.*
- ✔ *Outlook can be used to create a Document Workspace site.*

True/False

T F 1. Forms are created in Design view.

T F 2. Dial-up is the fastest connection Outlook can make to your server.

T F 3. If you are connected to your Exchange server, the Cached Exchange Mode ensures that all of your mailbox folders are up to date.

T F 4. The option that takes the most time to update your local mailbox is the Download Headers And Then Full Items option.

T F 5. A label is a field or window that provides a way for users to enter data into the form.

Multiple Choice

1. When you design a form, you can add _____ that create text boxes (for entering fields) and field labels, lists, check boxes, option buttons, and more.
   a. labels
   b. controls
   c. contacts
   d. All of the above

2. When you are finished customizing a form, _____ it.
   a. publish
   b. save
   c. label
   d. design

3. A _____ folder doesn't hold anything.
   a. saved
   b. control
   c. virtual
   d. public

4. A _____ folder can contain messages or information that can be shared with designated users.
   a. search
   b. control
   c. public
   d. published

5. _____ are sent to you as e-mail messages that notify you that selected content on a SharePoint site has changed.
   a. Alerts
   b. Notices
   c. Change notes
   d. Links

Short Answer

1. What are your connection options when you use Cached Exchange Mode?
2. How do you add a ready-made field to a custom form?
3. What is the difference between the Find and advanced Find functions?
4. What is the advantage of using a Search Folder rather than the find function?
5. How can you set additional mail options?
6. Identify three Outlook forms that you have used.
7. What are the available roles?

On Your Own

Exercise 1

Make your Contacts folder a public folder. Grant your class partner access to your Contacts folder and set the permission level to Editor. Create a folder called AW Appointments, and put it in your Calendar folder (not the server's Calendar folder). Put the appointment Attend the Public Relations Award Banquet in the AW Appointments folder. Publish the AW Appointments folder and give your class partner Reviewer permission level to the folder.

Exercise 2

Restart Outlook, and set it to work offline. Create a note reminding you of a dentist appointment next week. Connect to the server.

One Step Further

Exercise 1

Restart Outlook, and set it to work offline. Send two e-mail messages to your class partner. Set Outlook to work online and retrieve your new messages.

Exercise 2

Design an Outlook form that enables you to store survey information with the usual contact data. Write three questions and provide appropriate places to enter the answers in the form. Save the form.

Exercise 3

Outlook also enables you to set delegate access to your folders. Use Outlook's Help to determine why you would set delegate access.

LESSON 12
Managing Contacts and Tasks

After completing this lesson, you will be able to:
- ✓ *View and send task information for other users.*
- ✓ *Send and receive instant messages.*

KEY TERM
- instant messaging

Good communication is a vital part of all business activities. When you work with others, it is important to update the status of assigned tasks. This can be performed through Outlook task features and exchanging e-mail messages. However, it may be necessary to communicate quickly or convey information that is located on your computer. Instant messaging is ideal for small pieces of critical information.

In this lesson, you will learn how to use Outlook status reports and send and receive instant messages.

IMPORTANT
To complete some of the exercises in this lesson, you will need to exchange e-mail messages with a class partner. If you don't have a class partner or you are performing the exercises alone, you can send the message to yourself. Simply enter your own e-mail address instead of a class partner's address.

Viewing and Sending Task Information for Other Users

THE BOTTOM LINE
Outlook lets you assign a task to a contact and track its progress through status reports.

Accepting, Declining and Delegating Tasks

When you assign a task to someone else, you usually want to stay informed about the worker's progress as the task is completed. Remember that only the owner of a task can update the information about the task. Therefore, after you assign a task to someone else, you cannot update the task information. However, you can receive updates as the task is completed. Outlook enables any task owner to send a status report to the task requester who assigned the task. This simplifies the reporting process and enables you to keep a fingertip in the task without looking over the worker's shoulder.

A task can only appear in your task list once. If you want two people to perform the same task, the name of the task must be different for each person. For example, if you want Holly and Jay to call clients about a presentation, you create two tasks. One task is "Call clients A-M." The second task is "Call Clients N-Z." Assign the first task to Holly and assign the second task to Jay. This also prevents you from accepting a task assignment with the same name as a task that already appears on your list.

◆ Be sure to start Outlook before begging this exercise.

View and send task information

To demonstrate the ways in which you work with task information, in this exercise, you assign a task, accept a task, send a status report, receive a status report, and then view a list of tasks assigned to others.

1 Go to the Tasks folder. On the Standard toolbar, click the New Task button.

The task window is displayed. The insertion point is already in the Subject box.

> **IMPORTANT**
>
> The task you receive must not be the same as the task you send or you won't be able to accept the task. Coordinate task names with your class partner before creating one of the suggested tasks or create a unique task name.

2 Type **Work with Jay to create a slide presentation for the annual meeting.**

or

Type **Work with Holly to create a slide presentation for the annual meeting.**

Lesson 12 Managing Contacts and Tasks 349

Figure 12-1

New task

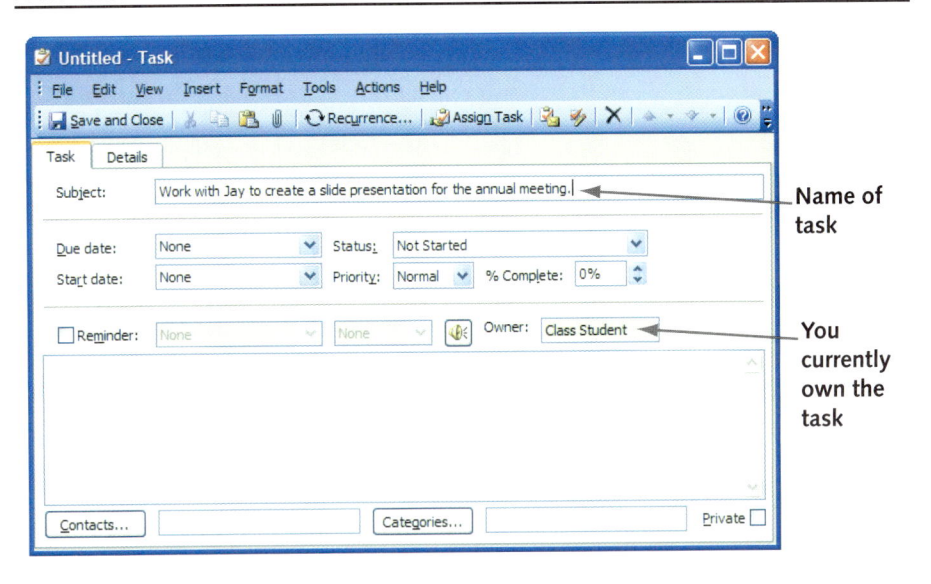

[Screenshot of Untitled - Task window with Subject "Work with Jay to create a slide presentation for the annual meeting." — labeled "Name of task" and Owner "Class Student" labeled "You currently own the task"]

3 On the Standard toolbar in the task window, click the **Assign Task** button.

A Task Request window, which is similar to the task window, appears. A note at the top of the window indicates that the task request has not been sent yet.

Figure 12-2

Task Request window

[Screenshot of Task Request window with "This message has not been sent." note]

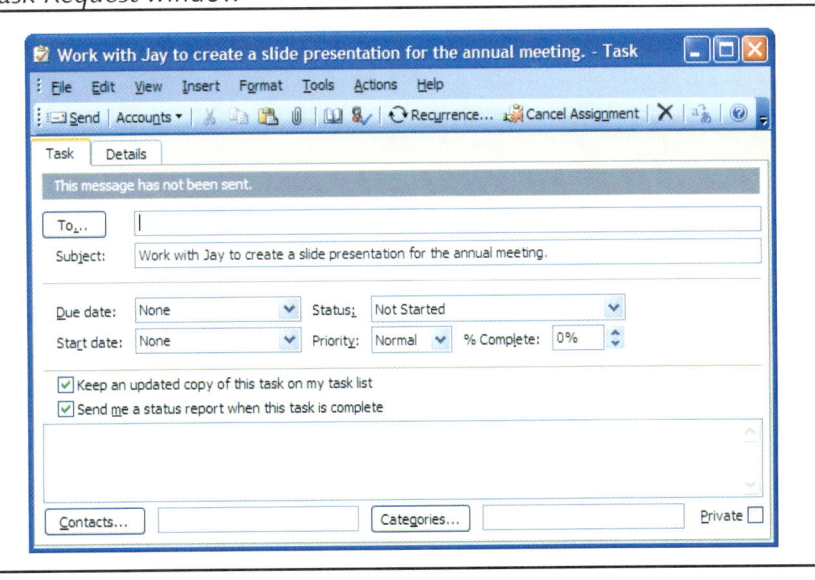

TROUBLESHOOTING

The addressee cannot be the same as the sender. If you don't have a class partner, use a second address entry for yourself that has a different e-mail address.

4 **Click the To button.**

The Select Task Recipient dialog box is displayed.

5 **In the Select Task Recipient dialog box, click your class partner's name, and click the To button. Click OK.**

The Select Task Recipient dialog box closes. Your class partner's name is displayed in the To box.

> **TROUBLESHOOTING**
>
> An alert box might be displayed. It states that the task reminder has been shut off because you are no longer the owner of the task. Click OK.

6 **On the Standard toolbar in the task window, click the Send button.**

The task is sent to your class partner.

7 **Go to the Inbox. Click the Send/Receive button.**

A task sent by your class partner arrives in your mailbox.

Figure 12-3

Task Request received

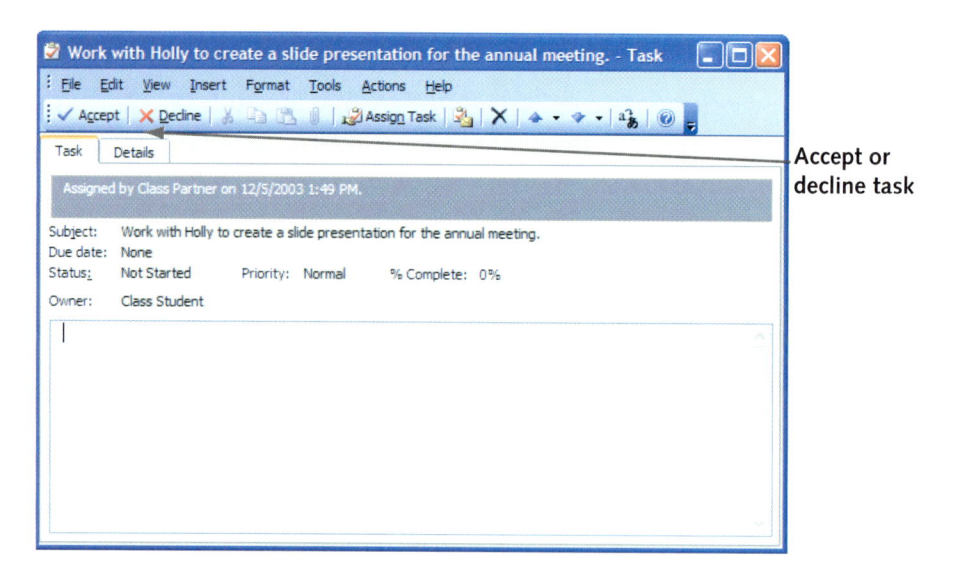

8 **Select the message and click the Accept button.**

The task is added to your task list. An alert box is displayed.

Figure 12-4

Alert displayed when task is accepted

Lesson 12 Managing Contacts and Tasks 351

9 **If necessary, click the Send The Response Now option and click OK.**

This alert box gives you the opportunity to send a comment when you accept the task.

10 **Go to your task list. Double-click the task.**

The task is displayed in its own window.

11 **Change the value in the % Complete field to 50%. Click the Send Status Report button.**

The default report, containing the status and percent complete, is displayed.

Figure 12-5

Status report

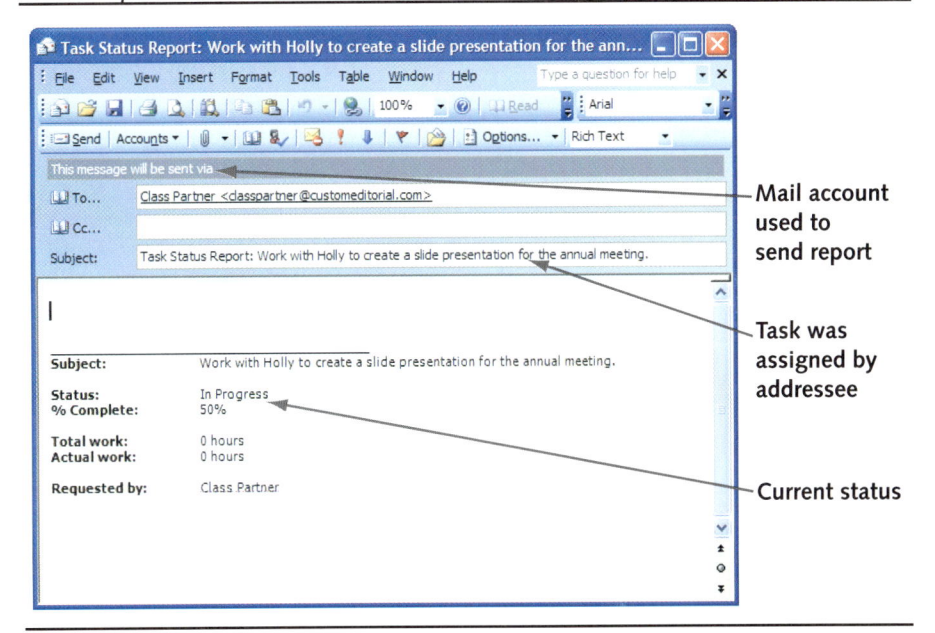

[Screenshot of Task Status Report window with annotations:
- Mail account used to send report
- Task was assigned by addressee
- Current status]

12 **Click the Send button.**

The status report is sent to the task requestor.

13 **Click the Mail button in the Navigation pane. Click the Send/Receive button.**

You receive the status report sent by your class partner.

14 **Click the Tasks button in the Navigation pane. Open the View menu, point at Arrange By, point at Current View, and select the option By Person Responsible.**

Tasks are grouped by the individual assigned to complete the task.

ANOTHER METHOD

If you don't want to use the automated status report feature, you can create a template and use it to create a status report that can be sent to any contact, not just the task requestor.

◆ **Keep Outlook open for the next exercise.**

352 **Lesson 12** Managing Contacts and Tasks

QUICK CHECK

Q: How do you choose to send a status report?

A: Click the Send Status Report button.

QUICK REFERENCE ▼

Send a status report

1. Update the status of the task.
2. Click the Send Status Report button.
3. Click the Send button.

Sending and Receiving Instant Messages

THE BOTTOM LINE

Instant messaging provides quick, easy communication with any contact who has the feature enabled.

The business environment has changed in the last decade. A few years ago, employees who worked closely with others had to be located near the other people on the same project. If you were reassigned to a different project or a different department, you emptied the contents of your desk into a box and moved to a different cubicle. Today's businesses are less traditional. Many employees work at home, connected to the office through computer networks, the Internet, and the telephone. Alternative communication methods have developed.

E-mail plays an important role in business communication, but sometimes it just isn't fast enough. Instant messages meet the need for instant communication without the expense of long-distance phone calls or the delay of e-mail. **Instant messaging** is a private, online chat that occurs through your network or the Internet. When you establish an electronic connection to another person, you can type directly into a message window. When you press the Enter key, the words are displayed in the message window of the user you selected. The user can respond quickly by typing into the message window on his or her computer. Instant messaging is just as effective if your messages go to the next room, across town, or across the ocean.

IMPORTANT

Outlook automatically supports instant messaging through Microsoft Windows Messenger, Microsoft MSN Messenger Service, or Microsoft Exchange Instant Messaging Service.

Some setup is required for instant messaging. You must exchange e-mail addresses associated with the instant messaging service. (This e-mail address doesn't have to be the same as the address used to send and receive e-mail.) You will need to add the e-mail addresses gathered from friends and co-workers to the information stored for your contacts. They will also have to add your instant messaging e-mail address to their accounts.

Lesson 12 Managing Contacts and Tasks 353

To enable instant messaging:

> **IMPORTANT**
>
> By default, instant messaging is enabled. This procedure is only necessary if instant messaging has been disabled.

1. Open the Tools menu, select Options, and click the tab labeled Other.

2. In the Person Names area, select the option Enable The Person Names Smart Tag and Display Messenger Status In The From Field. Click the Apply button.

3. Click the OK button to close the Options dialog box.

Figure 12-6

Enable instant messaging

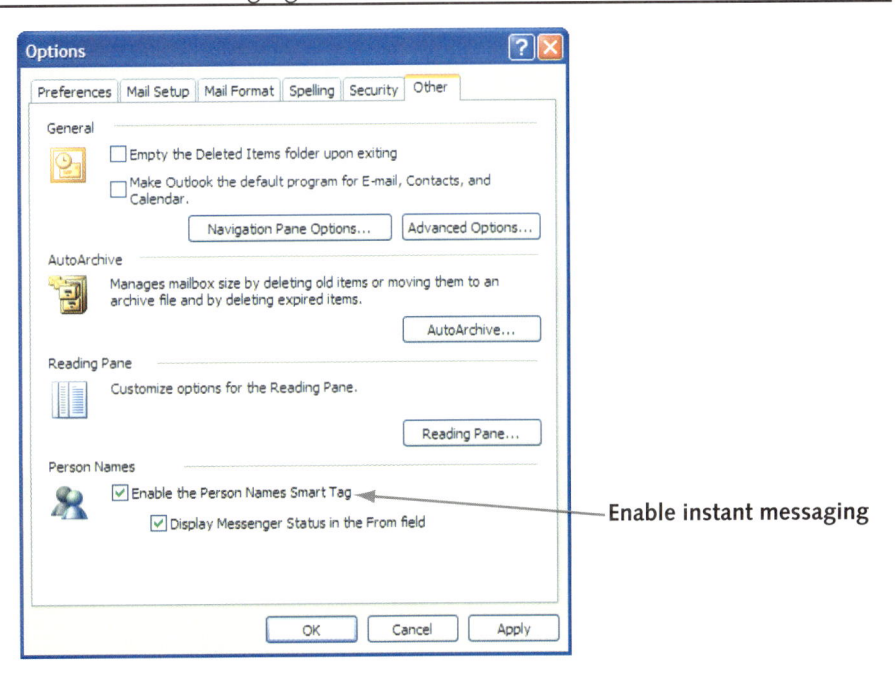

CHECK THIS OUT ▼

Status: Busy
If you are online but you don't want to receive instant messages, change your status to busy.

After instant messaging is installed, you can be logged in automatically to the instant messaging service when you start Outlook. If they look, your friends or coworkers who are online and logged into the message service will know that you are also logged into the service and available for instant messages.

Send and receive an instant message

You will now send and receive an instant message.

1 **Click Contacts in the Navigation pane. Double-click the contact record for your class partner.**

The contact information for your class partner is displayed.

2 **Click in the IM Address box and type the e-mail address your class partner uses for instant messaging.**

This address may not be the same as the address used for e-mail correspondence.

3 **Click the Save And Close button.**

The instant messaging information for your class partner is saved.

4 **Double-click the contact record again.**

If your class partner is online, a yellow bar is displayed below the tabs.

5 **Click the yellow bar.**

The Instant Message window is displayed.

6 **Type a brief message and click the Send button.**

When your class partner responds, the reply is displayed in the Instant Message window.

◆ Close the instant message application.
◆ If you are continuing to the next lesson, keep Outlook open.
◆ If you are not continuing to the next lesson, close Outlook.

QUICK CHECK

Q: Which instant messaging service does Outlook automatically support?

A: Outlook automatically supports instant messaging through Microsoft Windows Messenger, Microsoft MSN Messenger Service, or Microsoft Exchange Instant Messaging Service.

QUICK REFERENCE ▼

Send an instant message

1 Double-click the contact record.
2 Click the yellow bar indicating the contact is online.
3 Type a brief message and click the Send button.

Key Points

✓ You can track the progress of a task through Outlook status reports.
✓ Outlook enables you to communicate quickly by sending and receiving instant messages.

Quick Quiz

True/False

T F 1. The name of every task must be unique.
T F 2. You can update the status of a task you assigned to someone else.
T F 3. You can receive a status report for a task you assigned to someone else.
T F 4. You can send an instant message through your network.
T F 5. The e-mail address you use for instant messaging should be the same as the address you use to send and receive e-mail.

Multiple Choice

1. To send an instant message, you need a(n) _____.
   a. e-mail address for the recipient
   b. Internet connection
   c. telephone
   d. All of the above

2. Instant messages are displayed _____.
   a. in the Outlook contact window
   b. in the messenger window
   c. on the desktop
   d. in the Outlook e-mail window

3. Status reports are sent to _____.
   a. the task owner
   b. all users
   c. the person who assigned the task
   d. All of the above

4. The _____ updates the status of a task.
   a. task owner
   b. manager
   c. task supervisor
   d. All of the above

5. Outlook sends status reports via _____.
   a. instant messages
   b. e-mail
   c. fax machines
   d. All of the above

Short Answer

1. Who receives a status report?
2. How do you send a status report?
3. Why should a task name be unique?
4. When you assign a task, why can't you have the same e-mail address as the addressee?
5. How do you enable instant messaging?
6. Identify the information needed to exchange instant messages.
7. How do you know that a contact is online?

On Your Own

Exercise 1

View your current task list. Add two new tasks. Assign them to other students. Filter your task list to determine who is responsible for the tasks on the list.

Exercise 2

View your current task list. Request a status report from the contacts responsible for any tasks on your list.

One Step Further

Exercise 1

Add a new contact record. Exchange instant messages with the contact.

Exercise 2

Write five rules employees should follow if they use instant messaging.

Exercise 3

Investigate the options that affect instant messaging in Outlook.

APPENDIX A

Setting Up Outlook

When you install Microsoft Office Outlook 2003 on a computer and run it for the first time, the Outlook 2003 Startup Wizard prompts you for information about yourself and asks whether you want to set up an e-mail account. If you supply all the required information, you might not have to change your user or e-mail information in the future. However, you can add to this information or change settings later if you enter any of the information in your user or e-mail profile incorrectly or you don't know what information to provide. This appendix explains how to use the Outlook 2003 Startup Wizard, how to create a user profile, and how to specify which profile Outlook should use when it starts.

Using the Outlook 2003 Startup Wizard

The Outlook 2003 Startup Wizard can detect and import e-mail account information and address book information from many e-mail programs, enabling you to keep your e-mail accounts and contact records in one program.

If you are upgrading from an earlier version of Outlook, you will not have to specify your e-mail address, e-mail server, or other information about yourself. The Outlook Startup Wizard will use the previously installed version's settings to configure the settings for Outlook 2003.

If Outlook has been installed on your computer but has never been started, the Outlook 2003 Startup Wizard appears automatically when you start Outlook the first time. This wizard guides you through the installation step by step.

As you install and set up Outlook 2003, you need to provide several pieces of information. You may need to contact your Internet Service Provider or your network administrator to find out some of the information.

Data	Description
Type of account	Microsoft Exchange Server is often used by businesses with an internal network. POP3, IMAP, and HTTP provide Internet e-mail access.
Incoming server	This server is used for mail messages coming to your computer. Depending on your situation, the incoming server may be the same as the outgoing server.
Outgoing server	This server is used to send e-mail from your computer. Depending on your situation, the incoming server may be the same as the outgoing server.

(continued)

User name	This name identifies you to the server. It may be assigned by the network administrator or the Internet Service Provider.
E-mail address	This text identifies the address that you use to receive e-mail from others. The usual format is yourname@mailprovider.com.
Password	This prevents others from receiving your e-mail. It may be set by the Internet Service Provider or your network administrator.

(continued)

After collecting this information, you can install Outlook 2003 or upgrade your current version to Outlook 2003. Follow all the prompts on the screen. Don't forget to register your copy of Microsoft Office 2003.

Creating a User Profile

Microsoft Office Outlook 2003 enables you to establish e-mail accounts for different people who use the same computer. When you run Outlook for the first time and respond to the prompts by entering information about yourself, Outlook creates a user profile—a collection of Outlook settings that describes the e-mail accounts and settings for a particular person.

If you use Outlook at work, you might use more than one method of sending and receiving e-mail. For example, Adventure Works has both an interoffice network and access to the Internet. On each computer, the network administrator sets up Internet mail (for e-mail) and access to the company's internal e-mail.

The user profile that you set up in Outlook is not the same as the user profile that you set up in Microsoft Windows. A user profile in Windows identifies personalized startup and desktop settings that take effect when you log onto Windows using the name and password for the user profile. By contrast, a user profile in Outlook enables you to send, receive, and store e-mail messages.

If you share a computer with others, you need to set up a user profile for yourself. This enables you to send and receive your own e-mail messages and prevents others who use the computer from viewing your messages. Creating a separate user profile also prevents you from receiving another user's messages.

Create an Outlook profile

1 On the Windows taskbar, click the Start button, and point to All Programs. Point to Microsoft Office and Microsoft Office Outlook 2003.

Outlook is launched and displays the Outlook 2003 Startup Wizard.

2 Click Next.

The Account Configuration dialog box is displayed. Verify that Yes is selected.

3 Click Next.

The Server Type dialog box is displayed.

4 Select the type of server you will connect to for e-mail services and click Next.

The next wizard dialog box is displayed. The dialog box is based on the type of e-mail account you selected.

> **IMPORTANT**
>
> If you need to set up the Microsoft Exchange Server or Microsoft Mail services but you don't know the names of the items you are supposed to specify, check with your network administrator. If you need to set up an Internet e-mail account and need help, either your network administrator or your Internet service provider (ISP) should be able to help.

5 Continue through the wizard. In the last wizard dialog box, click Finish.

The Outlook application window is displayed.

Selecting a User Profile When Outlook Starts

If more than one user profile is set up on a computer, you must select which profile to use when Outlook starts. You can set up the profiles so that you use a specific profile each time Outlook starts, or you can have Outlook prompt you to select a user profile each time.

Select a user profile

1 On the Windows taskbar, click the Start button and click Control Panel.

The Control Panel is displayed.

2 Double-click the Mail icon and click the Show Profiles button in the Mail Setup dialog box.

The Mail dialog box is displayed.

3 Select the Prompt For A Profile To Be Used option or the Always Use This Profile option.

If you select the Always Use This Profile option, the drop-down box listing the available profiles is activated.

4 If you selected the Always Use This Profile option, select a profile from the drop-down box and click OK.
or
If you selected the Prompt For A Profile To Be Used option, click OK.

The new settings will take effect the next time you start Outlook.

Glossary

actions   Part of a rule that determines what Outlook does with a message, such as delete it, forward it, or move it to a folder upon receipt.

Address Book   A repository for storing names, e-mail addresses, and phone and fax numbers. Use the Address Book to quickly insert e-mail addresses in the To and Cc boxes when you compose a message.

Address Cards   The default view of Contacts in which the contact's basic information is displayed.

alert   An automatic notice sent to you as an e-mail message to notify you that selected content on a SharePoint site has changed.

Appointment Area   The place within the Calendar where you enter and schedule activities. It can be displayed by day, work week, week, or month.

appointment   Scheduled activity that does not involve using Outlook to invite others or reserve office resources.

archive   A process in which older Inbox and Sent Items messages and attachments are combined into a single file, compressed, and stored in a folder on your hard disk.

arrangement   Ways to group and view related items in an Outlook folder. Each arrangement focuses on a different characteristic of the items. For example, you can base your arrangement on the date the message was received or the individual who sent the message.

attachment   An external document included as part of a message.

AutoPreview   An Inbox view that displays each message header and the first three lines of each message.

Cached Exchange Mode   A feature that simplifies the switch between working online and working offline. It creates a copy of your mailbox on your computer. If you are connected to your Exchange server, the Cached Exchange Mode ensures that all of your mailbox folders are up to date.

Calendar   A component of Outlook that you can use to create and schedule appointments, meetings, and events.

category   A keyword or phrase associated with an Outlook item that helps to organize and group the items according to common usage (such as Business or Personal).

chat   In NetMeeting, a window that you can use to type messages to other participants and to view messages that you've received. In a chat window, messages are sent and received instantly.

conditions   Part of a rule that determines the requirements that must be met for a message before an action can occur.

contact A record of a person's or company's addresses, phone and pager numbers, and e-mail addresses. The record can include personal information, such as birthdays and anniversaries, as well as company information.

contact record All the fields entered for a contact, such as name, company, and phone number.

Contacts folder An address book and information record where you store, sort, and arrange contacts. The Contacts folder is often referred to as Contacts.

control A field or window component that typically provides a way for users to enter data in a form. Lists, check boxes, option buttons, and text boxes are common types of controls.

Date Navigator A wall-type calendar that is displayed in the Outlook Calendar. The Date Navigator can be used to switch to different days, months, and years in the Appointment Area.

Deleted Items folder The folder where deleted messages (and other deleted Outlook items) are stored until the folder is emptied.

delivery receipt A notice in the form of an e-mail message, verifying the date and time the recipient received the message.

Design view A view of a form that allows you to modify the appearance of the form.

desktop alert Displayed briefly when an e-mail message, meeting request, or task request arrives, this small box contains information about the Outlook item that arrived.

distribution list A single address book entry that contains several individual addresses.

Drafts The folder that stores incomplete messages so that you can complete and send them at a later time.

e-mail Any communication that is sent or received via computers, either over the Internet or through a messaging program used with an organization's internal network.

event Activities that usually make you unavailable at the office for at least a day, such as a vacation, convention, or off-site meeting. Events are displayed as a banner in the Appointment Area.

exceptions Part of a rule that determines the provisions for a message that, if met, will exclude a message from an action.

export Move information from the current program to another.

field A single item of data, such as a person's name, e-mail address, or phone number.

file Any document stored on a disk, such as Word documents, Excel spreadsheets, Microsoft Access databases, and pictures.

filter The process of specifying criteria and using Outlook to display only those items that match your criteria.

flag A small icon placed next to a message to remind yourself to follow up on an issue. You can flag an outgoing message with a request for someone else to follow up with a reply.

Folder List A list of folders and subfolders. Click an item on the list to display the contents of the selected folder.

folder Container that can hold files and additional folders. In Outlook, folders are used to divide Outlook into different functions. For example, you can receive messages in the Inbox folder and create contact records in the Contacts folder.

form A collection of fields and field labels for a particular record, formatted and organized to support a particular use.

formatted text Text that appears in different sizes, colors, styles, and alignments.

forward Send a message that you received to one or more other users who might be interested in the message content.

group A set of items with something in common, such as e-mail messages from the same sender or tasks with the same due date.

HTML An acronym for Hypertext Markup Language, which is the formatting language used by Web browsers to format and display Web pages.

iCalendar (Internet Calendaring) A component of Outlook and an Internet standard format that lets you send meeting requests over the Internet to people outside your company's network.

icon A graphic representation of an attached file or document.

import Bring information from one program into the program you're using.

Inbox The folder that contains received e-mail messages that have not been deleted or moved.

instant messaging A private, online chat that occurs through your network or the Internet.

interoffice mail Messages sent and received via computers that are connected within a local area network (LAN).

item Information displayed in Outlook. For example, in the Inbox, each message is an item; in Contacts, the contact record (phone and address information about an individual) is an item.

Journal A folder in Outlook in a timeline format that records when you create, use, and modify Microsoft Office documents and Outlook items.

junk e-mail Unsolicited and unwanted e-mail that is used for advertising purposes. It is also known as spam.

mail queue A list of messages received by a mail server, organized in the order in which the messages are received.

map Match an application's field names with field names that hold similar information in Outlook.

Master Category List A list of available categories you can use to group or find items. Outlook provides ready-made categories, but you can add your own custom categories.

meeting Type of appointment in which you use Outlook to request the attendance of other people or schedule resources. Recipients of an e-mail meeting request can accept, decline, agree tentatively, and propose a different time.

message header The top of an e-mail message that includes the name of the sender, the subject of the message, and the date and time when the message was sent.

Microsoft Exchange Server A messaging system that enables members of an organization to exchange and share information with users on a local area network and the Internet.

Navigation pane Provides access to the contents of folders that are available in Outlook, such as the Inbox and Calendar.

NetMeeting An add-on program, supplied with Internet Explorer, that you can use to conduct meetings over the Internet or over an intranet by using text messages, sound, video, or all of these elements.

news server A computer that is configured to accept messages from newsgroups.

newsgroup A collection of related messages that are constantly being sent and responded to by people within the group.

newsreader A program used to access newsgroups and view their content.

note Brief text item that can be saved, edited, and moved independently of the Outlook window.

Office Assistant An animated character that provides access to help topics for Microsoft Office applications.

Outbox The folder that contains messages waiting to be sent from your computer to the server.

Outlook Today An Outlook folder that summarizes the current items in specific Outlook folders.

owner The only person who can edit a task. You are automatically the owner of any task you create until you assign it to another person.

ownership The ability to edit a task. Ownership indicates that the owner is responsible for completing the task. Ownership can be assigned to others.

permission A set of instructions set up to control who can view and modify the contents of your folders.

Personal Folders file A file that contains all your Outlook items. It is stored on your computer.

Plain Text Generic text that can be read by any e-mail program. Use Plain Text when you do not want to include any formatting in your messages.

posts Messages that appear in a newsgroup, which you can read or send.

private Outlook items that can't be seen by other users.

private store A file that contains all your Outlook items. It is stored on a server.

profile Set of data required to enable Outlook to access your e-mail accounts and address book. It includes the name of your e-mail account, the servers used to send and receive e-mail, and your passwords.

public folder A folder that contains messages or information that can be shared with designated users.

publish The ability to name and save a custom form to a folder that Outlook can locate when you want to use the form to create a record.

read receipt A notice in the form of an e-mail message, verifying the date and time the recipient read the message.

Reading Pane A section of the Inbox window that displays the text of the selected message.

recall Send a message regarding a previous message requesting that the recipient disregard it. The original message may be automatically deleted.

recurring appointment An appointment or meeting, scheduled in the Calendar, that occurs multiple times or at regular intervals.

reply Send a response to the sender of the message. It might include a copy of an original message

Rich Text A standard method of formatting text with tags that can be understood by most word processors and newer e-mail programs.

roles Levels of involvement a user is assigned when working with public folders.

rule A set of conditions, actions, and exceptions that define and control the process for managing incoming e-mail messages.

search folder A virtual folder that shows you the messages that fit the search criteria.

Sent Items folder The folder that contains messages already sent.

shared attachment A document that creates a Document Workspace, a SharePoint Services site centered on the document where recipients can open and edit the attached document.

shortcut Icon that appears on the Navigation Pane. When you click a shortcut, Outlook displays the contents of the corresponding folder or file.

signature Information, such as your title, phone number, or address that is automatically added to the end of each e-mail message that you compose and send.

sort Arrange messages in ascending or descending order by the criteria you specify, such as by sender, subject, or flag status.

stationery Ready-made designs, including images, backgrounds, and borders, that can be applied to an e-mail message.

subscribe Add a newsgroup to the Folder List.

task list The area in the Tasks folder that displays tasks.

task A personal or work item to be completed. You can assign a task to other users.

TaskPad An area in the Calendar in which you record tasks that you need to perform. This area is integrated with the Tasks folder.

Tasks folder An Outlook folder used to create, edit, and organize tasks.

template In Outlook, an e-mail message that can be used as a pattern to format similar e-mail messages.

thread In newsgroups, a post and every response to that post.

vCard A virtual business card containing contact information that can be sent to others via e-mail so the recipients can view the contact information or add it to their Contacts folder or Address Book.

virtual folder A folder that doesn't actually hold anything except a reference to items stored in another folder.

Web beacon A program embedded in a message that informs the sender that you have read or previewed the message.

Whiteboard A blank screen used in NetMeeting that simulates marker boards used in classrooms or conference rooms. Use the mouse pointer to draw on the Whiteboard.

Work Week A view for the Calendar that displays the days you work each week.

Index

A

Accept meeting, 168
Accept task, 201–203
Access database, 249–256, 259
Actions, 283
Active appointment, 162, 164
Active Projects folder, 239–242
Active task, created from note, 220
Active Task view, 189–190, 204
Add Holidays, 297, 299–300
Add Holidays To Calendar dialog box, 299–300
Add New Shortcut button, 240
Address. See Web address
Address Book
  create distribution list in, 267–271
  defined, 124
  insert or add addresses to message from, 127
  list of contacts in, 268
  use, to send e-mail, 124–127
Address Cards, 94, 110–111
Addressee, 21
Add To Navigation pane dialog box, 240–241
Advanced E-mail Options dialog box, 327–328
Advanced Find dialog box, 333
Alert
  defined, 339
  display, from SharePoint site, 339–342
  displayed with accepted task, 350
  rules for, 339
Alert box
  for assigning tasks, 200
  for duplicate record, 133
  for meeting cancellation notification, 168
Align Left, 24
Align Right, 24
Alphabetical order, tasks sorted in, 190–191
Always Show Full Menus check box, 6
Annual events, 162

Appearance, customize, of e-mail message, 56–62
Appointment Area
  additional information displayed in, 157
  appointment scheduled in, 147
  create recurring appointment in, 151–153
  defined, 141
  delete appointments in, 158
  events displayed in, 148–151
  use, to schedule appointments and meetings, 176
Appointment Recurrence dialog box, 151, 308–309
Appointment(s), 176
  active, 162
  add details to, 147–148
  change time or duration of, 157
  defined, 140, 146
  delete, 158–159
  difference between, and meeting, 146
  edit, 156–158
  increase duration of, 147
  organize, by using categories, 159–161
  reminder for, 154–155
  schedule, 146–151
  scheduled in Appointment Area, 147
  set level of importance for, 156
  set private, 304–305
  See also Event; Recurring appointment
Arrangement(s), 34, 69
  active appointment, 162
  annual events, 162
  attachment, 33
  available for Calendar view, 144
  categories, 33
  by category, 162–163
  conversation, 32
  date, 32
  e-mail account, 33
  event, 162
  filtering, 72–76
  flag, 32

Index

folder, 32
from, 32
importance, 33
organize, by using arrangements, 161–164
organize appointments by using, 161–164
recurring appointments, 162
size, 32
subject, 32
to, 32
type, 32
Ascending order
   sort contacts in, 121–122
   sort messages in, 69, 71
Assign task, 198–201, 203
Attachment arrangement, 33
Attachment Format, 52
Attachment Options task pane, 343–344
Attachment(s), 35–37
   defined, 27
   messages sorted by, 70–71
   open, from Reading Pane, 36
   send iCalendar as e-mail, 315–317
   shared, 342
   size of, 29
Attach Original Message, 57
Attach the Business Car (vCard) To This Signature box, 131
Attendance, modify meeting, requirements, 310
Author, 337
AutoArchive setting, 88–89
AutoComplete, 21
Automatic Formatting dialog box, 84
Automatic Picture Download Settings dialog box, 272
AutoPreview, 32

B

Background color, 297, 299
Bell icon, 148
Blocked senders list, 86
Bold, 24
Broadband, 324
Browse dialog box, 257
Bullets, 24
Business Address field, 254
Busy status, online, 353
By Color, 224–225

C

Cached Exchange Mode, 325–327
Calendar, 139–180
Add Holidays, 297, 299–300
   advanced features of, 295–322
   background color, 299
   background color of, 297
   change time zone setting, 301–303
   customize options for, 293–301
   day view, 142
   default display, 301
   defined, 140
   four sections of, 141–142
   Free/Busy options, 297
   integrate, with other Outlook components, 176–178
   navigate within, 141–143
   print, 172–173
   resource scheduling, 297
   save, as Web page, 174–176
   start time, 297
   See also Date Navigator; iCalendar; Multiple calendars; Side-by-side calendars
Calendar display area, 293
Calendar File Name dialog box, 174
Calendar folder, 12
   defined, 7–9
   Organize pane in, 160
   Task completed in, 177–178
Calendar Options button, 144
Calendar Options dialog box, 296–300, 303
Calendar view, change, 144–146
Calendar window, components of, 148
Carbon copy, 21
Categories, 52
   organize appoints by using, 159–161
   organize tasks by using, 195–197
Categories arrangement, 33
Categories dialog box, 118
Category, 162–163
   assign items to new, 114–117
   change existing, 117–119
   defined, 114
   use, to organize contacts, 114–117
   view contacts by, 110, 112
   See also Master Category List
Cc button, 21–22
Center, 24
Change Automatic Download Settings, 86, 272
Change Your View list, 223–225
Chat, 311
Choose Form dialog box, 265–266, 332
Color-coding message headers, 83–85
Company, view contacts by, 110, 112
Completed task status, 190
Conditions, 273, 275–276
Confidential message option, 54–55
Confirm Delete dialog box, 159
Confirm File Replace dialog box, 219
Connection. See Remote connection
Contact(s), 52, 93–138
   create and edit new, 98–102
   create letter for, 134–136
   delete and restore, 105–107
   details of, 96
   number of Web addresses for each, 102
   sort, 121–124
   use, to send e-mail, 127–129
   use categories to organize, 114–117
   use folders to organize, 107–109
   use Views to organize, 109–113
   view, 94–97
Contact information, send and receive, via e-mail, 129–134
Contact record, 98–102, 116
Contacts folder
   as component of Navigation pane, 7–8, 10, 12–13
   defined, 93
   export contacts of, to Excel file, 256, 259
   return deleted contact to, 106–107

Contact window, 329
Contributor, 337
Control, defined, 330
Control Toolbox, 330
Conversation arrangement, 32
Create A New Category Called box, 160
Create Microsoft Personal Files dialog box, 248
Create New Folder dialog box, 193
    create folder in, 77
    grant permission to folder in, 337
    for organizing e-mail messages, 277
    use, to organize notes by folder, 226–227
    view multiple calendars, 318
Create Or Open Outlook Data File dialog box, 248
Create Rule button, 80–81
Create Rule dialog box, 80–81
Create Signature dialog box, 67–68, 130
Customize Current View option, 109
Customize dialog box, 284–286
Customize e-mail, 49–92
Customize Outlook Today option, 243–246
Customize View dialog box, 122–123
Customize Views: Messages dialog box, 70–75

D

Data record, 332
Date. See Selected date
Date arrangement, 32
Date Navigator, 297
    create meeting, 165
    create recurring appointment in, 151, 153
    defined, 141–143
    delete and restore appointments in, 158–160
    schedule appointment in, 148–150, 176
    set meeting reminder in, 154
Date/Time Properties dialog box, 301

Day-Timer calendar, 173
Day view, 142, 144
Decline meeting, 168
Decline task, 201–203
Decrease Indent, 24
Default
    change calendar, settings, 296
    messages filtered by, 74
    Microsoft Word as, e-mail editor, 24
    note yellow by, 224
    Outlook mail folders, 243
Default editor, Microsoft Word as e-mail, 262–265
Default message, 32
Default Search Folders, 334
Deferred task status, 190
Delete contact, 105–107
Deleted items, 76
Deleted Items folder, 209–210
    for deleted appoints, 158–159
    drag notes into, 228
    empty, 88
    as safeguard for deleted messages, 45–46
    set to empty permanently or delete contacts, 105–106
Deleted Items Folder Upon Existing check box, 105
Delete group, 240
Delete message, 45–46
Delete note, 228–229
Delete task, 209–210
Delivery receipt, 281–284
Descending order
    sort contacts in, 121
    sort messages in, 69, 71
Design Form dialog box, 330–331
Design view, 329
Desktop alert, 281–282
Detailed Address Cards, 110–111
Detailed List view
    click, to change task view, 185–186
    marking tasks as complete, 204–205
    sort tasks in, 191
    tasks displayed in, 197
Details, add, to appointment, 147–148
Details tab

add task details to, 187
    enter complete date in, 204–205
    use, to add information about contacts, 95–97
Dial-up connection, 324
Display May of Address, 97
Distribution list, 267–271
Distribution List dialog box, 270–271
Document Workspace, 342, 344
Do Not Deliver Before, 52
Do Not Include Original Message, 57
Double arrows, 5
Download Full Items, 325
Download Headers, 325, 327
Download Headers And Then Full Items, 325
Download Pictures area, 86
Draft, 27, 76
Drafts default mail folder, 243, 246
Drag message, 78–79, 82
Due Date, tasks sorted by, 191
Due Date column, 182–183, 188
Duplicate record, 133

E

Editor, 337
Edit Signature dialog box, 67, 131
Edit The Response Before Sending, 201, 203
Electronic note. See Note(s)
E-mail, 19–48
    advanced, features, 262–294
    customize, 49–92
    defined, 19
    Internet, account, 22
    message notification, 328
    send and receive contact information via, 129–134
    set advanced, options, 327
    specify, options, 50–56
    as threat to privacy, 271–272
    use Address Book to send, 124–127
    use contacts to send, 127–129
    See also Instant messaging; Message

E-mail account arrangement, 33
E-mail Accounts Wizard, 326–327
E-mail Options dialog box, 57–59
E-mail toolbar, 21, 24
Empty "Deleted Items" folder, 46
Enable instant messaging, 353
Encoding, 52
End time, 148, 297
Event, 148–151
Event arrangement, 162
Excel, 259
Excel database, export Outlook data to, 256–258
Excel file (.xls), 256
Excel spreadsheet, 27–28
Exceptions, 283
Exchange Server, 273
Exchange server access, 324–325
Expires After, 52
Export, 256–259
Export To A File dialog box, 257
Extension
 .oft, 264
 .pst, 248–249

F

Fax Viewer, 35
Field, 328–329
Field Chooser, 330
Field label, 329
File, 27–30
Filter, 72, 85–87
Filter dialog box, 73–76
Filtering arrangement, 72–76
Filter List, 86
Final Import A File dialog box, 252
Find feature. See Search
Find pane, 333
First Rules Wizard dialog box, 275
Flag, defined, 25–26
Flag arrangement, 32
Flag for Follow Up dialog box, 25
Flagging messages, 25–26
Flag icon, 25
Folder arrangement, 32
Folder list, 11–13

Folder(s)
 create, 76–78
 defined, 7
 grant permission to, 336–339
 move messages between, 78–82
 new, created in Inbox, 77
 organize notes by, 225–228
 organize tasks by using, 193–195
 use, to organize contacts, 107–109
 See also Personal folders
Follow-Up Flag, view contacts by, 110, 113
Font, 24
Font Color, 24
Font Size, 24
For Follow Up folder, 334
Form, 328, 332
Formatted text, 56
Formatting toolbar, change appearance of heading from, 266
Forward, 37–39
Forward note, 221–222
Franklin Day Planner, 173
Free/Busy Options, 297
From, 74
From arrangement, 32
FW:, 71

G

General tab, 95–97
Global AutoArchive setting, 88
Go menu, add news to, 284–286
Group, 239–240

H

Have Replies Sent To, 52
Heading, change appearance of, 266
Help topics, 15
Hide
 Journal, 235, 237–238
 Navigation pane, 237–238
 Office Assistant, 135, 274
Hide Journal, 235
High-priority message, 26, 55
HTML. See Hypertext Markup Language

HTTP. See Hypertext Transfer Protocol
Hypertext Markup Language (HTML), 57, 86, 174–176
Hypertext Transfer Protocol (HTTP), 22

I

iCalendar (Internet Calendaring), 297, 314–317. See also Calendar
Icon
 add, to Outlook, 2–3
 bell, 148
 defined, 25–26
 note, 215–216, 222
Icons view, 223
IMAP. See Internet Message Access Protocol
Import, 259
 Access database into Outlook, 249–256
 defined, 249
Import A File dialog box, 251
Importance, 51
Importance arrangement, 33
Importance down arrow, 53
Import and Export Wizard, 250, 257
Import and Export Wizard dialog box, 250
Inbox, 20, 76
 message headers in, 31
 new folder created in, 77
Inbox default mail folder, 243, 246
Inbox folder, 7–8
Include And Indent Original Message Text, 58
Include Original Message Text, 58
Incoming message, control, 272–273
Increase Indent, 24
Information
 create and use Outlook forms, 328–332
 grant permission to folders, 336–339
 manage, 323–346
 modify mail service, 327–328

Index 369

searching for, 332–336
use Outlook with Windows SharePoint Services, 339–344
view and send task, for other users, 347–352
working offline, 324–327
Inherited company address, 103
Inherited company name, 103
Inherited phone number, 103
In Progress task status, 190–191
Insert File dialog box, 29
Insert Item dialog box, 28
Instant messaging, 352–354. See also E-mail; Message
Internet, 23, 297
Internet Calendaring. See iCalendar
Internet Connection Wizard dialog box, 287–288
Internet e-mail account, 22
Internet Explorer, 175, 273, 312
Internet Message Access Protocol (IMAP), 22
Internet (RPC over HTTP), 324
Internet safety, 286
Internet service provider (ISP), 22, 289
Interoffice mail, 30
ISP. See Internet service provider
Italic, 24
Items, 114–119

J

Journal, 8
 defined, 206
 hide, 235, 237–238
 manually record task in, 206–209
Journal Options dialog box, 206, 208
Junk e-mail, 85–87

L

Label box, 148
LAN. See Local area network
Large Messages folder, 334
Last Seven Days By Categories, 223
Letter, create, 134–136

Letter Format tab, 135
Letter Wizard, 134–136
Letter Wizard dialog box, 135
Local area network (LAN), 30
Location, view contacts by, 110, 112–113
Location box, 148–149, 156, 166
Low-priority message, 26

M

Mailbox Cleanup, 88
Mail folder, 7–9, 12
Mail Format tab, 262
Mail queue, 30
Mail service, modify, 327–328
Manage Alerts tab, 340–342
Map, defined, 250
Map Custom Fields dialog box, 252–255
Mapping feature, 97
Mark task, as complete, 204–205
Master Category List, modify, 119–121
Master Category List dialog box, 121
Maximum button, 3–4
Meeting, 176
 accept, 168
 cancel, 306–311
 change start times, 306
 change status of attendee, 306
 change to NetMeeting, 306
 change to recurring series, 306
 decline, 168
 defined, 140
 delete, 168
 difference between appointment and, 146
 modify attendance requirements, 310
 new, request, 306
 plan, 164–172
 propose, times, 297
 schedule online, 312
 schedule online, using NetMeeting, 311–314
 Tentative option, 168
 update, 305–311
Meeting request
 new, 307–308
 respond to, 168–171
 send, 165–168

Meeting Request window, 165
Meeting resources, reserve, 171–172
Memo Area, 147–148
Memo box, 166
Memo style, 40–42, 192
Menu. See Personalized menu
Menu bar, 4–6
Message
 attach note to, 221–222
 control incoming, 272–273
 control outgoing, 273
 delivery receipt of, 281
 privacy protection, 271–273
 read receipt, 281
 rules for, 273–280
 send, to newsgroup, 288–289
 send iCalendar as, attachment, 315–317
 send same, to several individuals, 267–271
 send Web site address in, 24–25
 task request in Inbox as e-mail, 201
 track, 281–284
 See also E-mail; Posts
Message area, 21
Message header(s)
 color-coding, 83–85
 defined, 21
 in Inbox, 31
 reading messages, 35–37
 select multiple, 45
Message Options dialog box, 50–56, 282
Message priority, set, 26
Message(s), 24
 add signature to e-mail, 65–69
 archive, 88–89
 attach file to, 27–30
 check for, 30–31
 compose, address, and send, 20–24
 customize appearance of, 56–62
 delete, 45–46
 drag, 78–79, 82
 flagging, 25–26
 format of outgoing, 59
 formatting, 24–25
 high-priority, 26, 55
 low-priority, 26
 maximum length of, 23
 move, between folders, 78–82

print, 40–42
read, 35–37
recall, 44–46
reply and forward, 37–40
search, 42–43
sort, 69–72
sorted by attachments, 70–71
view, 32–34
See also Draft
Message template, create and use, 262–267
Message toolbar, 21
Message window, 21
Microsoft Access database. See Access database
Microsoft Excel. See Excel
Microsoft Exchange, for online meetings, 311
Microsoft Exchange Instant Messaging Service, 352, 354
Microsoft Exchange Server
 for delivery receipts, 283
 desktop alerts in, 281
 mail sent in, 30–31
 recall and update message in, 44–45
 required for voting options, 51
Microsoft Exchange Service, 325–327, 336–337
Microsoft Expedia Web site, 97
Microsoft Internet Explorer, 314
Microsoft MSN Messenger Service, 352, 354
Microsoft NetMeeting. See NetMeeting
Microsoft Office System document, 206, 209
Microsoft Outlook. See Outlook
Microsoft Outlook Help button, 14
Microsoft Search function, 232
Microsoft Windows Messenger, 352, 354
Microsoft Windows XP taskbar, 232–233
Microsoft Word
 as default e-mail editor, 24
 as e-mail default editor, 262–264
 Letter Wizard, 134–136
Mobile field, 103

Modified recurrence pattern, 309
Month, 144–145
Move Items dialog box, 80
Move Message option, 78–79
Move Note Selected Below To field, 225
Move To Folder button, 78–79
MSN Hotmail, 22
Multiple calendars, 318
Multiple categories, assign items to, 117–119
Multiple contacts, create, for same company, 102–104

N

Navigation pane, 259
 Active Tasks view on, 189
 Address Cards, 111
 Calendar, 141–142, 146
 Contacts button on, 106
 create shortcut on, 239–242
 customize, 235–238
 defined, 5
 to display task list in default view, 182–185
 e-mail, 31
 Folders List button on, 194
 hide, 237–238
 purpose of, 5
 to standard Outlook folders, 7–12
 Task button on, 176–178
 Tasks button on, 195
 window, 4
NetMeeting, 311–314
New Alerts dialog box, 341
New Distribution List dialog box, 268–269
New Mail Message button, 282
New Meeting Request, 312–313
New Message toolbar, 28–30, 39–40
New Note button, 214
New Outlook Data File dialog box, 247
News, add, to Go menu, 284–286
News account, set up, 286–288
News command, 285
New Search Folder dialog box, 334–336

Newsgroup
 defined, 284
 prepare to access, 284–288
 safety, 286
 send message to, 288–289
 subscribe to, 290–291
 view, 288–290
Newsgroup Messages, view, 288–290
Newsgroup Subscription dialog box, 288–289, 291
News server, 284, 289
News server name (NNTP server name), 286
New Task Request, 198
NNTP server name. See News server name
Note(s), 213–230
 active task created from, 220
 add new folder for, 226–227
 attach, to e-mail message, 221–222
 available view to display, 223
 convert task to, 219
 copy, 218–221
 create, 214–217
 defined, 213
 delete, 228–229
 edit, 217–218
 forward, 221–222
 icon, 222
 length of, 217
 organize, by Folder, 225–228
 organize, by view, 223–225
 save, 218
 task created from, 220
 on Windows desktop, 219
Note icon, 215–216
Notes folder, 11–12, 213, 223
Notes List, 223
Notes pane, note icon on, 216
Numbering, 24

O

Office Assistant, 3, 14–16
 defined, 14
 hide, 135, 274
Office Clipboard, 102
Offline, work, 324–327
.oft. See Outlook Template
Online busy status, 353

Index

Online meeting, 311–314
On Slow Connections Only Download Headers, 326
Options dialog box, 89, 105, 130
   Mail Format tab on, 262–263
Organization pane, crate new category in, 115–117
Organize pane
   add new junk e-mail addresses to filter in, 86
   to assign notes to folders, 226
   in Calendar folder, 159–161
   color-code messages in, 78–79, 83–84
   to organize contacts, 109
   to organize folders, 107–109
   to organize notes, 224
   use, to organize tasks using folders, 193–195
   Using Categories section of, 195–197
   using views in, 162–164
Other Elements tab, 135
Outbox, 23
Outgoing message, control, 273
Outlook
   add icon to, 2–3
   alter existing, form, 329
   create shortcut to launch, 232–234
   customize, 231–260
   export, data to Excel database, 256–258
   import Access database into, 249–256
   introduction to, 1–18
   mail folders by default, 243–246
   navigating within, 4–5
   set startup options, 232–234
   start, 2–4
   use, with Windows SharePoint Services, 339–344
   using e-mail in, 19–48
Outlook application, 232–233
Outlook Calendar. See Calendar
Outlook components, integrate calendar with, 176–178
Outlook Contacts, 255
Outlook.exe, 232–234
Outlook folders, 277
Outlook Newsreader, 286–288

Outlook Notes window, 214
Outlook profile, 3
Outlook Task folder, 176–178
Outlook template (.oft), 264
Outlook Today, 234, 259
   customize, 243–246
   defined, 243
   set, as start page, 243
Outlook Today Calendar, 243
Outlook window. See Window
Overdue task, 185
Owner, 198, 201, 337
Ownership, 198

P

Pager field, 103
Page Setup dialog box, 41
Permission, 336–339
Personal folders, 247–249
Personal Folders file (.pst), 247–249, 259
Personalized menu, 5–6
Phone list, 110–111
Plain text format, 57
Planner options, 297
Post Office Protocol 3 (POP3), 22, 281
Posts, defined, 284
Prefix Each Line of The Original Text, 58
Print
   calendar, 172–173
   message, 40–42
   task list, 192
Print dialog box, 41–42, 172–173
Print Setup dialog box, 41
Priority. See Message priority
Privacy, 271–273
Private, defined, 304
Private appointment, set, 304–305
Private store, 247
Properties dialog box, 338
Propose New Time dialog box, 169–170
.pst. See Personal Folders file
Public folder, 336
Publish, defined, 329
Publish Form As dialog box, 331
Publishing Author, 337
Publishing Editor, 337

Q

Quick Flags, 25–26

R

Range Of Recurrence section, 152
RE:, 71
Reading pane, 4
   body of message in, 33–34
   defined, 5
   message displayed in, 35
   open attachment from, 36
   task displayed in, 202
Read messages, 35–37
Read receipt, 281, 283
Recall message, 44–46
Recall This Message dialog box, 44
Receipt For This Message, 51
Recipient Info tab, 135
Recurrence Pattern section, 152
Recurring appointment, 158, 162
   create, 151–154
   defined, 151
   view, 163
Remember, 148
Reminder, 148, 154–155
Reminder dialog box, 154–155
Remote connection, establish, 324–325
Remote Mail, 325
Reply, 37–38, 61
Reply Group button, 289
Request A Delivery, 51
Request A Read Receipt For This Message, 51–52
Resize handles, 329
Resource scheduling, 297
Restore contact, 105–107
Reviewer, 337, 339
Rich Text format, 57, 61
Rights Management Add-on, 273
Role, 337, 339
Rule, 79, 85
Rule Description list, 276
Rules And Alerts dialog box
   create rule in, 274, 280
   manage alerts in, 340
Rules Wizard, 273–280, 291
Rules Wizard dialog box, 274, 278
Run Rules Now dialog box, 273

S

Safe Recipients List, 86
Safe Senders List, 86
Save As dialog box, 264
Save As Web Page dialog box, 174–175
Save note, 218
Save Sent Message To, 52
Schedule, appointments and events, 146–151
Search, 332–336
Search Folder, 332–336, 344
Search for the word(s), 74
Search messages, 42–43
Search Text dialog box, 276
Second Import A File dialog box, 251
Security Settings, 51
Security tab, 86
Select a Stationary dialog box, 62–63
Select Attendees And Resources dialog box, 166, 171, 307
Select Contacts to Export As vCards dialog box, 131
Selected date, 147
Select Folder dialog box, 245
Select Members dialog box, 268–271
Select Task Recipient dialog box, 199–200, 350
Send copy to, 21
Send/Receive button, 283
  click, to check for new messages, 31, 202
  use, to send and receive e-mail immediately, 23
Send Status Report button, 351–352
Send The Response Now option, 201–202
Sensitivity, 51, 54
Sent Items, 76
Sent Items folder, 42, 44–45
Sent To, 74
Set Up A Newsgroups Account link, 287–288
Shared attachment, 342–344
SharePoint site, 339

Shortcut, 8, 12, 259
  to active projects, 242
  create, on Navigation pane, 239–242
  create, to launch Outlook, 232–234
Shortcut menu, to organize notes, 224
Short Tools menu, 6
Show An Additional Time Zone check box, 302–303
Show Time As, 148
Side-by-side calendar, 317–320
Signature, 65–69
Signature For New Messages box, 263
Simple List view, 187
Size, of attachment, 29
Size arrangement, 32
Sort, 69–72
Sort contacts, 121–124
Sort dialog box
  sort contacts in, 123–124
  sort messages in Inbox in, 70–72
  sort tasks in, 192
Standard Calendar toolbar
  current day displayed in, 143
  Meeting Request option, 172–173
  for navigating within calendar, 141
New Appointment button, 149
  to select meeting request, 165
  set recurring appointments, 153
  use, to change calendar view, 144–146
  use, to delete appointments, 158–159
Standard toolbar, 4–5
Start Date box, 188
Start Time, 148
Start time, 297
Startup options, 232–234
Stationary, 62–65
Status, tasks sorted by, 191
Status bar, 4–5
Status report, 351
Streamlined Calendar folder, 297

Styles, print, 172–173
Subject arrangement, 32
Subject box
  for assigning tasks to others, 198, 200
  description, 188–189
  description of, 148–149
  for requesting read receipt, 282
Subject column, 182–183
Subscribe, 290–291

T

Table style, 40–41, 192
Task button, 176–178
Task details, add, 187–190
Task folder, defined, 181
Task list, 177–178, 181–185
  create, 182
  print, 192
  sorted according to contents of column, 190
TaskPad, 141–142, 176
Task Request received, 350
Task Request window, 349
Task(s), 181–212
  accept or decline, 201–203
  alert box for assigning, 200
  alert displayed with accepted, 350
  assign, 203
  assign, to others, 198–201
  change view of, 185–186
  convert note to, 219
  create, 182–185
  created from note, 220
  defined, 181
  delete, 209–210
  manually record, in Journal, 206–209
  mark as complete, 204–205
  organize, by using categories, 195–197
  organize, by using folders, 193–195
  overdue, 185
  owner, 198, 201
  ownership, 198
  sort, 190–192
  status of, 190–191

view and send, information for other users, 347–352
See also Active task
Tasks folder
  contents of, 7–8, 10, 12
  create note and move into, 219
  use, to organize tasks using categories, 195–196
Task tab, 187–188
Task Timeline view, 186
Task window, 183, 187
Template, 256–267
  benefits of, 267
  create, 262–265
  defined, 262
Templates folder, 262
Tentative option, 168
Third Import A File dialog box, 252
Thread, 288, 290
Time, 74
Time zone, 297, 301–303
Time Zone dialog box, 302–303
Title bar, 4–5
To arrangement, 32
To box, 282
To button, 21
Topic, 21
Tracking tab, 309–310, 316
Track message, 281–284
Translate, 24
Type arrangement, 32

U

Underline, 24
Undo Move, 79
Uniform Resource Locator (URL), 25
Unread Mail folder, 334
Update meeting, 305–311
URL. See Uniform Resource Locator
Use Microsoft Word To Edit E-mail Messages box, 262–263, 265
User Templates In File System, 266–267
Use Voting Buttons, 51
Using Categories section, 159
Using Folders link, 228
Using Views, in Organize pane, 162–164
Using Views link, 223–224

V

Validated address, 272
vCard, 129–134
View(s)
  Active Tasks, 189–190, 204
  available, to display notes, 223
  change, 228
  change task, 185–186
  Detailed List, 185–186, 204
  newsgroup and newsgroup messages, 288–290
  organize notes by, 223–225
  Simple List, 187
  task, 185
  use, to organize contacts, 109–113
Virtual folder, 333, 336
Virtual private networks (VPN), 324
VPN. See Virtual private networks

W

Waiting On Someone Else task status, 190
Web address, 174
  for each contact, 102
  include, in e-mail message, 24–25
  send, in e-mail message, 24–25
Web beacon, 272–273
Web browser, 24–25, 100
Web page, save calendar as, 174–176
Week, 144–145
Where am I, 74
Whiteboard, 311
Window, 3–5
Windows Clipboard, difference between Office Clipboard and, 102
Windows desktop, 219
Windows Explorer, 28, 233–234, 262
Windows Media Services broadcast, 311
Windows Picture, 35
Windows SharePoint Services, 339–344
Work Week, 144

X

.xls. See Excel file

Get a **Free**
*e-mail newsletter, updates,
special offers, links to related books,
and more when you*
register online!

Register your Microsoft Press® title on our Web site and you'll get a FREE subscription to our e-mail newsletter, *Microsoft Press Book Connections.* You'll find out about newly released and upcoming books and learning tools, online events, software downloads, special offers and coupons for Microsoft Press customers, and information about major Microsoft® product releases. You can also read useful additional information about all the titles we publish, such as detailed book descriptions, tables of contents and indexes, sample chapters, links to related books and book series, author biographies, and reviews by other customers.

Registration is easy. Just visit this Web page and fill in your information:

http://www.microsoft.com/mspress/register

Microsoft

Proof of Purchase

Use this page as proof of purchase if participating in a promotion or rebate offer on this title. Proof of purchase must be used in conjunction with other proof(s) of payment such as your dated sales receipt—see offer details.

Microsoft® Official Academic Course: Microsoft Office Outlook 2003
0-07-225577-3

CUSTOMER NAME

Microsoft Press, PO Box 97017, Redmond, WA 98073-9830

System Requirements

> **Important**
>
> This course assumes that Outlook 2003 has already been installed on the PC you are using. Microsoft Office Professional Edition 2003—180-Day Trial, which includes Outlook, is on the second CD-ROM included with this book. Microsoft Product Support does not support these trial editions.
>
> For information on how to install the trial edition, see "Installing or Uninstalling Microsoft Office Professional Edition 2003—180-Day Trial" in the "Using the CD-ROMs" section at the front of this book.

Your computer system must meet the following minimum requirements for you to install the practice files from the CD-ROM included with this book and to run Microsoft Outlook 2003.

- A personal computer running Microsoft Outlook 2003 on a Pentium 233-megahertz (MHz) or higher processor.
- Microsoft Windows® 2000 with Service Pack 3 (SP3), Windows XP, or later.
- 128 MB of RAM or greater.
- At least 2 MB of available disk space (after installing Outlook 2003 or Microsoft Office).
- A CD-ROM or DVD drive.
- A monitor with Super VGA (800 X 600) or higher resolution with 256 colors.
- A Microsoft mouse, a Microsoft IntelliMouse, or other compatible pointing device.